SCHOOL CHOICE IN AN ESTABLISHED MARKET

For my parents, Barbara and Tony

School Choice
in an Established Market

STEPHEN GORARD
School of Education
University of Wales, Cardiff

Routledge
Taylor & Francis Group

LONDON AND NEW YORK

Contents

Figures and tables

Preface

This is a book about school choice. It examines the trend towards markets in UK schools by dispassionately outlining the varied economic and political arguments both for and against increased parental choice. It then describes how choice actually takes place - including when the choice takes place, who has the final say, how many schools are considered, and which choice criteria are reported. One of the basic premises of the book is that the full effect of reforms in education policy cannot be seen for at least a generation. In order to understand some of the longer term implications of competition between schools, the work therefore includes a range of fee-paying schools which are competing in a very volatile localised market in South Wales. Schools were selected to represent the purported diversity of the school "market" - comprehensive, state primary, church, convent, community, for-profit, and traditional fee-paying schools.

"School Choice in an Established Market" destroys forever the cosy myth that fee-paying schools are large successful charitable institutions catering chiefly for a select group of privileged families. A typical fee-paying school is, in fact, a privately owned coeducational urban day school with fewer than a hundred pupils, perhaps even fewer than twenty pupils. It is based in poorly converted residential accommodation with few facilities. It offers a restricted curriculum which is short on sport, technology and other practical subjects. It is, of course, not part of the Assisted Places Scheme, nor a member of any association such as the Headmasters Conference or the Independent Schools Information Service. Perhaps most surprising of all to some readers, the school is very cheap and may be used by a high proportion of pupils from working-class or recent ethnic minority background. The "reluctant" private sector is growing and it gives the reader an insight into perceptions of state schooling in the light of recent reforms, from those on the outside.

The findings are partly based on the largest survey of its kind, with over 100 variables gathered from 1,300 respondents using 33 different schools. This gives them a general applicability unprecedented in previous school research. The survey included every reason for choosing a school suggested by past studies in the UK in order to avoid bias through suggestion or omission. The book is therefore the first to reveal those patterns underlying the complex and seemingly idiosyncratic reasons for choice which have been reported in other studies. Although this has been attempted before in an *ad hoc* way, this study is the only one to eschew pre-defined categories of choice criteria and to base the categories on those discernible from the responses of the choosers, using multivariate statistical techniques (such as principal components analysis). The results are a surprise. The relevance of convenience, pupil selection and the schooling of friends and family have all been seriously over-estimated in the past. A desire for a "traditional" education and a safe environment for the child are the primary general motivators underlying school selection, pushing academic matters and the school facilities into third place.

"School Choice in an Established Market" is also the first book that allows the voices of children to be fully heard in the context of debates about the values, consequences and mechanics of the process of choosing a new school. By gathering the views of parents and children independently via observation, interview and survey, it has been possible to compare them directly for the first time. The scale of the difference in the perceptions of each generation, coupled with the fact that the choice process is so complex (described here as having three discernible steps), leads to the possibility of conflicts within the family.

The schools' own procedures for marketing themselves and deciding between competing applications when over-subscribed were examined and compared to their actual facilities and outcomes. Now, a full school generation since the Education Reform Act 1988 is the first time that a proper analysis can be made of the established market. The results may be a surprise for the complacent, which is perhaps why the findings have been picked up and featured in local press stories and TV current affairs programming.

The key findings are that:

- **Parental choice of school does not work in South Wales.**

A recent study of the process of secondary school choice in 700 families using 33 schools concludes that the current market in state schools, supposedly based on rational choice and diversity of provision, will neither improve educational standards nor decrease social stratification.

- **Schools in the region are basically very similar in organisation** and even more similar in terms of the image projected by their marketing material.

- **Families seriously consider very few schools**, mostly one or two. The geography of South Wales, the lack of public transport and the low population density in some areas may mean that "choice" is a misnomer.

- **Selection by mortgage still operates**. The majority of places at oversubscribed secondary schools are automatically allocated to local primary feeder schools who operate a catchment area. Schools in middle-class suburban areas, for example, are therefore still populated by children from families who can afford to live nearby.

- **Formal sources of information, such as league tables of results and prospectuses, are of little consequence.** One brief visit to a school can make the decision, prompted perhaps by a smell in a corridor, or the style of the furniture according to some accounts.

- **Verbal reports from significant others, such as friends, relatives, current teachers, elder siblings and even casual acquaintances are more significant.** Such reports can be based on recent experience but can also be exposed as myth and prejudice.

- **Choices are often made by default long in advance, making a mockery of annual current performance indicators.** Moving house to be in the catchment area for a feeder school, the domino effect for younger siblings, and the reflection effect of parents' own schooling all show how far in advance some choices are made.

- **Children are made to feel more involved in the choice process than they actually are.** Nearer the time, children are presented with a subset of the schools available, perhaps composed of the parents' chosen school and another patently undesirable one.

- **Families do not want schools to be selective.** Selection on academic, social, religious, ethnic and even gender grounds were generally rated as not important.

- **The safety and happiness of the child is more important than academic outcomes, facilities, convenience and traditional teaching styles.** This finding shows up a flaw in many analyses of schooling in which only the long-term outcomes are considered to be relevant. For the children especially, the move to a big new school can be a frightening event and what all parties want is the assurance that life at school will be OK.

- **The supposed market in schools appears to be pulling all schools of whatever type towards conformity.** The need for number-related funding (or survival in the fee-paying sector) encourages all schools to attempt to appeal to all prospective "clients" rather than targetting a niche.

- **The fee-paying sector in South Wales is proportionately one quarter of that of England, making it one of the smallest in Europe after Sweden.** In the fully established market of fee-paying schools which is an out-and-out fight for survival, the trend towards similarity is dramatic, with all schools trying to attract all potential "clients".

- **The fee-paying sector has been misportrayed.** Most fee-paying schools in South Wales are very small, newly-founded, and poorly provided, existing in cramped converted accommodation with no facilities for sport at all. They are relatively cheap and totally non-selective, taking anyone able to cross the threshold of affordability. They provide no clear advantage in terms of certification.

- **Fee-paying schools are often used by the same kinds of families as the local state schools** (apart from in a very few traditional private schools). In fact, most fee-payers have used local state schools before deciding to look elsewhere.

- **The most universal reason for using a fee-paying school is dissatisfaction with state schools.** This is often based on a bad experience in a previous LEA school, such as bullying or disruption during the dispute over SATs. Some families wish to avoid the requirements of the National Curriculum, particularly with regard to the Welsh language and religion. This may be one reason why the for-profit schools are disproportionately used by families of recent non-Christian ethnic minority origin, where the child already speaks a language other than English at home.

Acknowledgements

Although the chief responsibility for this work remains with me, the study on which this report was based would not have been possible without the generous and enthusiastic assistance of the participants. I would like to thank the schools for their trust in me and their interest in the project, the parents and children who responded to the questionnaire, and everyone who took part in an interview, however briefly.

The training grant which funded the project was provided by the Economic and Social Research Council.

I would also like to thank everyone who assisted me with the work by reading chapters and providing advice and criticism, including Brian Davies, Tony Edwards, Gareth Rees, Jane Salisbury, Reda Abouserie, Anthony Packer and David Allsobrook.

A huge thank-you goes to See Beng Huat who helped with the layout, but whose crucial role was telephone support and therapy in the first year.

The final and chief acknowledgement goes to John Fitz, who seemed to know instinctively how I preferred to work. He advised me, included me, helped me with publications, and treated my ideas with more respect than they probably deserved. Thanks.

List of abbreviations

AP	Assisted Place
APS	Assisted Places Scheme
CCF	Combined Cadet Force
CTC	City Technology College
DfEe	Department for Education and Employment
DoE	Department of Education
ECA	Extra-curricular activities
ERA	Education Reform Act 1988
FTE	Full Time Equivalent
GM	Grant-Maintained
GSA	Girl's Schools Association
GCSE	General Certificate of Secondary Education
HMC	The Headmasters' Conference
HSB	High School and Beyond
INSET	In-service training
ISIS	The Independent Schools Information Service
KS	Key Stage
LEA	Local Education Authority
LMS	Local Management of Schools
NCDS	National Child Development Study
PACE	Programme of Accelerated Christian Education
PASCI	Parental and School Choice Interaction
PCA	Principal Components Analysis
PR	Public Relations
SES	Socio-economic status
SPSS	Statistical Package for Social Scientists
TES	Times Educational Supplement
VAT	Value Added Tax
WJEC	Welsh Joint Education Committee

Part One
INTRODUCING THE RESEARCH

Introduction

Selection of a new school is a fundamental and life-changing process for all children, whoever makes the selection and however the choice is made. It is a continuing concern of social science research, since the conditions under which the process is played out are forever changing. Previous research has naturally tended to concentrate on the schooling of the majority, and the influences and implications pertinent to compulsory state-funded education. Given the existence of fee-paying schools in the UK, it is understandable that some previous work has also addressed the related issues of who uses these schools, and why they elect to pay again for something which is provided free at the point of delivery. However, perhaps through a concern with the schooling of elites, such work has focused on a very different kind of fee-paying school to the majority of those available today, which are either small businesses run for profit, or even smaller religiously motivated concerns. Therefore although reference has been made in earlier studies to a "market" in education, most have been content to consider only a part of the full range of schools available in their chosen focus area. Earlier work has also tended to concentrate on differences in educational opportunity and outcomes for individuals, in terms of occupational class, gender, and ethnicity. More recently, a new direction in school choice research has emerged, which adds to the earlier mixture a more detailed investigation of the processes involved in choice, played out at the level of the family. This new direction required a re-evaluation of the methods used in investigations by social scientists, and has led to a melding of what were previously seen as competing research paradigms. In addition, the long-term effects of changes in national educational policy are rarely predictable, since they are implemented at a local level, often alongside other reforms with which they interact. Nor are the effects readily apparent even a year or so after implementation (e.g. McPherson and Willms 1987). It is therefore only now, one school generation after the Education Reform Act 1988, that its true effects can be seen in what is now an "established market". This is the background against which this book appears.

The programme of research on which this book is based was carried out at the School of Education, University of Wales, Cardiff, between 1994 and 1996 (Gorard

1996a). It is an investigation by survey and follow-up interviews, with both parents and children, of the process of choosing a new school. It represents a new approach to the study of school choice, focused on the long-established market for fee-paying schools in Wales. The study involved 794 families and 33 schools in South Wales. All of the families were just making, or had just made, a choice of a new school. The schools represent the range of all school types in the region, both state-funded and fee-paying. The parents and their children were surveyed separately, so that most families made two returns, with an overall response rate of 79%. The survey instrument included questions on the families and their characteristics, how they go about choosing a school, and what their reasons were. Semi-structured interviews were then held with the parents of some of these families, using an interview schedule based upon themes raised in the survey. A picture of the schools themselves was built up from official publications, visits, observation of lessons, interviews with selected staff, and analysis of the literature sent to prospective parents. The data so obtained was analysed in terms of its content, and coded by categories which emerged from the survey, or which were grounded in the data itself.

In general the work is seen as significant on three counts. Its timeliness in the light of recent educational reforms, and so its relevance to the marketing and management of schools and the indications it gives of the longer term effects of supposed markets in state-funded education. The lack of previous research concerning proprietary and grass-roots fee-paying schools, which are outside the major private school associations, along with the distinctiveness of the fee-paying sector in Wales as compared to England (this is the most substantial survey ever undertaken of the fee-paying school sector in Wales, and one of the largest of its kind in the UK). The use of sampling techniques and methods of analysis which are rare in this field, making the results more generalisable to a larger population, more reliable, and ultimately more revealing than in much previous choice research. The blend of large scale survey, and semi-structured interviews, as well as the inclusion of children as participants in their own right, uncovered some aspects of the family micro-politics of choosing a school that have not been previously addressed in the literature.

In summary, this is a study of the process of choosing a new school. Recent educational legislation, the increased marketisation of education, and demographic and economic trends, invite further development of earlier work on school choice, and make a "snapshot" of the situation particularly appropriate at present. The success of the legislation concerning parental choice of schools will depend to some extent on how the schools and their clients respond, and this is one of the issues addressed by this study. According to Tomlinson (1994), a market experiment is being tried out in the "laboratory" of education. The policy which is being tested is largely based upon an economic model of "rational choice theory" (Boyd *et al.* 1994), which although growing in use in other social sciences, has been little studied in educational research.

Following the 1980 Education Reform Act which introduced the notion of parental choice as a central part of education policy via the Assisted Places Scheme (APS), the 1988 Education Reform Act introduced Local Management of Schools (LMS), Open Enrolment, Grant Maintained Schools (GM), City Technology Colleges (CTCs) and league tables of school performance (Lowe 1988). Now,

4

parents may also send their children to schools in education authorities where they are not resident. The Parents Charter 1991, and the 1993 Education Act all helped to create, or strengthen, market forces in education (Douglas 1993). Within a funding system for schools which is *per capita* based, school survival in the state-funded sector is thus increasingly subject to the vagaries of parental choice.

It is, therefore, important to undertake research into what parents want from schools for a number of reasons. Firstly, such research can show educationalists and policy makers what the likely long-term effects of the recent reforms will be. It can indicate whether parents have a broad consensus about an "ideal" school, generally all wanting the same type of school, or whether choice and diversity are indeed linked (see Glatter *et al.* 1997). It can demonstrate whether the current performance indicators for schools are the appropriate ones - the ones that parents actually use in making a choice - or whether they are simply the easiest to quantify and publish. Above all, if improvement of standards via increased choice is to take place, it must be shown both that parents can recognise high standards in schools, and that schools can respond to parental influence. At present, unfortunately, as some recent research notes, "too often, schools are taking action to influence parental choice based on unsupported assumptions about what parents want from schools, and why they choose them" (Coldron and Boulton 1991 p.169). Schools do not seem to be seriously interested in discovering what will attract parents (Smedley 1995), and there is insufficient study of parents' perceptions of what makes a school good, and how they judge it (Echols and Willms 1995).

The research questions

This study partly arose from the personal experience of the researcher working in one of the fee-paying schools in Wales. The school was in a poor state of repair with falling pupil rolls and increasing debt. Although it supposedly selected students at intake by academic ability, participated in the Assisted Places Scheme, was a member of the Headmaster's Conference and had become one of the most expensive schools in Wales with a very low pupil to teacher ratio, nevertheless the public examination results were poor - worse than the national average for all schools at A level in fact. The question naturally arose - why are parents and the Local Educational Authority and the government paying so much money to send children here? What is the school offering? Are there other schools like it? Did the parents really know what it was like before they chose it? These, and similar, questions became the foundation for the research reported here, although the scope and nature of the project naturally evolved over time.

Below is a list of the research questions which prompted the study, and which are addressed in this book. Perhaps the largest, most all-embracing question, however, is - whether there is a discernible pattern in the relationship between the types of schools available, the families who use them, the way they choose them, the reasons they give for doing so, and the responses of the schools?

The process of choice
> How do families select schools?
> What role do the children play?
> Are there common reasons for school choice?
> What are the links between these reasons?

Market forces in education
> How much choice is there?
> How much diversity is there?
> How much do families really know about the schools?
> Does what parents want make sense educationally?
> Are market forces leading to improvement?

Fee-paying schools
> Why do families elect to pay for education?
> What kind of families are they?
> What type of schools are there in the private sector?
> Why is the private sector in Wales so small?
> Why are private schools generally so small?
> Is private schooling better than state-funded education?
> Do different types of families use different schools?

The work is primarily an empirical study of a region of schools and their users, driven by the kind of questions outlined above. It is the outcome of a gradual maturation in the approach to studying school choice in the UK. The study builds slowly, with deliberately simple steps to a rounded picture of an entire system of regional schooling with results that will surprise the complacent, and to grounded models of family choice that may well be applicable to other sectors of education, perhaps even to other public services, in which choice is relevant. The findings of previous studies of school choice are used to define potential choice criteria, which form the basis of the questions for the survey, which are then analysed to create underlying choice factors, and linked by models of the choice process to stories from the interviews. The results are finally placed back in the context of the previous work from which they sprang, and compared to the actual provision of the schools chosen by the participants. Instead of relying upon a prior theoretical position, or attempting to explain the position by means of metaphors which are impossible to refute empirically, the study is designed to be deliberately simple. Simplicity should make the results easier to understand, so enabling criticism and encouraging progress.

The organisation of the book

The book is arranged in four sections. The introductory section contains a brief consideration of the concept of markets in education, a review of some past research into the workings of the market and a critique of the methods used in some of this previous research. The second section outlines the methods used in the research on which this book is based, describes the types of schools encountered in the established market and the families who use them, and lists the key results from a large-scale survey concerning the process of choice. The third section uses stories from selected participants in the study and shows how the process of choosing a school is played out at the level of the family. The final section is a summary of the findings and their implications for policy-makers and educationalists.

1 Markets in education

Introduction

This chapter examines the trend towards increased "consumer" choice in school education, considering arguments both for and against this as a policy in the context of recent changes in this respect in the UK. Its objective is to establish the need for further work in the area of school choice, and to explain the difficulty of predicting the likely outcome of marketisation for the UK state-funded school provision. The chapter is in three main parts, starting with an outline of some of the varied arguments that have been used to promote choice in education. There have been at least three different strands in the push for greater "consumer" choice. One of these stems from the view that market forces will have a beneficial effect on the provision of what is seen as public service industry (e.g. James and Phillips 1995). Another is that allowing greater freedom of choice will end the reality of selection by mortgage, and give even the most disadvantaged sections of society a fair chance of using the best schools. The third strand is, perhaps, the simplest of all. It does not matter what the intended effects of a choice programme are, choice is a good thing by definition, according to views such as the libertarian perspective of Erickson (1989). Since the state only intervenes in the home life of a child - its clothing, shelter, and food - in case of neglect or abuse, it should behave in the same way with education. Description of these interwoven strands is followed by discussion of some of the criticisms of these arguments, and the chapter concludes with a brief critique of economic rational choice theories and their relevance to the marketisation debate.

Choice in education

There is some evidence that recent increases in population movement have led to more changing between schools in many children's lives (Van Zenten 1995), so there are more choices of school to be made than in the past, and choice of schools looks set to become more and more important in the future. There are good theoretical arguments both for and against increased control of school choice for the individual, and it is unlikely that the debate on this issue will be decided by theory alone. Some education writers quite reasonably take a political stance on this issue but many of the reasons given, even, or perhaps especially, by politicians for the recent legislation in the UK, are educational. In this light, the recent reforms in the UK, as elsewhere in the world, can be seen as a massive educational policy experiment, although the UK is perhaps in a minority in using an entire generation of the nation as its "guinea pigs". It is too early to tell what the full effects will be, but it is beginning to look as though the reforms are likely to be both less effective than originally suggested by some, and less damaging than feared by others.

Although this chapter is chiefly concerned with parental choice of state-funded schools in the UK, several other liberal democratic states have introduced legislation relevant to increased school choice in the last 15 years (OECD 1994). These schemes are all different in important respects, and highlight the need to distinguish between market theory as a general concept, and each version of its implementation in education. In the USA for example, choice of school can mean selection from several mini-schools on one site, or between educational programmes affecting entire states (Levin 1992). Many of the supposed advantages and disadvantages of market forces that have appeared in the UK can be seen as arguments for or against the specific set of legislation enacted here, rather than dealing with the concept of choice *per se*.

All school choice schemes, however, have given the *de jure* role in choice to the parents alone, without much obvious consideration of the alternatives. Although parents may be beneficiaries of the custodial role and income-generating potential of their child's education, and the majority may genuinely have the best of altruistic intentions, it does not necessarily follow *a priori* that they have the necessary competencies to decide on an appropriate school. Should parents really have the right to select a school that protects a minority sub-culture for example, and so deprive the child of a more normative education? Should they be able to select a school based around a narrow and fundamentalist religion, and risk the charge of indoctrination? And what happens if parents do not value any kind of schooling? Children from rural families used to be regularly kept away from school, during harvest and other crucial agricultural periods, by their parents, as evident from this complaint by an earlier Amish farmer, "once he goes to school and gets a little education, he's no good on the farm any more" (Coleman 1990 p. xii).

Closer to home, pressures to keep children out of school, or to leave early, are not merely due to poverty, and the need for the child to help in the family business (Gorard 1997a). In Wales, one writer claimed that "the main reason was the lack of appreciation by parents of [education's] importance for the future welfare of their children" (Evans 1971 p.262). Another pressure comes from not wishing to over-educate children, or prepare them for a type of job that would require leaving the rural area in which their family lives. Truancy, still worse in Wales than England according to one account (Reynolds 1990), is perhaps condoned, and maybe even encouraged by some parents. Where do they fit into an economic model of rational choice theory, and can a free market be fair to their children?

"Life contingency" is a concept originally used in occupational choice, to explain why people may make a choice for reasons other than its manifestly desirable qualities (Ginzberg *et al.* 1951), but it can also be seen to apply to the much newer field of school choice. Thus debate about the value of school choice is really about whose values should apply, and can only be answered by deciding on an answer to the preliminary question - what is the problem that choice is a solution to? A large number of reasons have been used to argue for, or justify, the increase of parental choice of schools. A few are strictly educational, some are economic, but many are based upon notions of justice, equality, or equality of opportunity.

Justice for all

Perhaps the first, and most obvious, argument is that school choice has always been available for parents in the UK to some extent, as it has in the USA (Witte 1990$_a$). In a system of allocating places to schools based upon a catchment area, parents had the right to move house and so come within another school's catchment area. Some cases were even reported of families renting pseudo-accommodation in another area to their home for this purpose. Parents could also opt out of the state-funded school and send their child to a fee-paying school. All of these choice strategies required finance, and so the catchment system provided choice only to those who could afford it. The Education Reform Act 1988 (ERA), and associated legislation such as the Assisted Places Scheme, has now given every child a *de jure* right to attend any school in the country including a number of fee-paying ones, and so can be seen as extending the luxury of choice, and diminishing the privilege of the elite, or at the least, sharing those privileges more evenly.

Central, or even regional, control of local schools imposes the policies and values of the state. Even where that control is established democratically, the prevailing majority view represents a dominant interest group which is potentially damaging to minority groups, whether based on religions, languages or cultures (Ball 1993). Parental choice of schools, on the other hand, can be seen as a local form of referendum having prospective parents as the electorate, but with the constituencies so small that local voices can be truly effective, and each school can, in theory, cater for a different set of "clients". In this way, the "dictatorship" of uniform public monopoly schools can be broken. Evidence that dissent to majority norms was being suppressed in the public school system was seen in the USA in debates surrounding censorship of books which tore some schools and communities apart (Arons 1982). Some parents wanted their children exposed to, and others wanted their children protected from, certain books, facts, and courses. This is reflected in Wales today in stories of parents choosing a fee-paying Catholic school, so that their child will not be taught about contraception and of schools cutting material about such matters from their textbooks (personal observation) and in the refusal of one school to visit an exhibition that included dinosaurs since their existence contradicted the school's teaching on the date of the beginning of the world (Wales on Sunday 1996).

One example of the perils of a public monopoly dictatorship is provided by the debate over the merits of coeducation. In the UK most state-funded schools are coeducational, and in the USA they are so by law (Coleman 1990), but according to some, there is mounting evidence that many girls perform better academically in single-sex schools. The public monopoly may therefore be seen, in this case, as favouring boys, and so denying equal opportunities to girls. Another well known example, educational "reproduction", is referred to by Cookson when he states that "the life arithmetic of the overwhelming majority of children is that their social class destination will be identical, or very similar, to their social class origin. This is a reality of American education" (Cookson 1994 p.90). This conclusion is backed up by the Institute of Economic Affairs (Maynard 1975) and Spring (1982) who both found no empirical evidence that compulsory state education, in either the UK or the USA, had been instrumental in decreasing poverty or increasing equality since its inception. One possible reason for this is the social stratification that routinely takes place in schools using a catchment system, and thus it can be argued that one part of the solution is to provide greater equity by a programme of increased choice coupled with open enrolment.

Choice programmes in the USA have therefore been particularly popular, and seen as particularly relevant to, the poorer sections of society, such as immigrant, minority, and one-parent families who have been deserting the large inner-city schools (Levin 1992). Ironically similar motivations may lie behind some families' use of fee-paying education, in opting out of the majority norms, or rejecting the inferior urban education available. A scheme to provide compensatory education for low-income families, particularly from minority backgrounds was rejected as "elitist" in the USA in 1984, as it involved the use of private schools (Peterson 1990). There is however, evidence that low-income families benefit from this approach, since "within the inner city there are private schools, including religious schools, that deserve public support because they are educating disadvantaged students at a time when public-sector schools are in disarray" (Cookson 1994 p.128). The private Catholic schools in the USA take a very high proportion of children from apparently disadvantaged backgrounds (Gaffney 1981, Coleman and Hoffer 1987), and like the grass-roots schools described in this book, the pay-what-you-can Steiner schools, and home-schooling materials in the UK, they are within the budget of most families who are prepared to make the commitment. In Milwaukee, the strongest pressure for an increase in parental choice is coming from the ethnic minorities and the poor (Cookson 1994), and in Scotland a much higher proportion of one-parent families, who are frequently economically disadvantaged as a group, exercise their choice by making placement requests (Willms and Echols 1992).

Several common reasons used to advocate both choice and diversity have been based on religious/philosophical grounds, but even these can be seen as a reaction to denial of equality by the majority on a class basis, since "religious involvement is and has been stronger on average for those who are less advantaged" (Coleman 1990 p. xx). Some dissenters have a religion other than the majority one sponsored by the state in the UK, and enshrined in the National Curriculum, while others have objected to theistic practices altogether (e.g. Bentley-Ball 1982). In the USA, where the constitution prevents religious worship in schools and thus enforces secular education, some dissenters have objected to "liberal progressivism" on moral grounds (Arons 1982). In the past, liberals have objected to "attending a daily act of worship", "taking the pledge" or "saluting the flag", which still takes place in many education systems in the Pacific rim where attendance at a state-funded school entails a daily vow of loyalty.

According to Keith Joseph in 1976, leaving systems to market forces is more effective than state intervention, provided of course that the free interplay of supply and demand is not impeded (Edwards *et al.* 1992), and to some extent this claim is now being tested in education. The claim that parental choice of schools will lead eventually to an overall improvement in standards is seductively simple. It can be summarised as follows. Public monopoly schools, mostly large comprehensives in the UK, have been too similar to allow a real choice, and they have been alleged to differ chiefly in their standards of attainment. Greater diversity is needed. According to Coleman (1990) the demand for diversity can be seen in the range of summer camps available in the USA, and the lack of coherence in the private sector which has military, Quaker, and progressive schools as well as the traditional boarding schools. However, this demand has clearly not been reflected in state controlled schools. In the UK, the terms of the Education Reform Act 1988, so the argument runs, allow greater diversity in provision, and have the capacity to create a situation where schools differ in their organisation, their curriculum, their mission and their specialisms, as well as in their standards. "Good" schools should be popular, and since funding is basically linked to pupil numbers, a form of natural selection will cause popular schools to thrive, and poor schools to close. With the continuance of each school linked directly to the satisfaction of clients, it should be more responsive to their wishes, which will eventually lead to an overall improvement in both provision of choice, and educational standards, since "schools that did not provide students with skills would not last long" (Cookson 1994 p.125).

Since the link between the budget and satisfaction of individual consumers is more clearly broken in non-choice public schools, the organisation often appears to aim for "profit in kind" such as prestige and avoidance of conflict (Boyd *et al.* 1994), which can detract from its effectiveness. The efficiency of allowing "consumer" dissatisfaction with such schools to be expressed by what Hirschman (1970) defined as "exit", is described by Witte (1990b) - "one does not have to say exactly what is wrong or what should be done to correct it; one does not have to argue, persuade, or cajole teachers or administrators; one only needs to find a suitable alternative". In the USA the rapid decline of some urban schools when rejected by the middle-classes shows the power of choice in those areas in which it has been implemented. Chubb and Moe (1990) argued that state democratic control of schools leads to an extra tier of bureaucracy in education, which can be unwieldy and impersonal, making schools unresponsive to their users. A market involving parental choice, and local control of schools by parents is one answer to such a problem. Such a scheme allows parents to express their dissatisfaction by "deselecting" a school, but also to use their "voice" on the governing body (Hirschman 1970). This is necessary because a market in schools is considered different to many other commodity markets, since conventional wisdom has it that it is not good for a child to move school frequently. This common convention creates the equivalent of "loyalty" to a school for many parents, which is said to keep "exit" at bay and so activate "voice". Parents are more likely to remain loyal, it can be argued, if their chances of changing the current situation at the school are favourable, compared to the risks of exit.

Choice advocates also argue that choice, by itself, can create a dynamic for the culture of the school as a society (Cookson 1994). Teachers, parents, and pupils in such schools feel that things are better than in non-choice schools. They may adopt some of the cultural characteristics of private institutions, such as a sense of mission for the staff, a sense of ownership for parents and greater community participation. However, if most schools are to improve there must be a link between choice and school responsiveness. Schools must be prepared to make changes as a response to the newer demands of the market, and some early evidence suggests that they are. For example, Woods (1992) studied three schools and found that a number of changes were made as a direct result of perceived pressure from parents, including policies on school examinations, homework, safety of possessions, breadth of curriculum, banding, more exclusions, and attention to uniform. Although having implications for marketing, these changes are substantive, not simply cosmetic. Whether these changes constitute improvement is, as yet, unclear, but they do show that some schools are prepared to respond positively to market forces.

Perhaps the final argument for the implementation of choice in education is that such a policy is generally popular. For example, Gallup found a clear 2 to 1 majority of parents were in favour of school choice in a 1993 poll in the USA (Riley 1994), and the early impact of the 1981 choice legislation in Scotland was maintained, with the number of placing requests doubling from 1982 to 1985 (Adler *et al.* 1989). People generally want to have some control over the kind of school that their child attends.

Problems with marketisation

Opposition to the notion of using market forces to drive improvements in education is as varied as the approaches of advocates. Whatever the long-term consequences, for good or ill, of the recent changes in the UK, some children will find themselves stranded in failing schools. Although such schools may eventually close, any improvement in standards through market-driven evolution will require "casualties". It is therefore possible to argue that the children in these schools are the forgotten victims of the choice process, although it is also possible to claim that the schools they attend were failing anyway, as evidenced by their decline in roll since the advent of choice, and so, although there has been no impact for the rump, choice has actually reduced the number of casualties. Some opposition is based upon predictions of likely consequences other than those intended by proponents, such as an increase in social stratification, but much of it meets the economic model head on and argues that choice simply does not work. In addition, some evidence of the benefits of markets in education, such as that provided by Chubb and Moe (1988), has been questioned (e.g. Bryk and Lee 1992). In the Netherlands, a country with a very high proportion of private schools, no standard numbers, and considerable freedom of choice, unpopular schools do not disappear. They simply become very small. In fact, most private schools are very small (Cookson 1994).

When Adam Smith developed the proposition that an economy of selfish agents making choices for their own benefits can be organised and made to work for the common good, he did so merely as a statement of logical possibility (Hahn 1988). This does not mean that it must be so. Many pre-conditions would need to be met. Assumptions include that the agents must be economically rational, knowing what they want, and how to get it. Above all the market must be genuinely free. These and other assumptions are usually not met in practice in any real market; witness the abolition of slavery, or the concept of industrial patents. The possibility of rational choice is examined in the third part of this chapter, after a discussion of some of the other limitations to a free market in education.

Education is not marketable

One problem for the model of consumer choice in education is that it operates maximally in urban or suburban environments. Low population density and travel restrictions mean that many families in rural areas effectively have no choice at all. Early reports suggest that active choice, or deselection of the local school, is consequently much higher in urban areas than rural (Adler *et al.* 1989), and in areas where there are more schools (Echols *et al.* 1990). Some rural areas are in fact still running a pure catchment area system, allocating places by proximity where a school is over-subscribed (Hammond and Dennison 1995) and there is little evidence that patterns of enrolment in primary schools have been affected by the market since 1988 (Menter *et al.* 1995). This is further complicated by administrative rules relating to school transport. Although there is free transport provided by the LEA for any pupils living more than three miles from school, this often only applies to transport to the closest school, which makes a mockery of the concept of free choice for many families. Some parents are of course still prepared to pay for transport, or to drive themselves, but such a strategy is likely to have social class implications. It is clear that for choice to work, travel costs must be taken into consideration in any plans to retain equity of provision.

However, it has been observed in the USA that it is largely the inner-city schools that have been deserted by participants in choice programmes (Fowler-Finn 1994), suggesting that it is in fact these schools which are leading to the greatest dissatisfaction. Such a possibility may be backed up by the observation of Echols *et al.* (1990) that use of private schools is proportionately four or five times more likely in cities than small, or single school, communities. Although there is a financial component here as well, relating to the payment of fees, there is again the suggestion that the chief dissatisfaction is with city schools in the UK. Perhaps parental choice is an urban solution to an urban problem? Families in some rural areas may be no better off in terms of choice, but they will also be no worse off. They will have the restricted choice of home schooling, which is a growing trend in some rural areas (Meighan 1992), and which could *in extremis* force a local school to close. It is not clear then, whether the opposition to choice based upon the uneven distribution of schools and population density assumes that school choice is a "good thing" of which some are being deprived, or whether it is a "bad thing" in which case those in rural areas, where it is impossible to implement, are better off, and can hardly be used as the basis for an objection.

One of the major reasons for the imposition of universal state education in the USA may have been the need to foster a sense of unity in a new culture through a sense of shared experience (Coleman 1990). Society values cohesion, which is one reason why racial integration is practised, and why there is suspicion of "bilingual education programs that appear intended to maintain a non-English linguistic subculture" (Coleman 1990 p. x). State education in the USA has also been used to break down the power of families, and to liberate children from narrow horizons, religious dogma, and the "slavery" of poverty, and above all to mitigate the potential divisions in society arising from the diversity of immigrants, who once formed the majority of the population. The situation in the UK is somewhat different today, but there are parallels in the desire for devolution and "own language" education in some regions, as well as the voluntary racial segregation discussed below. The creation of a market, by allowing diversity, may "splinter" the schooling of this country, and lead to greater disunity. The balance between the "benevolent dictatorship" of the state and the promotion of individual liberties is, as ever, a delicate one.

Other suggestions are that a free market in schools is not possible because of the likelihood of a monopoly being established. Schools are not "for profit" organisations, their product is unlike many others, and it is not the parents who are the main beneficiaries of schools anyway (Maynard 1975). A producers' monopoly of schools could be established in a free market, since the market itself is of fixed finite size and, unlike the markets for "genuine" consumer goods, it cannot grow without a population increase. There are also economies of scale in the provision of education services, so that larger schools can provide cheaper services *per capita*, using the money saved to fund further improvements over their smaller rivals. Thus, the early successful schools will be able to establish a "natural" monopoly. Such an outcome is possible, although it is also possible that assumptions about market size and economies of scale do not apply here. The length of time spent in education is not necessarily a constant, and successful schools may persuade more pupils to stay on at 16+ or to return in later life, for example. Economy of scale may only apply within the scale defined by the existing plant, and if a school expands beyond that to become split site, its character as well as its unit costs may change. Above all, there is no reason to assume that a state monopoly, as existed before 1988, is preferable in any way to one established in a market by popular schools with low unit costs.

A more serious objection is that market schools do not provide typical consumer goods, since their quality is chiefly determined by the quality of their customers (National Commission on Education 1993). Education as a produced commodity is not homogeneous in the same way as many others, such as breakfast cereals (Garner and Hannaway 1982). There is imperfect competition between schools (e.g. because of travel constraints), and imperfect information on which "consumers" may judge them. As described above, "exit" is a mechanism of control in a market organisation, but this is not an option that consumers of education are likely to use very much. The disruption caused by moving school is too great for it to be very effective. Perhaps the biggest obstacle is that schools are not run for profit and so, if demand outstrips supply in any school, it will lead to problems. In the UK, 85% of a school budget comes from age-weighted pupil numbers. A school is not like a mainstream business and cannot necessarily expand to meet demand, nor can it raise its prices since state education is a free service at the point of consumption. Rather than raising prices or expanding its customer base, an over-subscribed school may simply raise admission standards. Parents in the UK can choose a school, but do not have a right to use the school of their choice, unless it has spare places. In this situation, the school may become more selective in its pupils entry requirements. Such a policy would presumably allow the school to produce better public examination results, by increasing the ability of its intake, but without actually improving teaching standards. As the relative supply of pupils dwindles, power of selection moves to schools, who can drive up the entry requirements, and reduce the effort required to maintain superiority over other schools in terms of raw indicators. Thus a market can lead to complacency and demotivation for successful schools, emulation of their conservatism by those less successful, and so to dis-improvement overall. The theory that choice in an imperfect market leads to selection by schools, and so to social stratification, is an important one, discussed more fully in the next section.

Market theories of education see the consumer as the clear beneficiary, but may do so to the neglect of the external benefits. A whole society could benefit from the custodial or socialising roles of schools and this benefit could be greater than any private value. Market forces would thus be inappropriate since they would not preserve the interests of society as a whole. At a local level, parental governance of schools could lead to problems since the parents are assumed to be "selfish agents" in many versions of choice theory. If they are only concerned for their own child, they may act in such a way that short-term benefits override the collective good of the organisation for which they have been elected (Witte 1990$_b$). It is also administratively more convenient for the state to simply assign a compliant population to local schools, as exemplified by the complaint that some LEAs found planning impossible because choice in Scotland produced such volatility with unpredictable swings in enrolment (Willms and Echols 1992).

One of the pre-requisites necessary for competition to lead to an improvement in educational standards is the correct mixture of "alert" and "inert" clients (Hirschman 1970). Those parents who are more alert to educational rights, problems, and opportunities provide the stimulus for change either by exercising their "voice" to the governors of the school, or by signalling their dissatisfaction through exit. Unfortunately it may be the parents most likely to bring about change who are also those most likely to leave (Willms and Echols 1992). It therefore falls to the more inert parents, those perhaps less attuned to the situation, to provide the basis of loyal clients who give the school time and a "dollar cushion" for any improvements to take effect. Both are necessary. If most parents are "inert", choice does not stimulate competition. If most are "alert", it may cause problems for schools trying to expand, and so suffering in the short term, leading to another exodus, and not enough stability for any substantive measures to be seen to take effect. Improvements in schools can take years to become obvious in the form of quantifiable outcomes (McPherson and Willms 1987), which will be too long to wait for a selfish agent with only one shot at education.

Evidence on the existence and proportion of these two types of families in society is conflicting. On the one hand, the Carnegie Foundation report claims that "in states where school choice has been adopted, less than 2% of parents participate in the program; and parents who transfer their children to another school do so mostly for non-academic reasons" (Cookson 1994 p.71). There is, however, an indication that the number of parents prepared to become involved in choice is growing in both the USA (Cookson 1994) and Scotland (Echols *et al.* 1990), and that the poorer families are becoming just as involved as any other section of society. It may be that some families are natural consumers, used to making choices, and these are the minority, or perhaps the elite, reported in early results, but that others are not necessarily "inert". Some families may simply be slower than others in becoming aware of their rights to choose and appeal, in which case the proportion of "alert" clients would be expected to grow continuously, and there is already evidence that this is happening in the UK.

"Choosers tended to select schools with higher mean socio-economic status and higher mean levels of attainment" (Cookson 1994 p.92), which may be a rational attempt to boost a child's attainment (Echols *et al.* 1990). Unfortunately, in terms of pupil ability, a "favourable school context" measured by mean pupil SES is a "zero-sum resource" (unless society becomes more affluent) . What one school gains, the other loses. The policy of parental choice may therefore benefit choosers in relation to everyone else without necessarily improving standards overall, and as the number of alert families increases, the proportion gaining any benefit at all may drop. Since much of the information available on schools necessarily relates to past, not present, performance, the feedback to schools based on migration could anyway be incorrect, and might encourage the wrong changes. Effective schools in disadvantaged areas may be tempted to change to prevent losing pupils, while less effective schools in better areas might be made complacent by the attractiveness of their high mean SES (Willms and Echols 1992).

A major defect in the UK school market envisaged by the ERA 1988 is contained in that same legislation. Although parents may now express a preference for a school, and even help to run it, they are compelled to use a curriculum, testing policy, and funding strategy set by the government (Hartley 1994). Although schools can deploy their own budget, its level is determined by the number of pupils it attracts. This condition is set by the government, and implemented using national benchmarks. Teachers may retain their own pedagogy, but only within the constraints set by national curriculum, testing and assessment. The introduction of choice reforms at the same time as others giving greater central control over education has inhibited the very diversity felt necessary by some for an evolutionary market strategy to work.

Witte (1990$_b$) does not agree that publicly funded "state monopoly" schools have necessarily been uniform, and unresponsive, which is one of the charges made by choice advocates. Schools in the USA generally vary by size, years of intake, location, racial composition and income, plus testing and curricula, and they are complemented by the fee-paying sector. On the other hand, choice schools are now engaged in rivalry for expansion and survival, which may be leading to a "dull uniformity" of provision in the UK (Tomlinson 1994). All schools are aiming to follow majority trends, and none is responding to the diversity among parents by providing a distinctive kind of school, and then targeting their potential consumers (Woods 1992). Parental involvement in schools is more to do with the policy and vigour of the individual school than the policy of school choice (Riley 1994). In fact, parents who have made a choice may be less likely to be involved in school, perhaps because voice is more often used when exit is impossible.

Perhaps the reason that schools are being so unadventurous and unresponsive is that they do not have good processes for learning or responding to changes from outside (Levin and Riffel 1997). This is not due to ill-will or incompetence but "long-ingrained patterns of thought and behaviour" (Levin and Riffel 1995 p.1), which is why it might be that the advent of choice will be both less beneficial than advocates suggest, and less harmful than critics fear. Thus it can be argued, "any evidence that this... strategy [of competition through choice] leads to the expected improvement is hard to find" (Brown 1994 p.55). School effectiveness research suggests that the true effect of a school can only be judged after its intake, and the socio-economic character of its catchment area is removed from or controlled for in later results (Brown 1994). Intake achievement remains the single most important factor affecting subsequent achievement. Any slight improvements found in some studies could, anyway, be temporary and in the nature of a "Hawthorne" effect.

Choice leads to stratification

One of the other findings from early choice research that does not seem open to dispute is that there is still a real danger of significant social stratification in schools. Choice may have led to a larger elite, but they are still enjoying a better education at the expense of others (Tomlinson 1994, National Commission on Education 1993). In both Israel and the USA, students of "higher" social class are more likely to be enrolled in the schools of their choice (Goldring 1995), and this result is true across all ethnic groups. In Scotland, choice is more common among better educated and higher social class families (Echols *et al.* 1990), being linked to home-ownership and socio-economic status (Adler *et al.* 1989), and more prestigious occupations (Willms and Echols 1992). This trend is likely to be increasing the segregation between schools in terms of mean socio-economic status, and all of the pupil characteristics that have been found to be associated with it. Choice may therefore be maintaining and even reinforcing social inequalities linked to class background (e.g. Ball *et al.* 1996).

In addition to the problem of only some parents being alert to choice, there is the additional one of schools being perhaps too conscious of it. The introduction of a market could change the values prevalent in education (Ball 1994), so that schools may no longer be run primarily in the interests of their users (if they were before). A policy of "improvement" through selection of intake may make sense for a school in the market, but it is only cosmetic, not making any school more effective. It must also be reflected in a decline in results elsewhere. In reality the schools would be making the choice, and not the parents. A policy of selection by schools can therefore also lead to segregation by first language, gender or social class, as schools use profiles of an "average" successful candidate in order to predict future success. Children from homes whose first language is English, or whose parents are university educated, for example, might be seen as statistically more likely to be of value to the school, because of an established link between these characteristics and examination performance. The recent rise in exclusions, and associated appeals, suggests that schools may be trying to screen out what they see as problem pupils (Ball 1994).

There is already some evidence that school responses to market demands are discriminating against black families and groups (Blair 1994). The content of the National Curriculum encourages a narrow definition of national identity, in history, geography, literature and especially in the orders for religious education which emphasise Christianity. "Britishness" underpins many of the changes, and schools may unwittingly pander to the racist sentiments of their ideal consumer. The free market denies that there are in fact unequal starting points for families, and so does nothing to increase equity in education, appealing as it does to individual effort and "bootstraps". Muslim parents can query a definition of diversity that allowed Judaic or Catholic state schools, but denied them aid for state voluntary schools. Schools opted out of LEA control are allowed to draw up their own criteria for pupil selection, especially if they are performing well and become over-subscribed. In 1992 the Commission for Racial Equality found that Watford Boys and Watford Girls Grammar schools had indirectly discriminated against Asian parents in its entry procedures (Blair 1994). Parents were asked to write their reasons for choosing the school, but only those submitting six or more reasons were admitted. Some parents may not have had the literacy, cultural capital, or simply the confidence to produce so many reasons. In Dewsbury, white parents removed their children from a primarily Asian school, and justified their "exit" on racial grounds. Ball (1993) suggested that ethnic minority students will become more liable to exclusion from school, leading to a loss of real choice for them. Since the Reform Act, LEAs no longer have same authority over appointments in schools, and thus cannot impose a policy of equal opportunity. This is a particular problem, since most governing bodies are still predominantly composed of white middle-class males. Discrimination may also apply to black teachers not deemed acceptable to white parents. In the Dewsbury case, a court ruled that the right to choose overrode the Race Relations Act in the UK according to Dooley (1991), as evidenced by the "white flight" from Dewsbury middle school in the 1980s, and this may have set a dangerous precedent for the selection and promotion of teachers as well (Blair 1994).

Some of the original resistance to one proposed choice programme in the USA, a compensatory voucher scheme, arose from the fear that it might be used in part to counter the effects of the end of racially segregated schooling in 1954. However such an argument is not valid as such in the UK, which has never had compulsory racial segregation, or integration, in schools. In any case, a liberal programme might have to accept the possibility of "racist" choice as an integral part of any free-market. To argue that parents of minority religions and languages, which often correlate very strongly with racial differences, should be allowed to dissent from majority schools, is to permit voluntary racial segregation in schools. Separate Muslim schools have been seen by some as "sexist" in nature, as well as encouraging even further racial segregation in schools (Dooley 1991). This freedom to choose on possible ethnic grounds is one trade-off that policy makers thus have to consider when creating neo-liberal choice programmes. It cannot really be countered by racial classification and admission quotas, since these are messy, relying on the unrealistic concept of "pure" race and are, anyway, contrary to the spirit of the right to choose.

The paradox of choice programmes is that, although they are more popular in the USA with poorer urban families, recent immigrants, non-whites, and less prestigious socio-economic classes, these may be the very types of families who are least likely to use their choice, with the smaller better educated families in fact being more active (Lee, Croninger and Smith 1994). Because the poorer families are the ones that generally have access to the urban schools with the worst reputation, choice is often seen as negatively rooted, as being choice away from something (Goldring 1995). This is more likely in the USA than the UK, where the disparity in educational expenditure between US districts, financed by a local property tax, can vary by as much as 10 to 1, with the wealthier residential areas contributing solely to the upkeep of their own schools (Lee, Croninger and Smith 1994). Perhaps one of the reasons that researchers in the UK are less enthusiastic about choice is that, before 1988, expenditure was already more evenly spread between schools than in the USA. Another may be that, whereas US visions of progress may be based upon individuals, their freedoms, and right to advancement, in the UK visions are focused more readily on whole segments of society.

Although Ball (1993) conceded that not all of the effects of the ERA were necessarily intended by policy makers, he also stated that "the implementation of market reforms in education is essentially a class strategy which has as one of its major effects the reproduction of relative social class (and ethnic) advantages and disadvantages" (Ball 1993 p.4). Raw scores in league tables of results reinforce selection of pupils by ability in over-subscribed schools. As the market eliminates under subscribed schools, surplus places may be eliminated, reducing the pressure on schools to compete for students. Schools will seek to maximise their performance measures and minimise their costs per head, and thus will recruit more able students and turn away those with difficulties, and concentrate their resources on the most able. Therefore the indicators may have a political purpose other than to raise standards, perhaps to further a policy of "cultural restorationism" (Ball 1994). Selection of pupils by schools becomes possible, indeed rational, and might be "'a selling point'; what you get is who you go with", so that unlike in most markets, who the customer is makes a difference. As the value-in-exchange of education depends on how much one holds relative to others, it leads to a system of winners and losers, so that the market is not neutral. It requires access to possibilities (time, transport, literacy, numeracy, child care facilities) which are unevenly distributed in society. Those with little education, or on low incomes, may only access the lower level of information concerning schools, and so the system could lead to social reproduction (Bowe *et al* 1994$_b$). This reproduction could then be justified by claiming that non-choosers are bad parents, and reinforced by sending money to popular schools.

Several points can be made against this thesis, in addition to the evidence cited above that the proportion of alert clients is growing, especially among the poorer and minority families. Since income and wealth are unequally distributed in society this will inevitably lead to unequal access to education in a free market. Poorer families will have fewer funds for travel, and additional contributions to schools, and less opportunity to move. However this has always been true, even under a catchment system, and can be seen as an argument for greater equality in society or for raising the overall mean SES, and not one against parental choice *per se*. Since inequality is undesirable in its own right, its existence should not be accepted as a "given", and then used to argue against choice. Education, by itself, cannot be expected to solve major societal injustices.

The government could intervene in the financing of education to encourage greater equity by guaranteeing loans, or introducing negative income tax, but this would not necessitate intervention in the provision of education itself. It could still allow a market to operate, but one in which the "players" are more equal, and it could enforce a policy of allocating places at over-subscribed schools by random draws.

Alert "players" may then apply to slightly less popular schools, to increase their chance of first-choice allocation in a satisficing school, which could increase the proportion of first-choice allocations altogether, as well as reducing social stratification. Allocation of contested places could even use a stratified random selection (i.e. with target proportions set by whatever strata seem appropriate, including ethnic background, gender, ability and socio-economic group). Anyway, although research on parental choice has not yet reached an agreement on how schools are chosen by parents, it is clear that public examination results are not the only, nor even the major reason for choosing a school, so a popular school would be misguided to select pupils on ability alone. There is of course a danger that parents themselves will select a school on the basis of its current social class, gender, or racial breakdown, but such an outcome must not be confused with selection by schools, which it has been by some previous writers.

A policy of selective intake by schools only makes sense in a market in which their places are in high demand. In terms of organisational survival, any pupils are better than none. The evidence that schools seen as successful will be overloaded with applications, suggests that there are many parents not happy with their current neighbourhood schools. This is, in itself, evidence of the need for improvement in schools, and of the enthusiasm of parents for their increased choice. It is not at all clear that a policy of not allowing the parents in the less desirable schools to express their dissatisfaction is preferable in any way. It is also not clear that demand must necessarily outstrip supply. Some surplus places must remain in the system anyway, to provide the incentive for schools to compete in the market. Many parents appreciate small schools, so the paradoxical situation might arise that although small schools are popular, popular schools are large. The market might then see a natural evolution of schools to an optimum size, above which they cease to be popular.

The basic problem at present lies in the ability of schools to turn pupils away once their standard number, a completely arbitrary figure, is reached. It is this which may lead to selection, and could be prevented by supplementary legislation, such as that in the Netherlands, or that proposed by a former Secretary of State for Wales, allowing successful schools to expand. There are still spare places in the system, in the sense that there is provision for more pupils than actually exist. There are therefore more than enough teachers, buildings, and other resources to provide an education for all pupils in the school of their choice (this is not to say that there are, in fact, enough resources for a good education). The main problem with resources in the current parental choice scheme is that they are often in the wrong place. However, this is also not a criticism of market theory as such. In a free market, popular schools would be allowed to grow indefinitely, and unpopular ones would close. Some of the resources from under-subscribed and closing schools could be transferred to popular ones. Teachers contracts would need transfer clauses, and schools would need to offer incentives to attract more and better staff. Most schools use some "temporary" accommodation, and in future such accommodation could be organised so that it can be switched easily between sites. Many schools operate on split sites already, and have devised organisational and timetable strategies to minimise disruption. Such strategies could be used by a popular school which has outgrown its plant and takes over a nearby less popular school. It may be that as schools grow and begin to operate on split sites, in "portakabins" and employ teachers from "failing" schools, that their attractiveness may decline, and an equilibrium be reached without a single pupil having to be turned away.

The limitations of rational decision-making

At the core of a programme of school improvement through market competition lies the notion of parental choice. If parents make good choices, the model works well, at least in theory, and if they do not, the market fails to deliver. The market includes a belief that people are rational choosers, and will select schools that are academically superior, and as yet "there is little evidence from the private sector that parents will choose schools that.... are not in the best interests of children" (Cookson 1994 p.125). Market research reveals the stated preferences of respondents, and assumes that their choices are a kind of revealed preference (Sen 1982). The discussion here will concentrate on how people make decisions in general, and whether they are likely to make "good" decisions about schools. Psychological research on decision-making has emphasised the study of actual decisions being made, and because of its methodology has tended to highlight the factors other than logic that lead to them. At one extreme, people can be seen as rational, violating optimality by simple errors, and at another as primarily emotional and driven by unconscious motivation. The attribution work of Schachter and Singer (1962), and others, show how susceptible people can be to unconscious, perhaps even subliminal, cues when making judgements of people and situations. Courts are well aware of the strength of primacy and recency effects in the presentation of material.

In fact, "people are usually seen as trying vaguely to be rational but failing frequently to appreciate normatively appropriate strategies" (Eiser and van der Plight 1988 p.76). This usually means that a decision-maker is rational up to a point of "good enough", or that they are using bounded rationality, or "satisficing" in coming to a conclusion, as opposed to a formal cost/benefit analysis. There are many reasons for this, such as lack of time, subjectivity, computational ability, distractions, existing values and commitments, "groupthink", stress, and notably a lack of understanding of probability. Most decisions involve uncertainty about outcomes, and even premises, and so to some extent all real-life decisions can be seen as being based on probability. Classical probability theory, however, is based on long-run frequencies of many "trials", but most decisions are one-off cases, and they correctly involve subjectivity, in the sense that the value of an outcome may differ between individuals and over time (Eiser and van der Plight 1988).

One model of such decision making is the Subjective Expected Utility theory (SEU), which suggests there are five stages in a decision:

1. list all possible courses of action;
2. list all possible consequences for each;
3. assess the attractiveness of each outcome;
4. assess the likelihood of each outcome;
5. calculate the SEU of each course of action as the sum of [the probability times the utility of each consequence].

However, this rational model has only limited descriptive validity, since studies show that most people ignore SEU in making decisions, even after the method has been explained to them (Eiser and van der Plight 1988). It may be that such a calculation exceeds most peoples' calculational ability, especially as very few personal decisions, even major ones concerning choice of school or a house purchase, are represented formally on paper, despite the improvement in the quality of decisions that can be achieved by the use of balance sheets, cost/benefit analysis, and iterative computer simulations. Using a heuristic or short-cut leads to bias, partly due to the psychological factors outlined above, but the biggest flaw may be that the probabilities and the value of each outcome are not seen as independent in the way that theory suggests.

This misinterpretation of probabilities is a common flaw in heuristics (Eiser and van der Plight 1988). Any reduction in the probability of an outcome from 100% certainty produces a greater loss of its perceived attractiveness than an equivalent drop in probability from an originally lower figure, so that perception of probability is not a straight line function. Paradoxically, low probabilities are often greatly over-weighted in decisions, such as insuring for fire damage, or entering a lottery, but they can also be neglected entirely. One reason for this may be that risks from easily pictured causes, such as plane crashes, are more likely to be in the media than more common risks, such as diabetes, and so are exaggerated in subjective estimates. Decisions also depend on the phrasing of the problem, and the frame of reference of the subject. For example, losses loom much larger than gains, so that most people prefer to make £100 than to have a 50% chance of gaining £200, but the same people would prefer a 50% chance of losing £200 to definitely losing £100.

A further problem arises when probabilities have to be multiplied, as they would in practice in most real life decisions. Even professional mathematicians, who have correctly stated that successive tosses of a coin are independent, have been found to believe that a run of HHHHTTTT is less likely than HTTHTHTH (Eiser and van der Plight 1988), and teachers have stated that "1 2 3 4 5 6" is less likely to win the British national lottery than "3 12 17 28 44 47" (personal observation), for example. In addition, there is common misunderstanding of the "law of small numbers", so that small samples are often seen as equally representative as large ones when the results are expressed as proportions or percentages. This is good news for the small private schools regularly topping league tables of examination results in Wales with a 100% pass rate for seven candidates, for example. In one experiment, most respondents rated the probability of two independent events happening together as greater than one of them in isolation. For example, when told a story about a strong independent woman, she was rated by participants as being more likely to be a feminist cashier than a cashier (Eiser and van der Plight 1988), which is, of course, absurd. For these, and several other, reasons there must be considerable doubt about the ability of parents to make rational decisions which involve judgements of future uncertainty.

Assessing the value of an outcome can be as difficult as assessing its probability, and combining the two in the fifth step of SEU theory is very complex. Accuracy and reliability decline as the information load increases, and in general, people "limit themselves to one salient dimension whilst screening out dimensions that suggest a different solution" (Eiser and van der Plight 1988 p.99), particularly where they have already made a public commitment to one solution, or feel compelled to agree with a consensus. Since school choice is so complex, such findings suggest that parents will judge schools on one major criterion only. This has important implications for the results described in this study.

In practice, to make a choice based on the effectiveness of a school, one needs to be clear what the objective of education is, but this is something that even professional teachers and research academics cannot agree on. Parents cannot be expected to make such choices according to Thiessen (1982), who illustrated this point by saying that "just because... many families might prefer programs emphasizing... the classics... or the sayings of Chairman Mao, but do not find them served in the local public schools, it does not follow that anything is amiss in the school and that somehow the child's right to an education... has been abrogated" (Thiessen 1982 p.79). The perceptions of school effectiveness may differ substantially amongst parents, systematically varying by occupational class for example (Woods 1996), in which case school choice could lead to a fragmented market, social stratification and almost certainly little improvement in standards. The link between theory and the reality of choice is broken. Even if parents are capable of bounded rational decisions in theory, they may not have sufficient information to make them. For example, Raven (1989) pointed out the difficulties for parents in acting out the role of consumer of education. In order to be able to choose effectively, parents need access to the options available, convenient geographical access to more than one school, valid information about the alternatives, help to articulate their needs, familiarity with present educational programmes, the capacity to understand the information, and the time to consider and review it.

A MORI poll in 1993 found that whereas most parents were happy with their child's local school, most also felt that the education system as a whole was poor (Young 1994$_c$). Such a result casts doubt on the rationality of parents, in general, as judges of education, since this overall picture cannot be true. One explanation is that the finding is a result of media criticism of schools and teachers, leading to a public opinion that something was wrong overall with education, although parents' knowledge of their local school suggested otherwise. HMI [as it was then] was surprised to discover that parents with children attending schools identified as "failing" and liable to direct take over by the Secretary of State, have been satisfied with the school. Such findings also cast doubt on the competence of parents to judge the qualities of a school. Hughes *et al.* (1994) recalled a comment made by the then Education Secretary on national radio. He stated that the educational views of the National Confederation of Parent-Teacher Associations (claiming to represent over 8 million parents) were "Neanderthal". Such a statement shows little respect for the views of parents, and is hardly consistent with a belief that parental choice will improve standards in education. This attitude can perhaps explain some of the ambivalence and contradictions in Conservative education policy for the 1990s.

Willms and Echols (1992) analysed the relationship between choice and school effectiveness in the area of performance in national examinations. They divided the effect of a school into type A contextual success, sensitive to the characteristics of the intake, and type B, a truer comparative effectiveness with equivalent pupils. Parents making placement requests (choices) were not sensitive to this distinction, and tended to choose schools with type A benefits, particularly a high mean SES.

Willms and Echols (1992) concluded that "parents' choices are rational in the sense that they increase their children's likelihood of success" (Willms and Echols 1992 p.340) but that the effects are probably not as great as they appear on the surface, since parents are using the raw performance indicators, and so are choosing the past pupils of a school, and not the school itself. There may be an element of superstition involved in sending a child of whatever ability to a school in which other children of unknown ability have previously done well in examinations.

Conclusion

It is difficult to decide on the likely outcomes in the debate about school choice, especially as the different schemes proposed vary so much, and the UK legislation appears to contain contradictory elements. Since the results of policy changes can take a long time to become clear, this provides further justification for using the established market of fee-paying schools in order to help try and predict what the effects may be in the state sector. Also, given that choice is seen by some as an antidote to stratification and social reproduction in education, and by others as a major cause of it, it will be interesting to see to what extent fee-paying schools are elitist, and to what extent they are compensatory. Finally, as it is not clear whether parents are capable of making rational choices about schools, even when they behave as "self-interest maximising" individuals, doubt must be cast on the possibility of using increased choice as an engine for improving school standards. Again, the fee-paying sector can shed some light on this, the quality of the choices made by families, the extent to which the schools are driven by their "consumers'" preferences, and ultimately the comparative quality of the schools.

2 The prevailing evidence

Introduction

This chapter describes the results of some of the previous research into school choice. The first section looks at possible patterns in the relative responsibilities of those involved in selecting a new school. The different groups considered are parents and children, boys and girls, day pupils and boarders, and families of differing social backgrounds. The second section considers the process of choice, and reviews some of the evidence about when families start to consider the next school, how many schools they consider, and how they obtain information about the schools. The third section discusses a range of work which provides data about the possible reasons for school choice, and on which the survey instrument for this study is based. On the questionnaire form used in the present study, a question appears relating to each of the findings cited here. In this way, the chapter provides both a basis for the research, and a background against which its results can be judged.

Who chooses?

Before considering the reasons for choosing a school, it is necessary to consider who is actually doing the choosing. One obvious division within the "consumers of education" is between the parents and the pupils. Some researchers believe that the real decision-makers are the children themselves. In one study, for example, 60% of children claimed to have chosen which secondary school to attend, while only 14% had no say in the final decision (Forster 1992). Studies by Walford (1991[a]) and Thomas and Dennison (1991) showed that between 50 and 60% of children claimed that the school was their choice alone, with a further 20 to 30% claiming that it was a joint choice with parents. The question of who chooses is important for several reasons, not least of which is that adults and children may use different information sources about schools, and therefore rate the importance of school characteristics, such as mixed and single-sex schooling, differently (Smedley

1995). Such results also suggest that it is important to consult pupils in research concerning school choice (e.g. Gorard 1996$_b$).

On the other hand, another study found that 80% of parents said that the decision had been a joint one with their child (Woods 1992), and while Fitz *et al.* (1993) reported that the wishes of able children were the single most important factor in the choice of a secondary school, the clear implication of this finding is that the process of choice is at least a joint one. Similarly, David *et al.* (1994) found that although the child was involved in choosing in the majority of cases (eight out of ten pupils had visited the prospective school, and two out of three had read at least one brochure), they were rarely solely responsible. These findings are in line with those of Smyth (1993), Devlin and Knight (1990), and the OECD (1994), who found that 79% of parents claimed joint choice with pupils, whereas only 2% of pupils decided alone, and West *et al.* (1995) who found that the child has the main responsibility in only 18% of cases. All of these studies agreed that pupils are important in the choice process, but the debate concerns the amount of autonomy they have in making that choice, with the first group suggesting that in many cases the child is the main agent, and the second suggesting that the parents and the child act together.

These differences may be explained in several ways. The researchers involved may have been dealing with different groups of families, varying by age or gender of child, occupational status, educational background, and sector of education (OECD 1994). It may also be the case that both parents and children are overestimating their own contribution in self-reporting (Gorard 1997$_b$), or that parents may find it difficult to distinguish between taking the child's preference into account (West and Varlaam 1991), and allowing the child as a person to choose. All of these possibilities are examined in the present study.

Which members of the family are involved in choosing the school is related to social class, as assessed by the occupation, housing and education of the parents (Coldron and Boulton 1991, Ball *et al.* 1992). Middle-class, professional, educated, home-owning families are less likely to leave the choice of school to the child alone. Edwards *et al.* (1989) concluded that the views of pupils are less relevant in the choice of a private school, perhaps because of the payment of fees. Since it might be expected that users of fee-paying schools are more likely to be middle-class, as defined by occupation and education, these two results agree, and may partly explain the differences above. Adler *et al.* (1989) found that families from urban districts, home-owners, and those of higher socio-economic status were more likely to make placement requests within the Scottish state-maintained sector. Echols *et al.* (1990) confirmed this and added parental education, and disposable income, to the list of characteristics linked to a predisposition to make choices. Those families not making placement requests in Scotland tended to have more general views on schools than the in-depth analysis of some active choosers (Macbeth *et al.* 1986). They were more likely to use the nearest school, and to use convenience as the main reason. West (1992) also found that middle-class parents, and parents of high ability pupils appear to use different criteria to other parents in making a choice, and this was confirmed by David *et al.* (1994). Parents from different social backgrounds may therefore have different views on school choice, with active choosers tending to be middle-class, and professional, considering both

28

state and private schools, and paying more attention to discipline and academic standards, than convenience (Smedley 1995).

On the other hand, Johnson (1987) suggested that parents had very similar reasons for choosing the private sector as were shown by other studies to influence choice of specific maintained schools, and Coldron and Boulton (1991) reported that the three most popular responses were consistent for all social groups in their study (but see Chapter 3).

There may also be differences between families with one and two parents, and between the views of the two parents (Bauch 1989). David *et al.* (1994) showed that about 40% of the children ready to move to Year 7 in their focus schools were not from traditional nuclear families. Over 25% lived with a single-mother. They found that mothers were almost always involved in the choice, and this agreed with the conclusion of Madsen (1994) that mothers are more active in the initial research, while fathers are more involved later, perhaps in a verification process. Both studies found differences between the choices of mothers and fathers, such that fathers are more concerned with the sports programme, but David *et al.* (1994) found that mothers and children picked the same school as each other more commonly, and for similar reasons, than the father. However, both parents are still involved in most cases (West *et al.* 1995).

Hunter (1991) also found significant variation in priorities and use of choice factors between different ethnic groups and between parents of boys and girls. As an example, 86% of those who used single-sex education as the main criterion for choice were parents of girls. Most respondents who expressed a concern for the gender mix of the school wanted single-sex for their daughters, and coeducation for their sons (West *et al.* 1995), and parents of sons and daughters showed other differences in their views on choice (e.g. David *et al.* 1994). Selection of the same school already being used by older siblings was more important for girls, whereas the child's preference was reportedly more important for boys in one study (Coldron and Boulton 1991). Bauch (1989) reported further differences emerging according to income, race, religion. The OECD review (1994) showed marked differences in choice criteria between countries. All of the above studies show that "consumers of education" cannot be seen as a homogeneous group, and so help to justify further research in different sectors and regions, as well as providing relevant variables for the survey design in this new study.

The process of choice

Previous research suggests that the range of possible schools considered by families will vary depending upon the geographical position of the family home, their ability to travel, the possibility of relocation, and whether a fee-paying school, particularly boarding, can be considered (Hammond and Dennison 1995). Many families do not have a realistic choice because of low income, or isolated rural position, as the OECD (1994) reported for areas like Sweden and Scotland. This was confirmed by Fitz *et al.* (1993) who stated that a third of the parents in their study felt that they had no real choice of schools because of travel problems. It is important to recall when discussing school choice, that it relates to a majority of, but far from all, families, and that the availability of options for choice is probably the single most important determinant of parental choice behaviour (Echols *et al.* 1990).

In addition, David *et al.* (1994) reported that 50% of parents, presumably the majority of those faced with a real choice, only started thinking about secondary school in the last year of their child's primary education. Unfortunately, it is not clear from their figures, how many of these families were concerned with choice for their eldest child. It might be expected that the process of choice was very different for first and subsequent children, if the family had not moved or materially changed circumstances in the interim. In their study, 25% of parents considered only one school and 50% applied to only one school, perhaps representing that group with no real choice. Similar results are reported by West *et al.* (1995), with only 10% of respondents considering five or more schools.

Visits to schools for open days, interviews with the Head, or community activities are commonly seen as the one of the most influential sources of information for the choice. Also influential, and perhaps even more common, is the local reputation, as conveyed by other parents, personal acquaintances, and the previous school Head (GPDSA 1995). The implications of the Education Reform Act 1988 have led to an increase in the production and distribution of prospectuses, which after visits, and personal acquaintance with a school, are the most common and useful sources of information (Hammond and Dennison 1995). Headington and Howson (1995) suggested that brochures have the potential to become a key marketing tool for state schools, and there is evidence that schools are giving increased priority to marketing, even if they seem to be using marketing models from non-educational settings, which may be of little value (James and Phillips 1995).

League tables of truancy and examination results, newspaper articles, advertisements, and exhibitions are so far relatively unimportant to most families. In fact, some studies report that many parents see them as misleading (Smedley 1995), and many of those who have considered examination results may have used alternative sources in non-standard formats, such as school brochures (West *et al.* 1995), or hearsay (Macbeth *et al.* 1986), rather than the press. Children very rarely cite official sources of information when asked about choosing a new school. Instead, they tend to rely on anecdotal evidence (Smedley 1995). Transfer to a new secondary is often attended by myths, such as "the school where they flush your head down the toilet on your birthday" (Measor and Woods 1991 p.59), and these may be the kind of unacknowledged sources of information which will confuse any investigation based upon a model of rational choice. Although the overall influence of having brothers and sisters at a school may be slight, because not all families can be so influenced, 72% of families making a decision for a child with an older sibling felt that the school of the sibling had influenced the choice (West *et al.* 1995).

It is not clear that an economic model of decision-making with its rational cost-benefit analysis is applicable or appropriate to the educational context (see Chapter 1), nor is it clear that parents and pupils wish to act as consumers when selecting a school (Bottery 1992, Bowe *et al.* 1994a). Hughes *et al.* (1994) found in their interviews that only 12% of parents saw themselves as consumers of education, even when the concept had been explained to them. Parents do not seem to behave, or do not want to behave as public-choice theory describes. Many families probably make a default choice based on a very cursory examination of available information. Apart from the 10% of parents who select the private sector, only another 10% of parents may actively research alternative schools and forms of schooling (Clark and Round 1991). There is some evidence that these "alert clients" are more likely to be middle-class and have better than average educational qualifications.

So perhaps one third of families have no real choice, while only one fifth seem to have the ability, resources, and motivation to make an informed choice, although even some of these may be making an "unreasoned" choice of a particular private school based upon tradition (Fox 1985). The majority of parents do not have a sophisticated process of selection. Most of the sample questioned by David *et al.* (1994) were unclear about the characteristics of different school types. Young (1994$_c$) concluded that "parents and children rarely choose schools on the basis of well-informed comparisons". Another researcher agreed that "many parents selected schools on 'gut level' feeling" (Madsen 1994 p. 17), and that "in most cases, all of the parents knew immediately that.... was the school for their child" (Madsen 1994 p. 19). It is important to remember therefore, when analysing the questionnaire results, that most parents do not select schools in anything like the check-list manner that such returns may seem to suggest. In fact, it may be that as many as 75% of parents only ever consider one school and make a choice without even visiting it (Smedley 1995).

There is little support here for an economic model of school improvement through rational choice based upon published performance indicators. Only a few schools are considered by most families, little consumer research is done, and local reputation and impressions based on short visits are paramount.

The reasons for choice

In a recent review of studies of parental choice in the UK, the author stated that "the studies are remarkably consistent in their picture of why parents avoid particular schools" (Smedley 1995). This "negative" motive plays a large part in school choice, with 75% of parents in one study naming a school that they were trying to avoid, because of its bad reputation (West and Varlaam 1991). It has been suggested by some authors that there are unrelated reasons for avoiding and selecting a school, with the safety of the child paramount in the avoidance of particular schools (e.g. Smith and Tomlinson 1989). If safety is assured, other factors such as academic standards come into play, because "for parents a good school is one where children pass examinations, a bad school is one where they break up the furniture" (Smith and Tomlinson 1989 p.63).

Some studies and reports have attempted to group the "positive" reasons for choice. For example, the OECD (1994) carried out a review of many school choice studies, and decided to categorise the findings into four groups of reasons for choosing. These were academic (e.g. results), situational (e.g. travel), ethos (e.g. management style), and selection (e.g. single-sex). Coldron and Boulton (1991) also created four groups, of which only two were the same as the OECD. These were academic, school organisation (same as ethos), security (e.g. no bullying), and sources of information (e.g. sibling at school). On this basis there are a very large number of different ways that the reasons for choice can be grouped coherently. West *et al.* (1994) used five headings to group the common reasons for choice, and their groups were different to both of the above. The differences between these three classifications, and others, highlights the need for a more systematic procedure than was used by any of these studies, and provides further justification for the factor analytic approach of this study (see Chapter 5). For the present, the following review considers choice criteria in five groups, the four from the OECD review and one from Coldron and Boulton - academic, situational, ethos, selection and security. Most researchers have produced reasons coming into one of these categories, with the major differences between studies being the relative importance of each. The inclusion of the relevant variables in the standard questionnaire for this study was suggested, and is justified by, the work described here.

In order to assess the value and impact of parental choice in a market for schools, it is essential to know how these choice criteria can be judged by a potential "consumer" (see Chapter 1), and whether other research has suggested that such reasons are important to school life and school outcomes. If parents are judging schools on the basis of desirable criteria that are impossible to assess or, even more critically, if they are judging them on educationally undesirable criteria, the market cannot work as a stimulus to school improvement, and may not even be able to satisfy the individual chooser. This tentative linking of school choice and school effectiveness research is a relatively new departure (but see Woods 1996). One type of study usually considers what parents look for in schools, and the other considers what the characteristics of a good school are and attempts to measure them. Few studies attempt to combine the two. The question arises whether what parents look for are what make a school effective, and if so, are there ready measures of such characteristics publicly available?

A subsidiary question concerns the reasons why families choose to turn their backs on the free education provided by the state, and pay for the schooling of their children. This theme also runs throughout the chapter. Using pupils from both state and private schools in England, matched by parental occupation, Roker (1991) found that those in private schools certainly believed that they were getting a better education. This was expressed in terms of the quality of the teaching, the facilities, small classes, and the higher ability and motivation of pupils, but was seen to lead eventually to better final results. The pupils were more confident, and families assumed almost automatically that the child would continue to A levels and hopefully, to university. Only one interviewee from 67 was intending to leave school at age 16. Their confidence is even more remarkable in light of the fact that most were applying for oversubscribed courses, such as veterinary science, at prestigious universities. This finding was backed up by those families who had used both sectors, and were shocked by the large classes, poor teaching, and low motivation in the state sector. They believed that the "investment" of the parents in schools gave the children an extra pressure to perform, and the adults more influence in the running of the school. On the other hand, pupils objected to the view that mere attendance at a private school gave an advantage - they still had to work hard. Similar views were expressed by families in a study by Johnson (1987), also in England. Families using both types of schools, reported that private schools were better, even where they had not thought so initially. The private schools generally had teachers with higher qualifications, more scale posts, and smaller classes. Whether this is actually so, whether it is true in Wales, and whether parents are capable of making valid judgements about such matters remains to be seen.

Accordingly, for each of the five groups of criteria, this chapter considers how they may be assessed and compared between schools, and between sectors, and whether they are of educational significance. For example, to realise that a child is happy or badly behaved at school, or has failed an examination for example, is relatively easy and trivial *a posteriori*. The difficult thing for a family faced with the choice of prospective schools is to decide whether these things are true of existing pupils at the school, whether they are likely to be true of future pupils, and whether they are of any consequence for their own child *a priori*. How difficult such a decision is can be seen from the fact that educational professionals are still debating how to measure relative examination success, and whether the management style of the Head affects educational outcomes, for example, and yet it is precisely such questions that consumers may be required to consider when making a choice.

Academic criteria

Academic criteria are some of the major reasons for school choice according to public-choice theory, perhaps because they seem relatively easy to quantify and so compare between schools, and to some extent research has confirmed this (David *et al.* 1994). In summary, schools are selected by some parents because they believe that their child will fare better academically at a particular school or type of school (Hammond and Dennison 1995, Goldring 1995, Woods 1992), and English public schools give their pupils an academic advantage according to 23% of parents in a study by Fox (1990). Such an advantage is usually envisaged as greater certification, perhaps leading to a better chance of entry to a later school, sixth form, university or career, depending on the age of the child. Haertel *et al.* (1987) claimed that in the USA, examinations are seen by parents as the most important criterion of school effectiveness, and so the major determinant of school choice. The same reasons, especially better preparation for college were consistently found in a study of private schools in the USA (Bauch 1989). Parents and pupils at fee-paying schools seemed to agree on the importance of academic results, according to Edwards *et al.* (1989). Of fee-paying parents, nearly 60% cited better examination results, better chance of entry to higher education, and better career prospects, as important in school choice. Pupils may also see the best school as the one gaining the better examination results, and so leading inevitably to better career prospects. In a study of girl's private schools, Walford (1986) found that a desire for better academic results was the major reason for their choice. Girls moving to HMC sixth-forms often did so because they believed the new school to have better links to the universities at Oxford and Cambridge.

Such an academic advantage could be realised by schools in a variety of ways. High expectations of pupils by teachers were considered important in Catholic private schools in the USA (Gaffney 1981) and in British selective schools (West 1992). West (1992) also reported the importance of an atmosphere conducive to work, which may, in turn, be linked to an emphasis on public examinations, good quality teaching staff (Hammond and Dennison 1995), a good choice of subjects, and the range of facilities available (Woods 1992). The relevance of each of these has been confirmed by at least one other study (Clark and Round 1991, Fox 1985, Harris Research Centre 1988, Hunter 1991, GPDSA 1995, ISIS 1992, Smith and Tomlinson 1989, West and Varlaam 1991).

The quality of the facilities in the school were the most important criterion for choice, in the findings of David *et al.* (1994) for parents, and for pupils this included art, science, computing and sports facilities. An increased range of facilities also increases the likelihood of the provision of a specific activity or curriculum area, which was important to some respondents (Hunter 1991). This range could be in the form of additional services and facilities (e.g. music room, laboratory, gymnasium) not available at a rival school (Fowler-Finn 1994), or a swimming pool, computers, and school dinners (Forster 1992). Other targets are specific A level subjects, and facilities for art, music and sport (Walford 1986), Welsh language teaching (Packer and Campbell 1993), and extra-curricular activities in general (Edwards *et al.* 1989).

On the other hand, there are many of the studies of choice in state-funded education which have not found academic criteria to be particularly important. These criteria always appear, but often way down the "rankings". Coldron and Boulton (1991) claimed that the happiness of the child was the crucial consideration, and that academic attainment was in at least second place. Fowler-Finn (1994) found in a study in the USA, that despite the enactment of a choice programme specifically aimed at improving academic standards, the quality of education, the quality of teaching, and even the academic progress of pupils were not mentioned by most parents in making their choices. Forster (1992) agreed that very few parents mentioned examination results, or the curriculum, as a factor, and Adler *et al.* (1989) came to the same conclusion for Scotland. Discipline was the major factor in secondary school choice, and examinations were not.

In fact, an over-emphasis on examinations, described by Smith and Tomlinson (1989) as having narrowly academic views, was found by them to be a source of dissatisfaction to some parents. Some parents may be looking for an atmosphere in school which is not too competitive and over-powering for a lower ability or unmotivated child, or one with a specific learning difficulty. In addition, the reintroduction of a limited form of selection by ability in some state-funded education may produce a renewed market for private schools taking in the equivalent of the old 11+ "failures". Some private schools in this study certainly see special educational needs, or learning difficulties, as a growing market area (see Chapter 6).

Academic school effect?

An academic advantage might be gained from attending a particular school where children make better academic progress and gain better examination results than they would have done at another school, but a claim to that effect would be hard to substantiate. There is some evidence that pupils in private schools, for example, perform better on average on many raw score measures of academic outcome (e.g. Halsey *et al.* 1984, ISIS 1995b, Statham and Mackinnon 1991, Walford 1990) and many of these figures are impressive, but what they do not show is that the private schools were being more effective with equivalent pupils, even though some observers have sought to make the connection between the independent sector and academic excellence. As one centre-left organisation put it, "it is clear that children often have a better chance of doing well if their parents can afford to send them to a good independent fee-paying school and decide to do so. About 7% of our children are in private sector schools. The level of resources put into independent schools is usually much higher than that available for schools maintained by the state so that, apart from anything else, pupil-teacher ratios are much lower and pupils can receive more individual attention from teachers. Facilities are also usually more favourable" (National Commission on Education 1993 p.7). As is shown in Chapter 6, such a description does not apply to a typical private school in Wales, and one of the reasons for doubting the validity of the claim that private schools produce better results, is that the figures used to justify it usually refer only to a select group of schools, such as those represented by GSA, HMC or ISIS.

Another reason for doubt is the distinction between school outcomes and school effects. Although it may be that some proportion of the variance between schools in public examination results is school related (Reynolds and Cuttance 1992) and that private schools have a greater academic effect (Chubb and Moe 1990, Coleman *et al.* 1981), the absolute size of the effect is small (Cookson 1994, Halsey *et al.* 1980). Whether a school is private or not is probably less significant to outcomes *per se* than the social and ethnic background of the pupils, and the levels and quality of staffing. This background obviously continues to be present throughout the years of schooling "contaminating" any attempt to measure a school effect. Evidence that background continues to play a part in progress, and not merely initial attainment is given by Mortimore and Mortimore (1986) who cited studies showing greater academic progress by socio-economic class. To some extent this is related to differing attendance rates, which could be related to poverty, ill-health, poor housing, the number of siblings and the number of parents, as much as school specific factors. Gray and Jones (1986) considered that over 80% of school examination results could be attributed solely to the ability and background of the intake.

In fact, Lake (1992) has suggested that the main determinants of later GCSE performance are already discernible in candidates at the age of five. The catchment area of a primary school proved to be of more significance than its quality of teaching since there was a correlation of 0.94 between school success at GCSE, and the percentage of pupils on free meals at primary age, as a proxy measure of social disadvantage linked to poor literacy levels in the family. Different types of school, such as comprehensive and selective produce comparable academic results according to Rutter *et al.* (1979). Any differences found in their study between schools and school types were much less than the major differences between outcomes for different subjects, or departments, within each school. Walford (1984) subtracted variance due to family background and higher average school leaving age in the private sector from examination results, using figures from the Halsey *et al.* (1980) study. If these two factors are ignored, the difference between sectors for men born in the period 1933-1942 was not significant. The sole advantage of private education may be a higher retention of pupils at 16, and even this may be parentally determined. For men born 1943-1952, the school effect was larger but still very small. Much greater variance was shown between types of private school. After allowing for prior attainment in one study, a school effect in the form of

35

variation between schools was apparent in specific subjects only, but variation on whole school measures was insignificant (Tymms 1992). Redpath and Harvey (1990) even found evidence of the reverse - that maintained schools gave an academic advantage over private ones when considering only children from service-class families. Such pupils were shown to have higher rates of application, and higher rates of acceptance to higher education from state schools.

Haertel *et al.* (1987) found similar results in the USA and concluded that longitudinal studies showed only a very small academic advantage for pupils in private education (except for minority pupils). The variability between sectors in USA was also dwarfed by that within each. Coleman *et al.* (1966) found no measurable school resources or policies that showed consistent relationships to school effectiveness. The major links to achievement were home related variables, such as SES and parental education. After prior achievement, socio-economic background, mothers' education, number of siblings and gender were "partialled" out of the results, the remaining variance was most likely to be random error.

One of the largest longitudinal surveys in this field was the High School and Beyond survey (HSB) in the USA, which demonstrated better results for pupils from private schools (Witte 1992), but academically the private school effect was still smaller than the effects of family background, student characteristics, and taking more advanced courses. Most such elite private schools are in the suburbs. They tend to be much smaller, taking fewer blacks and Hispanics, and having more highly educated parents. They offer more advanced academic courses, have higher expectations, give more homework, show fairer discipline, and display less fighting and abuse of teachers, less truancy, and fewer problems with drugs (Witte 1992). One of the reasons for the small difference between schools at the level of High School in the USA, may be that very little of what the standard tests measure is actually learnt over the two years from tenth to twelfth grade. These years show very little improvement for anyone at all, so these are mostly "wasted" years compared to the first seven grades. Thus the potential for gain or loss in secondary schools is not large. Unlike other analyses of the same data, Witte (1992) found only a very small link between achievement and school organisation criteria, such as autonomy. Evidence of enormous measurement errors in some questions of the HSB survey, such as the family SES, as reported by students, and also in the "gain" scores, "suggest considerable uncertainty in the results of prior studies of public and private school differences" (Witte 1992 p. 388).

It is clear that the use of league tables as school performance indicators is totally dependent upon the application of a satisfactory value-added model, taking into account the factors described above (Bellin *et al.* 1996). However, even if this becomes possible, the performance of individual schools differs from year to year, has a differential effect on various sub-groups of pupils, and different outcomes by subject of study and department (Thomas *et al.* 1995). There are anyway major problems in using examination results as a "global" measure of school effectiveness. Individual schools may be differentially effective for particular social classes, or one gender, or some minorities (Gaffney 1981). Nuttall (1986) has shown that assumptions of comparability between sexes of candidates, examining boards, modes of examining and subjects are anyway not valid. Others agree that some syllabuses are easier than others (Blackburne 1994), and that school outcomes do not show much reliability from year to year (Reynolds and Cuttance 1992).

There is, perhaps, no such thing as an "effective school", merely a school that was effective last year. The school's annual league position may have no more significance than the number on the last turn of the roulette wheel.

Reserving the criticism of the British league tables for lack of added value, they are not even correct in the information that they do contain. Private schools have developed strategies for improving their position. Results subject to appeal do not appear in the tables, and the rate of appeals has risen dramatically since 1988. Private entries do not appear in the tables and local private schools are now "expelling" marginal candidates after the "mocks", but allowing them to return and sit their examinations as private individuals (personal observation).

Young (1994$_d$) suggested that it may never be possible to make league tables of results truly comparable, despite sophisticated research approaches of a kind unavailable to consumers. There is anyway little evidence that parents were actually aware of school examination results and their meaning, nor that they took any notice of them in choice of school (Smith and Tomlinson 1989) even when they claim to do so. Most parents simply do not seem to compare results (Morris 1994). The concept of raw-score league tables was even ridiculed in a peak-time television comedy (Spitting Image 27/11/94) by showing a school coming top of the league, and giving all their prizes to their only pupil, since all the others had been expelled. Since this sketch was presented without any background information at all, the programme makers presumably felt that most viewers would be aware of its satirical basis.

Good academic outcomes are not merely prized for their own sake, but are seen by some as leading to further success in later life. Although Haertel *et al.* (1987) showed that academic performance in the USA is only very weakly related to future earnings and job prospects, some families in other studies have mentioned getting on better in a career as a reason for school choice. Walford (1990) gave examples of the kind of figures sometimes quoted to show the validity of such choice criteria. In 1987 nearly half of Britain's' parliamentary M.P.s were from private schools. This was a much higher proportion than the proportion of pupils educated privately, and figures in other high ranking jobs including the judiciary and the armed forces were even more extreme. Similar results were given by Roker (1991), and Walford (1987$_a$). This could be used to argue that a private education does indeed help past pupils to get on in life, but it must be remembered that many of these M.P.s and judges were in school before 1944 and the advent of free universal education. A more complex longitudinal analysis would be needed to establish the proposition, and even then it could only establish that a private, or selective, education had been beneficial some 40 years previously. The figures also reveal that these "leaders" are mainly drawn from a small range of HMC-type public schools with a high rate of entry into Oxford and Cambridge Universities, and the argument, such as it is, is not applicable to the fee-paying sector as a whole. To send a child to a proprietary school in Wales, for example, solely on the basis of this evidence would not be rational. This conclusion is supported in a more recent analysis of the education of "celebrities" quoted in Massey (1993). Of these, 1,800 out of 3,100 had been to private schools, but only 369 of the 2,500 such schools in the UK were represented. As the other 1,300 celebrities came from more than 1,000 state schools, these figures also confirm that it is particular private schools rather than private schools in general, which should be seen as relevant.

Blackledge and Hunt (1985) stated that there is little relationship between educational attainment and later occupational position, even though many people believe that there is. Perhaps this is due to what they call a "crisis in credentialism". There are not enough administrative sinecure jobs to go around, and it is precisely these jobs to which general success in school leads. This assertion is supported by the National Longitudinal Study of the Class of 1972 in the USA. A study of the pupils from proprietary schools in the cohort, found no relationship between certification and later annual earnings. Such schools may even reduce the wage rates for men, and the study concluded that "there are no benefits of proprietary schools at all" (Grubb 1994 p.351).

Even the benefit shown above, that pupils in fee-paying schools tend to stay at school longer, may be unrelated to the schools themselves. It is possible that the career trajectories of pupils from private schools reflect the aspirations of parents, who are concerned with the education, employment, and ultimate social class destiny of their children. In other words, they view education primarily as a process of social and cultural reproduction. For example, Ashford (1990) found a clear relationship between pupil career and parental employment status. Employed parents were more likely to have a child staying on at school after 16, and this finding was unaffected by the condition of the local labour market. Similarly, Emler and St James (1989) reported that parents in skilled and non-manual occupations gave their children greater encouragement to stay on at age 16. These, and the local labour market may be stronger determinants than the attractiveness, or benefit, of the school itself. However, even the age of leaving school may not be a major determinant of later occupational success, since the local labour market is still more important (Bynner 1989), and this influence can over-ride differences between classes, genders and races (Gray and Sime 1989).

As a more direct, non-educational benefit, some private schools in the USA may have a charter or external authority to lift students into selective private colleges, even without better results (Cookson 1994), and this causes confusion in any assessment as "much of the literature concerning private schools has been extremely naive because the authors have failed to take into account the distinction between educational amount and educational route" (Cookson 1994 p. 95). It is agreed that links between education and economic outcomes are weak, as "what one learns in school has little to do directly with one's earning power" (Cookson 1994 p. 112). The end of closed scholarships to Oxford and Cambridge from public schools has done much to end such blatant privilege in the UK (Salter and Tapper 1981). Schools may merely sort their intake by class, and so preserve the inequality in their backgrounds. Farber (1969) went so far as to argue that outcome grades are the very antithesis of education. He cited 46 studies in the USA, comparing college grades and subsequent performance, and found no justification for basing admissions to higher education on those grades.

Whether reproduction occurs because those families with cultural capital (Bourdieu and Passeron 1992), and those familiar with an "elaborated code" (Bernstein 1977), can privilege their definition of reality and ordinariness, and so determine a form of education in which their children are more likely to be successful, is not clear. It may be that the "restricted code" is itself sufficient to explain later poorer career prospects, with what happens at school producing no additional noticeable effect. This latter model is a more parsimonious explanation of results, such as those from Bates (1990), who compared the "vocational trajectory" of working class girls from an FE college, some wishing to become care assistants, and others wishing to be fashion designers. Only some families were prepared to tolerate the training period necessary, when they could offer financial support to the youngster through college, and had the physical space at home for college work, and the more elusive "career toleration", in which the family and its values do not censor the form of work or training. These were all likely to be the better off families, forming an "upwardly mobile" working class. Representatives of the colleges interviewing the prospective students used such factors as confidence, eloquence, smartness, and family support, as indicators of successful completion of the course. They therefore appeared to prioritise the course success, but their role was to screen students for the required social and cultural resources, and so they were playing an invisible role in social reproduction. Perhaps the situation is as simple as explained by Meighan (1986), in that the rules which define "good" education, and perpetuate the unequal distribution of power and privilege are mainly in the hands of those who are themselves the products of private, and selective, schools.

One determinant of school academic effectiveness may be the quality of the teachers (DES 1988). In the state sector, 27% of teaching is done by non-specialist teachers, (i.e. those with no main or subsidiary qualification in the subject), with the figure rising to 40% for Technology and 50% for Science, and this is seen by some as a barrier to effective teaching (National Commission on Education 1993). High quality teachers and teaching may be important for academic outcomes. Although it is true that staff in private schools have traditionally had no teacher training (Salter and Tapper 1981), the situation is changing. In 1982, 90% of teachers in HMC schools were graduates. Advertisements for staff in private schools generally ask for more than good graduates. These schools have been described as "*greedy*", requiring all staff to help with time-consuming activities such as community service, cadet forces and cricket umpiring. The danger for researchers, and "consumers", is that they may confuse the quality of teachers with their qualifications. Although education beyond 'A' level in the subject taught is desirable, it is not the sole nor necessary determinant of teaching success. Rutter *et al.* (1979) also found that the quality of teachers had a significant effect in schools, but their description of high quality teachers was of those who behave as they would wish pupils to behave, who have high expectations of the pupils, and who display good classroom management skills. All of these skills are independent of teacher subject specialisms. They also found that better performance was linked to high staff turnover, but it is perhaps unsurprising that this is not mentioned as a factor in parental choice.

Some studies have found no direct connection between teacher qualification and school effectiveness. Coleman *et al.* (1981) for example, found that private schools in the USA had teachers with poorer qualifications, and Gaffney (1981) found that Catholic private schools had more poorly paid teachers than state schools, if credentials and experience were matched. Both studies found that despite this apparent handicap, the private schools produced better results. None of the studies cited mentioned the quality and level of support staff, nor the proportion of lessons taught by non-specialists, nor the provision for INSET. All of these are likely to affect the quality of teaching, but are perhaps too little publicised for all parents to decode, and none appear in the literature from the focus schools in this study.

One study made a direct comparison of parent satisfaction with teachers in both sectors (Turner 1983), and found proportionately more complaints about teachers in state-maintained schools. State school teachers generally set less homework, offered less help outside lessons, and had poor class control and insufficient subject knowledge. In contrast, Walford (1986) found that 76% of pupils and parents were satisfied with the quality of teaching in private schools. Most of their complaints were about pupils not being made to work hard enough, and poor lesson preparation by teachers. The same departments and teachers appeared repeatedly, suggesting that there was some reliability in the complaints.

Even the relevance of the scale of provision in the two sectors is in dispute. Walford (1990) provided some evidence that, in 1987, private schools were better equipped. For example, the average number of microcomputers in state schools was one per 260 pupils. Private schools had on average ten computers per 260 pupils. On the other hand, Gaffney (1981) and Coleman *et al.* (1981) found that Catholic private schools in the USA had worse facilities and equipment than others but still obtained better results. Both studies also found that parents did not consider facilities to be important, although it is possible that the pupils themselves would rate the provision of facilities more highly. Rutter *et al.* (1979) agreed that facilities are not a determinant of school effectiveness. Griffiths (1991) looked specifically at small private schools in South Wales and found that in general these schools were not offering better facilities than maintained schools in the region, perhaps worse.

The popular image of a fee-paying school is one that provides a great range of subjects and extra-curricular activities, and that is more likely to offer specialised curricular areas. In confirmation, Walford (1990) showed that in 1987, the range of sports on offer in private schools was greater than in the state sector. As an example, pupils could choose from a menu of 23 sports available at Rugby School, which had a sports hall, a swimming pool and 86 acres of playing fields. Although SHA (1990) reported a decline in sport and extra-curricular provision in schools from 1986 to 1990, private schools still do more, and 29% had reported an increase in extra-curricular activities since 1980. However, Walford was discussing the provision in a large long-established boarding school, of a kind which is not typical of the fee-paying sector in Wales (Gorard 1996$_a$), and even in the elite schools there is evidence that the academic pressure created by league tables, and the fear of litigation in event of an accident after legislation such as the Parents Charter and the Children's' Act, has led to staff being more reluctant to take games and fixtures (Spencer 1994). The traditional difference in "extra-curricular" activities between the sectors may be decreasing.

Many private schools anyway do not conform to the popular image, and the proprietary schools in the UK are similar to the Catholic schools in the USA, in that they do not have the funds for elaborate provision of inessentials. Griffiths (1991) pointed out that the small size of the private schools in South Wales effectively reduces the range of curricular and sporting options available to pupils. She also argued that smaller schools have fewer staff and therefore less likelihood of having a particular interest or skill (like chess, ancient Greek, or orienteering) represented. None of these schools offered Welsh, unlike their maintained rivals. In fact the private schools in Wales offered a more limited curriculum overall, partly because of financial constraint, and partly because there were too few pupils in any one age group to make certain activities viable (e.g. to form a rugby team).

In summary it is not always clear that differences in terms of academic effectiveness or privilege actually exist between the two sectors, or between the schools within them. Where these differences do exist, it is not clear that they apply to the whole school, nor that they are constant year-on-year, nor that parents and children would be able to judge them adequately given the academic disputes over their measurement.

Situational criteria

Situational, or convenience, criteria, have been shown to be very important in school choice, particularly for state-funded schools, lower-income groups, and the children themselves. In families where the child's preference is important, proximity to home, and having friends in the same schools are also important (Woods 1992). In one study of choice within state provision in the USA, the location of the school was substantially more significant than any other characteristic (Fowler-Finn 1994). A desirable location could be also be attractive, in a well-to-do leafy suburb, but other work has suggested that proximity is the most desirable characteristic of the location of a school, which is linked to ease of travel (Hunter 1991). To those families who claimed that location and ease of travel are important, must be added those who appear to have no choice of school at all, perhaps because of isolation and travel difficulties (Fitz *et al.* 1993). Geography alone can determine the school attended. Coldron and Boulton (1991) and West (1992) found that proximity was a major determinant of choice, and the former suggested that it was linked to convenience for parents, the safety of the child's travel, and the likelihood of friends and relatives also going to the school. Convenience for parents was also the motivation, in many cases, for sending all children to the same school (Packer and Campbell 1993), which may then come to be seen as part of a family tradition of using a particular school (Walford 1986).

Many studies have found that for pupils, in addition to proximity, the most important reason for choosing a school was the presence of friends, or relatives, in the school (Forster 1992, Terrell and Clinton 1992, West and Varlaam 1991, Alston 1985). Ball *et al.* (1992) suggested that such situational criteria are more important for working-class families, where the child's' wishes may be more decisive within the constraints imposed by travel. The criteria used by working-class families are more likely to be practical, and with immediate effect, whereas middle-class families may consider longer-term and more idealistic notions. Since the pupils have a larger say in working-class families, it is not surprising that these class differences also relate to the differences observed between adults and children.

On the other hand, Hammond and Dennison (1995) found that travel was not very important, especially for the more affluent families, in rural areas, who, presumably, did not have much choice about whether to travel or not. Similarly, some studies of choice in fee-paying schools, although recognising situational criteria like family tradition and location, have reported that academic reasons are more significant (Edwards *et al.* 1989, GPDSA 1995). In this context, it is

41

interesting to note that it may be as much the choices influenced by children in working-class families using immediate situational criteria, as any kind of middle-class flight, that is leading to the suggested social segregation and stratification in education due to market effects, for "it is possible that schools are being selected by like-minded parents for similar reasons with the knock on effect that their children will go to the same schools as friends - who may well be of a similar social group" (David *et al.* 1994 p.136).

In fee-paying schools, boarding can also be a situational variable. Some parents may select a boarding school because it is a good school for other reasons, or because they like the discipline of boarding, but Fox (1990) found that 4% of parents at HMC schools expressed a specific need to send the child to a boarding school, and these were often armed services families, or parents in the process of separating.

Situational school effect?

There are practical everyday reasons for choosing a school, such as ease of travel, and these are perhaps the easiest for any prospective parent to judge when making a selection. Convenience or ease of access (which includes proximity, travel and location) is perhaps the most commonly cited reason for selecting or rejecting a state-funded school. West (1992) also found that 11% of pupils had siblings in the same school, and 44% had friends from a previous school going to the new one. In many cases, these links were cited as the main determinant of school choice, and it is suggested in Chapter 3 that these two variables are related to convenience. Convenience may be less significant for parents considering private school because of the possibility of boarding, and the higher probability of car ownership, or a non-working spouse who can take and collect the children.

As well as the convenience of using the same school for several children, private school users may also have a family tradition of using a particular school, or type of school. This is most marked in what may be termed "sector loyalty", although in the schools studied by West (1992), 4% of current parents were also ex-pupils of the same school themselves. Halsey *et al.* (1980) found that 57% of pupils who were privately educated at primary school continued to private secondary schools, but there was also evidence of significant cross sector movement, while Boyd and Cibulka (1989) showed that the relevance of family tradition may be diminishing. In the same year, Edwards *et al.* (1989) found that only 39% of fee-paying parents had been to private schools. Even in the major public schools, half of the parents had been to state schools, and 75% had used state schools for other children, and over 30% of boys in HMC schools had been to a state primary previously (Walford 1990). So it is clear that although sector and school loyalty does exist, it is a relatively small-scale phenomenon, at least in the private sector.

Boarding is mentioned as a requirement by some parents, and for these few it is often the main reason for choosing a private school. However, boarding is also available, and perhaps more comfortable within the maintained sector (Whitehead 1994). There are also a number of parents who believe that boarding is the natural and preferred method of schooling, even though that number is dropping. Dean (1994b) reported an ISIS census showing a drop of 5.2% in the proportion of boarders in that year. The drop in 1993 was 6.2%. On the other hand the number of foreign boarders rose by 9.6%. This trend of reduced numbers, and a higher proportion of foreign pupils has been going on for some time. Whitty *et al.* (1989) reported that 20% of privately educated pupils were boarding, 65% of whom were boys, but boarders had dropped to 14% of privately educated pupils by 1993 (Dean 1994$_a$). Walford (1993) stated that boarding had declined by 2% for girls and 12% for boys from 1982 to 1989. Boarding was already in decline from 1974 to 1984, while foreign pupils increased from 2591 to 4389 in the same period. Boarders coming from same the county as the school rose from 7% in 1967 to 33% in 1982. By 1982, 60% of boarders' parents lived within 40 miles of the school (Walford 1986). This suggests a decline in the number of families with a specific need for boarding, and probably also explains part of the increase in demand for weekly boarding.

In summary, although the situational criteria described here, such as distance from home, do differ between schools, and are relatively easy to judge compared to educational effectiveness, they are unlikely to produce a great impact on a market for schools, either in terms of differing enrolment patterns, or school improvement.

Organisational criteria

Included in this category of school choice criteria are some characteristics which may be relevant to that elusive quality called "school ethos", as well as school size, management style, and the level of the fees. Organisational criteria have been seen as important by researchers into school effectiveness, but have not always been shown to be as important to parents faced with school choice. For example, although some parents, in a study by Hunter (1991) reportedly wanted parents to be welcomed in the school, a happy school atmosphere and the use of uniform, all of these comments came after prompting by the researcher. None were in the unprompted list of reasons. Similarly, West (1992) found that the ethos of the school, and the physical environment were important reasons for choice, but only to pupils who had already attended the school for some time. It may be that ethos is a somewhat nebulous *post-hoc* justification of what may otherwise be seen as a poor choice, or that it is too difficult to assess quickly with *a priori* information. Good school ethos, and high quality of leadership (i.e. management) are both mentioned by parents in a study reported by Clark and Round (1991), but even so they are far from the most important reasons given for the choice of a school. The study by Edwards *et al.* (1989) did report the school ethos as being among the most frequently mentioned criteria, but it was only one of several reasons with identical frequencies. Atmosphere/ethos was the second most common criterion according to parents in David *et al.* (1994). The reputation of the school, or a "good reputation", appears as an important reason for choice in several studies (Hammond and Dennison 1995, West 1992), but it is not a reason that fits very well with any others. It has the ambiguity of reasons such as "good discipline", but it is also, to some extent, a source of information about a school, like a brochure, and not a reason. It needs to be broken down, or otherwise examined, to decide what it is that the school has a reputation for.

Griffiths (1991) has done some of the little work appearing so far from fee-paying schools in Wales. These small schools seemed to cater for those parents who did not approve of recent educational changes in teaching practice. The schools emphasised tradition by having an old-fashioned uniform, with sporting cups and old photographs on prominent display. Academic gowns were frequently worn or visible on door hooks. There might be a coal fire in the Head's study. Classrooms had desks in reassuringly traditional rows. Such schools apparently offered the status of being known to pay for education, the confidence that comes from an awareness of privilege, less shame in being of weak ability because one form entry precludes streaming, better discipline, smaller classes, better atmosphere, freedom from fear of bullying in comprehensives, easier access to Head, and sensitivity and responsiveness to parents' views. All of these reasons have been confirmed by other work, including the higher status of private schooling (Walford 1986), small classes (ISIS 1992), small schools (Fowler-Finn 1994), and traditional uniform (Packer and Campbell 1993). It has been suggested that parents like small classes so much that the private sector is almost deliberately small scale (Johnson 1987).

The traditionalist, or perhaps restorationist, parents may want more than simple icons of tradition like desks and honours boards. The physical environment and buildings are relevant (Cookson and Persell 1985), as is the style and approach of the headteacher (Madsen 1994). Gaffney (1981) reported on private Catholic schools in USA, and showed that parents were looking for the teaching of moral value, discipline, respect and care for others. On the other hand, a few parents definitely do not want tradition in schools, and there are a range of styles of school within the UK private sector for them to choose from, including Summerhill, the London Free School, and Steiner and Montessori schools. Child (1962) suggested some of the reasons for using these progressive schools, which may be widening a child's interests, developing their personality, liberal discipline, or seeing school as an end in itself. A particular problem in much educational research is this neglect of the life of the children while at school, and an over-emphasis on what happens after or as a result of it. In a study of girl's private schools, Walford (1986) found that one of the reasons given for girls' choice of an HMC school in the sixth form was that they wanted to get away from boring petty restrictions and a childish ethos in their current single-sex school.

The major defining factor of the private sector is the payment of fees for tuition. Although there is no evidence that the level of fees is a major factor in the choice of school within the sector, it is likely that the existence of a fee is a major determinant of choice between state or private education in the UK. Statham and Mackinon (1991) stated that 6% of private pupils were paid for by the Assisted Places Scheme in 1990. Many schools within the scheme received applications for APs far in excess of the number available. This suggests, on the face of it, the existence of a significant number of parents who want to use private education, but who cannot afford the fees (even though much of this demand could be explained as multiple applications by fewer families). If so, inability to pay the fees could be important to many parents who make the default choice of the maintained sector. In a US study, 50 to 60% of parents mentioned affordable tuition fees as an important factor in selecting a private school (Bauch 1989).

Organisational school effect?

These are the criteria discussed above concerning the ethos, and management style of the school, as well as the cost in the case of fee-paying schools. The level of

44

fees to be paid is rarely mentioned as a factor in the choice of a particular private school, and is anyway hard to compare between schools. Parents know that they will have to pay "an arm and a leg" anyway. Some schools have higher fees but provide text books, stationery and meals without extra charge, others have low basic fees but charge extra for many items. Scholarships and bursaries may be influential in attracting pupils but this may be as much to do with a feeling of pride as the actual cash value. The number of applicants for the Assisted Places Scheme suggests that there are parents who would like to consider private schools but who cannot afford to. These parents are presumably not otherwise able to make a free choice of sectors, so that fees are an important part of their choice, but not in their choice of a specific school. However many of the Assisted Places are going to parents who would consider private schools anyway. Edwards *et al.* (1989) found that many APs had gone to pupils from "artificially" poor families. Many APs went to families with a private school "tradition", as several had siblings in private schools and 30% would have gone to the chosen school anyway without the assistance. These families were rarely of manual working-class background as decided by parental occupation. Overall, 10% of pupils in private schools had a single parent, but the figure for AP pupils was 40%. This reinforces the conclusion that many APs are going to families with middle-class occupations, but who have a temporarily low income because of death, divorce or unemployment. However, there is also some evidence of change here, for although only 39% of fee payers parents had been to private schools, a mere 13% of APs parents had.

Gaffney (1981) found that Catholic schools generally spend less per pupil than state schools in the USA, but gain better results, and this finding was confirmed by Coleman *et al.* (1981). In the UK in 1991, on the other hand, the unit cost of private secondary schools was £3,206, while that of state secondary schools was £1,926 (National Commission on Education 1993), with equivalent figures for primary schools. It is not clear whether these figures should be seen as a measure of quality or of inefficiency. Spending more does not, in itself, guarantee better education. In Wales there is no correlation between the level of fees, and examination results in private schools. In fact, in the present study, the private school with the worst GCSE results, has the second highest fees, and the school with the best GCSE results has the third lowest fees (Chapter 10).

Buildings and the physical environment of the school are rarely mentioned by parents, although some particularly attractive structures still provoke comment. Rutter *et al.* (1979) found that school effectiveness was not related in any way to the problems of operating a split site, nor to the age and size of the school buildings. Gaffney (1981) confirmed this by reporting private Catholic schools in the USA with very poor buildings in comparison to rival maintained schools. These still produce better outcomes and are accordingly popular with parents.

According to Witte, private schools in the USA are more efficient and more responsive as they operate without district offices, having higher morale, and more teacher/parent involvement (Witte 1990). Responsiveness and openness to parents (including ease of access to Head) are desirable characteristics of a private school for some writers, and a common characteristic of effective state schools for others (Bolam *et al.* 1993). Parents who have friends, who also have children at the same school, appear more proactive in dealing with the school, as well as being more involved with learning at home (Madsen 1994), but the opportunities and benefits of parental involvement with school decrease as the child gets older. Coleman and Hoffer (1987) showed that private schools in the USA appear to extend opportunities to parents to become more involved in the school, while one third of parents in USA private schools help to make decisions in areas of policy, goals and curriculum (Bauch 1989). However, this may not be the function of the school itself, as private schools may be attracting parents who are more highly motivated, or who have more time to be involved in school life anyway.

In fact, parents generally do not participate in the governance of private schools in the UK. While the schools may feel that as commercial concerns they must be responsive to parents' views, it is also the case that most parent or parent/teacher associations are limited to social and fund raising activities, which is unlikely to lead to high efficacy (Madsen 1994). Parents are not represented on the governing bodies, nor are they allowed to be Governors or Trustees of private schools, in their own right. In general, the governors do not even hold an annual meeting for all parents, which is now a statutory requirement in the state sector. There is little enough democracy in most maintained schools, despite work showing that pupil participation in the running of the school has a beneficial effect on outcomes (Rutter et al. 1979). There is generally even less in private schools. The parents and pupils in private schools are also deprived of several rights and opportunities given to every family in the maintained sector by the various Education acts. Some schools required parents to sign a contract stating that "the head has complete discretion in the imposition of sanctions" (TES 1994b).

A well-managed school, with an inspirational Head, is not often cited as a factor in school choice, even though the DES (1988) included a stimulating headteacher, and clearly written aims and objectives in their summary of an effective school. Bolam et al. produced a DfE report in 1993 with similar findings. These authors also reported that an effective school has a clear vision, arrived at collaboratively, and strong purposeful leadership. Rutter et al. (1979) also found that firm collaborative leadership had an effect on school outcomes, although others have concluded that leadership style is important in some contexts only (Brown 1994). The impact of the principal is perhaps more likely to be on student and teacher attitudes to school, than on student achievement (Hallinger and Leithwood 1994). Indeed, "it has almost become an article of faith that the capacity of schools to improve teaching and learning is strongly mediated by the quality of leadership exercised by the principal" (Hallinger and Leithwood 1994 p. 208). In their review, several studies from 1983-1993 found a (small) impact on achievement, while others found none. It was clear that no single leadership style was appropriate for all schools, even though this work concentrated only on state-funded primary schools.

Small schools and classes are seen by some as an advantage for a school, and a recent advertisement for private schools claimed that "educationalists and politicians argue whether class size matters. Parents don't" (ISIS 1995b p.5). This conclusion is supported by recent work with state-funded primary schools (Bennett 1996). Private schools in South Wales do tend to be much smaller than maintained ones (Griffiths 1991). In 1991 the teacher to pupil ratio in the private sector in South Wales was 1:12. The average in the maintained sector for Wales was 1:18. By 1994 the average pupil:teacher ratio in private schools was 9.6, whereas it was 15.9 in state secondary, and 22.3 in state primary schools (Welsh Office 1995a). So, private schools in Wales do have smaller classes than all other types of schools, apart from special schools. However, these figures might not be comparable since sixth form teaching is traditionally done in smaller groups, and private schools generally have larger sixth forms. 'A' level classes in private schools are, in fact, often larger than in state schools, because of their higher retention of pupils (Walford 1986). There is also a higher proportion of labour intensive boarding, and extra-curricular, duties in some private schools.

It is not at all clear that school size is of much significance anyway. While Hargreaves *et al.* (1996) suggested several reasons, including daily contact with the headteacher, why small schools can be confident about their effectiveness, Rutter *et al.* (1979) found no link between the size of the school, or the size of the teaching group, and academic outcomes. Walford (1990) and others have confirmed these results. On the other hand, Coleman *et al.* (1981) found that the private schools had larger classes, and produced better academic results. There may be pastoral advantages to a small school linked with a friendly non-threatening environment, but these have to be balanced by the reduced range of subjects and extra-curricular activities provided, and the lack of expensive communal facilities, such as swimming pools. Even those optional subjects offered in small schools cannot always run, since classes of one student are not feasible in some subjects, such as drama. A smaller school also has fewer staff with less opportunity for staff responsibility, fewer incentives and less INSET cascading. Morgan (1990) confirmed in relation to Welsh schools, that small schools often had problems with their curriculum breadth, and the maintenance of a sixth form. Although parents tend to like small schools, seeing them as happier, and with better discipline, in fact, their lack of employee promotion possibilities tends to reduce staff quality, and the small groups in some subjects may not stimulate each other sufficiently.

In conclusion, it is not at all clear that there are many organisational criteria that can be as easily assessed by prospective parents as the situational criteria, and which can also be seen as undoubtedly beneficial for the education of their child or for society as a whole.

Selective criteria

To some extent, in an era when league tables of results are used as school performance indicators, and these results are presented in raw form, a desirable school is presented as one with high ability pupils. Thus market forces may be seen as driving parents to select schools with such "desirable" pupils. For example, the most popular schools in a Scottish study were those with above average attainment and high mean pupil SES (Echols *et al.* 1990). However, selection may be by gender or religion, for example, as well as by ability (Hunter 1991). Although each of these criteria for selection may not be inter-linked they can all have an effect on the social mix of the school, and so might lead indirectly to social selection.

Fowler-Finn (1994) found evidence that state schools were selected in the USA by some parents for their ethnic mix. In this case, it was mainly middle-class white parents with their own transport, avoiding schools with higher black and Hispanic populations. This "white flight" could be a significant factor in school choice, evident in both the USA and the Netherlands (Cookson 1994). Gaffney (1981) found a complementary trend in private Catholic schools in the USA. Minority groups, like blacks and Hispanics, formed 70% of their pupils. They appeared to achieve better results on average at this type of school than at the state-maintained equivalent. Their parents may have selected such a school for its apparent academic advantage, or perhaps because their children would be denied equal opportunities in a state school. There is some suggestion that a similar phenomenon is apparent in the UK (Rogers 1992). Social and racial selection is a sensitive and difficult area to research, since respondents may not always admit their true motivations. Walford (1986) suggested that such reasons playing a part in the decision may not be readily admitted to a researcher, or may only be discussed informally, which is one of the reasons for the follow-up interviews in the present study. The kind of reasons involved might include social exclusivity, in avoiding the tenants from a particular council housing estate, or wishing to avoid ethnic or racial groups. In Wales, the choice of Ysgolion Cymraeg [Welsh medium schools], and English style private schools may add another dimension to this form of selection (Gorard 1997_g).

A study of HMC schools found evidence of both social and ability selection (Fox 1989). Mixing with more desirable pupils, mixing with pupils who want to learn, and wanting the old school tie were all mentioned as relevant by parents, with the last presumably seen as leading to useful social contacts for later life. The same researcher (Fox 1990) discovered that 20% of the parents using HMC schools felt that private education was naturally better but advanced no reason, which she described as "unreasoning support for the private sector". These were simply the type of schools that "people like us" used.

Johnson (1987) suggested a link between selection by ability, and parents of high-ability children. Such parents mentioned the demise of the grammar school and direct-grant systems as reasons for using a fee-paying school. Schools offering special provision for high ability pupils were also seen as attractive to parents in the study by West (1992), as long as the policy was published and included enrichment, acceleration and differentiation. Specific reasons were given for the choice of a private education including the high ability of a child, and poor experience or reputation of state schools. Among the reasons given by parents of Assisted Place pupils for the choice of a private school were that comprehensives were too slow, "holding back the able pupils", and that the existence of a "critical mass" of able pupils leads to pressure and higher expectations (Edwards *et al.* 1989). Evidence from an ISIS survey (GPDSA 1995) suggested that dissatisfaction with state provision has increased since 1989, as a reason for choosing private education.

In several developed countries the existence and choice of private schools is dominated by the parents' right to choose a particular religion or denomination (Cookson 1994, Walford 1989). The importance of this in the USA can be seen in the finding that, in several studies, over 50% of parents cited religion as their main reason for using private schools (Thiessen 1982). Religious values were also given for choice of the mainly Catholic private schools by Bauch (1989). In the UK, the government has continued to deny funding for state schools of several minority religions, such as Islam (Pyke 1996_b), and followers of these religions can only turn to private schools in order to escape the Christian domination of the state sector.

In one study, more than 20% of parents were using single-sex education as the major factor in choosing a school (Alston 1985). Most of these were of Asian origin or were parents of girls. Edwards *et al.* (1989) also found that a significant proportion of girls felt that their private school offered a gentler, safer environment for them, often by being single-sex. The relevance of single-sex provision in selecting a school, especially for girls, appeared also in West and Varlaam (1991). These studies were concerned with pupils in Years 6 and 7 (10 and 11 year-olds). By the age of 16, Walford (1986) found that several girls in single-sex schools now favoured the presence of boys in the sixth form.

Selective school effect?

These are reasons for choosing a school based upon the attributes of other pupils allowed to attend, and they are taken to include the traditional use of private schools. Traditional or "unreasoned" support for the private sector is a description by Fox (1989) of the lack of reasons given by some families who do not really consider any alternative to private education. The assumption they make is that private education is necessarily better, even though there may be no evidence to suggest that such an assumption is warranted. In any assessment of the validity of parents' choice of private schools, it is important to remember the wide variability between the best and the worst. Walford (1990) stated that in 1987 there were 2,400 private schools in Britain, but that most research had concentrated on the major schools, particularly the "public schools" and that this tended to disguise the range within the sector. Whitty *et al.* pointed out that small schools benefit "unjustifiably from the halo effects thrown over the whole private sector by its market leaders" (Whitty et al. 1989 p. 13), while a further study stated that "although there is no direct relationship between level of fees and quality of education received, those at the lower end of the spectrum sometimes offer little more than snob appeal, and have poor facilities and teaching" (Walford 1993 p.5). The mere act of paying for a school, does not make it more desirable.

However, the National Child Development Study provided some evidence that selection by ability may be of benefit to high ability pupils (Steedman 1983b). Despite reservations about the findings, the public examination performance of pupils at selective grammar schools was better than for equivalent pupils at comprehensive schools. Similarly, after appropriate correction for the ability of the intakes, pupils at comprehensive schools appeared to perform better than those at secondary modern schools. This suggests that the quality of results for matched pupils is related to the proportion of high ability pupils (Rutter *et al.* 1979), or to the school mean ability (Willms and Echols 1992, Tymms 1992). However, the NCD study found no differences between the overall results of a system of grammar and secondary modern schools compared to a system of comprehensives. In effect, what is gained by those at grammar schools is lost by those elsewhere. Naturally, parents may only be concerned with the individual benefits to their child, and a rational choice strategy could therefore be to select the school with the highest mean ability, as judged by raw examination scores, or the difficulty of a selective entry examination.

Parents may also wish their children to be taught with others from families like their own, and so look for a fairly narrow and homogeneous social background in the intake, perhaps to insulate them "from the perils of the youth culture" (Edwards and Whitty 1995 p.1). Dean (1994$_a$) reported a MORI poll showing a dramatic increase in the class divide between private and public education. Fewer manual and white collar workers were using the private sector than ever before, despite the AP scheme, which has not really had its desired impact of broadening the scope of the private sector. The proportion of managerial and professional parents is still growing. However these class structures are fluid. It is not the same families using the same type of schools over generations, and over half of all families using private education were doing so for the first time. Halsey *et al.* (1980) found significant cross sector movement between state and private schools, but the abolition of selective grammar schools may have changed that. The introduction of Welsh medium schools, the Assisted Places Scheme and the re-introduction of selection in GM schools and CTCs may change it again. Edwards *et al.* (1989) found that 85% of fathers of full fee paying pupils were in social classes 1 or 2, and only 10% of fathers in the AP scheme were in social classes 6 and 7 (the pattern for mothers was similar except that more had no employment). Cookson and Persell (1985) reported that in USA private boarding schools, 85% of fathers and 75% of mothers were graduates, and 90% of fathers had managerial or professional jobs. Fewer of the mothers worked than the national average, but those that did were more likely to be professional or managerial. These families generally had a higher income than average. Fewer blacks, but higher proportions of both Jews and Asians attended these schools.

Equal opportunities (and lack of racial prejudice) are cited by Gaffney as influential in the USA private sector. Pupils from black and Hispanic backgrounds perform better in Catholic private schools than they do in state schools (Gaffney 1981). This agrees with the findings of Coleman and Hoffer (1987) that poor and minority pupils perform better in private schools, and are therefore more likely to continue in education after school. In summary, fee-paying schools do seem to be attracting a privileged elite, but not one which is self-replicating over generations. It remains to be seen whether the research cited concerning elite schools, full fee-payers, and boarders is directly relevant to the situation in Wales. Whether social selection takes place in some schools or not, it is not clear that it can have any direct benefit, whether to the families involved, or to society as a whole.

Some parents may select schools on the basis of the family religion, but there is little evidence that religious schools are more successful than others in retaining religious values over time (Walford 1984), or that attending a school of a particular faith makes a difference to whether children remain in that religious community after school (Pyke 1996$_a$). Child (1962) suspected that this is because many overtly religious schools are not actually living their values, and so their teaching is seen as hypocritical. Interestingly, followers of "world-renouncing" religious ethics (e.g. Baptist, Pentecostal, and Brethren) do appear to be disproportionately successful in worldly affairs such as careers (McEwen and Robinson 1994). It is possible that early Bible study, patterns of family socialisation stressing obedience, and moral separation from the world, could be a form of Bourdieu's cultural capital. In this way, early training in the family would prepare the child to learn and believe what they are taught. These evangelicals are highly upwardly mobile in social terms, and believe that their academic success comes from God, more than those of "normative" religious views. At GCSE, they perform better in linguistic subjects, but at A level no difference is apparent. McEwen and Robinson (1994) suggested that this may be because other students have a greater critical ability which is stifled in the children of evangelicals, but which is not relevant until A levels and beyond.

Selection by gender mix of school is relevant in a society in which sexism is still regarded as a problem. Girls use fewer household resources but perform more housework than boys, particularly so in families of lower social class (Emler and Abrams 1989). The gap between the pay of men and women in equivalent jobs still exists and is higher in Wales than elsewhere in the UK (Eurostat 1995). Such inequalities are also apparent in schools, where they are reinforced by sexual harassment of the kind described by Larkin (1994). Lee at al. (1994) confirmed this in a study of classroom sexism incidents in private schools in USA. Most incidents were initiated by teachers, and their frequency was similar between single-sex and coeducational schools, irrespective of the gender of the teacher. The forms of sexism differed, the strongest being in boys-only schools and chemistry lessons in coeducational schools. The fact that sexism is inherent in girls schools with mainly female staff shows that it is not only males involved.

"Mixing makes the girls brave and resourceful and the boys courteous and helpful", so said a teacher in the USA in 1915 (Tyack and Hansot 1990 p.243), but many feminists now see the coeducational schools as contributors to sexism and male domination. There may be a revival of interest in single-sex education for girls, partly because of this new feminist approach, but ironically also because of cultural restorationists who favour girls schools that offer a traditional "girlie" curriculum away from the danger and distraction of boys. These last might include those parents setting up Muslim private schools for girls only, who may be more concerned with controlling the experiences of their daughters than improving their educational chances (Walford 1995).

Single-sex education in the UK was criticised by Dale (1974) who felt that segregation by sex was artificial, and claimed that coeducation was to be preferred for the happiness of the pupils, and was not at any cost in attainment. Steedman (1983a) has used the data from the National Child Development Study to confirm part of this. Having controlled for the type of school, ability at 11, and home background, she found very little difference between the examination results for girls in single-sex and mixed schools. A more recent similarly careful comparison of results in public examinations for mathematics in Northern Ireland, found no significant difference between the performance of girls in single-sex and mixed schools (Daly and Shuttleworth 1995). The authors suggested that media reports to the contrary mainly refer to elite single-sex schools, such as those of GSA, termed by them the "headline-grabbers", and compare these to non-selective mixed schools. Walford (1986) found that similar proportions of girls take mathematics and science 'A' level in HMC schools, as in those belonging to GSA/GBGSA. These figures are also true for higher education (if medicine is included as a science). The findings of Bone (1983) are not so clear. Although single-sex provision appears to produce better academic results for girls, and less stereotyped choice of courses and careers, the effects are tangled up since most single-sex schools are also academically selective (Steedman 1983a), and all pupils have also been to primary schools, most of which are mixed. After allowing for background variables in the NCD study, such as the ability and social class of pupils, much reduced differences in attainment were evident (Steedman 1983$_a$). Pupils moving to single-sex at 11 schools already had higher scores at age 7, while pupils in mixed schools were more likely to have a father in a manual occupation. There was a slight advantage to girls in single-sex schools, but not for boys, and not for either in mathematics or English, and there was no evidence that girls performed better in science away from boys (Steedman 1983$_a$). However, all of the data were based upon a comparison of O-level results, and it cannot be assumed that the findings would generalise to pupils of lower ability.

Dale had actually found that boys did better, and girls did slightly worse, in mixed schools, but argued that the social advantages outweighed the depressed girls performance (Dale 1974). Spender (1989) felt that pupils made more sex-stereotyped subject choices in mixed schools, and Spender and Sarah (1988) reviewed studies showing that boys generally demanded more teacher time than girls in the classroom. This could further disadvantage girls in coeducational schools, who will have fewer female role models in school. They ask the question - "when males are dominant, is it sensible/useful/desirable for women to be educated with men?" (Spender and Sarah 1988 p. 13). Walford (1993) found that, allowing for prior academic achievement, girls in coeducational private sixth forms achieve fewer A levels, even though HMC boys schools are attracting the most able girls.

It is, therefore, not yet clear whether girls and boys perform better academically separately or not. Spender (1989) claimed that regardless of outcomes, single-sex schooling is a breathing space for girls from the message that they are unworthy, since sexism is still prevalent in the workplace (Budge 1994). Coeducational private schools often have a much higher proportion of boys, while girls schools are more likely to contain role models as a head of science or mathematics. In HMC schools only 10% of the staff are female, and none are heads. In 1984 there was not even one female head of an academic department. Figures quoted in Spender (1989) show quite clearly that despite the intervening Sex Discrimination Act of 1975, and an increase in women teachers, the proportion of women in authority in schools has continued to drop from 1965 to 1986, and this trend has continued at the same time as an increase in coeducation. Perhaps the message is that although governing bodies and education authorities see women as suitable candidates for the headship of a girls school, men are more suitable for any school in which there are male pupils. In Wales, 4% of male secondary school staff are headteachers, while only 0.3% of women are, and a staggering 40% of male primary schools teachers are heads, while only 8% of women are (Welsh Office 1995$_a$).

Cresser (1993) believes that the admission of girls to former boys-only schools is prompted more by a need to restore falling rolls than by any deep seated belief in coeducation. Delamont (1980) claimed that although all schools are conservative in nature, propagating a morality of family values that is less liberal than society, HMC schools were the worst in this respect. Girls do appear to have a lower status in HMC schools. One HMC school in Wales allocated one matron to each girls boarding house and two matrons, a housemaster, and three assistants to each boys house in 1992. Although this may have been due to staffing problems, such problems were not addressed, and the provision was declared "adequate and fair" by the Head (personal observation). Day girls are often used as a secondary market, filling in spare places after option schemes have been fitted around the boys. Terminology is also still a problem - fire regulations ask "boys" to evacuate the building, and signs direct visitors to the "masters' common room" in a school in Wales today (personal observation).

In summary, selection by class background, religion, ability, and gender all take place in school choice, but there is no conclusive evidence that any of these strategies are effective in terms of outcomes, or indeed in any other terms.

Security criteria

An important reason for parents when selecting a state-funded school is discipline. This usually means that they want the other pupils to have and display discipline - to be well-behaved - and one of the major motivations for this is concern for the safety and security of their own child. In this way, discipline is also linked to bullying, and the happiness of the child. Discipline can also be something taught to their own child (Fox 1990), and some parents may want lenient, rather than harsh, discipline in schools (Smith and Tomlinson 1989).

Good, or presumably firm, discipline was relevant in studies as various as those by Alston (1985), Bauch (1989), GPDSA (1995), Harris Research Centre (1988), Hunter (1991), ISIS (1992), Packer and Campbell (1993) and Walford (1986). In Scotland, Adler *et al* (1989) reported that discipline was a major factor in secondary school choice, and far more important than any academic criteria. Smith and Tomlinson (1989) interviewed Year 7 pupils and their parents, and asked them to suggest areas of satisfaction and dissatisfaction. Dissatisfaction was most commonly expressed over disciplinary matters, including the poor behaviour of other pupils, while satisfaction was more commonly expressed over academic matters.

West (1992) found that where the child would be happiest; the child's preference, and better discipline were all mentioned by respondents, but given less prominence overall than other school choice criteria. On the other hand, their "child's happiness was of paramount importance" according to Forster (1992). This may mean that the child's preference was important, or that the parents were looking for evidence from the school that their child would be happy there. A friendly school with a happy atmosphere was also considered important, which could be achieved with the help of a caring staff, or friendly teachers.

A threatening atmosphere, and bullying were off-putting to the pupils in the study by David *et al.* (1994), and this could be the reason for selection of a single-sex private school by some girls (Edwards *et al.* 1989). Fear of bullying at the local state school was a major reason for choice of fee-paying school in a study in South Wales (Griffiths 1991). It is clear that many parents "feel very protective towards their vulnerable 10 year old children" (Smedley 1995 p. 97), and are looking for a school in which their child will be happy and safe. Few studies mentioned pastoral care specifically, although it may be related to a happy atmosphere, or the desire for a small school.

Security school effect?

Security criteria, such as good discipline, well-behaved pupils, and a happy school atmosphere may be desirable characteristics for schools, but they are extremely hard to assess in a way that leads to rational comparison between institutions. Good discipline may mean tough, fair, or lenient. Most parents appear to refer to firm discipline, but Rutter *et al.* (1979), for example, described the use of rewards and remedies rather than punishments as a factor which has a beneficial effect on school outcomes. There is also a problem in identifying good or bad pupil behaviour, as indicated by a study (Corrigan 1979) of the "festering" activities of boys on housing estates in Sunderland. Their actual behaviour was very similar to the free-time house/study behaviour of public school boys (e.g. water fights, minor vandalism, drugs and drink). However, the working-class children were far more likely to be seen as badly behaved, and so to become involved with the judicial system.

A happy atmosphere, or a friendly school and a pleasant learning environment may have an effect on school outcomes (DES 1988), although the quality of pastoral care arrangements does not appear to (Rutter *et al.* 1979). But the type of school effectiveness research cited here tends to overlook the fact that the years spent at school are an end in themselves. Much of the research on school effectiveness in Britain appears to assume that schooling is only a means to an end, although for pupils it is a major part of their life. Jenks *et al.* (1972) concluded that "some schools are dull, depressing, even terrifying places, while others are lively, comforting and reassuring". If school life is viewed as an end in its own right, these difference are crucial.

One "terrifying" aspect of school can be bullying. Massey (1993) gave an insight into the scale of the problem, by pointing out that 'Childline' received 10,000 calls from children during the first six months in 1992, mostly concerning bullying and sexual abuse. There is no evidence that the situation is better in private education, and there is a feeling that it might even be worse. Although schools may advertise their policy for dealing with bullying, they are unlikely to present figures for its occurrence. In fact, most private schools would probably prefer not to mention bullying, or even its absence, in their promotional material. Like happiness, behaviour, and discipline, parents can really only judge bullying by the local reputation of the school, intuition, and the public behaviour of pupils outside school, all of which can be misleading.

Conclusion

Despite the differences between several studies cited here, it is clear that children do play a significant role in choosing, that families do not behave as "ideal consumers" content to use published school performance indicators, and that a wide range of choice criteria have been reported. The relative importance of these criteria varies between sectors, classes, and generations. Little work has been carried out with the full range of fee-paying schools, or in Wales. It has already been argued that there is a need for a new approach to researching school choice, and recent changes in education may, anyway, have made much of the earlier work of less relevance today. Most methodological approaches used in the work cited here have both advantages and disadvantages, and there may be no best method or approach. Some studies are from outside the UK, and some are of the state-maintained sector. Some involve only boys from HMC public schools, or girls from GSA and GPDSA schools, which are not representative of the fee-paying schools in Wales.

Some studies have used as few as 12 respondents, and some have involved over 15,000. It is difficult to assess whether studies of overseas private schools, HMC and GSA schools, or English state-maintained schools are more or less likely to be applicable to choice of the fee-paying sector in South Wales. Thus the findings are used chiefly to determine the variables to be studied in this work, in terms of questions to appear on the standard questionnaire used in this research. Each "variable", such as ease of travel, forms the basis of at least one prompt in the following study. The grouping of the variables into five categories - academic, situational, organisational, selective, and security - provides the start of a framework that can be used for later analysis. They are potential factors, that might be expected to emerge from the later principal components analysis, and as such they are hypothetical constructs awaiting testing (Comrey 1973).

However, the picture remains a confusing one. Very few of the reasons for selecting a school given by families in previous research are educationally relevant, different between schools, and easy to judge, even for academics. Selective criteria, for instance, may involve variation by ability, background or gender of pupil, or even family religion, in terms of school intake. Such criteria are relatively easy to judge, but they have no universal importance, since they are, by their very nature, of more significance to some groups than others. There is also no compelling evidence that schools chosen in this manner are any more effective than non-selective schools. Situational variables, such as proximity, are similarly easy to judge, and likely to be more universally popular with families than selection, according to previous work. However, reasons for choosing a school such as proximity to home are unlikely to cause major improvements to schools in a market system. Organisational and management criteria may be clearly linked to school effectiveness by research, but they are harder for families to judge *a priori*, and are consequently less popular reasons for choice. Security and academic reasons are both important in making a choice of school, according to the work described here, and while one is more relevant to the quality of life in school, the other is more concerned with the outcome of schooling. The reality of both reasons are hard for families to judge, which is why the simplest, and most visible, aspects of these criteria, such as size of class and league table results, may take on added but perhaps unwarranted importance in school choice.

3 The need for a fresh approach

Introduction

This chapter presents an exegesis of some of the existing key research on school choice. It proceeds to call for greater precision in survey design, a more sophisticated analysis of data and rigour in the interpretation of results in this field of research. It shows that even the best of the previous work may be flawed and it establishes some parameters for the methods used in this study. It contains a brief examination of the "state of the art" in UK school choice research, which is presented partly as justification for another study of school choice and partly to establish the need for a new methodological approach to its study (Gorard 1997$_c$). The chapter considers a range of methods common in previous choice research in the UK, in terms of their sampling strategies, instruments and techniques of analysis. In each section it offers examples of recent published work to illustrate the practical problems and pitfalls. It must be stressed that the work portrayed here has been selected not just for its suggested weaknesses, but because it is typical of an entire paradigm of school choice research. The examples come from some of the best and, perhaps, the most respected studies of their type. An indication of their importance in the field, despite their drawbacks, can be seen in Chapter 2 where their findings are discussed in more general terms, along with those of other researchers. Another reason that these particular examples are used is that, because they are respected, they are naturally quoted in subsequent work by other writers. Dennison (1995), for example, quotes both Coldron and Boulton (1991) and Gewirtz et al. (1994) despite the somewhat problematic nature of some of their work discussed below, as though their findings can be accepted at face value. The later paper, thus, ends up by using their concepts in an attempt to explain new findings. In this way, errors in the literature are in danger of propagating (Gorard 1997$_c$), and further threatening the already poor cumulation of knowledge in social science.

Quantitative or qualitative research?

There are currently thought to be two common approaches to the study of school choice, loosely based upon the two methodological paradigms, often referred to as quantitative and qualitative (Popkewitz 1984). The first approach is perhaps the most common approach world-wide, since it is used in market research (Cox *et al.* 1989, Gabbitas 1992, Tyrell 1992), as well as in academic studies of school choice. In general, this approach is to produce a summary list of reasons for school choice, and assess the popularity of those reasons statistically. It is argued here that in addition to simplifying, and so perhaps trivialising, the complex process of choosing a school, such an approach requires a precision in measurement, a sample size, and above all, a more complex analysis of results than is usually demonstrated in UK research. The second approach is a narrative or interpretative one, portraying the complexity of the choice process for individuals, by using the accounts of the choosers themselves. Such an approach is not new or ground-breaking, despite some claims to the contrary, as text books on qualitative methodology for educational researchers have been around for more than twenty-five years (e.g. Filstead 1970), but the dispute over its relevance continues. It is argued here that the findings of such work cannot always be meaningfully generalised from the individual cases to a larger population. There is also an inherent problem in using a grounded theory approach, such that merely plausible results may be accepted as valid, especially when they fit neatly into an existing language of description. An example of each of these dangers is explored later in this chapter.

It is clear that the two research paradigms are seen by some as dichotomous, so that working with lists, tables, and numbers is not seen as dealing with qualities, and looking for patterns in observations and interview transcripts is not seen as having anything to do with frequency counts. Clearly, statistical treatments, and the identification of general trends in data, both deal with measuring the occurrence of qualities in a study. Hermeneutics and discourse analysis, for example, can deal with quantities, even when these are expressed, not as cardinal numbers, but as terms such as "some", "few", "many", "most", or "none". This supposed split in research methods is more a matter of degree than anything, but is part of a larger split in social science between those concerned more with explanation, and those concentrating upon prediction (Frazer 1995). The distinction between the two methods may be an illusion according to some observers (West *et al* 1994), and a growing number of methodological eclectics "heroically" ignore the division, and attempt to use elements of both approaches (Cohen and Manion 1989). Happily a philosophical background for these researchers is beginning to emerge. They are the "new realists" (Frazer 1995), accepting the imprecision of measurement, the impact of subjectivity, and the dangers of reductivism, and so striving for even greater rigour in their studies, in the form of "triangulation" between the methods within one investigation. Social processes are complex, making them difficult to study, but it is important not to exaggerate their complexity compared to other areas of study, such as physics or history. The act of describing a process must of necessity simplify it, so that a paper of 10,000 words, even if it describes how only one family chose a school, is a huge simplification. However, in the same way that complex problems do not always have complex solutions, complex processes do not always need complex descriptions. Different levels of abstraction are appropriate for different purposes. Research can seek to both explain and predict. This is, perhaps, what is denoted by the new realism.

Since both approaches to studying school choice have common elements, they are dealt with together in the next two sections on sampling and instrument design. The final two sections briefly consider the uses in this field of statistics and qualitative analyses, respectively.

Problems of sampling

Perhaps the first problems encountered in researching school choice, whether using interview, survey, or observation, are those of selecting the sample to be used. There are practical problems such as negotiating access, and cost, which encourage the use of "opportunity" samples. Such samples can be reasonable, but they are reasonable only in terms of what is intended by the sampler. Research is not a census, nor is it a history, or the setting out of a mere story. The purpose of a sample is to allow generalisation of some sort to another, probably wider, population, or sampling frame. In designing such a sample the main methodological issues are representation, volunteer bias and, and size.

To be used to draw statistical generalisations from, a sample must represent as far as possible the population or cases to which its findings are transferred. There are at least three main ways of achieving this. A priori, the sample can be selected at random, or it can be selected on a stratified basis, having the relevant characteristics in the same proportions as the sampling frame, where the relevance of characteristics is determined by prior theory. A posteriori, the sample, having been determined by any method, and then characterised, can then only be used to generalise to populations with the same characteristics. Very little educational research in the field of school choice, as described in Chapter 2, is based on random sampling. Some attempt is generally made to show stratification but there is seldom a formal attempt to characterise both sample and frame. In reality, most samples are opportunity in nature, and so researchers must be cautious in generalising from them. For example, some researchers have made claims about the independent, or private school, sector in the UK, based upon sampling the high profile, readily available elite schools. This is likely to have contributed to the popular notion that the private sector is dominated by wealthy traditional foundation "public" schools. In fact, such a sample is totally unrepresentative of the much larger number of poorly resourced proprietary and grass-roots schools reported later in this study. Such research should therefore be cautious concerning claims made about the private school sector as a whole.

A study of school choice by Coldron and Boulton (1991) is used to illustrate several points in this chapter. The first concerns the quality of the sampling. The sample they used was 222 parents of Year 6 pupils. At first sight this is a reasonable number and substantially larger than in several other studies, but as with any study, there are several potential problems which need to be addressed before any conclusions can be drawn from this sample. It is not clear from their report how the sample was selected, what the sampling frame was, and what the response rate was. Thus, it is not possible for the reader to estimate the size of any potential non-response error, nor of any sampling error, and so the results are not generalisable to the population of parents who choose schools, nor even to some smaller clearly defined sub-population of parents. There is also no mention of the characteristics of the sample, such as the proportion of parents in the survey for whom the child in question is the first child, although it is likely that the selection of a school for a subsequent child is subject to what Johnson (1987) termed the "domino effect", whereby the second child follows the first unless there is a major reason for dissatisfaction with the first choice.

Another criticism of the representativeness of samples in many studies is that of "parentalism". Perhaps because it is the parents' right to choose that is embodied in the Education Reform Act 1988, even researchers who have reported a key role for children in school choice, have often only asked the parents for their views, or even for their views of their children's views. Such an acceptance of a parent's view of their child's view is evident in a study by West *et al.* (1995), in which parents were asked about their child's reasons for choosing, and which found that 83% stated that the child wanted the same school as the parents [according to the parents]. An example of this also comes from Coldron and Boulton (1991). Even though the researchers were interested in the views of the pupils, only "parents... were asked to report their children's reasons for wanting to go to a particular school" (Coldron and Boulton 1991 p.175). It is not clear, in this case, why the 10 and 11 year old children were not felt able to speak for themselves. It is, however, hardly surprising that the authors concluded that "from these figures it appears that children chose mainly on the same basis as their parents" (Coldron and Boulton 1991 p.175), since the two sets of views they were comparing were in fact both from the parents. The inaccuracy of parents and children's reports about each other was shown by Pifer and Miller (1995), and so the value of the two findings above are clearly called into question, despite having already been cited in subsequent papers by other authors.

Related to the issue of representation is that of volunteer bias. Not all institutions and individuals asked to take part in a piece of research will agree, often because they are too busy. By necessarily using only those prepared to take part, a study is already open to the charge of bias. Questionnaires may be more readily completed by those who are more literate, or more opinionated. Interviews may be granted by those who are more confident, or linguistically gifted, or who have greater leisure time. David *et al.* (1994) provided a clear example of the importance of this issue. They questioned pupils and parents about school choice, but only 50% of parents responded, giving them two notional groups of pupils - those whose parents were interviewed, and those who were not. There was a clear difference in the results, with the first group of pupils putting more emphasis on educational reasons, while the second, whose parents refused interviews, gave primarily convenience reasons. This is indirect evidence that the responses of the two groups of parents would also be different, if they could only be compared. Happily, David *et al.* (1994) managed to interview some non-volunteers subsequently, and found that they were indeed different to the volunteers, being more concerned with the child's' wishes, but otherwise being less active in making the choice. This is very valuable, and under-publicised, evidence of the dangers of sampling bias. Protection against this volunteer bias comes partly from making participation as easy as possible, and following up the non-respondents as far as possible, so increasing the participation rate.

The third major issue of sampling concerns size. The sample must be large enough to accomplish what is intended by the analysis, perhaps of the order of five or ten times the number of variables for some methods of analysis. Small samples can lead to loss of potentially valuable results, and are equivalent to a loss of power in the test used for analysis (Stevens 1992). Cases in the sample are lost at several stages of a study, and so redundancy needs to be built in. Surveys will have some forms not returned, some questions not answered, some answered unintelligibly, and some transcription errors, for example. Some interviews will be refused, rushed, or interrupted, or their recording will be indistinct, and there will be some transcription errors. Therefore data will be lost before analysis is even started. As soon as data is cross-tabulated, to look at the responses by gender for example, the number of cases drops again, often at an alarming rate. Taking an extreme case from the current study, although the total number of respondents was 1,267, only the adults were asked about their religion, and only 272 of these gave intelligible responses to one of the other questions in which responses were made on a three point scale. If parental religion is coded on a seven point scale, any analysis of responses to the second question in terms of religion, has fewer than 13 cases per cell, on average, making any test of significance very weak. Such alarming calculations highlight the need for a very large initial sample, in order to draw conclusions of a bivariate or multivariate nature.

Table 3.1
Estimated sizes of occupational group cells

Occupational group	Gave reason	Did not give reason	Number of cases
Professional	9.25	9.25	18.5
Employer	9.25	9.25	18.5
Semi-professional	9.25	9.25	18.5
Total			55.5
			(or 25% of 222)

The Coldron and Boulton (1991) study also provides an example of the problems that this dwindling of cases can cause, in coming to the conclusion that the three most popular responses to the main choice question in their survey were consistent across all socio-economic groups. It was not made clear in their paper how, or whether, this consistency was tested, nor is it clear that the sample size was large enough to make such a comparison. Socio-economic groups are hard enough to assess, and prone to error anyway, using scales often devised primarily for single-earner two-parent nuclear families and traditional male occupational groups. These researchers used the father's occupation only, and divided the responses into seven categories. Only 90% of the 222 parents responded to the socio-economic class question, and 25% of these respondents fitted into three of the seven categories. So, on the best possible and most generous interpretation of equal sized groups and measurement of a variable with only two possible values, such as the presence or absence of a reason in the responses, there would be fewer than 10 cases per cell for these occupational classes (Table 3.1). The values in Table 3.1 are very sensitive to changes, and since the transfer of one case from one column to another represents a difference in frequency of 10% for that class/variable cell, it is not clear how sure the authors can be when they state that the "response of 'best for education' was given by a much higher percentage of those in the professional and semi-professional categories" (Coldron and Boulton 1991 p.175). Such small values are also very sensitive to non-response bias and sampling error for the same reason.

Detailed calculations such as these are usually ignored by those analysing the results of interviews. An example of this type of work is provided by Gewirtz *et al.* (1994), outlining the stories of three families faced with the choice of secondary school. The stories were taken from the transcripts of 136 "loosely structured" interviews, lasting between thirty minutes and two hours, with families in three different LEAs, "from a range of socio-economic and ethnic backgrounds" (Gewirtz *et al.* 1994 p.7). It is clear that the time taken to collect the more detailed data from interviews, means that the breadth of this study was less than that of the study of 222 families discussed above. This number is sufficient if the participants are indeed seen as "real people" as stated by the authors, and the stories they tell are used merely to illustrate the point that choice is a complex and individual process. However, as an attempt is also made to generalise from the data any comments made above about reliability and the generalisation of results, apply with even more force to this study. It is clear from their comments about the range of families studied, that the authors wish to see their results as being of relevance to a wider population than the 136 individuals concerned, although insufficient evidence is given of the sampling strategy used to make such a claim. There is an underlying tension in this study, between concentration on the individuals on the one hand, and seeing them as representative of a class of families on the other. The three families in the paper were chosen "because they illustrate what we have identified as three broad groups of families..." (Gewirtz *et al.* 1994 p.7). Since the study eschewed any quantitative analysis, no account was given in this paper, or in the authors' more recent book, of how large these groups were, how their characteristics were measured, and why these three families were chosen as typical. In these circumstances, it is not possible for the reader to make any generalisations from the stories to the group, and so, interesting as the stories might be, the exercise loses any greater impact.

In summary, a good sample is representative of a wider population, and is large, with a high participation rate. The point has been made that it is risky to accept the generalisations made from previous work, without first considering their sampling strategy. Pressure of space in research journals, and their emphasis on a full description of what is termed the "theoretical" basis of the work in prevalent discourse (but see Gorard *et al.* 1997), often do not allow authors to describe their sampling, or indeed any methodological issue, at the level of detail that they might prefer. There must be a danger therefore that the ever-increasing number of journals in the UK will publish a growing number of studies reporting findings which readers will not be able to accept safely, precisely because of this lack of detail.

Instrument design

The quantitative or "shopping list" approach to school choice research has been criticised by some writers as having being "captured by the discourse" of the market

(Bowe *et al.* 1994ₐ), and of being, in essence, market research. It is superficially similar to the market research undertaken by schools themselves, and by organisations such as the Independent Schools Information Service (ISIS 1992), and the authors of the Good State School Guide (Clark and Round 1991). This means that even if the researchers are not captured by the discourse of a market approach to schooling, their surveys may be seen as market-oriented by the respondents. This type of research can over-simplify the process of choosing. In such work, parents are asked to list, or rate, the important criteria they use when choosing a school. Unfortunately, the use of lists, and the willingness with which parents respond to them, may incorrectly suggest that the choice process was approached in just such a check-list manner, and this trap must be guarded against. By emphasising why people choose schools, it ignores how they go about it. Another problem is that researching school choice often appears to assume that choice exists, but, in a related context, it was found that "other respondents denied the premise of choice among alternatives. Such respondents corrected for the rational bias built into the interview and revealed the limitations of any model which assumes entirely independent, unconstrained, and carefully weighted decision-making" (Lortie 1975 p. 41). The value of studies, however, lies in beginning to clarify the issues of relevance to parents. All of these problems are addressed in later chapters.

The list of choice criteria can be pre-fixed by the researcher and presented to the participants, but this generally leads to at least one of three further problems. The list can be incomplete, in the sense of not containing all possible reasons for choosing a school, which can lead to serious omissions in the data, and so bias the later analysis. Evidence of the importance of this comes from the present study. In one of the focus schools, over 20 questionnaire forms were mistakenly issued with one page containing 25 of the 73 suggested reasons, missing. Some of the criteria left out were "good public examination results", "firm discipline", "small classes", and "no bullying" which were all found to be very important overall in the selection of a new school. Not one of the affected respondents suggested any of the 25 missing reasons in their comments on the form, and so presumably without them as a prompt did not notice their lack. Other studies use reduced lists throughout, by design, and any omissions may well bias the study (Kim and Mueller 1987ₐ), by making other criteria appear more important than they truly are (Maddala 1992). In one such study, for example, Dennison (1995) used only 25 criteria in a survey from the outset, and this list excluded religious preference and the size of the school, for example, which have both been shown to be important to some families in other studies (Chapter 2). Another study "considered many aspects of choice" (Coldron and Boulton 1991 p. 170), but clearly made no attempt to include all possible reasons for choice. Variables such as the size of the school, the size of the classes, provision of religious education other than Christian, retention rate at 16+, rate of entry to university, career prospects, and several others cited in previous studies were ignored. It is strange that this phenomenon of potential bias through omission is not more widely discussed in the school choice literature.

A second problem with the use of pre-fixed lists is that they may suggest reasons to respondents which they might, in retrospect, feel are important, but which they did not consider at the time. Thirdly, some studies reduce the size of their list of reasons by collapsing some categories. They do this on theoretical and common sense grounds, with the obvious danger of imposing their own values directly onto the data at an early stage of analysis.

Alternatively, the list can be constructed by the participants, rather than the researcher who simply provides a prompt and a blank sheet of paper, but this method also has disadvantages. It relies more heavily on the imperfect memory of the respondents, and retrospective recall of their motivation. It is likely to over-represent the views of the more literate and highly motivated, and will probably produce as many differently worded responses as there are respondents (Oppenheim 1992). The ambiguity of the written word will make further analysis, or reduction, of the choice criteria very dangerous. Coldron and Boulton (1991), for example, use the relatively simple example of "good discipline" to make this point about ambiguity effectively (also see Coldron and Boulton 1996). Is good discipline meant to be firm, lenient, or fair? It is not for the researcher to decide in the first instance. In a study by West *et al.* (1995) the parents' responses were put into categories from a "wide range", including such responses as the "good reputation" of the school, which could be a source of information, or a reason for choosing a school. Their interviews did not unpack this complexity, and, as with discipline above, there is no report of what the reputation is supposed to be a reputation for. Most terms used by parents are similarly non-specific, because they are an attempt to summarise a process. Some studies use survey instruments with both open-ended, and structured "list" versions of the same basic questions, in order to obtain the advantages of both approaches, but sometimes without avoiding the disadvantages of either.

The Coldron and Boulton (1991) study carried out a survey of parents with children in Year 6, using a questionnaire with a mixture of prompted and open questions. The researchers grouped all similar responses [i.e. responses considered to be similar by the researchers], and calculated their frequencies to determine which were the most common reasons for choosing a secondary school. Yet, since the similarities used to group the criteria were judged by the authors, and not calculated directly from the data, the resulting frequencies can also be seen as the product of the researchers opinions. Similar studies have produced very different groupings by the same procedure (OECD 1994, West *et al.* 1995, Glatter *et al.* 1997$_a$). Therefore, in each case, the outcomes are basically a report of what the authors thought were the most common criteria for choice, as partially admitted by Glatter *et al.* (1995), and then supported by the rhetorical appeal of a frequency calculation. However it is not true to say, except in a very trivial sense, that "researcher bias in the interpretation of parental views on school choice is present, however, whatever approach is taken - whether researchers make decisions in advance.... by giving pre-coded categories which are then reported without grouping, or whether 'highly disparate and individualised parental replies have to be made more manageable by grouping them into a limited number of broad categories'" (Glatter *et al.* 1995 p.11). The bias is present only if researchers do not take into account the actual relationships detectable between the various elements of their data, by a procedure such as factor analysis, used in this study and also in a recent study in the USA supervised by Pat Bauch (personal communication to the author). For example, Glatter *et al.* (1997$_a$) reported that "nearness to home/convenience for travel" was more influential for parents in choosing a school than the behaviour of the pupils.

Their argument was based upon frequency counts of the responses to their standard PASCI questionnaire. However, while nearness or convenience appeared as only one of the items to be rated, pupil behaviour appeared in two items - one relating to behaviour inside the school, and the other to outside. Now it may be true that these are different choice criteria, but it may also be true that parents use the more easily visible pupil behaviour outside school to gauge behaviour inside, and it may also be true that some parents want a school close to home for reasons other than convenience for travel (one woman in the present study liked to be able to look into the playground from her bedroom window). If the PASCI questionnaire had separated convenience and proximity, but included only one item about behaviour, the results would, in all probability, have been very different. In this way, the findings of even such a large study with an excellent sample are effectively determined in advance of any data being collected.

In one section of the Coldron and Boulton study (1991), respondents were asked, unprompted, for their reasons for choice. No limit was made on the number of reasons given. Payne (1951) recommended that questions should try to state how many ideas are expected from each respondent, or else it is likely that the more convinced and more articulate respondents will be over represented, if the question is unstructured. If some groups of respondents, those with the most "cultural capital" for example, produce more reasons each, at least some respondents will produce more reasons than others, and this is borne out by the fact that their 222 respondents gave 380 reasons between them, and 380 is not exactly divisible by 222. Therefore, even if all reasons can be assumed to be simple and unrelated constructs, which they patently are not, but which ought to be a necessary precondition for their frequencies to be equitably compared, they cannot all be given equal weight. However, there is no way of calculating appropriate weights for them in this methodological approach. It is not reasonable to assume that both of two reasons given by one respondent are each equally as important as one reason given by another. Neither can it be assumed that each is only half as important. Such considerations begin to give a clue to the complexity of the analysis of the choice process.

There is no mention of where or how this questionnaire was administered, nor is any measure of the complexity of the language calculated. The authors themselves also pointed out that families may not share the same vocabulary as each other, or their readers, and suggested the difficulty of dealing with non-specific responses such as "better discipline", which could mean opposite things to different people, or "the child's preference", which is ambiguous concerning the amount of control given to the child (Chapter 2). Any grouping of such reasons is necessarily *ad hoc*, and open to criticism. It is therefore, not possible to say how well separated the informed respondents were from the uninformed. The number of reasons given in the unprompted questions was reduced to 30, by collapsing some into others. The authors correctly stated that such a procedure was dangerously open to misinterpretation and bias, but even so the list of 30 reasons "is only partially illuminating" (Coldron and Boulton 1991 p.171) because it is so long and unstructured.

Having stated that the reasons are difficult to group, because they are too vague, unrelated to each other, or belong to more than one group, the writers go on to make the contradictory claim that "it seemed *clear* that academic/educational..."

reasons should be one group (Coldron and Boulton 1991 p.172). It is however not clear from the survey responses, whether each reason stated in the questions, and each suggested by the respondents should be treated as a discrete entity, or whether they overlap. Further doubts about the validity of treating the reasons as simple constructs, sharing no common variance, arise from their Table 1. Three of the reasons, including "minority language spoken" were cited as representing one case each, whereas another entry, representing six cases was described as "other" reasons. It is not clear why three of the individual reasons were treated separately for analysis, while six others were grouped together, but the decision to do this has significant implications for the shape of the results.

Perhaps in an attempt to avoid the dangers of simply collapsing and arranging categories of choice criteria, and the limitations of the list and hierarchical analyses of such criteria, while they remain unclear and overlapping, Coldron and Boulton lead on to an example of a network relationship (Figure 3.1). They selected 12 of the variables, and attempted to show the relationships between them schematically (Coldron and Boulton 1991 p.177). Even at this level the diagram is not easy to interpret, and would become unhelpful if all choice criteria were included. It is not clear, for example, whether the variables included are meant to overlap or not, i.e. whether they are composite or elementary.

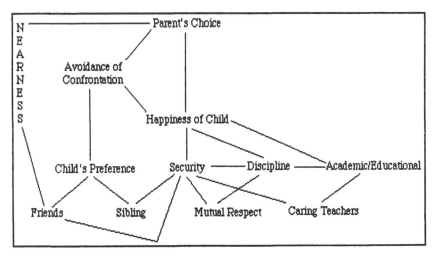

Figure 3.1   Relationship between common criteria for choice

For example, although it may be true that "nearness" (proximity to school) and having friends using the same school are related, it is not clear how, nor is any attempt made to establish this systematically by the use of formal network analysis, as described by Knoke and Kuklinski (1982). In this diagram, nearness may be desirable to make travel easier and safer, and having friends at the same school allows pupils to travel together which is convenient for parents and safer for pupils. Thus both reasons may in fact be a subset of ease of travel. On the other hand, nearness may be valuable, since it means that more local friends will be likely to be using the school, making the induction into senior school easier.

Nearness, may then, be a subset of having friends. The two reasons may, on the other hand, merely intersect. Theory and common sense alone cannot even decide how the variables are related, much less measure how much variance is explained by each, and the authors made little attempt to justify this particular arrangement. This is where a technique such as factor analysis, used in the present study, can help. It produces a small and manageable number of underlying variables, based more precisely on the associations among the data themselves. Although these resulting "factors" are theoretical constructs, they are grounded in the empirical results. It is the opinion of one writer that "a score resulting from an ably performed factor analysis is a much more sensitive and foolproof assessment... than a raw score on any 'real' variable" (Jackson and Bogatta 1981 p. 15).

After collapsing the number of reasons to 30, Coldron and Boulton presented the percentage of respondents citing each reason, despite the facts that the reasons are no longer in the words of the respondent, they may not be discrete, they may be more important to some than others, and several important reasons are anyway left out. They then collapse the 30 reasons into four categories made up by themselves, and claim of two of these categories, for example, that "the prioritizing of security criteria above academic/educational criteria to these open responses is very *clear*" (Coldron and Boulton 1991 p.173). The four categories of reasons are derived from, but not used in four other British studies of parental choice. The OECD (1994) carried out a review of many more school choice studies, and also decided to categorise the findings into four groups of reasons for choosing. These were; academic (e.g. results), situational (e.g. travel), ethos (e.g. management), and selection (e.g. single-sex), of which only two are similar to those of Coldron and Boulton (1991), who also have *proximity* to home which is additional to their four categories. The differences between these two classifications, thus, reinforce the conclusion drawn above about the PASCI questionnaire, and highlight the need for a more systematic procedure before conclusions can be drawn concerning the relative importance of one category or another.

Ethnostatistics

"Ethnostatistics" is a term used by Gephart (1988), to describe the study of the use of statistics, particularly in social science research. It is clear that "producing a statistic is a social enterprise" (Gephart 1988 p.15), and that the stages of selecting variables, making observations and coding the results, take place in everyday settings where practical influences arise. Statistical textbooks describe ideal procedures to follow, but several studies of actual behaviour have observed different common practices among researchers, and the divergence between ideal and actual is probably increasing because of the increased accessibility to statistical software packages, and a tendency to see them as "expert systems" rather than convenient calculators.

Computers are making decisions for researchers that they may not even be aware of. A statistical package can easily find a Pearson r correlation coefficient for nominal data, and nowhere in its output will there be a warning that the result is nonsense. There are Ph.D. theses on the shelves of university libraries today which have used a two-tailed t-test after predicting the direction of difference between two means, or using two different methods of dealing with missing values in the same analysis, when calculating correlation coefficients as part of factor analysis, for example (personal observation). In both of these examples, the authors had simply used the default settings of SPSS, one of the most popular statistical packages. Before selecting a technique therefore, researchers should thoroughly scrutinise the assumptions underlying it, paying particular attention to the "invisible" default settings that allow the package to make decisions for researchers, without them even realising it. The defaults are there for convenience only and should not replace the decisions themselves. Some assumptions may, of course, be violated without too many problems, but it is important to be aware of them before deciding on their violation. Understandable reasons for omitting this stage of the analysis might be ignorance, over-reliance on a package, having no feasible alternative, or invisibility through familiarity. The dangers are increased because, for some, statistics have an under-stated rhetoric of their own, able to persuade specific audiences of their objectivity (Firestone 1987).

In general, survey analysis usually proceeds as though the cases in a survey are independent of each other, with an equal probability of selection, or, in other words, that random sampling has been used. Alternatively, clustering and stratification techniques can be used to select cases, and produce a sample that is similar to a good random sample, in which all population elements must have a known non-zero probability of selection. If any other method of selecting a sample is used, standard techniques of analysis can be inappropriate (Lee *et al.* 1989). The use of bivariate statistical tests, such as chi-squared, has another major underlying assumptions which is so well-known and obvious that it is often ignored - "*the* logic of these tests makes two strong assumptions: first, that the sample from which the data have been obtained is a random sample from a specific population and secondly, that just one hypothesis, formulated beforehand, is being tested. In most social science research, neither of these assumptions holds good" (Gilbert 1993 p. 72). The problem of sampling was dealt with above. The other potential problem, of the over-use of a test mathematically designed for one-off use, dramatically increases the chances of error, and so leads to spurious results (Stevens 1992). Imagine a study that asked parents 10 questions about themselves and their family, such as their occupation, and then asked them 20 questions about their choice of school. It is possible, using a computer, to run a test of significance for all 20 questions in relation to the 10 family characteristics, and then select only those results that show a difference at the 5% level of significance. These are the results published, but the 5% significance level paraded in the publication was intended for testing one hypothesis, and is now meaningless, after 200 such tests. If a 5% chance of a Type I error [rejecting a null hypothesis incorrectly] is accepted for each test, then the chance of at least one Type I error in 200 such tests is over 99.99%. Multivariate statistics, such as multiple regression, and factor analysis, although having problems of their own, can reduce the chance of such errors by reducing the number of variables, or combining the probabilities into fewer calculations.

Most research on school choice quite properly uses only basic statistics, calculating frequencies and chi-squared, means and F-tests. Despite this apparent simplicity, several studies have errors at the level of calculation, so that even where an appropriate test is used, the answers can still be wrong. In fact it may be that it is the very simplicity of the statistics used that makes them so seductive, but also inadequate to express the complexity of their topic. Coldron and Boulton (1991) looked at the differences in the frequency of responses from sub-groups of parents, such as those in different occupational groups, and those with boys and girls. They stated that for two of the groups of reasons, there were two differences worthy of note between parents of boys and girls, but that in three others, "there were no differences in frequency of citation" (Coldron and Boulton 1991 p. 173). No null hypotheses, or tests of significance were mentioned in the article. As an example, they stated that "the child's own preference of school was mentioned more by parents of boys (15) than of girls (7)" (Coldron and Boulton 1991 p. 173). Since they also reported that 46% of the 222 respondents were parents of girls, it is possible to construct a 2 by 2 contingency table for their results, as in Table 3.2.

Table 3.2
Cases for suggested gender differences in choice (1)

	Preference	No preference	Total
Boys	15	105	120
Girls	7	95	102
Total	22	200	222
Chi squared	DF	Prob.	
1.96253	1	0.16124	

Examination of the values in Table 3.2 reveals that the expected frequency of parents of boys citing the child's preference is 12 (i.e. 54% of 22), while the actual frequency is 15, which was treated by the writers as significant enough to be worth mentioning, without explaining how they made the judgement. One way would be to use the chi-square test for 2x2 contingency tables and two independent samples (Siegel 1956). Such a test shows no significant difference between the two genders in this respect, with over 16% probability of the difference being due to chance or an error in measurement, and yet these supposed differences between boys and girls have already been quoted in other research papers as a valid result, as explained in the introduction.

To show that such incidents are not isolated, a further example of a similar problem is described. West et al. (1995) used a sample of 70 families, and, like many studies, considered the differences between sub-groups of respondents. They stated that "all differences are significant at the 0.05 level or beyond unless otherwise stated" (West et al. 1995 p.38), although there is no description of the tests used. Using the chi-squared test for independent samples, as above (Siegel 1956), one of the differences that they describe is not significant at the 5% level when recalculated, and is unlikely to be so using any other available test, since the number of respondents in each cell for comparison is too few for the size of the observed differences. In the study, 51% of the sample are boys, and 69% of parents of boys rejected schools on the grounds of discipline/behaviour, but only 47% of parents of girls did so. Making the most generous assumption of a 100% response rate to these questions from the 70 cases, the 2 by 2 contingency table is as in Table 3.3. From these figures, West et al. stated "more parents of boys than girls did not want their child to go to particular schools because of the discipline/behaviour of pupils there". Yet, the frequencies they cited have almost a 6% probability of occurring by chance, and to claim therefore that there is a gender difference in this respect is incorrect, especially as more than one hypothesis was being tested with the same data.

Table 3.3
Cases for suggested gender differences in choice (2)

	Discipline	Not discipline	Total
Boys	25	11	36
Girls	16	18	34
Total	41	29	70
Chi squared	DF	Prob.	
3.61107	1	0.05740	

These papers are not unique in containing errors of analysis, and it is recognised that all writers make such mistakes from time to time. These two examples may differ from many others only in the amount of detail that they provide, making it easier for readers to re-analyse their data. However, the errors are there, and they have passed both the proof-reading, and the peer-review stage of publication. Also, being key articles, the errors in the findings are already propagating through the literature, via the citation process.

Problems with qualitative analysis

The discussion above identified several of the methodological problems in attempting to capture the process of choice for academic study in the form of numeric data. Other groups, such as that based at King's College London, approach the research of choice from a different perspective, which is represented by Ball *et al.* (1992), Ball (1993), Bowe *et al.* (1994b), and Gewirtz *et al.* (1994). They also criticised the approach taken by Coldron and Boulton (1991), but for them it was not the potential flaws in the details of the design but the entire concept of listing criteria for choice which was the problem. Bowe *et al.* (1994a) argued that much social research in this area has been "captured by the discourse" of the market and they saw the list, hierarchical, and even the network approaches as fundamentally flawed. They argued that such a consumer approach ignores how the choice is made, which may be integral to whether and why it is made. They concentrated instead, on the process of choosing, and agreed with the view of another author that "families do not tend to make decisions on the basis of criteria ranked in the way implied by neat lists" (Woods 1992 p. 208).

One problem for the market research approach to choice outlined above, is the danger that the instrument used will bias the results, and that it "actually distorts what it purports to set out to discover" (Bowe *et al.* 1994a p. 71). However, an experimenter-effect is not a new suggestion, and ironically it is more commonly associated with face-to-face interviews than with surveys (Adair 1973), and must be considered in any kind of design. However, this is not to suggest that researchers such as Coldron and Boulton actually believe that parents generally use such lists for the purposes of making the choice, even unconsciously. Some parents do, but the list itself may also be valuable anyway as a partial reconstruction of the motivations underlying the choice. To use an analogy, we are all aware that a list of components is not the same as a machine, but we would not deny the value of such a list to someone trying to understand or repair the machine. This analogy cannot be extended to imply that choice is mechanical, but merely to illustrate that understanding is seldom "gestalt", and to defend the value, in principle at least, of a partial solution. It is anyway not clear that researchers such as the Kings group have discovered rather than suggested much more with their own approach, other than that the process of selecting a school is difficult to research.

The second, or "holistic", strand in British school choice research tends to use face-to-face interviews rather than surveys, but suffers from many of the same defects as the first. Its value is that it reminds us that the cases in surveys are real people with genuine anxieties in an often perplexing situation. The samples used are often smaller than with the list approach, and less clearly defined, while the analysis is sometimes even less sophisticated, and more prone to error, with the obvious danger of accepting "findings" which can not be replicated merely because they are plausible. The researchers may seek to avoid such criticism by eschewing statistical analysis, and seeing each case or narrative as an individual. If this so, interesting though the stories may (or may not) be, few lessons can be learned of a more general nature, except perhaps the dangers of over-simplification. In fact many researchers, while avowedly holistic in their introduction, do attempt to generalise from the few cases available to them, even though traditional extrapolation of qualitative data is unlikely to be either valid, or helpful (Firestone 1990). Some use their interview data as a "mini"-survey, and face the same problems with statistical treatment as described above (e.g. West *et al.* 1995).

Some writers resort to metaphors in an attempt to help explain the process of choice, but the danger of using these, and their associated "flowery language", is that they may obscure whether the statements made are trite, or else impossible (Phillips 1992). They are seemingly immune to criticism, since the models used are seen as exploratory, or heuristic, but once analysed logically, relativist and naturalist polemics are often flawed, or trivial (Phillips 1992). Reports which set out to sound clever, to use metaphors as fundamentally flawed analogies, and which cannot be gainsaid with ease are unhelpful to progress in this field. They confuse the necessary complexity of the subject under study with contingent complexity in explanation. Those who are relativists, for example, have to make clear whether there are, indeed, multiple truths which conflict and which are all true, which is to abandon logic and make progress impossible, or whether there are merely different perspectives. Objectivity and truth, like social justice, are ideals. They are ideals to which research can aspire, whilst realists, as well as relativists, realise the enormity of that aspiration. Observations are value-laden, but this does not make all points of view equally justified.

The following example is given of the danger of accepting mere plausibility in qualitative analysis. Gewirtz *et al.* (1994) theoretically defined three different types of families and their levels of engagement with an educational market and then illustrated these with three in-depth case studies drawn from a larger set of interviews. The three categories are "privileged" families who wish to make a considered choice, and have the capacity to do so, "frustrated" families who also wish to make a choice but have limited cultural capital to invest in the process, and the "disconnected" who are uninterested in choice and who automatically accept their local school. The groups were defined theoretically rather than statistically, even though the authors claimed they had no set theories when starting the analysis, and their groupings were apparently grounded in the data. Their model used two axes of variation (Figure 3.2).

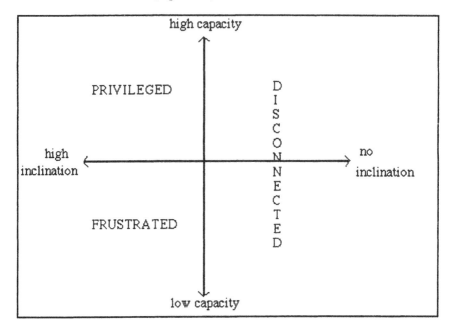

Figure 3.2 Theoretical positions of families in the marketplace

One axis is presumably identical to the dimension already identified in the quantitative work of Willms and Echols (1992) in Scotland, using over 5000 pupils, and bivariate statistical techniques, where they used the term "alert client" to represent parents expressing a preference for a placement at school, and "inert client" for those who accepted the designated school. These terms were borrowed and really only used in the title of the paper, and although perhaps unfortunate, they do express a real difference in the practice of school choice (see Chapter 9). To change these terms to "high inclination" and "no inclination", as was done by Gewirtz *et al.* (1994) is anyway insufficient on its own to "spring" them from the capture of market discourse. The other axis, on the other hand, is a new construct, portraying the abilities and resources that a family can bring to bear upon the process of selecting a school, including educational background, leisure time, and travel (Chapter 2). However, such characteristics have already been found to be related to the "alert clients" by Willms and Echols (1992), and the later authors agreed that "in practice, however, inclination and capacity are linked" (Gewirtz *et al.* 1994 p. 19).

Thus, there could be only two classes, or two ends of a continuum measured on one axis in which inclination and capacity are covariant. Alternatively, there could be four classes of families, or two ends each of two separate continua, each representing one quadrant of the model. It is therefore not clear why Gewirtz *et al.* (1994) only acknowledged three groups, named "privileged", "frustrated", and "disconnected", since three is not a number of groups derivable from their theory. Their disconnected group could also be sub-divided into those, presumably meant to be exemplified by the disconnected family in their paper, who have neither the desire nor the abilities to engage with the market, and those who have the same kind of resources as the privileged, but who do not make a reasoned market choice. This last group has already been identified in previous work, and includes users of the famous English public schools for whom family tradition is more important than anything (Fox 1990, Edwards and Whitty 1995), and who therefore make an "unreasoned choice". This group also includes those families using state schools "who decide not to exercise their options" (Echols and Willms 1995 p.144), whether out of political principle, or practical considerations such as keeping the family together. Even though one of them may be inconvenient for their own analysis, the Gewirtz model clearly predicts four classes of families.

In addition, the three cases chosen by Gewirtz *et al.* (1994) to illustrate these categories [from a larger number of cases so that it can be assumed that these exemplars are some of the clearest available] can be more easily explained by the number and ages of the children in the family. The privileged family were interviewed about their eldest child, and the frustrated family were interviewed about their only child. Both of these families showed a strong wish to engage with the market, and they differed chiefly in how free a choice they appeared to have, because of their different resources. The disconnected family showed markedly less interest in researching alternative schools, and using their new rights as consumers, but they were interviewed about their second child, and it was clear that they were content to use the same school for her, as for her elder brother. One reason for their disinclination to engage in the choice process could easily be that for them, but not the other two families, this was the second time around, and this would have nothing to do with their ability or inclination to exploit the market. The researchers should have been aware of the likelihood of a "domino effect" (Johnson 1987), but it is quite clear that the term "disconnected" is intended by them to mean more than merely a family content with a previous choice. It is strange that these authors, who expressed a desire to see the process of choice clearly for individuals, and acknowledged that families cannot be assumed to use the same vocabulary as the researcher, should have not viewed this difference as a likely explanation for the attitude of their disconnected family. The family in question may, or may not, have had the capacity to exploit the market, but one reason for their disinclination to engage in the choice process could easily be that for them this is the second time around, and they may not have had the ability to express this to the researchers. Since there is no longitudinal study of their behaviour with different children, and no quantitative analysis of the characteristics of other disconnected families, it is not possible to judge whether an explanation based upon the number and ages of siblings has any greater general value for their work. The subsequent book by the same authors contained further examples of families that they classified as disconnected, but in only one of these examples is it possible to decide on the birth order of the child, and in this case, as in the paper, the child in question is a subsequent child (Gewirtz *et al.* 1995). In fact, there are some indications that this whole category of disconnected families is based upon a few who empower their children more than others, particularly where the child is not the first in birth order. In the first example of a disconnected family in the book, the mother says "we've decided we're going to look at the two schools" (Gewirtz *et al.* 1995). So this mother, who is supposedly not engaged with the market, and was chosen by the authors as the standard bearer of the disconnected, is aware of a greater range of options, but has limited serious consideration to two schools. It is shown later in this book that two schools is higher than the average number considered by the predominantly middle-class families participating in the present study, and so the figure can hardly be seen as indicative of a lack of engagement with the process of choice.

The paper described above and the relevant chapters in the 1995 book show the tension inherent in some qualitative work, of seeing narratives as valid in their own right, but of also wishing to draw general conclusions without a sufficient sample - and the dangers of steering between the Scylla of pointlessness and the Charybdis of invalidity. Using so-called qualitative methods is no excuse, *per se*, for mere "speculative theory" which is ungrounded in bodies of data (Strauss 1987). To paraphrase the title of another paper by Ball (1995), this study seeks to emphasise the urgent role of *data* in educational research, and its primacy over theory in the first instance.

Conclusion

As a reminder it is stated again that the work cited here has not been chosen as a "soft" target, but because it is highly respected, showing that as even these studies may have methodological problems, there is scope for improvement in much choice research. Some previous work is based on poor "opportunity" samples, which were neither stratified nor random, from an undefined population, so that it is not clear how the results could be of any general value. The samples are often small in comparison to the number of variables, and the response rates can be lower than 50%, with the very real danger of over-representing certain sections of the population. The statistical treatment of results is generally simple, leading to mean responses, or frequency tables, and comparisons between cells. Often the frequencies are of the "collapsed" criteria, and therefore of dubious validity. It is not always clear whether the test of significance implied was only used on those comparisons presented as significantly different, or whether it was used more "globally" with the aid of software, and the interesting "results" extracted. Such multiple comparisons of a bivariate nature could be better handled by a multivariate analysis, since the significance levels cited are, of course, only for stand-alone tests, but this is rarely seen. Some papers have been published citing results as different, when a simple reworking of the significance test shows clearly that they are not.

The dangers of over-simplifying the process of choice, the problems with quantifying anything as vague as reasons, and the possibility of accepting a plausible or politically acceptable explanation of a small number of cases, are all shown above. "All methods have their limitations. There is no best method in the sociology of education, only suitable and feasible methods, so we should try as many as possible" (King 1987 p. 243). It therefore seems appropriate to use several approaches and data sources for any further investigation of this issue, within the context of a realistic paradigm. On the other hand, while it is accepted, and obvious, that social phenomena are complex, the research process assumes that later work will build on the simpler first steps of current endeavours which is, "reasonable, since one cannot study everything at the same time" (Strauss 1987 p.7). This has two implications for the present argument. Firstly, each generation of researchers must be reasonably sure that they can rely on previous findings in their field, and that the utmost care has been used in their production. Secondly, no researcher should be called to account merely for simplifying the description of a process. It may sometimes be necessary to simplify processes in order to find patterns and make progress, but in no way does such a simplification imply that the researcher is unaware of the complexities, some of which will hopefully be dealt with by subsequent work. A finding cannot be described as too simple. It can, of course, be rejected as wrong or incomplete, but the simpler it is, the easier it is to reject on these grounds, and therefore the better it is.

It is easier to criticise others for lack of rigour, or for refusing to simplify, and seeking to escape from such criticism into a metaphor of landscapes or whatever. It is much harder to address and attempt to solve the problems. This study hopes to do so to some extent, and the methodology used is described in Chapter 5. In summary this study uses a mixture of methods, documentary analysis, detailed interviews, and a survey with a large stratified sample of both parents and pupils, a questionnaire containing every reason suggested by the research outlined in Chapter 2, and a form of multivariate analysis that can help to decide which reasons are indivisible elements, and which are linked to each other. One of the purposes of this chapter is to show that further study is justified in this area, and another is to make the point that where the results of the current study differ from those published in previous research, it should not be automatically assumed that it is the previously peer-reviewed work that is correct.

4 The sampling frame

Introduction

After a rehearsal of some the key arguments for focusing on the fee-paying school sector in Wales, this chapter continues by describing the number and range of types of schools in Wales, and introducing some of the characteristics of education which are peculiar to the region. One section describes the provision of state-funded schools, and the ways in which the principality and its schools differ from England. Another section examines the fee-paying school sector in Wales, showing its distribution and size, and the size of its schools. The final section considers the users of fee-paying schools, and introduces a range of possible reasons to explain the very small size of the fee-paying sector in Wales, each of which was tested by the research. In this way, the chapter provides further justification for the research by producing some evidence of a specifically "Welsh" education culture, and by showing how the fee-paying sector is very different not only from that in England, but also from popular understanding of private schooling. The small schools described here are most definitely under-researched. Finally, by outlining the background against which this study takes place, the chapter creates the sampling frame for the schools described in Chapters 5 and 6.

State provision

Although many official documents and much educational research refers to England and Wales as one entity, distinguishable from Scotland or Northern Ireland, Wales, in fact, has a different educational system from England in several ways. Education in Wales is administered day-to-day by the Welsh Office, not the Department for Education and Employment. The majority of public examinations are taken using papers from the Welsh Joint Education Committee. Wales has its own version of the National Curriculum, and the provision of schools in the principality is even more homogeneous than in England. It is therefore not at all clear that previous research on school choice in England can be seen as entirely applicable to Wales.

The uniformity of schools in England was commented upon in a recent international study (OECD 1994), and although attempts have been made to vary the provision of schools since the publication of the white paper entitled "Choice and Diversity" in 1991, little has been achieved as yet. Simple inertia may partly explain this lack of response, but other contributory factors may be: the notion that diversity is the precursor of inequity; the British habit of ranking alternatives by worth (OECD 1994), and the "dead hand" of the National Curriculum. The situation in Wales is even more remarkable. Among the 2,048 schools of all types in Wales in 1994, there were no City Technology Colleges, or similarly specialist schools for drama, sport, or languages (Welsh Office 1995$_a$). There were only 15 Grant Maintained (GM) schools altogether. In fact, fewer than 1% of schools in Wales have opted out, compared to more than 4% in England, and even the larger number of GM schools in England has not produced much diversity of provision, since many seem to be reviving an academic model based upon tradition and selectivity (Fitz *et al.* 1995). Of the 484,322 full-time pupil equivalents in Wales in 1994, 57% are in LEA primary schools, and 38% are in LEA secondary schools (Table 4.1). Thus, only 5% of the school population are in GM, independent, and special schools combined (Welsh Office 1995$_a$).

Table 4.1
Types of schools in Wales 1993/94

	No. of schools	FTE pupils	Mean size
Primary	1693	274715	167
Secondary	217	185894	857
Special	59	3587	67
GM primary	5	947	189
GM secondary	10	8507	851
Independent	64	10672	167

Part of the reason for the particular lack of diversity in Wales could be its geography. The average population density in Wales is only 1.4 persons per hectare, compared to 2.4 for Britain as a whole (OPCS 1993). Much of Wales is still predominantly rural in nature, particularly Gwynedd and Dyfed (apart from the Llanelli area). The density in Powys LEA is 0.2 persons per hectare, which is the lowest in England and Wales and one third of the density of the next sparsest LEA which is also in Wales (Gorard 1997$_e$). Only 12 towns in these three counties have a population exceeding 5,000, and transport facilities are generally poor (Aberystwyth Policy Group 1990). Motorways, dual carriageways and Inter-City train services are generally confined to the north and south coastal regions and local rail routes such as the Heart of Wales line, have a diminishing service, being more suitable to tourists or shoppers than commuters. In selecting a school, families, particularly those from rural areas, may therefore face a choice from limited options of little diversity. Reynolds (1990) claimed that 40% of parents in Wales had no choice of secondary school, unless they were prepared to travel 40 or more miles.

Despite the isolated nature of parts of Wales, the population itself is in a state of flux. The 1991 census revealed that only 77% of residents were born in Wales, and that this population was not reproducing itself (OPCS 1993), although the overall numbers are rising due to in-migration (Aberystwyth Policy Group 1990). There is a steady outflow of young people from rural areas, and an equivalent inflow, the majority of whom are elderly and retired English people (Aberystwyth Policy Group 1990). Despite the fact that economic regeneration in the region, the arrival of Japanese factories, and EU support has meant an increase in non-Welsh in-migrants (Webster 1990), ethnic diversity is not as obvious as in other parts of Britain. In Wales, 98.5% of the Welsh population are still defined as "white" (OPCS 1993), compared to an average of 94.5% in Great Britain as a whole. In Powys, as an extreme example, 99.4% of the population are white. However, the recent scale of population change can be seen from one finding of the Aberystwyth Policy Group (1990) that one rural school with a roll of 800 took on 66 pupils new to the area in one academic year.

The impact of these population changes can be seen in the decline of the Welsh language so that the majority of Welsh language speakers now live in areas like Cardiff where the majority language is English (see Gorard 1997$_a$). However, the one type of state-funded school peculiar to Wales - the Ysgol Cymraeg or Welsh-medium school - has continued to grow in numbers in almost inverse proportion to the number of Welsh speakers (Baker 1990). The number of children speaking Welsh at home has fallen every year since 1986 to around 6% of population, yet teaching through the medium of Welsh takes place in 34% of primary schools (Welsh Office 1995$_b$).

A curriculum Cymreig

There are in addition to the above several differences between the National Curriculum for Wales, and that for England, with subjects such as history, geography, art and music having separate orders. The differences are in perspective as well as content, since, according to legislation, all pupils in Wales have the right to learn about Welsh language, culture and history (Jones and Lewis 1995). There is, or should be, a "general Welshness pervading pupil's learning experiences" (Jones and Lewis 1995 p.24). The National Curriculum for Wales also specifies that the teaching of Welsh (as a second language) is compulsory in all state-funded schools (Welsh Office 1995$_b$). All pupils, of whatever background, study Welsh from Key Stage 1 to Key Stage 3, in addition to another modern foreign language in Key Stage 3.

This legislation concerning Welsh language teaching faces several problems. In schools teaching through the medium of English, the Welsh language is taught in addition to all of the subjects that appear in the National Curriculum for England, which means that local pupils need to do better, just to reach the same attainment targets as in England, which is hardly fair. Welsh language in all schools, and throughout the age range, was originally to have been introduced sooner (Welsh Office 1990), but as with the Welsh language schools, lack of resources and sufficient trained teachers, among other factors, held up its implementation. For such practical reasons, 3.2% of schools still do not teach any Welsh, while the proportion teaching Welsh as a first language has dropped dramatically since 1986.

Welsh is now taught only as a second language in 63% of schools (Welsh Office 1995$_a$).

With reference to the growing number of in-migrants, the legislation makes the following minor concession: "Pupils who enter a school in the final year of KS3 or during KS4 may be exempted from the National Curriculum requirements to study Welsh if they have not studied Welsh in the school curriculum for at least one academic year in any of the 3 preceding academic years. However... the governing body and headteacher may decide that the subject should be taught. These regulations apply to pupils transferring between school within Wales as well as pupils moving to Wales" (Welsh Office 1994 p. vi). These regulations do not apply to fee-paying schools which has an important implication discussed in Chapter 10.

Fee-paying schools as an established market

This study uses the fee-paying school sector as an example of a localised, but long-established market, and examines the choices and justifications of the sector's users, and the responses of its schools. While this study focuses on fee-paying schools, it also includes state-funded schools, and will have some relevance to understanding trends in the more recently established markets in state-funded provision. The fee-paying sector may not be the ideal market from which to gain evidence, but it is at present one of the few available which allows researchers to see the long-term effects of consumer choice in education. As Levin (1992 p.281) stated, "debates on market choice in education have been largely confined to theory rather than evidence... because of the lack of voucher-type experience in the USA or comparable industrialized countries". In the absence of such evidence therefore, it can be argued that the literature on school choice remains merely indicative.

The fee-paying sector is not ideal for a test of an educational market for several reasons. The payment of fees introduces some constraints on who is able to consider such a school, and the usual condition of having to give a term's notice before leaving, or forfeiting a term's fees, reduces the readiness of users to switch between schools - to take the "exit" option (Hirschman 1970). Several fee-paying schools are also academically selective in their intake. These features combine to prevent school choice in the fee-paying sector from taking place in a "free" market. However, it is also true that there is no truly "free" market in the state-maintained sector. The limiting factors here include the National Curriculum and testing, the imposition of a "standard number" ceiling on school admissions, and travel constraints. In addition, several rural LEAs still may not inform parents of their right to choose, and many LEAs continue to use a system of "catchment areas".

There may also be a reluctance in the research community to draw conclusions from a sector of education which is seen as elitist and therefore politically undesirable. In a similar way, Edwards *et al.* (1989), in their early investigation of the Assisted Places scheme, found some LEAs so displeased with the scheme that they fell into the trap of seeing any research as either condoning it or advertising it. However, as early as 1982 in the USA, Garner and Hannaway stated that "the case for expanding school choice may not rest on the degree to which private schooling fits the competitive market model of economics; yet these are the arguments most commonly advanced" for it (Garner and Hannaway 1982 p.120). In the UK, a model of good educational practice embodied in some of the recent reforms may be seen as deriving from the successful but traditional private school sector in England. In fact, one observer concluded that "independent private schools can serve as a prototype for privatization" (Madsen 1994 p.12). Yet, in the same way that financial success in any market can lead to complacency, successful private schools may not, in fact, be truly effective, but since the reforms may be based on them, it is important to find this out, and to publicise it.

Work in the fee-paying sector was advocated by Hughes (1995), who found significant obstacles to the development of an educational market in the state-funded sector, but argued "there other areas, such as private education... where market forces may be more pressing. Studies of what is happening in these areas should throw some light on both how a real educational market might operate, and whether the further encouragement of market forces in the state sector is either practicable or desirable" (Hughes 1995 p.17). Parents using private schools might be assumed *a priori* to be more capable of making an active choice of school than some in the population (Echols *et al.* 1990). They may be more likely to have the transport and time, the literacy and numeracy, and above all the confidence and the "taste" to be able to make a choice. They are perhaps closer to idealised "consumers" of education, and this possibility is examined in the present study. If this is assumed to be so, and if they cannot be seen to have brought about an improvement in school standards through their exercise of choice, the prognosis for such an improvement in other sectors is poor. These purported qualities of users of fee-paying schools would also make them suited to a questionnaire survey, since they could be assumed generally to have the necessary literacy skills, and by approaching them via the schools themselves, they can be given the necessary motivation as well. In fact, such motivation is not misplaced. Although never intended to be a programme of market research, the quality of the survey, and the size and breadth of the sample were such that many focus schools were very keen to know the results. Some schools are already acting on its findings, and one has commissioned further work in a similar vein on the existence of its own micro-market.

Fee-paying schools can also be seen as a perfectly valid area of research in their own right, since "there is very little writing which seeks...to add and clarify our knowledge of policy and practice in Public schools through the results of academic research" (Roker 1991 p.3). There has been very little assessment of the relative effectiveness of fee-paying and other schools. If a market exists in the private sector, as some claim, and in an educational market, a popular school is a good school, as assumed by those advocating improvement via public choice, then a popular private school would be effective by definition. One possible reason for this is that "the opportunity costs of tuition for parents often loom larger than the opportunity costs of educational finance for state and local governments. Because parents of private school students always have a cheaper option available to them, private schools have strong incentives to keep perceived quality high enough to justify the expenditure" (Weiss 1990 p.111). An investigation of whether such a market exists, and whether popularity is indeed related to quality, is therefore of potential relevance to the school effectiveness literature. This possibility cannot be over-emphasised. If markets lead to improvement, as some claim, then a popular fee-paying school in Britain is an archetypal "improved" school, and its characteristics could be copied by other schools wishing to improve. Conversely, if such a school is relatively ineffective, then a doubt must be cast over the likelihood of marketisation leading to improved educational standards.

The market-place in South Wales

Some studies of school choice have emphasised the importance of local factors, even in a supposedly national market for schools, leading to the existence of regional micro-markets (Gewirtz *et al.* 1995). One of the findings of a review of choice studies by the OECD (1994) is that there may be different reasons for choice of schools in different countries, and in different sectors of education. However, they included no report of work in Wales, which is usually considered only in conjunction with its much larger neighbour, England. The provision of state-funded education in Wales shows marked differences from England. It is controlled by the Welsh Office, not the Department for Education and Employment. It has a different version of the "National" Curriculum, a separate Curriculum Council, very few Grant Maintained schools, no City Technology Colleges at all, and a growing Welsh language sector. All of these differences justify a major study of school choice in Wales, in its own right.

Research in the traditionally private sector of school education has concentrated on England, and the "famous" schools discussed by writers, such as Johnson (1987) and Fox (1985), are invariably English. The fee-paying sector of school education in Wales is small, smaller than official lists suggest, and becoming smaller every year. The range and stability of provision is reducing. The relative lack of provision and diversity in the fee-paying sector in Wales suggests that private schools in Britain, as currently constituted, are predominantly an English phenomenon, which may explain why such schools in Wales have previously been ignored in educational research (Gorard 1996$_c$).

More surprising is the fact that so little research has focused on the very many tiny private schools of the type predominant in Wales. Existing research has focused on the "elite" end of the sector (Walford 1993, Edwards *et al.* 1989). In a rare study of private schools in Wales, Griffiths (1991) confirmed that there has been little research at the "lower" end of the private sector, and pointed out that small businesses and charitable religious trusts are "sadly under-represented in the literature" (Griffiths 1991 p.85). However, even she appears to have relied solely on umbrella organisations like the Independent Schools Information Service (ISIS) in compiling her figures, and she complained of being refused access to Howell's School, Llandaff, in Cardiff, which is the largest, and arguably one of the most prestigious Welsh fee-paying schools. This apparent "blindness" to the less visible private schools permeates all levels of writing about fee-paying education. For example, a recent government publication on schools in Wales stated that the reader can find out more about independent schools from the Independent Schools Information Service (Welsh Office 1994$_c$). This is true. Advertising is the function of ISIS, but it only provides information about its 30 member schools in Wales, and it has fewer members proportionately in Wales than in the rest of the UK. The problem with relying on lists from organisations such as ISIS, the Headmasters' Conference (HMC), the Girls' School Association (GSA), and others is that they are selective. Only 1349 private schools out of over 2400 in England and Wales are members of ISIS for example (ISIS 1995$_b$), and of these the majority are charitable schools, while only 132 are proprietary, of which a mere 101 are limited companies. ISIS lists 30 private schools in Wales, whereas there are, in fact, 52. The remainder are, of course the proprietary and grass-roots schools, "a segment.... for which information is relatively weak" (Grubb 1994 p.351), and which are a key element in this present study.

A recent article devoted to schools in Wales stated that the Assisted Places Scheme is "completely irrelevant" to Wales since there are so few independent schools (Reynolds 1995). APs are scarce in Wales, but the real reason is not just that there are so few schools, but that there are so few schools that have been allowed to offer APs. There are only eight Assisted Place schools in Wales, out of 295 participants in the UK [although these figures have increased since the study]. A recent newspaper report, apparently advising readers on school choice, made the claim about fee-paying schools that "entrance to girls' schools is usually at 11 and to boys' schools at 13....If you are determined on this route, you will probably already have your children in a private prep school which specialises in preparing children for the appropriate examinations. Parents who cannot afford private-school fees are eligible to apply for help through the assisted places scheme..." (O'Connor 1995). As is shown by the present study, the fee-paying sector in Wales today is very different from this newspaper description. Preparatory schools are almost non-existent, very few pupils of either sex transfer between schools at age 13, few of the schools are selective, and hardly any offer APs. What all of the above statements show is that, perhaps because of the lack of research in fee-paying schools, some writers are making the same mistake over and over again in assuming that the most prestigious, high profile, and easier to contact schools are typical of the sector. They are not, and this research shows that they are not.

A difficult time for the fee-paying sector

Proposals to increase the diversity of schools in the state-funded sector have significant implications for fee-paying schools. For example, fee-paying schools can now "opt in" to government control (Walford 1995), while grammar schools and selective schemes are being re-introduced in the state-funded sector, and grant-maintained schools can now become Technology (or other "magnet" subject) Colleges. Loans are being offered to investors by the Funding Agency for Schools in order to create new Grant Maintained schools. Although the 1993 Education Act requires sponsors to provide 15% of the cost of a new school, even this sum can now be provided by a government loan for up to 15 years. The process by which a school opts out of LEA control has been made easier. The growth of these various schools may have recruitment implications for the fee-paying schools, especially among those parents nostalgic for the direct grant, and other selective schools of their own youth, and who would until recently have had to pay for such provision.

One effect of the "marketisation" of education has been the erosion of neighbourhood recruitment patterns in the state-funded sector, making it harder to target the marketing for potential pupils (Donelly 1993). Some schools in the state sector now report taking pupils from as many as 30 primaries. There is also an increased media awareness of schools and pupil outcomes. It is to be expected, therefore, that schools will be marketing more strongly than in the past. Devlin and Knight (1990) suggested that: the changes in demography; the ERA 1988; the creation of a public relations (PR) budget for schools for the first time under LMS, and the chance of generating greater resources, or a broader spread of parental involvement by a better relationship with the community, all require changes in marketing. As more schools put effort into public relations, the successful marketing of private schools is likely to become more difficult and resource-demanding.

A future Labour Government is now pledged to tighten the use and definition of charitable status. Some private schools are based on an endowment intended to be used to educate the poor. Labour might insist that the terms of the endowment are strictly adhered to if charitable status is to continue. They may make VAT payable on the fees, and would almost certainly also phase out the Assisted Places Scheme which is providing between 10% and 50% of the pupils in individual participating fee-paying schools. Private schools in Wales will need to plan for their survival under such conditions. These plans become urgent in the light of a 35% drop in the number of pupils of secondary school age from 1980 to 1990 which has led to increasing competition for pupils (Gaunt 1991), although an upturn in school population may be on its way (Eurostat 1995).

There are other changes in policy which may make survival more difficult for small fee-paying schools. For example, the funding for armed-services children at fee-paying boarding schools has been tightened, and the impact is beginning to be seen in the drop in boarding numbers (ISIS 1995b). Schools are admitted to this scheme merely by registering with the DfEe, so there is at present little accountability, but this could soon change. In some schools, between 50 and 70% of the boarders have parents in the armed forces, thus any change in this area could have a large impact on the rural boarding schools of Wales. This study, therefore, is taking place at a unique point in the history of private schooling in Wales, and may be describing a system in the process of changing beyond recognition.

The size of the fee-paying sector

In any attempt to assess the size of the private sector in Wales, the first decisions concern which schools to include in the category, and which sources of information to use. The term "independent", although preferred by the schools themselves is not appropriate in this context, since it is ambiguous and has also been used to describe devolved Sixth Form Colleges, and City Technology Colleges, which are not included in this study. The term "public" or "famous" school is not appropriate in this context, since it has been traditionally reserved for those long-established, large English boarding schools, usually belonging to HMC. Few, if any of the fee-paying schools in Wales could be described as "public", and none have the prestige usually associated with that term. The preferred term used throughout this study is "fee-paying" school, although the less descriptive term "private" is also used, for variety. Fee-paying schools are defined here as those in the traditional private sector which charge fees for academic tuition, and cater for at least five pupils of compulsory school age. These schools are registered as independent under Section 7 of the Education Act 1944.

When compiling a list of private schools in Scotland, Walford (1987_a) found several problems also relevant to this study in Wales. The sector was so volatile that "the difficulties even extend to the very basic question of the total number of such schools" (Walford 1987_a p.109). He found inconsistency in the treatment of senior and junior sections of the same school, and that their age range and their "age of transfer is not clear cut" (Walford 1987_a p.111). The private sector has no corporate identity (Johnson 1987), and associations such as HMC do not provide a unifying structure. Lists of schools published by umbrella organisations like ISIS are of limited use as many of the fee-paying schools are not included. Even in England, the Independent Schools Information Service is only sponsored by associations representing 56% of the private schools (ISIS 1994), and in Wales that figure is less than half. Proprietary day schools in areas such as Swansea, for example, where ISIS does not hold exhibitions for parents, have little to gain in terms of marketing from joining such an organisation. Some schools are so new, or so small, that they do not have a listed telephone number, and one small school in Wales even has no name. Many of these are schools that have developed from successful home-schooling schemes, and as such, they have defied much previous research. For example, Edwards and Whitty (1995) stated that fees in the private sector in England ranged from £3,300 to £8,400 p.a., and while it is true that fees in England are higher than in Wales (Gorard 1996_a), it is likely that their research was based only upon lists, such as those provided by ISIS, which both under-estimate the size of the sector, and over-estimate its cost. Perhaps one of the reasons for the concentration of previous research on "famous" schools is convenience. Changes in the provision of the smaller schools are so frequent, that any list of such schools is in the nature of a snapshot at a moment in time. However, to ignore such schools and concentrate on the more stable and neater schools is to bias any assessment of fee-paying schools in Wales. All of the schools in this study are independent and all charge fees. All of the Public schools are included, as are the "for profit" proprietary schools and the small faith-based schools.

The use of school lists from the Welsh Office, on the other hand, inevitably leads to an over-estimate, since they only make the distinction between state-funded and "independent" schools, and the latter category includes private nurseries that have no children of compulsory school age as well as those "independent" schools listed as being for "pupils emotionally or behaviourally disturbed" or "physically handicapped schools". These are primarily small residential institutions, often for statemented pupils, and they were excluded from this study. The Welsh Office list of "Registered Independent Schools (Wales) as at September 1994" has 61 entries, two fewer than in 1993, since three schools had since closed, two had merged, and two new ones had started. These "snapshot" dates also obscure the story of two schools which merged, and then separated again between the two dates. The changes in these nine schools in one year, at least 15% of the total, give an indication of the severe volatility of the sector. The number of pupils listed as being on the rolls of these schools is very approximate, apparently being based upon the returns of the schools themselves in the previous September, and then compared to the difference between live-births for each year in question, and the number of children in state-funded schools. The number of pupils actually in most schools during the study is smaller than the figure recorded by the Welsh Office. Pupils may be accepting places at more than one private school, or they are either dropping out after registration, and returning to state-funded provision, or else the number of children not at any school is being officially underestimated.

Two of the 61 schools on the Welsh Office list are, in fact, the Senior and Preparatory sections of the same school, which are listed separately as having different Heads, and neighbouring addresses. However, several other schools have junior sections with their own Heads, so to be consistent, all such schools are treated as one if they have the same owners, or governing bodies. One school took only two pupils of compulsory school age, and another did not charge fees, relying on voluntary contributions from an associated church. Neither of these was a fee-paying school according to the definition above, and the exclusion of these and the residential schools left 52 on the list of fee-paying private schools in Wales. The majority of the schools are in the south, mostly along the coast, with nearly 20% being in Cardiff alone. Several are on the north coast, but very few appear in Mid-Wales. The sector is divided geographically into two unequal "halves".

The schools themselves vary considerably in size, and so their numbers may not be good indicators of the size of the sector in different parts of Wales. Table 4.2 shows the distribution of the schools by county, and their intake in September 1994. It also shows that boarding is now almost non-existent in the southern counties of Wales, while it is still relatively strong in rural mid-Wales [these counties were replaced at the end of the study by new unitary authorities].

Table 4.2
The size of the private sector by county

County	Schools	Pupils	Mean Size	Boarders	% Board
Clwyd	10	1798	180	493	27%
Dyfed	7	940	134	219	23%
Gwent	6	1900	317	303	16%
Gwynedd	8	1098	137	349	32%
Mid Glam	5	627	125	40	6%
Powys	2	448	224	295	66%
Sth Glam	10	2512	251	41	2%
West Glam	4	484	121	-	-
Total	52	9807	189	1740	18%

The total of 9,807 pupils of compulsory school age in fee-paying schools is from a school population of 473,670 in 1992 (Welsh Office 1994a), equivalent to less than 2%. Private schooling is most frequent among 14 year olds, tailing off normally on either side of this age (Welsh Office 1995a). The number of schools has fallen to 52 from 71 in 1990, and the number of pupils has fallen regularly from a peak of 15,438 in 1960 (Welsh Office 1994a). The relative decline of the sector is even more marked in the light of a growth of the private sector in England since 1979. Also, since the Welsh Office figures include non-fee paying independents in their list, but exclude the growing number of pupils taught at home from their school population figures, the size of the fee-paying sector in Wales is even smaller than official figures show.

This figure of 52 schools makes the private sector in Wales very small in comparison to England, which has 2,247 independent schools plus a further 14 City Technology Colleges (DfE 1994), and it is even fewer than the 93 private schools in Scotland, described by Walford (1987). In England 7.9% of pupils attend independent schools (DFE 1994), making the sector four times as significant as in Wales. The size of private schools in England also tends to be larger with some schools having over 1,500 pupils, and an average size of 238 pupils, compared to 189, or even less, in Wales. Despite the differences in overall scale, Table 4.3 shows that the proportions of boarders, and boys and girls, are similar in England and Wales (Welsh Office 1994$_a$).

Table 4.3

Comparison of private education in England and Wales

	England	%	%	Wales
Pupils	538676	8	2	9807
Boys	284596	53	50	4884
Girls	254080	47	50	4923
Boarders	94062	17	18	1740
Boy boarders	58296	62	67	1171
Girl boarders	35766	38	33	569

The private sector in Wales is not only different in scale to England, but it is also much smaller than in the USA (13% according to Peterson 1990), France (21% according to Roker 1991), and the Netherlands (72% according to OECD 1994), perhaps because Church schools in the UK have been assimilated by the state system (Whitty *et al.* 1989). In fact, in Western Europe perhaps only Sweden has a comparable figure to Wales (Roker 1991).

Explanations for the size of the fee-paying sector

Fee-paying schools in Wales are rare, and those that exist are generally smaller than their state-funded equivalents, and their fee-paying equivalents in England (Gorard 1996$_a$). Possible explanations for this situation are discussed under three related themes - the relative performance of the schools, economic constraints, and local educational history. One could argue that there does not need to be a reason why so few parents wish to pay for an education in a country with free universal education. In the absence of evidence that private schools are better in some way for their pupils, there is no rational explanation for paying for something which is already provided free of charge. However, such an argument alone does not explain why Wales probably has one of the smallest proportion of private pupils in Western Europe. In order to discuss this question, it is necessary to first establish what kind of schools are available in the private sector, and who is using them.

Walford (1987$_a$) stated that the range of types of private schools in Scotland, and perhaps by implication England, was "considerable", from old-established boarding schools charging high fees, through ex-direct grant day schools, and religious schools, to specialist schools for overseas nationals in the oil industry, concluding that "clearly while some of these schools are in accord with popular views about independent schools, others are far from usual expectations" (Walford 1987$_a$ p.110).

The private schools in the focus area of this study are described in considerably more detail in Chapter 6. The analysis here considers all private schools and concentrates on their size, age range, gender mix, and whether they offer boarding places, based upon figures from the Welsh Office (1994$_a$). Instead of splitting conveniently into primary, middle, preparatory, secondary, or even all-age, the 52 schools actually span 34 different age ranges - with 3 to 6 years of age being the shortest span, and 2 to 19 being the longest - a similar range to that found by Walford (1987$_a$) in Scotland. This span is collapsed to 12 types for the sake of simplicity in Table 4.4 which shows that 39 of the 52 schools take pupils of both secondary and primary ages. This age range displays diversity of a sort, but the diversity is largely caused by the schools being in the process of becoming more uniform in their ages, by increasing their range at either end. These changes are probably taking place as a direct result of the recent 33% decline in the sector.

Table 4.4
The age ranges of Welsh private schools

Lowest age accepted	Highest age	Number of schools
2, 3, or 4	10 or 11	11
2, 3, or 4	12, 13, or 14	5
2, 3, or 4	15 or 16	8
2, 3, or 4	18 or 19	14
3	6	1
5 or 6	12 or 13	2
5	18	1
6	15	1
7, 8, or 9	18 or 19	5
8	13	1
10	16	1
10 or 12	18	2

Six of the schools are single-sex (three of each gender), five of them taking boarders, and four offering Assisted Places. Even these categories are not clear-cut. Some schools, while coeducational, take only boarders of one gender, or within a limited age range. Some of the single-sex schools take both genders in their pre-school classes. Some of the mixed schools, which were previously single-sex have only a few of one sex in certain age groups. In total, 17 schools offer boarding, of which only 6 are primarily for boarding, and eight offer Assisted places (although since this study was completed the Welsh Office have announced that a further 8 schools will participate from September 1996). Figure 4.1 shows the pattern of the sizes of schools, with most having fewer than 100 pupils. The smallest school has 8 pupils, and the largest has 652, still very small for a secondary school in Wales.

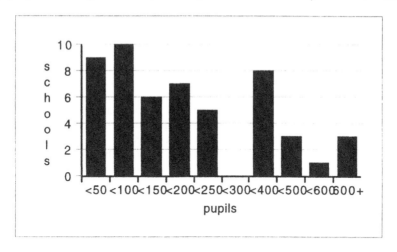

Figure 4.1 The number of pupils in each school

The number of boarders is dropping at an accelerating rate, and there is a clear trend towards coeducation in private schools, especially for boys (GPDSA 1995). Even in the traditional public schools described by Salter and Tapper (1981), the trend towards coeducation, day pupils, and weekly boarding with families living near the school, was already clearly visible. The number of home boarders is dropping even more sharply than these figures show, since there has been an increase in the number of foreign boarders (ISIS 1995b). The few remaining rural single-sex boarding schools are the ones most under economic threat, while the new schools being formed are mainly coeducational urban day schools (ISIS 1995b).

In summary, the clear majority of fee-paying schools in Wales take day pupils of most ages, and both sexes. For economic reasons, the current trend is towards making these schools more rather than less similar (Gorard 1996a). The position in the fee-paying sector is thus the same as that described by Glatter *et al.* (1997) for the state sector. If any movement is detectable in the new market-like environment for schools, it is in the direction of greater uniformity, and not diversity.

Who uses fee-paying schools?

Since many of the private schools in Wales are far from the popular image of public schools, the same may also be true of their users. Characterising such families is one of the objectives of this study (see Chapter 10), and this section unpicks some of the threads in this objective, and reviews some of the previous work shedding light on the users of fee-paying schools.

The defining characteristic of a fee-paying school is the payment of fees for tuition, and this is a barrier preventing universal access. The people of Wales might therefore be seen as uniquely unable to cross the purported threshold of affordability, and this might explain why the fee-paying sector is so small. Such an explanation might refer to the decline of the coal, iron and steel industries with its linked unemployment and regional poverty (Gorard 1997$_e$). If it were true that a smaller proportion of the population is able to afford private education, one would expect that cost would be a major determinant of whether a family used the private sector, and of which private schools were chosen. Indications of this would be great importance attached to the level of fees by parents and pupils, a high demand for the Assisted Places Scheme, heavy competition for scholarships and bursaries, a high dropout rate due to lack of funds, relative popularity of cheaper schools, and more private schools in wealthier areas. However, it is also true that this limitation of access due to cost may be more of a myth than a reality, since some schools have very low fees, many families are charged fees at reduced rates, and because of the introduction of the Assisted Places Scheme. Although ISIS (1994) quoted a fee range of £2100 to £8700, the highest annual fees for a day pupil in a Welsh private school are £5799, while the lowest are around £300. The range illustrates the absurdity of viewing all fee-paying schools as the prerogative of only the most privileged in society. The figure of £300 p.a. is only a third of the price of smoking 20 cigarettes per day. The answer to the question posed by Johnson (1987) whether there is a threshold of affordability below which private schools cannot be considered is probably "no", but the schools that most people can afford are probably not those of their dreams. The most expensive schools tend to be the older schools that also offer boarding, and it is possible that their prices are determined as much by the cost of the upkeep of aged living accommodation, as by their facilities and staff. The cheapest schools are the faith-based schools, which are aided either by donations from the congregation of a related church group, or by volunteer staff. Many schools have different prices for different age groups, and in the case of one proprietary school, the range is from £2460 at age 5 to £6450 at age 17.

Whatever the costs of the school, ISIS (1995$_b$) reported that more than 28% of pupils in their member schools are anyway given assistance of some sort with the fees, and that this number is rising every year. Most of this assistance comes directly from the schools themselves in the form of scholarships and bursaries (18%), the rest comes from Assisted Places (7%), and the LEAs (3%). The funding from LEAs is for pupils with special educational needs that cannot be economically met by the LEA provision, and this figure is also still rising every year. The special educational need can be as simple as the need for boarding. The scholarships are usually given to children chosen by performance in an entrance examination, and are based upon supposed academic potential, but there are also scholarships available for sport, music, and drama in some schools. The principle here is to charge others indirectly for the privilege of being schooled with scholars. The bursaries are usually based upon family circumstance rather than ability, and reductions in fees are offered for children of the clergy, the teaching staff, and families of existing pupils in financial or domestic difficulty. The principle here is that, even though the schools are under-subscribed, classrooms need to exist, and be staffed, heated and lit anyway, so the extra pupils do not cost much. Some pupils are sponsored by external agencies such as livery companies, multinational companies, professional associations, and the government, which pays allowances for the families of diplomats and the armed forces.

One of the intentions of the Assisted Places Scheme was to give free or subsidised places at private schools to academically able children from working-class and disadvantaged backgrounds (Fitz *et al.* 1986), with at least 60% of the places being taken by pupils who had previously attended state schools. There has been some success in mobilising working-class parents (Edwards *et al.* 1989), but the 60% target has been difficult to sustain (Johnson 1987), which has meant that the number of Assisted Places available each year has never been filled, despite having 235 candidates for every 100 places (Douse 1985). One reason for this apparent competition for places is that there is no central register, and so the same family can apply for more than one place. APs are being taken up by families who have a low income, by definition, but they are not necessarily inner-city deprived working-class, and are more likely to be a "submerged middle class" of artificially poor single parents after death or divorce, often with a good educational background of their own (Douse 1985). Of the new AP pupils, 20% already have a sibling at a private school and 32% have one or more parent with professional or graduate qualifications (Douse 1985), and these findings are similar to those of Edwards *et al.* (1989). Furthermore, 50% would have attended a private school anyway and up to 40% would have attended the school at which they obtained the Assisted Place (Douse 1985). In his study of six schools, Douse (1985) found no APs for disabled pupils and only one for a child of an ethnic minority, while 83% of the recipients were single parents and 41% were, or had recently been, unemployed. A further source of assistance "from the state" is the use of covenants, whereby a relative can pay the school fees from untaxed income (Robson and Walford 1989), although such a strategy is becoming less valuable as the rate of direct income tax is falling.

Echols *et al.* (1990) studied 126 users of Scottish private schools among 3,010 families, and found them to be much more likely to be in service and intermediate occupational classes than the working-class, according to the scale used by Halsey *et al.* 1980 and throughout this study. They were also much more likely to have at least one parent educated past the age of 16. The same study found that users of private schools were more likely to be in areas of high school choice, urban settings with seven or more alternative state schools, as well as in areas of no school choice at all, rural settings with only one state school. This suggests that there at least two types of private school users, consumerist families exercising their right to choose and those who are dissatisfied with their local school. Johnson (1987) found a range of themes of transfer to private schools, sometimes because of problems with a particular child, among families who are not natural users of the sector. A survey by the Institute of Economic Affairs found that most families in all socio-economic groups were prepared to pay for their child's education, perhaps because "people pay directly for better services for themselves more willingly than they would pay taxes that bore no relation to the services they received" (Maynard 1975 p. 6), and this is confirmed by a more recent MORI poll showing that most parents would use a private school if they could afford it (ISIS 1995b). Most users of private schools have no inherited wealth, and pay the fees from earned income (Johnson 1987, ISIS 1995b) and the number of private pupils with parents and siblings from private schools is dropping (GPDSA 1995) with at least 40% of user families where neither parent attended a private school.

Perhaps the two clearest indications that it is not inability to pay fees that has led to so few private schools in Wales are firstly, that the 1991 Census reveals similar levels of disadvantage in Wales as in the rest of Britain (OPCS 1993). The rate of unemployment and number of lone parents are close to the national average and while homes in Wales are less likely to have central heating and private bathrooms they are more likely to have a car than those in the rest of the UK (but these overall figures disguise the local differences between the more affluent M4 corridor and the depressed ex-mining valleys for example, see Gorard 1997$_e$). Secondly, if there were an underlying but frustrated desire for private schools, it is unlikely that the 136 Assisted Places available every year in Wales would never have been filled since the start of the scheme, which is what has happened (Welsh Office 1995$_a$). In summary, without wishing to dispute that some users of private schools are highly privileged, these are perhaps the most visible users, and there are indications that there are other users, in faith-based schools, or with special educational needs, or the 7% of working-class Assisted Place holders, who are far from privileged. It must be recalled that APs are only available in 10% of fee-paying schools, and that in addition to the half of the sector spoken for by ISIS, there is another half of non-elite, small, cheap schools.

Variations in performance

One simple explanation for the small size of the private sector could be that state schools in Wales have traditionally performed well in comparison to those in England, for example, where the fee-paying sector is larger. Therefore, so the argument runs, state schools in Wales provide little reason for dissatisfaction. If this were true, one would expect that Welsh state schools would compare very favourably with both English state schools and Welsh private schools in terms of effectiveness and pupil outcomes. Whether this is so is admittedly difficult to answer without considering the function of schools in society and the intention of parents in choosing a school, and without deciding on an objective measure of school quality. However, all of the indications are that, on any commonly accepted measure of school performance (Eurostat 1995, Hackett 1995, Istance and Rees 1994, Jones 1990$_a$, OHCMI 1993, Reynolds 1990, Reynolds 1991, Reynolds 1995, TES 1993, 1994$_a$, 1995) Welsh schools do not perform any better than private schools in Wales or state schools in England, in fact possibly the reverse (see Gorard 1997$_a$ for a fuller treatment of this complex issue).

There are, of course, individual variations, but private schools in Wales figure very prominently near the top of published league tables of performance, although the actual worth of such figures is disputed in Chapter 2. The little comparative work that has been done between the sectors has not referred to Wales, and this is a gap that should be remedied. If low rates of use of fee-paying schools are due to their relatively poor performance, one would expect the rate to be higher in areas where the state schools have the worst performance, but this is not so. The lowest retention and participation rates in Welsh state schools are in West Glamorgan, while the lowest GCSE benchmark figure (30% of pupils with 5+ GCSEs) is in Mid Glamorgan (Welsh Office 1995$_a$). Similarly, the largest number of school leavers with no qualifications is from Mid and West Glamorgan (Reynolds 1990), but it has already been shown that attendance at private schools in these counties is, in fact, the lowest in Wales. It is more likely that the absence of fee-paying schools in Mid Glamorgan, for example, as well as the poorer performance of its state schools is due to the class backgrounds of the intake. Mid Glamorgan has the highest ratio of working to middle-class families in Wales (Reynolds 1990). However, even this cannot explain all, since South Glamorgan which has the lowest ratio of working to middle-class families, and the most private schools, has the second highest number of school leavers with no qualifications. Perhaps the reasons are economic, but more complex.

Further economic reasons

If performance figures alone, based on the little research available, do not suggest that state schools in Wales are out-performing the private sector in a way that is not happening in England, perhaps the reasons for the lack of private schools in Wales are economic. The schools may be small because the sector is so small that many schools are in a volatile situation. Relatively small local variations in demand could cause the rise or fall of a school so that the sector is dominated by new schools seeking to establish themselves and older schools in decline. Using figures from ISIS censuses, there is evidence that the number of fee-paying schools in the UK from 1981 to 1995 exactly followed the pattern of economic growth and decline, but the percentage changes were smaller and lagged behind by about two years (GPDSA 1995). If the local fee-paying schools started from a base of a few small schools run as businesses, this link with economic cycles might lead to a volatile situation with schools opening and closing and little chance to become established. This is apparently what has happened. Walford found a similar situation in Scotland, where "the sector is constantly changing. Faced with a falling school-age population in Scotland, coupled with fee levels that have had to increase markedly faster than the rate of inflation...., several schools have found the need to merge with others or close.... while small local day schools come and go with the enthusiasm of the founders" (Walford 1987a p.110).

ISIS (1995b) also reported that the recession, and falling birth numbers in Britain as a whole, were "sorting schools out". Although the proportion of pupils in fee-paying schools has grown since 1979, the absolute number has gone down, and their nature has changed. More of the boarders are foreign nationals, but there are many fewer boarders overall. This means that one type of fee-paying schools is decreasing, but that in addition a similar number of new schools is opening while old ones are closing down due to changes in demand, with rural boarding schools in particular danger. Even many of the large, long-established schools may only be able to survive due to the Assisted Places Scheme, which although small in scale, accounts for over a third of pupils in individual schools (Edwards *et al.* 1989). The APs are only one of a range of financial measures helping the fee-paying sector, and others include exemption from income tax, VAT, and capital gains tax (Robson and Walford 1989). However, like the APs, these concessions are really only of relevance to the larger, richer, land-owning schools, of which there are very few in Wales. In 1982, for example, only 56% of private schools were registered charities, and these tended to be exactly the type of schools in the AP Scheme. The tax concessions are anyway of no value unless the schools receive rents from land, equity from sale of property, or other surplus income. The reduction in local authority rates only applies to charities, and is of particular help to those schools with acres of land (Robson and Walford 1989). Very few schools in Wales own acres of land.

It could be argued that schools are small because that is how their clients want them to be so that, ironically, small schools are popular. The difficulties of becoming established as a school may in part explain why the private schools in Wales are so small, but not why they are so few and why the number of children not attending any school is growing (Meighan 1992). Although the details are not in the public domain, there is a suggestion that at least some LEAs in Wales actively suppress the creation of new fee-paying schools, which may be denied permission to operate even when there are ready made premises available, such as at Cefn Mably or Miskin recently, and properly funded plans. This is considered further in the next section on the history of fee-paying schools in Wales.

The development of private education in Wales

If use of the private sector is found to be an advantage and is what its users are paying for, one reason why the sector is so small could be that Welsh people do not value educational advantage as much as the English. It could be that the British educational system has been a weakening factor in Welsh society, raising false hopes of better employment, leading eventually to emigration from the principality perhaps as a form of "brain drain". If this were true, one would expect the staying on rates of all schools in Wales and entry to Higher Education to be lower than in England. One would also expect that truancy rates would be higher, with little importance attached to educational reasons for choosing a school and that the private sector in Wales would be disproportionately filled by in-migrants from England and further afield. There is some evidence that all of these possibilities are true, in part (see for example Gorard 1997a).

In theory there was universal free elementary education available in Wales before 1889, although any higher standard of education, such as that required to enter a university, in practice required students to attend fee-paying schools. In that sense, all nineteenth century secondary schools were private. However, none of these were considered to be public schools in the English tradition. In fact, according to one writer "the elite among the Welsh landowning gentry had sent their sons to the great English public schools since the sixteenth century and would not have contemplated such provision in Wales. The thought of a Welsh Eton was an absurdity" (Jones 1990b p. 62). The middle and lower-middle classes were not sufficient in numbers to support many of the foundation schools, which were "few, relatively poor, compared with their English counterparts and far removed from the main centres of population in the nineteenth century" (Jones 1990b p. 63).

The Welsh Intermediate Education Act of 1889 established the secondary age intermediate schools which, although state supported, did charge fees and offered scholarships to the poor. Since there were insufficient wealthy middle-class families to support the selective intermediate schools in Wales, many reverted to being elementary schools, but some became boarding schools taking pupils from elsewhere, which was the origin of some of the present private schools.

A problem for some communities was that an intermediate education did not lead to a suitable local job in a primarily agricultural area. Suitable jobs were available in England, and that is where many young people went. For example, of 60 leavers from Penygroes county school, Caernarfonshire in 1938, 26 went to England because they could not find a suitable local job (Evans 1990$_a$). In industrial areas, the exodus was greater, and the majority of school leavers left their home communities. This was unpopular in some families, and so education may have been seen by them as an evil (compare the Amish farmers in Chapter 1). Jones quotes an Alderman of Cardiganshire as saying at this time "if you want to keep your children in the country, don't give them any education at all" (Jones 1982 p. 197).

After the 1944 Education Act, many intermediates became Grammar schools and no longer charged fees. In principle, selection was by merit but the population density was so low in rural Wales that it proved impossible to implement a viable tri-partite system. There were no properly equipped technology schools in South Wales at all (Evans 1990$_a$). Some pupils had to travel great distances to get to their selected school. From 1951 to 1955 the selection rate for the grammar school in Narberth was over 40% (compared to a more common rate of 10% in England). Jones (1982) gave similar figures for the 1950s in Wales, where 36 to 50% of pupils attended grammar schools compared to 18 to 25% in England. This was not because of a greater ability or a differing educational philosophy, but perhaps because there was no other secondary modern school within convenient travelling distance.

In the light of the foregoing, it is possible that the paucity of fee-paying schools in Wales is partly due to the fact that local people have not traditionally valued education as much as their English peers, partly the early lack of a numerous middle-class and the availability of boarding schools in England, and partly the preponderance grammar schools in Wales after 1944. What is clear is that for a variety of economic, social, and political reasons, private schools in Wales have a much shorter and less stable history than their more robust neighbours in England.

Conclusion

The discussion in this chapter serves three main objectives. The first is to justify a new study of school choice in Wales, by showing that the education system in Wales is sufficiently different from England, that the fee-paying sector is so much smaller than in England, and that the type of schools in Wales have not been fully addressed previously in the research literature. It also shows that this study needs to address the issues of the Welsh language and the Curriculum Cymreig, in addition to those associated with researching school choice in England. Questions relevant to this issue are therefore required for the survey instrument. The second objective is to establish the population, or sampling frame, for the focus sample of schools. This chapter makes a preliminary study of the users of private schools, and shows that the fee-paying sector is composed of more and smaller schools than is popularly supposed, but that the numbers of pupils enrolled may be lower than official figures suggest. The third outcome is a set of possible explanations, such as economic diversity, to explain why there are so few fee-paying schools in Wales, and some associated issues to be explored further in this study.

Research by Walford (1987$_a$) has shown that the sector in Scotland is tiny by comparison to England and Wales. One further purpose of this chapter is to divorce Wales from this comparison, and show that fee-paying schools in Britain, as currently instituted, are predominantly an English phenomenon. Another is to suggest that despite the existence of a long established market for fee-paying schools, the size of the sector in Wales is shrinking, and the schools are becoming more similar, perhaps as a "survival technique of the threatened" (Griffiths 1991). In this market at least, the forces are moving from choice and diversity towards constraint and similarity. The trend is towards mixed day schools with a wide age-range covering both primary and secondary age groups.

Part Two
RESEARCHING THE ESTABLISHED MARKET

5 Outline methodology

Introduction

This chapter describes, and justifies where necessary, the methods used in the present study, building upon criticism of the methods used in previous work, as outlined in Chapter 3. In summary, this study uses a mixture of methods, a large stratified sample, multivariate analysis, and a range of schools. It shows the value of combining documentary evidence, with a large-scale questionnaire and follow-up interviews, as suggested by Hammond and Dennison (1995). The aim of this study is "to use the quantitative data to generate and test hypotheses on the lines of the classic hypothetico-deductive model, and to use the qualitative data to explain the findings and processes at work ... that lay behind the statistical relationships" (Reynolds 1991). It involves children by asking for their views directly, rather than via their parents, and contacts families both during and after making the choice. This enables a comparison to be made between the attitudes of families before, and after, starting the new school. By looking at the characteristics of the schools themselves, it is also possible to illuminate any mismatch between professed attitudes and actual behaviour (Eiser and van der Plight 1988).

The chapter is divided into six parts. The pilot study is described briefly, with its implications for the main study. This is followed by a description of the sample, the instruments used in the main survey, the proposed analysis of the quantitative results, and a discussion of the quality of the data so obtained. The final section describes the collection and analysis of the more detailed interview and narrative data.

The pilot study

The process of negotiating access to schools in South Wales commenced in 1994, and embryonic versions of the questionnaires were piloted at that stage. Three schools took part in the pilot survey, while three provided findings from their own market research, and these two sources provided an interesting comparison. The pilot survey involved only families with children in Year 7. Questionnaire forms for pupils were distributed during normal school lessons, and the parents' forms were sent home with the pupils under a covering letter, and returned to the school. A total of 178 forms were returned, with an overall return rate of 90%.

Lessons from the pilot study

In one pilot school, the pupil questionnaires were administered by a member of staff with the researcher not present. This was convenient for administration, but had three major disadvantages. The pupils were more likely to see this as the school's own research, and thus feel inhibited in their criticisms. The teachers may have provided different explanations of questions in different schools, and may not have understood the purpose of the work, and so misled the respondents. This last problem was also encountered several times by the researcher when working in tandem with a form teacher in classrooms. The "ratings" questions asked pupils to rate the importance for them of a number of school characteristics when choosing a school. It was made clear by the researcher that the ratings should not be an appraisal of the current school, but a recollection of the characteristics of the "ideal" school sought in the previous year. In this light, it might be perfectly reasonable for a respondent in a single-sex school, for example, to answer that co-education was very important to them, although presumably outweighed by other reasons, or the opinions of others. However, more than one teacher was heard to encourage pupils who asked for clarification, to respond for the school. One such comment was "... well, it's about the importance of a sixth form, but we don't have a sixth form so you should put 'not important'". To remedy such problems in the main study, all forms were completed by pupils with the researcher present, and standard explanations were written, to be read out for each question.

Most questions given to parents and pupils were intended to ask the same thing, but several were paraphrased on the pupil form in order to reduce the level of reading competence required to complete it. It was difficult to paraphrase concepts such as "equal opportunities", "progressive education" and "traditional values" without being cumbersome, or losing precision. In retrospect, it was not clear whether both groups were actually answering the same underlying questions, which prevented clear comparison of the differences between children and their parents. In the main study, all questions are phrased identically for both groups. However, several questions were simplified for all, and made easier to answer, code, and analyse.

The sample

The initial unit of sampling and administration for the main study was the school. Schools were chosen for the sampling frame because it was easier to create a list of all fee-paying schools than to create a list of all families using fee-paying schools. Once schools had been identified and agreed to participate, the entire year group of relevant age pupils and their parents were surveyed.

The size and distribution of schools in the fee-paying sector of Wales is shown in Chapter 4, and it can be seen that the absence of schools in Mid-Wales divides the sector neatly into two. North and South Wales each have their own fee-paying schools concentrated near the coasts, and there is a large band of mid-Wales with no such schools at all. It is reasonable to assume that day schools in North Wales are not competing with any in South Wales. The region of South Wales was selected for study since it was the largest, and the most convenient. It was operationally defined as the area south of a line through Llandovery, Brecon and Monmouth. This line was chosen because there are no private schools north of these towns until Barmouth, which is in the northern part of Wales. The few schools in the far western portion of South Wales were excluded from the study, as being too difficult to access. The study region therefore extends from Chepstow, on the border with England, to Llanelli in the West.

The fee-paying sample

The problem described in Chapter 4, of out of date official lists of private schools, was also observed by Griffiths (1991), who decided that so little information about the population was available, with not even a pupil gender breakdown, that she could not take a stratified sample of the users of private schools. The problems are overcome here to some extent, by using the school as the unit of sampling. Even so, the sampling frame is only in the nature of a momentary snapshot. To give an indication of the pace of change in this sector, one of the schools approached for the study, closed suddenly during one summer holiday. The first that the staff learned of the sale of the business was by reading of it in a newspaper. The private sector in South Wales is facing the same pressures as in England. In the last two years, it has been marked by school closures, a decline in boarding, a decline in single-sex provision, and by schools extending the age range of their intake. Three schools have ceased to take boarders. One previously single-sex school now accepts girls in the sixth form and has announced an intention to become fully coeducational, while two others are now offering combined coeducational sixth form courses. The number of coeducational schools far outnumbers single-sex ones in South Wales. However, these categories are not clearly distinct. In addition to the recent changes noted above, five private schools in the region have a coeducational intake at age five, but will not educate boys after a certain age, usually seven or eleven. At first sight, these differences between schools are incompatible. Girls schools are admitting boys until a certain age and then becoming single-sex, while boys schools are becoming co-educational through the addition of girls to the higher age groups. As the existing boys-only schools are no larger than the girls schools, there are, apparently, not enough boys-only schools to cope with the excess. The anomaly is explained, in part, by the fact that many of the coeducational schools have more than 50% boys on the roll. Several ostensibly coeducational schools have complete year groups containing only boys. In summary, there are only three schools taking pupils of one sex throughout their age range, and only one that offers no mixed classes at all.

Three schools have plans to expand by nearly 50%, one by introducing a sixth form, one a GCSE section, and one by moving to a new site. Most private schools already take pupils of both primary and secondary ages. Many are also taking children as young as two years old. This may be a marketing strategy to maintain their market share of pupils, or a new use of existing facilities prompted by falling rolls, or it may be seen as an extended selection process for entrance to the main school. Thus the majority of private schools in the area have made major changes in two years, all tending towards similarity of provision. These changes tend to be more inclusive, in order to increase the potential "custom" of the schools. Boarding provision is declining, as the unit costs of its provision are greater, and is retained chiefly by those isolated schools which could not survive on the basis of their local catchment. One of these schools, for example, is 20 miles away from the nearest town of more than 5,000 people, and sheep clearly outnumber people in its environs.

It was understood from the outset that schools in the private sector might not welcome research conducted in the sensitive areas of recruitment, market image, and reputation. It was anticipated that some may not have the funds necessary for development, and would be wary of raising false hopes by what might appear to be consumer research. In addition, there remained the possibility that some would not relish further comparison with other schools in the area. There was a fear that the work could be haunted by the "ghost of Royston Lambert" (Walford 1987c) whose earlier unflattering work on English boarding schools made it harder for later researchers to gain access. Even the limited local study by Griffiths (1991) was constrained by the refusal to take part in the investigation of 40% of the private schools approached. In an attempt to allay these concerns, the schools in this study were assured that they would not be identified in any reports arising from the survey, although this clearly does not rule out other kinds of analysis based upon publicly available information, such as that presented in Chapter 10. Schools which expressed an interest were shown a provisional copy of the questions and asked for feedback on the acceptability of their phrasing. As a result, the rubric given to respondents was changed to make it clear that cooperation by the school did not indicate support for any of the ideas contained in the questions. The schools were offered an analysis of the results of their own respondents, and a summary of the results from the whole study and it was suggested that these might be of benefit to them for their marketing and development.

It is worth recording here again how helpful, friendly and tolerant the management, staff, parents, and pupils of all schools were. The atmosphere that this attitude created made the field work a real pleasure. In many cases, after communication and a brief discussion with the Head, the researcher was allowed to take entire year groups of pupils unsupervised for a pastoral or registration period. The age and experience of the researcher as a teacher for 13 years were undoubtedly helpful in gaining this measure of trust. Three of the schools that refused to take part in the survey did so because they did "not want to stir up a hornets' nest". Their replies show a lack of confidence in their provision and the goodwill of their parents and pupils. Unfortunately, all three of the schools are of one type - rural, single-sex, boarding schools. As this type of school is so scarce (see Chapter 4), it was not possible to completely replace these in the sample with the result that the findings which emerged may have less validity for these traditional fee-paying schools and that the sample is slightly biased towards girls and day pupils.

There are 29 fee-paying schools in the study area. All of them were contacted by the researcher and most have supplied publicity material as a result. Ten have completed a supplementary questionnaire about their size, cost, and make-up. Twenty of the schools were visited by the researcher, and of these, three took part in the pilot study, sixteen have taken a full part in the survey, and six have provided families for interview. Further details of the sampling frame, and the sample used are given in Table 5.1, using data from the Welsh Office (1994$_a$).

Table 5.1
The sampling frame and the sample

	Frame	Sample	Proportion
Schools	29	16	55%
Number of pupils	6425	3056	48%
Single-sex school	4	2	50%
Number of boys	3198	1260	40%
Number of girls	3227	1796	56%
Boarding schools	8	4	50%
No. of boarders	628	213	34%
Urban schools	17	10	59%
Rural schools	12	6	50%
AP. schools	5	2	40%

The 16 schools taking part in the study are an approximately 50% stratified sample of private schools in South Wales, and are also a reasonable 31% sample of all such schools in Wales. Of the schools in the focus area, 6 take pupils of only primary age, and 3 of these were surveyed (50%), while 23 take some pupils of secondary age, and 13 were surveyed (57%). The sample included the largest and the smallest schools in the region. Despite some reservations, and the fact that the sample is not random, it has many of the characteristics of a good random sample of fee-paying school users. The sample includes schools from Abersychan, Brecon, Bridgend, Cardiff, Machen, Monmouth, Penarth, Porthcawl, and Swansea. The sample includes 50% of the private schools in both Dyfed and Powys, 40% from Mid Glamorgan, 33% from Gwent, 25% from West Glamorgan, and 89% from South Glamorgan. It is unlikely that these schools have been so well characterised in any previous study.

The state sector sample

Some focus private schools provided information leading to the identification of local state-funded primary schools which had previously "fed" them pupils in cross-sector movement, and some state-funded secondary schools were additionally located by being mentioned as under consideration by parents of year 6 pupils in fee-paying schools. One of each such school was included in the survey, in order to provide a small sample for comparison with the results from the private sector, and to ensure that families considering cross-sector movement in both directions were included in the overall sample. An additional primary and a secondary state-funded school, neither of which were mentioned as having any cross-sector communication with fee-paying schools were also surveyed to provide a basis for comparison. The sample of state-funded schools contains two primary and two secondary, one urban and three suburban schools in two cities. However, although relevant, it cannot be seen as proportionately representative of its population in the same way as the fee-paying sample. No attempt has been made to map the entire sector, and no claim is made that the schools represent that sector fully. The four schools are, however, a reasonable indication of the character of mainstream Welsh state-funded education, and the kinds of schooling available to parents. Entire year groups had to be surveyed in order to find those families involved in a cross-sector switch. Having obtained the data representing the whole year group for the four state schools, they are used primarily for comparison with the results from the fee-paying schools.

The total school sample therefore consists of a stratified sample of 16 of the 29 local fee-paying schools and, in addition, four of the local state-funded schools with which they compete. A further 13 various schools, while taking no part in the survey, provided information about themselves, and allowed access for interviews and observations concerning their admission procedures.

Families

Although most research on school choice concentrates on parents and their views, there is clear evidence, given in Chapter 2, that pupils are very influential in school choice. David *et al.* (1994) questioned pupils, and found them to be a valuable source of often quite complex information. As pupils can be contacted at school, the response rate is likely to be high, and so their responses can be seen as truly representative. Woods (1992) agreed that there are good reasons for more research investigating pupils and their role in school choice, while King (1987) pointed out that "10 year olds can complete a simple questionnaire", and the importance of allowing them to do so was shown by Pifer and Miller (1995) in their analysis of data from the Longitudinal Study of American Youth, revealing the inaccuracy of the reports of parents and children about each other. This finding confirmed the view of Payne (1951) that respondents are generally more accurate about themselves than about others. So this study involves both pupils and their parents. Pupils were asked for their input to give them a sense of ownership of the work, to encourage them to deliver and return their parents' forms, because they are themselves under-researched, and because they could answer more accurately for themselves than their parents could.

The choice of a secondary school is likely to be the most fruitful area for research into parental choice, as most parents have more contact with schools at that time in their children's' education than at any other (Hunter 1991). Some previous research on parental choice of secondary school has focused on parents of pupils in year 7 - the 11/12 year olds who have already taken a place at school. One advantage of this approach is that a one year study can readily identify those who have chosen a particular type of school, and find out why. The population is easily defined and an appropriate sample can be devised. The research cannot affect or disrupt the process of choice, and, as Payne (1951) said, "answers to hypothetical questions may not be so valid in predictions of future behaviour as answers in terms of past experiences may be". The disadvantage of this age group is that there may be an element of justification of their choice in their recall, and their responses may be influenced by their *post hoc* knowledge of the school, and their drive to reduce dissonance (Eiser and van der Plight 1988). The researcher is also

104

faced with a *fait accompli*, and has lost the immediacy of the choice process (Dennison 1995).

The advantage of dealing with parents of pupils in Year 6 - those 10/11 year olds still at primary school - is that the researcher can be closer to, and more involved in, the actual process of choosing. In this way, the reasons of parents who do *not* choose a particular school can be more easily identified and such de-selection of schools is at present an under-researched area. In such a group, the element of *post hoc* justification is missing and, in addition, the researcher can investigate the process of choice as it occurs. This approach has a major practical drawback. A researcher looking at pupils going to a particular type of school cannot prejudge those who are likely to apply, or be selected, since this will bias the sample. Therefore, the sample must be wider and larger than with Year 7 to ensure that it includes a sufficient number eventually going to that type of school.

The decision concerning which year groups to study depends upon whether it is seen as preferable to consult families before or after their choice, but it is also complicated by the lack of consistency in the age ranges of the focus schools. In the event, this work uses respondents from both year groups, and attempts to preserve the advantage of both, while investigating any differences between them, which are anyway likely to be small (West and Varlaam 1991). The survey only involves families with children faced with a choice of school for next year, and those who have just moved schools. Some schools take the majority of their children in Year 1, or in Year 7. Some schools lose the majority of their pupils at the end of Year 6, at the end of Year 8, or at the end of Year 11. As far as possible, in schools with pupils of primary age, Years 1, and 6 were surveyed, although only the parents were involved from Year 1. In schools with pupils of secondary age, Year 7 was surveyed. In preparatory schools taking pupils to age 13, Year 8 was surveyed. In secondary schools with no sixth form, Year 11 was surveyed. In-depth interviews were also conducted with selected volunteer families whose child was in Year 6 in a study school in which there was no Year 7, or in Year 7 in a school in which there was no Year 6, or in Year 8 in a school in which there was no Year 9.

The parents and pupils completed the forms between October 1994 and November 1995. Responses are anonymous, which means that, although it is possible to compare the overall results of parents and pupils, it is not possible to link the responses of individual families. In retrospect, this loss of potential data may have been caused by over-sensitivity on the part of the researcher and in any further research of this type, a code numbering system could be used for the purpose of linking the pairs of forms, although this might involve other ethical compromises. The rubric to the questionnaire and the letter of introduction to parents makes it clear that respondents should feel free to leave out questions which they feel uncomfortable with.

In total, 1,267 usable forms were returned from 1,606 distributed in 20 schools. Most of these were fully completed. Fuller details of the respondents and their characteristics are given in Chapter 6.

The questionnaires

The questionnaires used in this study are totally original, although based upon the findings of previous research as described in Chapter 2, and designed upon established principles (Payne 1951). Technical and unusual words and homographs were avoided where possible. Questions of similar design were put together, and distinctive type faces were used for questions, answers and directions (Oppenheim 1992). The personal questions about respondents were placed either at the beginning, or the end, in two different versions of the instrument. Since face to face, telephone, and mail surveys produce similar responses to the same questions (Payne 1951), the choice of a hand delivery method was made for practical reasons, such as cost. The forms were only printed in English, which was the medium of instruction in all of the schools. However, it must therefore be considered a possibility that the response rate from the few parents in the region whose first language was not English was lower than average. All pupils completed at least some of the questions. Two children in different schools completed the questions verbally and had their answers recorded by a support teacher, because of problems with their reading. Two Japanese children in different schools spoke so little English, that although they were given every assistance, their responses were mostly incomplete.

The questionnaires were given to pupils during normal school time, and were completed immediately after a short explanation by the researcher. Whenever a pupil asked for clarification of a question, a pre-prepared explanation was read out at a volume that all could hear. The pupils were given a re-sealable envelope containing a questionnaire form for their parents, a letter from the researcher and, in some cases, a letter from the individual school supporting the research. The completed forms from the parents were collected from the schools in envelopes, although in some cases parents mailed them to the University. In an unusual case of twins at the same school, the mother and father completed two forms separately for their own amusement, and sent both in with a covering letter. Both were coded, and the decision to do this was partly influenced by a problem which arose when parents had children in the study years at more than one school. Such a problem is not mentioned in the literature, and although obvious in retrospect, had not been catered for in the design and was only noticed when a parent explained why they were returning an empty form. Since not all cases could be identified, and the numbers were likely to be few anyway, the problem was not regarded as important. All completed forms were processed, but future designs should be aware of the overlap.

The forms for children used the same questions about the reasons for choice, as the form for the parents. Otherwise, they were shorter and simpler. Pupils were not asked much about their family background, as they have not been shown to be reliable on such matters (Pifer and Miller 1995). Each form contains 606 words, at an average rate of six words per sentence, and takes between 10 and 30 minutes to complete. Its Flesch Reading Ease is assessed as 63.8, and its Grade level as 8.6 using Word 5.1 for Macintosh, defined as "standard" or not difficult writing (Microsoft 1991). Since the researcher was present throughout the administration of the pupil questionnaire, and an entire pastoral/registration period was devoted to it, it was also possible for standard explanations to be given to pupils who had difficulty in reading the form. Many pupils made relevant coherent comments on the form, or orally during its completion. In several schools, once the forms had been collected, a general discussion of some of the issues raised, such as bullying, ensued naturally. There is, as a result, no reason to doubt the competence of the majority of children to complete the questionnaire, or at least, no more so than for the adults.

The questions are highly structured in order to make completion and comparative analysis easier. Because open questions are more likely to cause problems of categorisation and so lead to false conclusions, or to over-represent the more convinced and more articulate (Payne 1951), the great majority of responses involve ticking an appropriate box. In order that the questions were not too restrictive, some are also of open design, eliciting responses not foreseen by the researcher. There are spaces for comments and many respondents felt free to give explanations and comments throughout, even where there was no obvious space for them on the form. Some parents attached letters to the form discussing points of interest and explaining their answers to some items, and a few included other documentary material justifying, or explaining, their decision. Parents were asked to write their occupations, and their post-code districts, but otherwise all respondents only wrote anything if they wished to make a comment, or if there was a category not foreseen in the design.

Instead of using standard methods of checking for "ignorant responders" (Payne 1951), the decision was made to treat all respondents as experts in this field. Unlike many surveys, the questions do not measure attitudes, since a decision is actually made by the respondents and no-one can know better than they how and why they make it. They may make a decision based on imperfect information or even on faulty reasoning, but they do make the decision, and the survey attempts to find out how and why. Where possible, the competence displayed by respondents is assessed by comparing their responses with the chosen school characteristics, but even this is difficult. For example, if they rate examination results as very important and then choose a school with poor results, it might mean that they are not very good at choosing a school with the desired characteristics. However, it could also mean that other equally important reasons over-ride exam results or that respondents are not being truthful in completing the survey. It is not possible to tell. This problem provides further justification for the interviews conducted as part of the research programme.

The questions and their associated variables, may be notionally divided into three types, those concerned with the characteristics of the respondent, those concerned with the process of choice, and those to do with the reasons for choice. Parents answered eight questions about their characteristics, including their own education, the education of their other children, their religion, occupation, and postal code district. They also answered nine questions about how they choose a school, including who is responsible for choosing, which type(s) of school they are considering, how many they are considering, and which information sources they use.

All respondents were asked to rate the importance of 73 possible reasons for choosing a school. The reasons are in no particular order, except that those apparently related in the sense that the same term appears in both, such as "wide range of sports" and "good reputation for sports", are kept separate. This is done to encourage the concentration of the respondent on each issue. It is common practice for questionnaires to use several questions to ask what is essentially the same question, and then to average the results per case to form an index, but this survey asked each question only once. There are two main reasons for this. Firstly, in order to avoid the problem of omitted variable bias (Maddala 1992), or variable selection bias (Kim and Mueller 1987a), a question is included for every reason found by the previous research cited in Chapter 2. This means that 73 questions need to be asked, and it is likely that the fatigue induced by asking each question more than once would outweigh the spurious advantage of creating an index. It is also likely that the completion and response rate of a longer form would be lower. Secondly, this technique of indexing is normally used because having only one measure is often unreliable, but the presumption that several sources are more reliable is a statistical argument based upon sampling theory (Anderson and Zelditch 1968). The method assumes that each measure used in an index has the same variability, and that this is due solely to random error. If either of these assumptions is false, and it is unlikely that either would hold in much published work, using only one question can, in fact, be more accurate (Anderson and Zelditch 1968). Any decision here is in the nature of a compromise, but although it is recognised that there will be a substantial error component in the responses, there seems little point in repeating the substance of each question.

Each response is in the form of a tick in one of three boxes, rated "0 : not important" to "2 : very important". Above the boxes, a continuous arrow is drawn from 0 to 2. Three boxes are used rather than the five (or even seven) more usual in attitude research, since this makes completion of the form easier for the respondents, particularly the children, who struggle with seven point scales. Any loss in sensitivity is likely to be spurious anyway. The three point scale, recommended for verbal scales by Sudman and Bradburn (1982) and by Hammond and Dennison (1995) increases the number of cases in each category and produces a more normal distribution overall. In addition, use of the more sensitive and powerful parametric statistical models proposed requires the data to be in equal interval, as opposed to ordinal, form. This means that the difference in importance between 0 and 1 must be the same as the difference between 1 and 2. Such a position is easier to maintain for the two differences on a three point scale, than for the six differences on a seven point scale, for example. During analysis, some analysts collapse the 5 or 7 points on their data collection scale to 3 anyway, so that for example, "strongly agree" and "slightly agree" are both coded as "agree". This may lead to some distortion, and it is better, where possible, to collect the data in the form in which it is to be analysed.

A simple data capture form was also designed to make it easy to collect comparable data on all of the schools involved in the study. Although most of the information concerning schools comes from observation, interview, and literature in the public domain, the 33 school representatives were also asked 30 questions about the structure, composition, curriculum, and history of each school.

The analysis of the results

Coding

To a large extent, the coding system is implicit in the schedule. The most open-ended question, concerning occupation, was the most difficult to code. The intention was to use this information to judge the occupational, and therefore the social, class of the respondents. This study is not alone in facing the problem of defining the class of the emerging non-nuclear families, and the increasing proportion of dual-income families. David *et al.* (1994) felt that it was not clear that current definitions of class accorded with traditional notions. Existing scales appear to have been designed to take account of only one (male) occupation per family. This causes several problems for the present study. Firstly, "women's occupations are usually defined in ways that make them appear more middle class" (David *et al.* 1994 p.143), and secondly it is not clear how to code a family with parents in two differing occupational classes. The decision was made to use the eight point scale of Halsey *et al.* (1980), using the classification of occupations defined by the Registrar General (OPCS 1970), and to categorise the family on the basis of the full-time occupation of whichever partner appeared in the most prestigious category on the scale. A new category was created for those who were unpaid, including unemployed, students, retired, and house workers. Even so, it is not easy to classify some families. Particular problems were caused by the distinction between higher and lower grade professionals, between directors of large and small businesses, and between marketing managers and sales staff. Respondents did not always provide sufficient information to make these distinctions, and may anyway have been tempted to use more grandiose titles than was absolutely necessary.

The coding system for some nominal variables was altered after the data collection. The data on occupational class, although recorded on a nine-point scale were combined by recoding onto a smaller scale of four points for analysis, since some of the cells created by the larger scale were too sparsely populated. The new collapsed scale is still that of the Oxford Mobility project, with divisions of groups 1 and 2 into "service", 3 4 and 5 into "intermediate", and 6 7 and 8 into "working" class.

The 73 ratings of the possible reasons for choosing a school are coded as real numbers, with an arbitrary zero point and undefined unit of measurement, which are the defining characteristics of an interval, rather than ratio, scale of measurement (Siegel 1956). Previous research may have treated these results as being on an ordinal scale, but to do so is to ignore a vital characteristic of attitudes which is that they "probably do not exist in a simple pro-con dichotomy but rather in gradations..." (Reynolds 1977 p.8), and to reject the use of the more powerful parametric techniques of analysis. The responses are anyway used to create a matrix of correlation coefficients, and even if they are thought of as being only on an ordinal scale, assigning numbers to them and using parametric tests would be unlikely to distort the resulting correlation values (Labovitz 1970). Much research literature uses parametric statistics anyway, without any apparent qualms about the metric used. Comrey (1973) is particularly reassuring on this point - "if the distributions for the data variables are reasonably normal in form, the investigator need have no concern about applying a 'parametric' factor analytic model without demonstrating that his scores are measured on an equal-unit scale" (Comrey 1973 p.198).

Univariate analysis

The response rate was calculated, the results were processed, cleaned, and then processed again. The frequencies and modal values of those variables measured on a nominal scale (e.g. "occupation of mother") were calculated (Frude 1993). The distribution of those variables measured on an interval scale (e.g. "the number of schools considered") was assessed, and it was shown that they followed an approximate normal distribution overall, which was not overly skewed. Their means and standard deviations were calculated, and the 73 ratings of the reasons for school choice were sorted into descending order on the basis of their means.

Bivariate analysis

With 97 variables in the study, the number of possible comparisons between any two of them is 9409, making a 5%, or even a 1% level of significance, of little value if all comparisons are made. This is a major argument for reducing the size of the data set, by reducing variables that show large common variance into a smaller number of underlying components by using factor analysis. To this end, a correlation matrix (Pearson's r) was produced for all of the interval variables, including an entry for each of the 73 choice variables in the questionnaires. This provides a measure of common variance between the ratings, so that any with little common variance can be excluded from multivariate analysis. Correlation is used as the first step in analysis to standardise the scores, and eliminate the problem of different means and standard deviations for each (Gorsuch 1972). As the data are non-continuous, many cases can score the same on one specific variable, which reduces the variance and the corresponding correlation coefficients, so any results are likely to underestimate the common variance. This is another reason for treating the data as being in interval form, since although the use of non-parametric rank correlation coefficients would reduce the effect of skewness and kurtosis, as there are only three values in the metric, there would be too many ties for rank ordering to be effective (Gorsuch 1972).

The nominal variables were converted into percentages for standardisation (Reynolds 1977), and cross-tabulated with each other (Gilbert 1993), and when the difference between the observed frequencies were markedly different from those expected, given the size of the sample, or where previous results suggested a difference, a chi-squared test of significance was carried out using the original frequencies, and the null hypothesis that the differences were due to chance was rejected, where appropriate, at the 5% level. Even so, the number of tests carried out was large and as looking for patterns in tables has been compared to looking for patterns of stars in the sky (Gilbert 1993), in addition to prior theoretical knowledge, some triangulation of these results was required for verification. Chi-square was used as a measure, rather than the easier to comprehend Goodman and Kruskall's tau, since it is more usual and it is not necessary in this study to predict row cell values from column values, or vice versa (Reynolds 1977). Where the cell sizes did not appear large enough for suitable analysis, categories, such as those on the scale for occupational class, were grouped together (Lee *et al.* 1989).

The mean of each of the interval variables was calculated for all sub-groups of respondents, as defined by their characteristics. For example, differences (and similarities) were sought between the responses from different schools, gender of pupils, year groups, fee categories, religions, parents and pupils, and between those who are making, and those who have already made, a choice. When the means showed a marked difference, or when a difference was expected on the basis of previous research, a one-way analysis of variance (or t-test), was carried out with the characteristic as the independent variable, using a 5% significance level. When appropriate a Tukey range test was applied to decide which groups were driving the difference found by analysis of variance (Levine 1991). This method computes a single value against which all possible differences between pairs of means can be compared.

Multivariate analysis

The bulk of the data are the ratings of 73 choice variables on an interval scale, and the major task of analysis was to reduce the size of this set to a smaller but more useful set of measures, referred to as "factors". These factors are intended to have an explanatory, and possibly a predictive, value. As well as making clearer why families choose particular types of school, it might be possible to use the factor scores to decide in advance which type of school would be selected. Such an analysis also requires the reduction of schools to a smaller number of types, or clusters.

Assumptions The assumption that the data used for the analysis were measured on an interval scale was discussed above, and, in his textbook, Norusis (1985) for example, presented an illustration of using factor analysis on consumer ratings of products, as though such a procedure is an everyday occurrence with rating data. Similarly, Kim and Mueller (1978$_b$) stated that factor analysis can be used even when the metric base of the variables is not clearly defined, as with attitude measurements. Apart from this assumption, the ideal basis for factor analysis is to have variables that are approximately normally distributed, which they are, even though the factor analytic model does not require it (Kim and Mueller 1978$_b$), with linear regression between all pairs of variables, although this ideal is also not always necessary (Comrey 1973). The sample is over four times the number of cases needed for PCA according to Comrey (1973), and the number of variables is less than 5% of the number of cases (Child 1970).

Principal components analysis Factor analysis, in general, provides the economy of description necessary in such a complex process as school choice, while retaining the majority of the variance in the responses (Child 1970). It is used to give "a better understanding of the complex and poorly defined inter-relationships among large numbers of imprecisely measured variables" (Comrey 1973 p.1), to explore the data more fully, and to set up new measures. These new measures minimise the number of variables for future analysis, while maximising the amount of information retained (Gorsuch 1972). Some information is lost in this procedure, but most of what is lost are the idiosyncratic, erratic, or irrelevant components of the variance in responses (Marradi 1981), and since the use of multiple tests tends to lead to spurious results, factor analysis can combat this by reducing the number of potential tests (Stevens 1992).

There are many different types of factor analysis, although they all have common steps. This section describes those common steps, and explains the decisions taken by the researcher at each one. The first step was to decide which variables to include in the analysis. A 73 by 73 matrix of Pearson correlation coefficients was produced, and examined for an intuitive feel for the data. As discussed above, other types of correlation or covariance matrices can be calculated (Siegel 1956), but the standard Pearson r is the most common, and the most appropriate to these data (Comrey 1973, Kim and Mueller 1978$_a$). One purpose of the analysis was to find a smaller number of satisfactory substitute variables, so substantial correlations between variables are required (Comrey 1973). All of the variables correlate significantly with several others, but there are marked differences between the number and size of these associations. A criterion was needed to determine which correlations are large enough to be worth further investigation, and which to exclude from the reduced correlation matrix (Marradi 1981). To exclude the clearly unrelated variables from principal components analysis can lead to a neater solution, but it can also damage the result. On the other hand, to include them would be to court unnecessary complication, and is contra-indicated by the principle of "garbage-in garbage-out" (Kim and Mueller 1987$_a$). With a large sample, such as in this study, several minor factors will appear as statistically significant, without contributing greatly to overall covariance structure (Kim and Mueller 1987$_a$). All researchers have to make a judgement at this point, and this one is based upon discretion. One way of increasing the proportion of "healthy indicators" in the analysis is to exclude all variables not correlated significantly with any other, at the 5% level. The advantage of this method is that it is case-sensitive, but since the number of cases is 1,267, correlations as low as |0.06| are flagged as significant, even though the proportion of common variance is negligible. Instead, the method chosen here was to select a figure for the size of common variance that could be useful for explanatory purposes, such as 10%, calculate the size of the correlation that represents it, such as |0.3162|, and exclude all variables that have no correlation of at least that size. The selection and discarding of measures at this stage is too important to be left to a computer, and is of necessity an iterative process (Marradi 1981), so a final decision cannot be made until all data are collected, and it is discovered which of the 73 choice variables are the more useful "pure factor" measures, and how many of them may be dropped as too "complex" for their explanatory power (Comrey 1973). Another use of the correlation matrix was to confirm that it was not an identity matrix, which would make factor analysis impossible (Norusis 1985). A third reason was to calculate and check Kaiser's measure of sampling adequacy.

The second step is to extract the unrotated factors underlying the variables. Two main decisions were made at this point - which method of factor extraction to use, and how many factors to extract. A common method of extraction for factor analysis is the centroid one, where the first factor is assumed to be in the middle of the two most closely related variables. This is a good method for retaining and exploring all of the variance (Maxwell 1977), but the principal components method is also good for extracting the maximum variance (Gorsuch 1972), and is chosen here for several reasons. It is more appropriate for reducing the number of variables, especially where the first few factors account for a large part of the variance, more useful as a prelude to further analysis, and better used when all variables are measured on the same metric with relatively low measurement error and variances of similar magnitude, as they are in this instance. Maxwell (1977) described principal components analysis as ideal in these circumstances, and further stated that, used for this purpose, "a principal component analysis is straightforward in the sense that no distributional assumptions need to be made about the observed variates" (Maxwell 1977 p.42). The principal components solution is often rotated to from other starting points (Gorsuch 1972), and Comrey (1973) pointed out that whichever method is used initially, the subsequent rotation of the factors leads to similar results anyway. Missing values for specific variables were dealt with by imputing a suitable estimated replacement value (Lee *et al.* 1989), based on the mean value for that variable.

The sums of squares of loadings for successive factors decrease (Comrey 1973), so they become less and less useful in explaining the common variance. Factors are extracted until the residual correlation is too close to zero, but generally as many factors are extracted as there are initial variables, in order to explain all of the variance. However, unless the measurement of the variables is wholly reliable, which they are not in this case, at least some of the variance is due to error. The total variance for each variable can be seen as the common variance, as assessed by the correlation, which itself contains an error component, plus its unique variance, and the variable-specific error component. To attempt to explain all of the variance, including that due to error, is unparsimonious, and the number of factors should be kept to a minimum (Cureton and D'Agostino 1983). On the other hand, several factors need to be extracted to create a good enough structure for rotation in step 3 (Comrey 1973), and forcing a solution into too few factors (e.g. fewer than 6) distorts the solution. It is possible to test each factor for significance (Gorsuch 1972), but since the test is case sensitive, with over 1,267 cases, even trivial factors would be statistically significant. Kaiser's criterion and Cattell's Scree Test both define a cut-off point for the number of factors extracted, and both give similar results when the number of cases and variables are large, although they also tend to be less accurate, and to overestimate the number of factors in these circumstances (Stevens 1992). The first of the two methods was used here, so that factors were extracted until the sum of the squares of the correlations of each variable with the factor (the eigen value) was less than 1.0. A factor with an eigen value less than 1.0 would explain less than 3% of the total variance in the responses to the 73 choice questions, which does not justify the additional complication of its inclusion in the solution. The scree test would be a more useful method of determining the number of factors in a study where a large number of "minor factors" are expected, and interest is focused on the major ones (Kim and Mueller 1978$_b$). It is not so appropriate in this exploratory study since the variables with low inter-correlations, which are liable to cause the minor factors, have been omitted from the analysis.

The next step is to rotate the factors to a solution, which although mathematically equivalent to the original, is more useful for explanatory purposes. The main choice is between an oblique rotation, allowing the factors to overlap, or an orthogonal rotation, forcing the factors in the solution to be unrelated (Child 1970). An oblique rotation would be necessary if higher order factors were to be derived, but the gain in generalisation from second order factor analysis is at the cost of less accurate results (Gorsuch 1972). As with many decisions in the analysis, and perfectly properly, a mathematical decision is taken for non-mathematical reasons (Comrey 1973). Several useful criteria for deciding on a method of rotation are: the ease of interpreting the results; the number of zero loadings; the speed of convergence; the restriction of each variable to only one factor, and the replication of factors across split halves of the cases (Gorsuch 1972). It was discussed in Chapter 3, with relevance to network analysis, that one of the problems in school choice research is that no-one knows which reasons for choice are related to each other, and for this reason alone, Varimax orthogonal rotations were used here (Stevens 1986). The intention was to produce a small number of clearly unrelated factors underlying the reasons for choice, with clearly differentiated loadings. This does not mean that an oblique rotation would not produce meaningful results, merely that they may not be so clear cut. A set of uncorrelated factors can also be seen as more parsimonious (Cureton and D'Agostino 1983).

The final step is to interpret the factors produced by the rotation. This involves both naming and explaining the factors, each of which can then be treated as a type of hypothesis which should be further tested. It is important to decide of each factor - is it valuable, or is it an artefact? One of the reasons for the use of the extended interviews was to see how they, and the choice factors shed light on each other, because one way of testing the factors is to see if they agree with the reality of people's experience. Another is to see if they are relevant to previous findings. Either way, the factors must be confirmed by an alternative analysis to have any genuine theoretical meaning, and so to have any usefulness (Gorsuch 1972).

Each variable has a final measure of communality, which is an estimate of the sum of the squares of all common factor variances of a variable. It gives the proportion of variance in the variable that can be accounted for by scores in the factors. So a variable with a communality near 1.0 is almost wholly explained by its common variance with one or more factors, but a variable with a communality near zero is almost wholly explained by its specific variance. The latter should be minimised by the exclusion of non-correlating variables, prior to analysis. Their exclusion does not mean that such variables are unimportant in school choice, although many of them actually are, but that they are irreducible, or elementary, and need to be discussed in isolation.

Each variable also has a final loading on each factor. The loadings are the correlations between variables and the factors, so the square of a loading can be seen as the amount of variance common to both. One very conservative estimate of the significance of these loadings is to use twice the critical values of alpha for a two-tailed t-test as a cut-off point (Stevens 1992). With over 1,000 cases, a value below 0.162 would emerge as significant, but it would not necessarily be useful. Comrey (1973) suggested that loadings of 0.55 are good, those of 0.63 very good, and those of 0.71 are excellent. He also agreed with Child (1970) that a reasonable cut-off point would be 0.3, with loadings below that figure being ignored in explanation of a factor. This study uses the more precise, and more stringent, figure of |0.3162|, which is the square root of 0.1, so that variables used in the final model have at least 10% common variance with the factors to which they contribute. However, the threshold for a loading cannot be defined rigidly in advance, as it really depends on where a sharp drop in values is noticed (Marradi 1981). As discussed above, since the variables are unlikely to be wholly reliable, they cannot correlate perfectly with any factor, but as a rule, if the loading of a variable is equal to the square root of its reliability, it is a "pure factor" measure, i.e. the variable and the factor are identical. For example, if a variable is reliable at a level of 0.81, and has a loading of 0.9, it is indistinguishable from the factor, and it is variables of this type that will be most useful in shaping the factor "space" (Comrey 1973). For a study with a relatively small number of cases, the quality of a factor must be assessed both in terms of the number and size of its loadings, so that, for example, Stevens (1992) suggests that a reliable factor must have four or more loadings of at least 0.6 when the number of cases is below 150. However, with cases in excess of 300 as in this study, any number of significant loadings can define a reliable factor (Stevens 1992).

Further analysis Once a satisfactory set of factors were derived from the data, they were subject to further analysis. The factor scores per case were calculated and saved. There is only one common method of calculating factor scores after PCA (Norusis 1985). These scores are defined as the sum of the case score on each variable, multiplied by the loading for that variable on the factor, for all relevant variables (Jackson and Borgatta 1981). Unfortunately, this procedure reduces the number of cases, since only cases with valid responses to all of the relevant variables are given a score for the factor. One-way analysis of variance, and t-tests were used to test for relationships between the factor scores and the nominal variables, as above (Levine 1991), and correlation coefficients were calculated between each factor score and other interval variables, such as those ratings not included in the principal components analysis.

School types

Where the absolute sample size is small, as it is with the schools in the study numbering only 33, grouping them into smaller clusters in terms of theoretical knowledge is an appropriate method before analysis (Stevens 1992). The qualitative data described in Chapter 6, led to the division of the schools into seven different types, based upon their common characteristics (Everitt 1980). As a follow-up, a principal components analysis was carried out on interval variables describing the characteristics of schools, such as size, age range, and gender mix. The choice of variables for this analysis is partly based upon theory, and partly upon what information is available, so that the conclusions of this analysis must be seen as indicative, rather than definitive but they do confirm the seven cluster model. Once the school clusters have been produced, they are tested for validity by comparison with variables not used in the analysis, and it is actually the successful triangulation of the results that justifies their further use.

The quality of the survey

Responses

A total of 1,606 forms were distributed to children and parents in 20 schools. Of these, 1,267 were returned, from 794 families, amounting to an overall response rate of 79%, which can be considered excellent, and indicative of the willing assistance of the schools and families involved. In fact the true figure is probably higher than 79%, because of the problem of identifying children from the same family in different study schools, as described earlier. Most forms were fully completed, but there were a few questions that repeatedly caused problems. Also, this overall rate masks clear differences between sub-groups. As the children's forms were generally completed by all pupils present on the day, during a school lesson, and under the supervision of the researcher, the return rate for children is over 95%. The children had to take a form home to their parent(s), ask them to complete it, and return it to school. Given that the form could therefore be lost at any one of several stages in the collection, and that some of the children had parents living overseas, the response rate of over 69% from adults can also be considered as excellent. The responses of parents in the various different types of school, and for Years 1, 6, and 7 were excellent. The return rate from Year 8 was poor, below 40%, but these data represent only one preparatory school, with a high proportion of boarders. The return rate from parents of Year 11 boys is also low, and this is due to the mislaying of forms by one of the two schools making returns for this age group, and so need not be seen as necessarily biasing the other results. The relative paucity of these responses must be taken into account in any conclusions drawn about families and choice in Years 8 and 11.

Table 5.2 shows the frequency of responses from both parents and children, broken down by the year group of the child in question. In total, 62% of parents, and 52% of pupils were asked about a choice they had just made, while 38% of parents, and 48% of pupils were asked about a choice they were in the process of making. The difference between the proportion of each generation is mainly due to the additional parents in Year 1, whose children were not surveyed. The proportion of the sample in each age group is a reflection of the frequency of the age ranges of intakes encountered in the school sample, and in the population. Preparatory schools, and secondary schools with no sixth form are uncommon in Wales.

Table 5.2
Frequency of responses by year group

Year group	Frequency	Percentage
Year 1	70	5.5
Year 6	452	35.7
Year 7	645	50.9
Year 8	46	3.6
Year 11	54	4.3
Total	1267	100.0

Although the proportion of pupil and parent respondents for each gender are closely matched, there are more girls, 57.1%, than boys, 42.9%, in the sample. The imbalance is partly a result of that in the sampling frame, caused by the existence of a larger number of private girls schools than private boys schools in South Wales. It is also true that the girls schools and coeducational schools were, in general, more willing to co-operate with the survey. On these measures, the respondents are a close enough match to the characteristics of the sampling frame for further analysis to proceed safely.

Distribution of the responses

The assumptions underlying the use of parametric statistics such as t-tests, and Pearson's r, with interval data are outlined above. It is also shown that under some conditions it is not necessary that all of these theoretical assumptions hold, and that in practice much research makes no mention of them. However, one major assumption behind all such tests, which can not be assessed before data collection is the shape of the distribution of the results. The use of the mean and standard deviation as descriptive variables, and the use of t-tests based upon them, are only appropriate where the data is approximately normally distributed, and not overly skewed (Guilford and Fruchter 1973). In this study, the assumption is made that the interval data relating to school choice is approximately normally distributed overall, but not that the answers to each question, nor for each sub-group of respondents, are so distributed. For example, it is not assumed that the responses of parents using Church schools to questions about the importance of religion would have the same distribution as the responses of other parents. The results from the background questions, such as number of children or number of schools considered, are almost uniform, but slightly skewed towards the lower range. A few results from individual questions on choice, such as the importance of no bullying, are highly skewed, and overall the results are skewed towards the top end of the scale, which might be expected since all of the questions were phrased as positive reasons for choosing a school (Table 5.3). The distribution of responses does show that respondents were prepared to discriminate, and not simply tick the middle box in most cases.

Table 5.3
Frequency of different responses

Rating	Frequency	Percentage
not important	22,177	27
important	25,516	31
very important	34,046	42
Total	81,739	100

Validity

The validity of a survey can be examined in a variety of ways, but most routes lead to similar concepts, and for convenience this study will follow the summary of Venkatraman and Grant (1986). However, validity may not be so easily divided into types as implied by books on methodology, and in general the quality of a survey is obvious, almost intuitively, to the reader.

Content validity Content or "face" validity is indicative of the instrument being a reasonable measure of what it sets out to discover, and this includes the relevance of the questions, the correct use of technical terms, and the appropriateness of the instrument for its intended users. An appeal is made here to expertise. The forms were designed by the researcher on the basis of the results of prior work on school choice, and using his own knowledge as a senior teacher involved in school admissions. The questions were read and criticised by two established researchers in the field of school choice, by the principals of many of the schools involved, and by the 178 respondents in the pilot study. In the light of their suggestions, many changes were made to the design, the wording of the questionnaire, and to its method of delivery. There are some indications that the reasons for choice coming towards the end of the pilot questionnaire were rated more highly. This could have been due to practice or fatigue effects in the respondents, although it could, of course, have been a genuine result. To test whether position affects the responses, and to see whether siting the characteristics questions at the beginning, or at the end as suggested by Sudman and Bradburn (1982), affected the response rate, two versions of each form were used in the main study. The second version is the same as the first except that the order of the questions is reversed. Although the numbers of respondents answering each version are not appropriate for a formal comparison, there is no evidence that the order of the questions has had any effect on the outcomes.

Many of the respondents made comments on the questionnaire form, or included a letter with their return, or in the case of pupils, asked for clarification. Such comments and questions back up the "qualitative" data from observation and interviews, but some of them also give an indication of the high level of competence of the respondents, and the intelligibility of the instrument.

Problems were discovered with a few questions. The question "Please list up to three schools that you strongly considered" caused problems with coding, and should have been more specific. The responses do not make it easy to compute the number of schools considered by parents. There is no reason to limit their responses to three, and some Year 7 parents listed three in addition to the school that their child is attending, effectively mentioning four. An indication that the number of schools "seriously considered" by respondents may be underestimated comes from some Year 7 returns saying that no schools were considered the previous year, and some which say that only one school was considered, but then give the name of that school as different to the one they are in. In both of these cases, it is assumed that the respondent interpreted the question as asking about the number of schools apart from the one they are currently in, and so the data are coded as one and two respectively. There were 10 other questions that frequently needed explaining to children, such as the importance of an equal opportunities policy, and standard explanations of these were read out in a voice audible to all, starting with the phrase "how important is it for you that...".

An indication of the suggestibility of the children comes from their comments at the end of the form. When initially explaining how to complete the form, the researcher used one of two example questions concerning the importance of food in the canteen, or a swimming pool, neither of which are actually on the form. Comments concerning these two aspects of school only appear on forms from schools where the example was given. Another indication of suggestibility comes from the atmosphere in the various classes. In one school, for example, four classes were surveyed on different days, and there was a very different atmosphere in each. Normally there was a buzz of chat during completion, but in one group, there was a strict silence enforced by the class teacher. This class finished the survey quickly and efficiently, with a very high response rate to all questions, but not one child made an additional written comment.

In several schools, at least one teacher was also present during administration, and although most of these were immensely helpful, some dealt with queries in a clearly biased way, as already encountered in the pilot study. As an example, in one of the grass-roots schools a teacher was heard to say, "the question asks about the National Curriculum, but we have our own, so it is 'not important'". In general, this was the biggest problem in the wording and administration of the survey - making Year 1 and Year 7 respondents consider what they had been looking for, and not what they ended up with.

One parent stated that it was "impossible to answer some questions until one's child has actually started at the school", even though the questions were clearly asking about what was being looked for from the school. Similarly, some pupils also made negative comments about their current or previous school, obviously hoping that things would change. Some of these were very specific, perhaps relating to a recent injustice felt by the child. For example, one Year 8 child felt that, "when you get fall [sic] mark in a test you should get a plus point". Another child in Year 6 was in favour of "separate breaks for infants and juniors" and "going to town without getting credits". There were also several joke comments, such as a request for "great detail on sex-education and drugs, alcohol etc.", "must have shops and night clubs close to it", and "how many good looking girls". One parent simply wrote "please" next to the question about reduced fees.

Generally, the pupils were happy to co-operate, enthusiastic to complete the forms, and keen to discuss the issues raised, possibly because they were missing assembly, or in one case a maths lesson. In one school, pupils were called in early from their lunch break to take part, but despite this, their attitude was still helpful. Only one boy, in one school, was uncooperative and sullen throughout. It is also clear from the ensuing discussions that some pupils know a great deal about the process of choice. Most of the Year 6, 8 and 11 respondents were in the midst of making a choice, and in one class, many were attending an open evening at a prospective school that day. Despite the flippancy and a few misunderstandings, the majority of comments, some of which are used later as illustrations, show that respondents took the survey seriously and understood the questions.

Convergent validity A second form of validation, convergent, is possible when data from different sources, or questions, are shown to complement each other, and so provide what is termed "triangulation of measures" (Venkatraman and Grant 1986). This study uses data from a variety of sources other than the survey itself, including interviews, observation, school literature, the schools' own market research, and previous academic research into school choice. It can be seen from the discussion of the results from these sources, especially the interviews, that sufficient triangulation was achieved to show that the results of the survey are mostly valid, although doubts are raised in the text about certain measures. Questions about behaviour or facts are, in principle, verifiable (Sudman and Bradburn 1982), and this claim can be made to include questions about intentions. Unfortunately, this verification is not always easy to achieve, and may not even be possible for ethical reasons. An attempt was made wherever possible to check the claims of respondents. In addition, there were large number of formal checks for the internal consistency of the data, including, for example, a t-test which showed that boarders were more interested in boarding facilities than day pupils, and a very high negative correlation between the respondents ratings of the importance of "single-sex provision" and "coeducation" in schools. The results of this study agree with much previous work and although there are some differences, it is contended that the differences are more likely to be associated with differences in time, scale, region, or sampling strategy than to indicate a lack of validity in this study.

Reliability Reliability, or internal consistency, is a measure of the consistency of the instrument under different conditions. However, using the same respondents for a re-test can distort the results, because of possible bias through learning and memory. Perhaps the strongest claim to the reliability of the survey comes from the small scale replication of the pilot with the main study. Although only around 40 of the 95 questions were the same on the two versions of the form, due to the changes described above, the results on these 40 measures are indistinguishable in most cases, despite involving different cohorts in different schools. Another measure of reliability employs the method of split-half analysis, which runs the same analysis either on two halves of the respondents (split-case analysis), or two halves of the questions. The first gives an estimate of test-retest reliability, while the second shows the internal consistency of the questions. The method of split half was used as a check in the creation of the principal components described in Chapter 7, so that the factors underlying the reasons for choice were calculated for every alternate case, totalling 633, as well as overall (Stevens 1992). The two split-halves give remarkably consistent results, which are also very similar to the overall results in Chapter 7. The same technique was used to calculate the frequencies or means, as appropriate, of the responses to all questions, for two halves of the cases, and the results were statistically indistinguishable from each other and very similar to the overall results. The second type of split-half test - splitting the questions - is really designed for psychological research with multiple questions intended to cover the same metric and scores like Cronbach's alpha show the level of measurement error in the scores for each cluster. Since this research is exploratory, the questionnaire is new, and it is not intended to include multiple questions, such a test is not entirely appropriate. It is worth noting, however, that if it is assumed that all of the questions on school choice are intended to measure the same thing - school choice - then an overall alpha score can be calculated, which turns out to the remarkably high figure of 0.91. The alpha for each of the seven factors derived via principal components analysis (PCA) varied from 0.80 to 0.63, and the Kaiser-Meyer-Olkin measure of sampling adequacy for the PCA was 0.92. All of these figures are perfectly acceptable. In fact the PCA was run hundreds of times in a variety of ways, using different methods of rotation, such as oblique, different methods of dealing with complex variables, such as second order analysis, and with different sub-groups of the cases, and just as with the split-case test, the results were very stable. The same seven factors always appeared in some guise. Given the size of the sample, in comparison to the number of variables, all sources agree that the solution described in Chapter 7 is a good one.

In the end, the chief ingredients of a good survey are like those of a good factor analysis, namely meaningful results and parsimony (Norusis 1985), and it is contended that this study has such ingredients and that the foregoing discussion shows that the results which follow should be seen as viable.

"Thicker" data

This study uses data from taped interviews, concentrating on those families who were making the choice for the first time, as it concerned their eldest child. Interviews with Heads, and pupils, and data on the way in which schools presented themselves to a prospective parent through publicity material, open days, and exhibitions are also used. The interview data was coded, and used to help understand and illustrate the findings from the survey. Each source and type of data suggested models, and frameworks for analysis, to be used with the others in a genuine triangulation process. The marketing and actual provision in the study schools was matched to what the participants reportedly wanted, to test the assumption that "if information about private schools were freely available to potential clients, we would expect to find that parents choose schools that have educational goals and philosophies like their own" (Garner and Hannaway 1982 p.120). Such a comparison can begin to consider how much parents actually know about the schools they choose, whether the factor analytic approach leads to a fair reconstruction of the reasons for choice, whether parents are making good choices, and so, ultimately whether it is possible for an educational market to improve standards.

Qualitative methods should not be distanced from other work in the field, as they can lead to better understanding of the data, while the quantitative methods can allow the researcher to generalise about results. The "quantities" used in social research are often "amounts" of qualities anyway. Thus, the two supposed paradigms should not be seen as a dichotomy, but as two strands of a more general investigative method. In this method, all relevant techniques of data collection and analysis co-operate, leading to confirmation (or disconfirmation) through triangulation, a richer detail in analysis, and new lines of thought springing from the surprises and contradictions encountered (Miles and Huberman 1994).

Interviews are often difficult due to time scarcity of both "actors" - McCracken (1988) gives a time budget of 738 hours to deal with 8 interviews - and the respondent's concern for privacy, but they were used here to balance the simplicity of the survey, since "the disadvantage of numerical scores is the risk of reducing something that may be rich and complex to a single index that then assumes an importance out of all proportion to its meaning" (Eiser and van der Plight 1988 p.4). The lucid and forthright comments of some respondents on the questionnaire show the complexity in the views of some families, and the serious problems many of them face in choosing a school. They highlight the need for a more detailed account of some cases, as "every scientific study is improved by a clearer understanding of the beliefs and experience of the actors in question" (McCracken 1988 p.9). The interviews employed in this study are of two main types. The first are informal, opportunistic discussions with Heads, teachers, parents, and pupils, recorded in field notes, during school visits. The second are pre-arranged, semi-structured, taped interviews with volunteer parents. In total, 47 interviews were held with a variety of "players" in the choice process, not including the prolonged discussions held with some groups of pupils immediately after completing the questionnaire.

Opportunity interviews

Methods, purposes, and even results were frequently suggested to the researcher by participants during the field work. Everyone who had worked in, or even attended, a school had a view on how, and why, other people chose schools. This, the friendliness of all involved, and their willingness to give up their time, were very seductive. The researcher was a 36 year old, ex-deputy headteacher. He wore a simple suit during all field work, as this was his "uniform" as a teacher, with which he felt comfortable. This appearance made it easy to gain access and trust in most schools and classrooms, but may have made it harder to remain distanced, and so reflective. He settled in the end for being treated as an uninvited consultant expert on school development, and concentrated upon making the schools "anthropologically strange" as far as possible, for himself (Measor and Woods 1991).

A major problem with these interviews was the lack of consistent length and pattern, with short interviews, such as at a school gate, or while waiting in a foyer, generating data of possibly doubtful validity (Burgess 1985). The problem of pupils being coached by teachers, as noted by Walford (1991$_d$), was encountered in the pilot study, and minimised in the main study by the greater rigour of the researcher. However, it is undoubtedly difficult to interview people in a half-hour slot, explain the purpose of the research, and get them to trust the interviewer. The aspect of trust was as good as could have been expected, and some individuals told personal stories of abuse, racism, and unfair treatment in an obviously unrehearsed way. These interviews were noted on paper in longhand at the time if possible, else they were noted in the researcher's car at the earliest opportunity, and then typed in a fuller form within 48 hours. The unprompted comments in such interviews and class discussions help to validate the questions in the survey, and suggested new ones for the pre-arranged interviews. The recorded comments and behaviours of Heads and their representatives were used to enhance the knowledge of each school and its mission (Chapter 6).

Pre-arranged interviews

These were arranged with the cooperation of six schools - three catering for only primary age, one preparatory, one secondary, and one all-age. Two were state-funded schools, two were proprietary, two were traditional fee-paying, one was rural, one was single-sex, and one took boarders. The families interviewed were all faced with, or had just made, the choice of a new school for their 10/11 (or 12/13) year old, who was their eldest child in many cases, since "parental choices in education are sometimes made only for the first child in the family" (Johnson 1987 p.121). The families were selected from a larger set of names and addresses provided by the schools, partly to protect the identities of the interviewees, and partly to concentrate on those with a relevant or particularly interesting story to tell. The sample includes families considering a move from fee-paying education to state-funded, and the reverse, including those who had made the change, and those who had decided against it, those looking for a boarding school in England, for a boarding school in Wales, a music scholarship, and an Assisted Place. They include a wide range of schools under consideration, with pupils expected to gain a scholarship, and those expected to have trouble with an entrance examination. In this way, although the interviewees cannot be seen as proportionately representative of a larger population, they do include many varied backgrounds and stories. The sampling strategy can be seen as a mixture of the methods of maximum variation, critical cases, theory based, and opportunistic, but with multiple cases where possible (Miles and Huberman 1994). As data from the survey came in and was analysed, it was felt important to try and contact more of the families for whom English might be a recent or second language, and an attempt was made to do this by contacting families on the basis of their surnames. Although a reasonable number of such interviews were arranged, some were very brief, several were cancelled, and on two occasions, no one was in the house at the agreed time of the appointment.

The interviews were held in the homes of the interviewees, except for one which was held at the University in the office of the researcher, while two were in the workplace of the interviewees, a burger bar, and a hardware store respectively. The recordings of these last two interviews are markedly inferior. The total elapsed time per case is between 80 minutes and 200 minutes. They took place between January and July 1995, while applications, entrance examinations, ISIS exhibitions, and school Open Days continued for entry in September 1995, and again in October and November 1995, after the new pupils had just arrived at school. They were recorded, with the permission of the interviewees, on a portable cassette tape recorder, and transcribed by the researcher. The comments of the interviewees were transcribed *verbatim* wherever possible.

The use of a questionnaire is vital for a long interview, to cover all of the terrain in the same order, and to help manufacture distance (McCracken 1988). Use of the structure allows flexibility, but does not lead to the collection of superfluous data, helps to reduce bias, and the similarity of the schedule to the survey makes comparison of the various sources of data easier (Miles and Huberman 1994). The standard questions were listed as a schedule. Some items are similar to questions in the survey, such as who made the final choice, while some are prompted by the early results of the survey, such as a discussion of the meaning and value of the choice factors, and others are completely new items, such as the detailed educational history of siblings. All interviewees were asked these questions, as far as possible in the same format, although the previous conversation made some of them superfluous, or insultingly repetitive, in which case they were dropped. Additional questions and comments were put to individuals, depending upon their narrative. The interviewer tried to remain non-directive and non-committal, but was on occasion open to the seduction mentioned above, as most of the interviewees were both lucid and emotional. In the longer interviews, both parties visibly

123

relaxed, with the interviewer becoming involved in household tasks, such as watering plants, during the conversation, and in one case being asked to drive the daughter of the house to a music lesson a few miles away.

Data on the schools themselves

Apart from the school questionnaire form, and the interviews with "actors", the main sources of data concerning schools were Welsh Office publications, league tables of School Performance, the schools' own publications, Local Education Authority documents, and the publications of fee-paying school associations, such as ISIS. The school literature was analysed, following the suggestions of Headington and Howson (1995). Some data were also available to the researcher as an individual, who worked in one of the focus schools in a senior management position, and in another as a relief teacher. This final group of data are not made public here, but they can be said to be "present" throughout, providing much of the initial motivation for the work, and presumably influencing the perceptions of the researcher.

Analysis

There are no clear guidelines for the "qualitative" analysis of data, and "seen in traditional terms, the reliability and validity of qualitatively derived findings can be seriously in doubt" (Miles and Huberman 1994 p.2). There is a very real danger of finding meaning or patterns in data, like the patterns appearing in random numbers, by relying on plausibility. Plausibility is not enough. In addition, it is difficult to assess the validity of many ethnographic conclusions or generalisations, as replication is generally not possible (Hammersley 1990). The value of interview data is sometimes discounted because of poor sampling, and because there is no recognised way of checking their reliability or completeness (Weller and Romney 1988). However, it is often apparent when quality data and conclusions are obtained, since quality data is unambiguous, economical about assumptions, internally and externally consistent, powerful in explaining, and fertile for new ideas (McCracken 1988). No claim is made that the interview sample is complete and representative of a larger population in the same way as that of the survey, from which it is taken.

The data from interviews, and comments from the survey were coded manually in two ways: as a complete narrative, by the type of respondent, and by the content and tenor of each section, as chunks of text. Approximately twelve codes, such as "gender issues", were initially used as a manageable number, and these were checked by, and discussed with two other researchers, so that they are to some extent consensual (Miles and Huberman 1994). None of the categories were determined in advance, and although some were suggested by the quantitative results, some, such as the concept of three steps in choice, were plainly grounded in the observations (Measor and Woods 1991). These results were used to create substantive theories (Glaser and Strauss 1970), which led to further analysis of the interview data, and to hypotheses to be tested by the further application of bivariate, or multivariate statistics, to the survey data.

The data from schools are similarly coded, using codes such as the method of funding the school, but the analysis is less detailed, or perhaps less visible to the researcher himself, which is in line with the approach recommended by some previous investigators (LeCompte and Preissle 1993).

Conclusion

The regional nature of the sample, the size of the survey and the use of pupils as respondents are probably sufficiently novel in their own right to justify this research on methodological grounds. However the use of different year groups, the mixture of interview and survey design, the inclusion of fee-paying and state-funded schools, and above all, the use of multivariate statistics to describe the relationships between data that until now have been only theoretical and metaphorical, make this a completely new venture in the field of school choice research.

This study is in part a response to dissatisfaction with previous work in the area of school choice. Social phenomena are complex, and a process like school choice with so many participants is, perhaps, particularly so. Participants describe the process in different ways, and it is not always clear whether this is a difference of perspective, or a clear difference in position. Some of the problems are evident in a study by Woods (1992). In that study, 33% of parents maintained they had no real choice of school, because of the difficulties of travel, while others claimed to have had a choice, but to have rejected particular schools as being too difficult to travel to. It is not clear that these two groups are, in fact, any different. They may be simply describing the same phenomenon in different terms, or it may be that a real difference here requires further study. One way of getting behind such responses is via a semi-structured interview, such as is used in this research. Another, is to look for concepts underlying the data, chiefly by examining correlations between cases, and variables. In all branches of social science, advances in measurement and analysis can lead to changes in theory, and this study introduces multivariate parametric statistics to the field, by treating many of the variables as being on an interval scale, perhaps for the first time in UK school choice research. Above all, the very complexity of the process under scrutiny necessitates rigour, precision, triangulation and simplicity from the researcher, as much as empathy and imagination.

The use of principal components analysis helps resolve much of the ambiguity concerning the relationship between the criteria for school choice that have been published in previous work. Although, following the style of previous researchers the potential criteria for choosing a school are provisionally grouped into a smaller number of key categories (Chapter 2), these categories are then tested by the PCA based upon the correlations within the data themselves (Gorard *et al.* 1997). Thus, the method can begin to explain the way in which the respondents themselves group the criteria, and the emergent groupings, or "factors", can therefore be treated in as "real" a way as any of the face variables. Merely theoretical categories and expositions, on the other hand, are likely to become polemic if based on imprecision. This can lead to criticism from equally imprecise sources, and therefore to a "tonnage of written materials rather than knowledge", which is what may be happening in the UK choice literature today. "In the social sciences, one cannot assume the correspondence [between concepts and measures], and so the factor analytic procedures [such as PCA] that have developed have come as both challenges to the self-assured and disruptions to those who had already arrived at conclusions" (Jackson and Bogatta 1981 p.5). It is hoped that this work can provide just such a disruption to the complacent, and that the care and judgement that previous researchers have shown in collapsing their choice criteria can be better used in this case, and in future studies, in interpreting the results. It may also be possible to use the resulting model to calculate a measure of the attractiveness of each school, for different types of families. Such a tool - a kind of school attractiveness function - would be invaluable for future civic and educational planning, if the move towards increased parental choice of schools continues unabated.

6 The schools and their users

Introduction

This chapter examines the sample of schools in more detail in terms of their demographics, facilities, image-making, management, and results. The stories from the individual schools in the study are used to create a range of seven distinguishable types of schools, and it is these seven types that are used for subsequent analysis. This device is used partly to reduce the number of variables, partly to increase the number of respondents in each cell of any between-schools comparison table, and partly to protect the identity of the schools, where the information given is not already a matter of public record.

The data involved in the survey can be divided into four areas of interest - the type of schools, the characteristics of the families, the way choice takes place, and the reasons given for making a choice. The final part of this chapter concentrates on the first two of these areas - the respondents, and their relationship to the types of schools that they use. One section shows the results from the questions concerning the respondents, their family, and background, and the final section relates these variables to the seven types of school. It should be noted that this chapter contains a brief summary of the characteristics of all respondents. Differences between sub-groups, such as adults and children, are discussed in Chapter 7, while the characteristics of those using fee-paying schools are described in more detail in Chapter 10.

The seven types of schools

In order to protect their anonymity, to reduce the number of variables in the analysis, and increase the number of respondents in each category, the schools have been provisionally clustered into seven different types, based upon data concerning them gained through official lists, interviews with principals, school visits, and their own publicity material. This clustering has been tentatively confirmed by a statistical analysis of the numeric data concerning the schools and their characteristics, described further in Gorard (1996a).

It is clear from the survey results that there are differences between the responses from the users of different schools, but the number of respondents from some schools is necessarily so small, due to their size, that it is difficult to draw firm general conclusions. One way of overcoming this problem is to place the schools into groups by type, but that leads to the problem of what the categories should be, since there is no relevant established typology. The researcher contacted all of the 29 fee-paying schools in the sampling frame in the course of the study, as well as four state-funded schools, and collected data concerning their characteristics. The sources of data are Welsh Office documents, Annual League Tables of Performance, the schools' own literature, a few official school histories, the researcher's own teaching experience in one state and one fee-paying school in the sample, ISIS exhibitions and publications, visits to the schools, lesson observation, and interviews with staff, pupils, and parents.

Each school provided different kinds of data about themselves, and to examine why would provide a book in its own right. Some schools send prospective parents several glossy publications, while some publish nothing. One school refused to make any information public, because of the danger that it might be misinterpreted. Some fee-paying schools attend ISIS exhibitions in force, while others do not belong to ISIS. Some schools allow visitors to walk around the premises unaccompanied, while others have security locks and require signing in and out, and the wearing of identification at all times. Due to these variations, the initial comparisons between schools, used to help create the types, are based upon five topics. These are not necessarily the most significant facts about a school, but they are used because they are readily available from all schools, using the above sources. The five topic areas are:

The pupils - their age, gender, number, and day or boarding status.
The teachers - their number, gender, and qualifications.
The school organisation - the number and gender of governors or owners, the headteacher, location, date of foundation, day length, and curriculum.
The exams - entry policy and pupil outcomes.
The fees charged - including membership of the Assisted Places Scheme.

The five types of fee-paying schools, tentatively identified through the qualitative analysis which follows, are summarised in Figure 6.1, and to these are added the two age groups for the state schools that also took part in the study. All fee-paying schools in South Wales are included in the analysis, even those that take no further part in the survey. In the next section, the types are validated by their differences in terms of qualitative data not used in the clustering, including their buildings, religious affiliation and the associations to which they belong.

Name	Summary of likely characteristics
State-funded primary	Free, religious by law, purpose built, National Curriculum, day, coeducational, primary
State-funded secondary	Free, religious by law, purpose built, National Curriculum, day, coeducational, secondary
Grass-roots	Volunteer-aided, fundamentally religious, converted accommodation, own curriculum and assessment, day, coeducational, all-age with mixed age teaching groups
Catholic	Registered charity, sectarian, converted accommodation, quasi-National Curriculum, day, mainly girls, mostly all-age to 16
Feeder proprietary	For-profit, secular, converted accommodation, quasi-National Curriculum, day, mostly coeducational, pre-school and primary only
Stand-alone proprietary	For-profit, secular, converted accommodation, quasi-National Curriculum, day, coeducational, pre-school to sixth form.
Traditional foundation	Charitable status, religious, purpose built, quasi-National Curriculum, boarding, recently single-sex, secondary or preparatory (some with junior sections), HMC/GSA, Assisted Places Scheme.

Figure 6.1 The seven school types

The focus schools themselves

In this section, the schools in the sampling frame are described in greater detail, to show the data upon which the typology is based (Gorard 1997$_d$).

State-funded schools

The four state-funded schools in the study have many similarities. They are all in towns or city suburbs, and housed in 1960/70s purpose-built accommodation, with additions, and some prefabricated classrooms. They all follow the National Curriculum, have "religious" assemblies, use uniform regulations and display a few notices in Welsh. Several families have children in two of these schools at the same time, and all four schools have large classes of over 30. The classes are so large that they are frequently taught as a whole group, even in the primary schools. The major differences between the primary and the secondary schools are in terms of the age of the pupils, obviously, but also in terms of size. The primary schools have approximately 500 pupils each, of which around half are infants. The secondary schools have around four times as many pupils.

Each time that the researcher visited a primary school there was something special going on. On one occasion the children were in their own clothes, while the staff were dressed as children from St Trinian's, in order to raise money for Children in

Need. On another, the hall was full of tins of food and other produce for a Harvest festival, and classes were engaged in arranging the display. Neither primary school has a room capable of taking all of the pupils, and so assemblies are held by forms, or years. The time and trouble necessary to arrange these are resented by the staff and by the head in one school. Despite the obvious fun taking place, both schools had a traditional feel, with children dismissed by rows. Because of the lack of a hall large enough, children were assembled in the playground. In one case this was to guess the length of a row of coins, and in another for a lecture on the size of footballs allowed in the playground, in which children were asked to imagine what the school could have bought with the £86 recently spent on replacing a window. Even six year olds are made aware of budgetary constraints.

The two secondary schools both have a reception area with a display of sporting cups, and other certificates that might be said to be rather elderly without being genuinely traditional. Both seem very aware of bullying and have a clear policy for dealing with it. In one school a log is kept of all reports of bullying, including the source, the victim, and the offender and having this formal record is very valuable when intervention takes place. One secondary school was the only school visited that not only employed staff to help children with learning difficulties but had a teacher sit next to a pupil during the lessons. This one-to-one relationship is very helpful to the child and allows the class teacher to progress at a faster rate but it must be very expensive. A class of 30, therefore, might actually have two adults present, for an average 15:1 ratio overall, which is close to the figure for the fee-paying schools. One child had the questions in the survey read to her by the support teacher, and answered verbally, as her literacy was so poor.

Each secondary school has two feeder primary schools, and all of the leavers from those feeders are guaranteed a place by the relevant LEA. In one of the schools, there are around 120 applicants for the 40 places remaining after the allocation to the feeder schools, and the decision as to who is successful is made by the LEA. Generally, all of the unsuccessful applicants go to appeal every year, which might surprise other researchers, such as Ball (1993), who feel that appeals are used only by a privileged minority. The LEA guidelines for acceptance are first, those living in the catchment areas of the two feeder schools, then those providing evidence of moving to those areas, then those with compelling medical and social grounds, and finally siblings of current pupils in years 7 to 9. It is quite clear from these rules that the LEA is, in fact, implementing a system of catchment areas for its secondary schools, and so selection by mortgage continues, even after the ERA 1988. According to the schools, some families understandably try lies and other strategies to obtain a place, such as using a phoney address. The sixth form of one school has a free entry policy, and the LEA considers that sending an older child to the sixth form in order to get a younger child in is an example of cheating, and so has changed the policy on siblings to apply to only Years 7 to 9. It is not clear why. The school is fiercely against cheating in the selection process, but once a child is in the school, their needs are rightly given priority. They are unlikely to be moved even after a deception is uncovered, but this does have the effect of encouraging cheating. In addition to implementing a covert catchment area, the LEA also prevents market forces from taking full effect by not allowing the school to expand beyond its standard number, to fill the consistent demand. The school has applied for money to expand under a separate Popular Schools Initiative, but the

Secretary of State for Wales, who reportedly wanted this initiative, has since resigned, and its future is not clear. Ironically the school does not see itself as being in competition with other local schools, does not want to "steal" pupils from them, and justifies its growth solely by pointing to the emergence of a new nearby housing estate.

Grass-roots schools

Six of the fee-paying schools in South Wales are new, springing recently from their local communities, often by way of home schooling. There are around 10,000 families in Britain whose children do not attend school (Meighan 1995), and this number is growing (Meighan 1992). Some of these families object to state education as being too secular, or conversely for teaching the wrong form of religion. Several religious groups offer such parents a ready prepared, and approved, set of curriculum materials, as well as training in their use. One is the Programme of Accelerated Christian Education (PACE), based in Swindon. Parents who are trained and prepared to teach their children at home, may then be approached by friends to take more children. At this stage the arrangement often becomes a school, and legally must register as such with the Welsh Office. Those schools which do not charge the parents any fees, but rely instead on funding from a church for example, have not been included in this study. The majority do charge fees, very low fees, and so they are actually and legally part of the private school sector. Some of them have been dubbed "reluctant private schools", and are attempting to gain state-funding (Walford 1995). In addition to the Christian Pentecostal schools, one of the 28 Muslim private schools described by Walford (1995) is in South Wales. These schools, the "reluctant private sector", are poorly funded, often supported by the direct action of parents as volunteer teachers, administrators, and maintenance staff, and they are the most volatile type of school, with several opening, closing, merging and splitting during the period of the study. The researcher obtained from one school a list of 12 families in Gwent and Mid-Glamorgan currently using PACE material at home, including both Jehovah's Witnesses and Mormons. The temptation to contact them, and possibly to study a new school in embryo was very strong, but resisted at that stage.

Both of the grass-roots schools taking part in the survey are mixed, taking children of all ages and abilities, and teaching them in groups representing several ages. They prefer to take only Christians, since they relate the stories of the Bible to all aspects of education, but appear, in reality, to take any applicants. Both are in small villages, in old mining areas north of Cardiff. Both are very friendly and open in nature. One school is a member of the Australian Christian Schools Group. It is 12 years old, taking 27 pupils from 4 to 16 years old, who are divided into smaller groups for teaching by the four members of staff. The school does not have a telephone but at least it has a name, which one of the others does not. The school is cheap, since the fees are supplemented by donations from the Church. It is housed in a Baptist chapel, but claims to be non-denominational, accepting pupils from families who are not members of the church, since "the fear of the Lord is the beginning of wisdom". Delegation to the school must be done carefully however, since "God has specifically demanded that children are educated by their family", which may explain why these schools remain small, and are constantly being reinvented as each home-schooling programme grows to the statutory minimum. Many of the children are characterised by the head as being "failures" from elsewhere, with a high proportion of fostered children. One child listened to the questionnaire, and answered verbally, as his literacy was so poor.

The other is a PACE school, using curriculum packs designed in the USA. The school is four years old. There are seven pupils, only one of whom is a boy, including three children of the three members of staff, ranging in age from 3 to 18 years old. Only the head is male and only he has a degree or a teaching qualification, with the other two staff having attended a one week training course at the Swindon headquarters. The staff are unpaid, and the site, of an old LEA primary school, is rented, so the fees of £86 per month, with reductions for subsequent children, make this school one of the cheapest in Wales. All of the children study in silence in one room, using the programmed instruction booklets with regular self-tests for Maths, English, and Social Studies that were originally developed for home-schooling. Pupils do not automatically progress with age, but must obtain near 100% in a summative test before proceeding to the next course. If the objectives for a day are met, there is no homework, and for consistent success there are privilege bonds which may be exchanged for rewards. Each child has two flags, one requesting a monitor, and one a supervisor, which they place out on their desks to attract attention without disturbing others. The work leads to the PACE qualifications, rather like student profiles, which do not appear in league tables but which the school claims have been accepted for university entrance.

Feeder proprietary schools

Six of the schools in the study area have the following characteristics in common. They are all fee-paying, taking pupils of primary and pre-school age, but with no senior section. As well as moving to all-age proprietary schools, and the state sector, a large proportion of their leavers move on to traditional foundation schools. These feeder schools are therefore fulfilling a similar function to the older preparatory schools. In fact, one of them was a preparatory school but has found that it is no longer worth retaining charitable status. All six schools are privately owned, in converted residential accommodation, mostly run by a female head. Three of them are between 10 and 15 years old, and three claim to be at least 70 years old, but this may be an attempt to create an "instant tradition", since it is not clear that they have been open during all of that period. All of them are notionally coeducational for at least some age groups, but at the time of the study, one contained no boys, and another contained no girls in at least one of the ostensibly coeducational years.

One school stands out, as it only takes children from 3 to 7 years, and so is "feeding" other primary schools. It is a private pre-school of 43 pupils, with some children of school age. The other five all take children from ages 3 to 11, with between 80 and 200 children on their rolls. They are not selective, as most children arrive before Year 1, but they may have an entrance test for children aged 7 or more. Their fees are all similar, ranging from £2145 to £2685 p.a., which is more than double the price of the grass-roots schools, even before the inevitable extras such as lunch, milk, ballet, music and drama. Their facilities are generally better than the grass-roots schools, but they generally have no land, no playing fields, and no intrinsic sports provision. Most of the staff are women, and most of them have a degree or a teaching qualification. The larger number of trained staff, and the division of children into year groups allows more traditional teaching, of more varied subjects. Most of these schools are in the suburbs, running private buses to rural areas to help enrolment.

Stand-alone proprietary schools

Four of the schools are similar to the feeder schools in several respects. They are privately owned, ostensibly coeducational, and non-selective, in converted extended residences, with usually only a small yard for recreation, and few facilities. In being prepared to take any child they are making more of a business, than an educational, statement. Like some feeder schools, some also run buses to rural areas. They differ chiefly from the feeder schools because they take pupils of both primary and secondary ages, and all have male heads. Two schools only take pupils to the age of 16. All of their fees are on a sliding scale, comparable to the feeder schools with which they are in competition at ages up to 11, increasing in one case to a figure of over £7000 p.a. at 18, but mostly stopping at between £3,000 and £4,000. Extras include books, sports, trips, lunch, examinations, insurance, and in one school, £175 for Science lessons. The schools range in size from just under 200 pupils to over 500, with between 20 and 40 teachers.

One school has recently been formed from the merger of two others, meaning that the site is split into three parts. The main school is like a rabbit warren of steep internal stairs, fire doors, and small rooms, supplemented by Portakabins for practical subject teaching. The structure of the school restricts teaching to traditional methods in small groups. The play area for children is small, and this means that children of vastly differing ages are thrown together. One parent removed her 10 year old twin daughters from a similar school after an unpleasant incident in the playground with a 15 year old boy. These restrictions are common to the stand-alone schools in the study. Most of the schools are members of an association such as ISIS, or IAPS, and most have respectable positions in local league tables of GCSE results. All of the stand-alone schools are in the suburbs.

Catholic schools

Three of the local fee-paying schools are based upon a Catholic convent. Like the stand-alone proprietary schools, they are also generally coeducational all-age schools, but, in addition to their Catholic basis, they differ because they have charitable status, like the traditional foundation and grass-roots schools. They are much larger than the grass-roots schools, having between 100 and 300 pupils, and cheaper than the traditional schools, at around £2,000 to £3,000 p.a. They are between 60 and 140 years old. One school nearly closed during the study, and has been taken over by some of the existing parents, so that, strictly speaking, it is no longer a Catholic school, but as the pupils are still broadly similar, and there has not been much time for any organisational changes to take effect, the school appears in this study as though still connected to the convent. It is the only one to have a male head, and the only one to still offer boarding. Two used to be girls' grammar schools, and one still only takes boys to age 11. They generally have better buildings than the proprietary schools, although these are sometimes in need of renovation. They also tend to have more land, and a greater range of subjects and facilities, offering such attractors as Italian, and the Duke of Edinburgh's Award Scheme.

The Catholic schools are non-selective, but achieve a respectable position in local league tables of examination results. One school boasts a 100% pass rate at A level, with an average of 19 points per candidate. The schools also claim to be non-denominational, with one saying that they will "warmly welcome all denominations and faiths", and another that their role is merely "to inculcate Christian principles and moral standards, the outward signs of which are good manners and respect for others". However, an RE lesson observed in one of the schools showed little eclecticism, or respect for other beliefs. Religious tolerance was taken to mean recognition that there are pupils of many backgrounds in a class, so that some Catholic concepts required greater explanation or emphasis. Two of the schools are in rural areas, and one is in a city centre.

Traditional foundation schools

Five of the fee-paying schools in South Wales can be seen as traditional private schools. In general, these schools are larger, and older, with charitable status, and higher fees. Two are large selective girls schools, with over 600 pupils, members of GSA and GPDST, founded in the nineteenth century, and both are supported by London livery companies. They have junior sections taking girls of primary age, and feeding the senior section. The fees are around £4,000 p.a., with lunch, music, ballet, rowing, and dance extra. One school takes boarders, and the other has just stopped taking boarders. Both have female heads, a predominantly female staff of over 70, nearly all of whom have teaching qualifications, and a predominantly male board of governors. They both own land around the school - up to 15 acres - and have swimming pools, sports halls, technology suites, computer laboratories, art rooms, and a theatre, or a library. As such, they are better equipped than all of the other types of private school and their standard in this respect is comparable to but perhaps better than, the state funded schools in the study. They offer a wide range of subjects and extra-curricular activities and manage to pack these into a refreshingly short school day. Both schools offer a variety of scholarships, as well as Assisted Places, and are near the top of their local league tables of examination results. One is in a city, while one is rural, but both run bus services to a wide area, and encourage applications from a very wide catchment. The day school has a list of 254 feeder schools.

Three of the other traditional foundation schools are either boys schools, or they have only recently started taking girls. One is a boys school, running some mixed sixth form classes. One is a boys school, with a mixed sixth form, which has just announced an intention to take girls throughout. The third was a boys school until the 1970s, started to take some girls as a survival measure, went back to being single-sex, and returned to taking girls in the late 1980s. In all three, any girls are very much in the minority throughout, and the impression gained is that the schools have not started to accept girls through a commitment to coeducation, but in order to boost their falling rolls. One school has declined in numbers by about 10 pupils every year since 1979. In some respects these schools are similar to the girls schools except for the gender of the pupils. They offer Assisted Places, have many specialist buildings, and their own land. The differences are that they are all rural, more expensive - between £5,000 and £7,000 p.a. - generally less successful, and smaller with between 200 and 550 pupils. All three are boarding schools, with male heads, belonging to HMC and ISIS. The one with the fewest boarders is also the largest and the most successful in terms of results and popularity. The other two have around 80% boarders, and this affects their ethos to a considerable extent. Boarding below the sixth form is in dormitories, with as many as 12 children together, sometimes in bunk beds. They have a longer school day, with day pupils allowed to leave at around 7 p.m., to go home and do their homework before returning for Chapel at 8:35 the next morning. Saturday school is compulsory, and there is a school Chapel service on Sunday. Religion is "central" and all offer scholarships to the clergy. They also claim to be open to applications from all, and tolerant of religious differences. However, attendance at Chapel is compulsory. Overall, the results from the boys schools are nowhere near as good as those from the girls schools and in one the 1993 public examination results are worse than the national average for all schools. This school has over one third of its teachers with no teaching qualification. All five of the AP schools were founded more than 100 years ago, in one case as early as the sixteenth century. All are ostensibly selective in intake, but the rigour of this selection process is understandably affected by market conditions.

Of the remainder, one is a traditional preparatory school offering boarding, and taking pupils to age 13, but with an increasing number now leaving at 11. It is therefore considering creating a full secondary section, in order to retain its market share. It has the same type of buildings and facilities as the above "single-sex" schools, although it too now admits girls throughout the age range. The other four schools are all similar in some respects to the "single-sex" schools, but they are all coeducational, none offer APs, and none are members of the more prestigious associations. They are similar to the proprietary schools in that they were, or may be about to be, privately owned, but at the time of the study they all have charitable status. They also tend to be in rural areas, with considerable land attached, unlike the proprietary schools, and it may be the rates payable for the land that encourages them to remain as charities, while the city schools are run for profit. They vary in size from 200 to over 500 pupils, and charge between £3,150 and £4,300 p.a. In some of the schools, especially those concentrating on the primary and early secondary age group, the majority of teachers have no teaching qualification, and the facilities are not particularly modern or well-kept.

Summary of fee-paying provision

The average proportion of male teachers in the private schools is 37%, which is similar to the proportion in the maintained sector, with the female teachers mainly working in primary schools. On average, 87% of governors of private schools in the region are male. Perhaps this figure can help to explain why 67% of the Headteachers are male, while 63% of the teachers are female (although the figure for the maintained sector is not much different, 62% male Headteachers, and 63% female teachers). Only one school has parents as governors, in the sense that they are governors because they are parents, and membership of the governing bodies is always by selection, not election.

Some of the small Christian schools do not enter pupils for traditional public examinations, preferring to use their own certification and it is therefore not possible to compare their outcomes on these measures. Otherwise, the figure used for comparison of GCSE results is the "benchmark" figure published in the press in "league tables", with all of its attendant defects (Chapter 2). In the private schools taking pupils to age 16, the top score in GCSEs for 1993 was 100% of pupils with 5 or more at grades A to C, and the bottom score was 51%, with an average of 80% compared to 33% for the maintained sector in Wales (TES 1993). The highest average A level score per candidate in a private school was 23 in 1993, and the lowest was 12. The average figure for the independent sector in the region was 18 points per candidate, compared to 13.3 for the maintained sector in Wales. At both levels therefore some private schools are gaining results that are nearly twice as good as others but very few are gaining better results than the highest ranked state schools. It is also noteworthy that Llandovery College, the private school in the study region with the worst examination record from 1992 to 1995, is consistently achieving sixth-form results below the average for the maintained sector, while charging one of the highest fees. The full league table of fee-paying schools in South Wales appears in Chapter 10. There is almost no correlation between the examination results of the private schools in Wales for the years 1993 to 1995 (TES 1995). However there is a small *negative* correlation between the results from 1993 to 1995, the level of fees, and the length of the school day. It is interesting to note that this is one market where the consumer does not get more by paying more, and may even get less, and that giving schools more curriculum time does not lead to better results.

The market and the right image

The fee-paying schools described above vary in terms of their size, cost, governance, age range, and location, showing the absurdity of treating all private schools as the same, as though they are all traditional schools. This diversity of provision is apparent even in such a small group as the 29 schools in South Wales and is in marked contrast to the similarity of organisation between state-funded schools in the same area (Gorard 1997a). However, the differences between the fee-paying schools, apart from their finances, should not be over-emphasised. There are no specialist schools for Technology, Sport, or Dance, for example, no progressive or Steiner schools, and none teaching in the medium of Welsh. Most are coeducational day schools, taking anyone who can pay, and adapting the National Curriculum to fit their circumstances. In addition, most private schools present themselves in their own literature in a similar way, with the exception of the few Pentecostal schools which have no literature. Griffiths (1991) found that the range and quality of prospectuses in the region varied enormously, and that "schools that were too well known locally to require aggrandisement were the ones that tended to offer the most basic of material" (Griffiths 1991 p.90). If that were true in 1991, it certainly is not now, and the quality of literature sent to parents is in almost direct proportion to the size and prestige of the school. Schools still do not advertise much, independently of their associations, since it is not cost-effective. It "takes a seven figure sum to change the public's perception" of a school, according to a local head who is also the director of ISIS. But the schools do spend money on their own literature, and the development of a house style, as do the state schools in the study. To some extent, this is a result of greater access to desk-top publishing systems, in-service courses on projecting the right image, and the appointment of marketing directors.

The analysis of school's own literature follows some of the suggestions made by Headington and Howson (1995) in their report of the content and presentation of state school brochures. They used several bases for comparison, such as adherence to the regulations for content in the 1980 Education Act, the Flesch reading ease, the use of aids such as lists of contents, the ratio of text and graphics, print and paper quality, size, and cover design. Headington and Howson (1995) using a much smaller sample, reported that there was a lack of standard structure which made comparison between the publications difficult, and also that schools generally underestimate the value of illustrations. Only one school of their four showed a child on the outside cover, and "colour was used sparsely" (Headington and Howson 1995 p. 91). Such conclusions are not warranted by the findings of this study, which are more in line with those of Gewirtz et al. (1995). Those schools that have publicity literature, also use a similar structure, and several use colour photographs lavishly. Some also have a marketing video. Nearly all of the covers show a few children, often of different ages and genders, amid some greenery, with one of the buildings as a backdrop.

The most common format for a local prospectus is an A4 size glossy brochure, of 10 to 16 pages, consisting chiefly of large colour photographs mixed with small sections of text. Several arrive in envelopes carrying their school logo, often as a franking mark. The brochures usually have a sleeve inside the back cover for the insertion of several sheets of paper of varying heights to allow the heading of each sheet to be read in *situ*. These inserts are commonly used to present information not included in the prospectus, perhaps because it is likely to change regularly. Generally included in this category are a list of staff names, their qualifications and subjects, a list of governors and their professions, the dates of terms and holidays, and the school fees, their methods of payment and concessions. The range of concessions quoted are government Assisted Places, named academic scholarships, bursaries, scholarships for music, drama, choristers and sport, concessions for children of clergy, or the armed forces, or for subsequent children from the same family living at the same address and attending the school at the same time. Different levels of fees are often quoted depending on the age of the child, and whether the child is new to the school. The fees are most often quoted as per term, and sometimes per month, presumably because these seem less alarming than the annual total.

Most brochures include a registration form to be completed by the applicant, and sent to the school with a non-returnable registration fee of between £20 and £75. Other less frequent inserts include uniform lists with details of stockists, invitations to Open Mornings, public examination results, photocopied newspaper articles, newsletters, school magazines, rules, a picture for the child to colour in, a school fees plan, and insurance leaflets relating to pupil safety, fees payment protection and even private medical insurance. Some mailings include a word-processed letter from the Head, making references to the child's name or age. These letters urge a visit to the school, and usually offer a guided tour during the working day. A few schools spend less on their brochures, which can be 10 to 20 A4 black and white photocopied sheets of paper stapled together. One school sent only one sheet of paper folded up into a black and white leaflet.

The more permanent contents of many of the brochures are similar. There are brief sections describing the history of the school, its facilities, its aims and objectives, an introduction written by the Head, and a location map noting local travel facilities. Most also have photographs and text relating to Drama, Music, Sports, Trips, and Societies, which are the most visually attractive school activities. Regulations concerning advertising standards presumably apply to school prospectuses, but it would not seem so from the claims made in some. One of the most traditional schools claims to be "in the vanguard of educational development". Another school that has no drama facilities, and has not put on a school play for four years, claims that it is involved in "regular" drama in such a way that the reader would also reasonably expect the drama to be frequent.

Three common themes are found in many brochures which might be considered a priori to present contradictory views. Schools claim to be traditional, reinforcing this message with the historical outline, pictures of old buildings and teachers in gowns, with the appearance of Latin or "Divinity" in the Curriculum, and an emphasis on uniform. The keywords "discipline" and "homework" appear frequently. At the same time, they claimed to be innovative and up to date, reinforcing this message with National Curriculum nomenclature, pictures of computer networks, technology suites or pupils in white laboratory coats, and descriptions of leadership development courses. One prospectus manages to put both ideas across together by stating that the school is "in the vanguard of educational development, while retaining a commitment to those standards and values that are both honourable and endurable". Another school claims that it can "marry traditional qualities to tomorrow's needs".

In a second theme running through most brochures, schools are pursuing, and according to them attaining, academic excellence. There is an emphasis on pupils achieving their full potential, on Common Entrance success, past pupil scholarships to Public Schools, public examination results, or entry to Higher Education. A few schools emphasise that they are "academically selective". Some schools have an entrance exam for pupils entering from outside schools, others hold a test "for correct placement". It is unlikely that many pupils are in fact refused entry by these schools, many of which are also offering help with learning difficulties. Pupils are probably also accepted at any age. In this case, entry is likely to be by interview and references only. The traditional January entrance exam for age eleven (and decreasingly for age thirteen) is of most use in determining initial placement in streams or sets, or for awarding scholarships, bursaries and APs. On the other hand, many schools describe facilities and specialist staff for pupils with specific learning difficulties. One school takes pupils with Special educational needs from the Local Education Authority. Others offer scholarships for non-academic talent such as sport, music, drama and public speaking. Academic excellence is said to be only one of the objectives of the school. All claim in some way to be educating the whole pupil. This is backed up by pictures of extra-curricular and leisure activities, and by descriptions of pastoral welfare systems.

A third theme relates to religion, class, and ethnicity. Most schools claim to have a Christian basis. Many feel quite strongly that they have a mission. At the same time, nearly all schools claim to welcome pupils of all faiths and denominations, and to teach tolerance and understanding of different cultures. One school claims that its purpose is the "Christian education of the middle classes". Another claims that it is open to all faiths and as an example of this supposed tolerance states that "pupils of other faiths attend our morning [Christian] assemblies". Only one appears to make a virtue of the fact that it is not open to all by stating that "all children in the school are British with English as a mother tongue".

Most schools also claim to be following the National Curriculum, but few list Welsh as either a first or second language, even as an option. Only one prospectus contains sections of text in Welsh. Two schools have a weekly assembly in Welsh. Otherwise the only concession to a Welsh ethos is a reference to one-day inter-house competitive Eisteddfodau in two brochures. Technology is the other National Curriculum subject most frequently missing in these schools. Combining these two "deficiencies" with variations in individual schools, it is not clear that any are strictly in line with a National Curriculum, from which they are exempt. The range of optional subjects in some schools is very large, and their prospectuses make it clear that pupils can study subjects which are not part of the standard timetabled option blocks. In some cases, this means that the school is offering help to individuals who wish to study a subject like music, Latin or Japanese, in addition to their 9 GCSEs, or 3 A levels. In other cases, sets appear to be taught outside the timetable because the school has a rigid option block procedure, and has not increased pupil satisfaction by implementing a choice-driven heterogeneous option pools system.

Several brochures describe parents associations which are mostly social and fundraising organisations. Most also mention the number of reports to parents, generally two or three per year with an annual parents evening. Some schools have termly parents evenings and a few emphasise that the Head is always available for a meeting. The lack of parental representation among the Governing bodies and the lack of any formal consultative procedure, makes the schools appear to be responsive to parents without being run by or for them and their children. Small schools make a virtue of their size, and emphasise the family nature of their institution. Several Heads imply that they would not want so many pupils that they could not know them all personally. One school states that it is "small enough to create a feeling of family". Another argues that "one of the advantages of our relatively small size is that pupils of all abilities have the chance of representing ... in inter-school matches". This situation may not necessarily be a selling point to a small boy faced with his first game of rugby against a team containing boys three years older than him, as was observed in one school.

The respondents and their schools

The findings described in the remainder of this chapter are based upon a large number of tables. For clarity and ease of reading, several tables resulting from the analysis are not shown in the text, and those that are shown are simplified, or converted into graphical form. The distributions of responses, and all cross-tabulations using these data, are shown as percentages, which are used to standardise the figures, and to make comparison between them easier. The statistical calculations are done with the original frequencies. It should be noted that this chapter only deals with the overall sample. The next chapter considers the process of choice, and the following chapters deal with issues and sub-groups of responders that arise from these data. In particular, Chapter 10 reviews the characteristics of those using the fee-paying sector in Wales.

There are nine variables relating to the background characteristics of each family, in addition to the generation of the respondent, gender, year group, and school type, as described above. This section briefly describes some of these characteristics and their inter-relationships for the whole sample. These findings, although of little wider significance in their own right, characterise the sample, providing the background, and basis, for further analyses in Chapters 7 to 10.

The simple variables

Most of the mothers, 74%, attended state schools themselves, while fewer than half of them have a degree. More of the fathers attended state schools themselves, 76.4%, but well over half of them have a degree, 61%. The number of parents with degrees is relatively high, since only 18% of the total population aged 25 to 59 in Wales have a degree (Eurostat 1995). The differences could be partly due to a higher return rate from more educated parents, which would be expected, or, as the question specified "degree or equivalent", respondents could be being liberal in their interpretation of the word "equivalent". It is also possible that it is linked to the relatively high proportion of users of private school, among whom there may be a better standard of education. The fact that more men than women have degrees was expected, as this is also the situation in the population for Wales as a whole (Eurostat 1995). The fact that a quarter of the parents have been to private school is surprising, given the relatively small numbers in the private sector in Wales, or even England, today. However, as the sample is heavily weighted towards current users of private schools, this suggests some form of "domino" or reproduction effect, in which the education of one generation in the family influences the next, as discussed further in Chapter 8. In the survey families, the child in question has, on average, one brother or sister of school age, who is more likely to attend a state school than a private one (Table 6.1). This figure shows that a large number of siblings of private school users do not go to a private school themselves. Both of the results concerning the schooling of other members of the family show that the concept of a family tradition of using a particular school, or even a particular type of fee-paying school, must be rare.

Table 6.1
Schooling of siblings

	Mean	Standard Deviation
Number of children	1.01	0.82
Number in private	0.43	0.66

The two measures of parents educational background - type of school, and level of education - both have a strong relationship to each other, and to the education of the partner, in those families where there is more than one parent. Mothers who went to a private school themselves, are more likely to have a degree and to have a partner who both went to a private school himself and who has a degree. As one example of these relationships, Table 6.2 shows that 84% of mothers with degrees have a partner with a degree.

Table 6.2
Mother's education by father's education

	Father degree	Father no degree
Mother with degree	84	16
Mother with no degree	39	61
Chi-Square	Degrees of freedom	Significance
95.31007	1	0.00000

Also, as expected, these two educational variables are strongly related to the occupational class for both partners. Parents with degrees, or who attended private schools are more likely to be in the service class, and much less likely to be working-class. As one example of this phenomenon, Table 6.3 shows that less than 1% of the fathers in the working-class families have degrees. Working-class families are also less likely to declare a religious affiliation, while declared Christians are most likely to be in the service class. Families with minority religions, such as Islam, are more likely in the intermediate class.

Table 6.3
Father's education by occupational class

Father	Service	Intermediate	Working	Other
has degree	79	20	-	-
no degree	37	53	8	2
Chi-Square	Degrees of F.	Significance		
77.68571	3	0.00000		

Parents who went to private schools themselves have, on average, more children attending private schools, whereas the children of graduate parents are split proportionately between the state and fee-paying sectors. This suggests that it is the type, rather than the level, of education received by a parent that produces a propensity to use fee-paying schools for the next generation. Table 6.4, for example, shows that in families where the father attended a private school, the child in question has almost twice as many siblings in private education, although no more siblings overall than in other families.

Table 6.4
Siblings' education by father's education

	Siblings in private school	Standard Deviation
Father attended private	0.67	0.72
Father attended state	0.36	0.63
t-value	DF	Prob.
3.87	151.15	0.000

Families with a larger number of children in private schools much more often come from a service occupational class background than from a working-class one (Table 6.5). This finding completes the link between the education of the parents, their occupations, their religion, and their children's schools. In addition, families with a Catholic or minority religion, such as Islam, tend to have more children in private schools, but this is chiefly because they also tend to have more children overall.

Table 6.5
Siblings' education by occupational class

Class	No. in private	Working class	Intermediate
Working class	0.15		
Intermediate	0.24		
Service	0.55	*	
Unpaid	1.00		
Source	Degrees of F.	F ratio	Prob.
Between	3	8.5957	0.0000

Families and types of schools

This section begins a consideration of the different types of schools used by the kinds of families described above. The validity of the model of seven types of schools is further confirmed by cross-tabulations of the types of school by the characteristics of their users, such as gender and age. While such confirmation is important it does not add to the descriptions of the schools given above.

As expected, those parents who attended private school themselves are more likely to be using a fee-paying school for the child in question, and this is especially true of those using traditional foundation schools. This generalisation is not true of the parents using grass-roots and Catholic fee-paying schools, who are even less likely to have been to a fee-paying school themselves than those parents currently using a state secondary school. Table 6.6 shows the relative frequencies for the fathers education, by way of example, but the figures for the mothers are similar, since the educational backgrounds of the parents are linked anyway.

Table 6.6
School type by father's education

	Father private	Father state
State primary	12	88
Grass-roots	14	86
Catholic	14	86
State secondary	18	82
Stand-alone proprietary	22	78
Traditional foundation	34	66
Feeder proprietary	38	62
Chi-Square	Degrees of freedom	Significance
29.12648	6	0.00006

The distribution of parents' degrees is more even than the school background of the parents, between fee-paying and state schools. However, since all of the educational background variables are so strongly linked, it is not surprising that parents using grass-roots, and to a lesser extent Catholic, fee-paying schools are less likely to have a degree, while those using traditional foundation schools are more likely to be graduates. Table 6.7 gives the frequencies for mothers education, for example. The pattern for graduate fathers is similar. Families with a child in any fee-paying school are more likely than users of any state schools to have other children in a fee-paying school of the same type. When this occurs, the two children do not necessarily use the same school, partly because of gender or age differences, although the reasons are more complex in some cases (see Chapter 9).

Table 6.7
School type by mother's education

	Mother degree	Mother no degree
Grass-roots	-	100
Catholic	32	68
Feeder proprietary	45	55
State primary	48	52
State secondary	53	47
Stand-alone proprietary	54	46
Traditional foundation	61	39
Chi-Square	DF	Significance
25.79635	6	0.0002

The relationships between school types, and the occupational class of families using them are generally in accord with the findings for class and educational background. The proportion of working-class families is higher in the grass-roots schools, but otherwise there is no overall difference between the state and private sector in terms of use by the working-class. The intermediate and service classes are fairly evenly balanced in both Catholic and state schools, but service families dominate the traditional private schools. The proprietary schools, which have a relatively high proportion of parents with a fee-paying background, also have predominantly service class users, despite having only an average number of graduates.

In a cross-tabulation of the school types by the main family religion, several of the religious categories are spread relatively evenly between the different types of schools, and there is no obvious difference between the state and private sectors as a whole, in this respect. There are, unsurprisingly, more Catholics in Catholic schools, although even there they are in a minority. It is noteworthy that the stand-alone proprietary schools are the only other ones to have less than half Protestant Christians on their rolls. These schools are overtly secular in style, but they do not have a very great proportion of those with no professed family religion. They are used more by those whose religion is not well catered for by the existing state provision, such as Hindus.

The grass-roots schools have the least balanced intake, although it must be remembered that the numbers using them are small. In reference to small religious schools, Walford (1995) suggested that by focusing on particular beliefs, they restrict entry to their roll to those of a homogeneous nature, which will lead to greater social and ethnic divisions between schools if they become more popular. There is some evidence to support that claim here. All of the pupils in all of the grass-roots schools surveyed were "white", and these were the only schools in which that was true. The highest proportions of "non-whites" were in the focus year groups at the stand-alone proprietary schools.

Conclusion

Recent legislation on education in Britain has looked to the independent sector as a model for improvement in the maintained sector. In theory, an attempt has been made to create a range of schools offering a diverse choice to parents and pupils. The rational choices made from the menu by these "consumers" should allow some schools to grow with success, and others to disappear as failures. It has been suggested here however, that such a process is more likely to produce conformity than diversity in patterns of schooling, with most schools attempting to appeal to most families. Market forces are likely to produce schools whose overriding priority is to survive, primarily for the benefit of their owners, investors or employees. There is little support from the fee-paying sector in South Wales for the theory that choice and diversity in schools are linked. The trend is towards medium sized co-educational day schools, with a maximum age span offering academic emphasis, all-round education, support for those with learning difficulties, sport, music, drama, art, Christian morality, multi-faith tolerance, and traditional educational values as well as educational innovation. Most schools are attempting to maximise their number of potential customers, by pushing many "buttons" in their advertising material - a situation referred to as "rhetorical convergence" by Glatter *et al.* (1995) - in some cases even to the extent of being misleading.

The existence of charitable status and support from Trust funds or livery companies for some schools gives these a subsidised advantage in the market place over those privately owned schools run "for profit", which could be seen as "unfair" in terms of market theory. The fact that the government has not admitted any of the privately owned schools to the Assisted Places Scheme, which is recognised as a major financial support for the independent sector, has increased the gap between them and the older charitable status schools [although since this study was completed, the Welsh Office has announced that 8 more schools will be participating in the scheme from September 1996, and some of these 8 were privately owned at the time of the study]. Free market forces do not appear to operate in education even in the private sector, and ironically it is the government's support for certain types of private schools that is part of the cause of this.

The seven types of schools described in this chapter are used as part of the more complex analysis in successive chapters. One result of this later analysis is to confirm the validity and usefulness of the typology. The five types of fee-paying schools, and the range of size, cost, and quality that they represent, display once again the absurdity of treating all private schools as though they were all "public" schools, catering for a very privileged elite.

In summary, there is a link between the predominantly Christian families in the service occupational class, their educational background, and their greater use of fee-paying schools for both generations. However, it would be misleading to imply that there is a simple state/private split. In many respects, such as parent education and social class, the users of Catholic schools are more like those of the state schools in this sample. It is, perhaps, the users of grass-roots schools who differ from others in most respects, with lower levels of education, and a higher proportion of working-class parents. Even so, the other types of fee-paying school are not seamless, since the stand-alone schools are catering for many more non-Protestants.

Traditional schools tend to be used by graduates from private schools in the service class and a very high proportion of their other children will also use private schools. Proprietary schools tend to be used by similar families but in which the parents are more often non-graduates. Grass-roots schools are used more by working-class parents than any fee-paying schools, and the parents tend to be non-graduates, from a state school background. Catholic, and the focus state-funded schools are more often used by families in the intermediate class who have no private school background but who are otherwise educated to a similar level as the majority of users of other school types.

Having established the characteristics of the families who took part in the survey and the types of schools they use, the next chapter describes how the schools are chosen, and derives a simplified model of the reasons given by these families for choosing a school. These four groups of data - families, schools, the process of choice, and the reasons for choice - are finally all linked together. Successive chapters look at the stories of the individuals behind these general findings and link the various strands of data together into analytical models of school choice.

7 The choice criteria

Introduction

Having established in Chapter 6 the kind of schools that the respondents use, this chapter moves on to describe the main findings from the questionnaire survey. The first section reviews how families go about making a choice of a new school in terms of who is involved in the choice, where they obtain information from, and how they go about it. The second section looks at the respondents' ratings of the importance of the 73 reasons for choosing a school, dividing these reasons into four groups of decreasing overall relevance to choice, from very important to not important. The third section looks at the correlations between these ratings to establish which of them are significantly covariant. In the fourth section, the ratings are reduced, by principal components analysis, to seven underlying factors, which are used to explain the patterned variance in the majority of the reasons for choice. Differences in the relative importance of these to different families, and links between the factors and other reasons for choice are discussed, as well the relationship of the factors, the patterns in the process of choice and the users of different schools.

In general, this chapter follows the same order as Chapter 2 in which reference is made to previous work in this field, and to which the present chapter refers. As with the family background variables in Chapter 6, some values are converted to percentages for presentation. In the interests of clarity, only selected examples of the results mentioned are included as tables within this chapter. All differences and relationships mentioned are significant at the 5% level, using chi-squared, Pearson's r, t-test, or one-way analysis of variance, as appropriate to the data.

The process of choice

Who chooses the school?

Over 50% of respondents claim that the choice of a school is a joint one, where neither the parents nor the child can be said to have the larger role, while fewer than

147

10% of respondents claim that the main role is taken by the child (Figure 7.1). This last is an unexpectedly low figure, given the findings of much previous research as described in Chapter 2 which tend to envisage the choice as being either the prerogative of the child, or at least, a joint process with the parents (e.g. Thomas and Dennison 1991). It should be noted that the question asked was "who has the major say in choosing", and that therefore both parties could have been involved in all decisions to some extent. However, the scale of the difference between this finding and previous studies requires further explanation. The figure is more unexpected, as this survey is unusual in including the views of children, who are less likely to neglect their own role in comparison to their parents. If anything, the inclusion of children would be expected to lead to a greater emphasis on a child-centred approach.

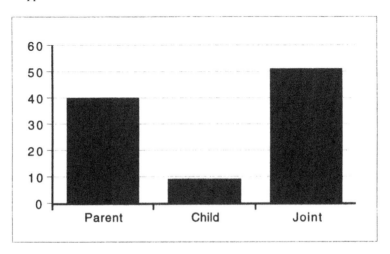

Figure 7.1 The main role in choosing a school

It could be that the difference is due to the occupational class, and parents' educational background, since there are some indications that it is especially working-class families who empower their children (Ball *et al.* 1992). It could be that, in previous work, parents have exaggerated the role that they gave to their children and that what has been discovered here is that children are more realistic, and know how little control they have had. It is also possible that asking families at different stages within the choice process would lead to different answers. Each of these possibilities is briefly discussed in this section, and then more fully in Chapter 9 which describes the process of choice as a three step procedure, in which the role of parent and child varies over time, as well as between families. However, some studies agree with this one, in assigning the greater role to parents. For example, West *et al.* (1994) reported that the choice was made by one or more parents 73% of the time, with the child alone only making the choice 7% of the time.

It is clear from Table 7.1, in which the frequencies of Figure 7.1 are broken down by the generation of the respondent, that it is only children who are claiming a major choice role for themselves whereas only 2% of parents report allowing the child to have the major say. It is not clear at this stage, which of the two generations, if any, is more reliable in this matter. However it is clear that the role of children has not been exaggerated by the parents interviewed in previous studies, in fact rather the reverse. Each generation feels that it is more involved in choosing a school than the other one reports, with parents claiming to be significantly involved in 98% of families.

Table 7.1
The main role in choosing by generation

	Parent's choice	Child's choice	Joint choice
Parents response	45	2	53
Child's response	36	14	49
Chi-Square	DF	Significance	
56	2	0.0000	

It could be argued that as the study focuses on fee-paying schools, with a greater proportion of service-class families in which parents may have a greater say, possibly because of the payment of fees, the finding with respect to choice roles is as expected and as found by other researchers such as Edwards *et al.* (1989). However, there is no evidence of a difference in the allocation of roles to generations when the parents' responses are cross-tabulated by occupational class (Table 7.2).

Table 7.2
The main role in choosing by occupational class

Occupational class	Parent chose	Pupil chose	Joint choice
Service	39	1	60
Intermediate	40	1	59
Working	43	7	50
Other	67	-	33
Chi-Square	DF	Significance	
8	6	0.2244	

The uniformity of choice roles across the three main occupational classes is impressive. This uniformity could be regional, and specific to South Wales or due to the exact phrasing of this difficult question, but there is no clear reason to accept either of these explanations. The lack of variation by class, and the differences in the reports of each generation indirectly support the third possibility given above for the difference between the findings of this study and others, in that the answer to the question of who really chooses may be sensitive to variations in the time of asking. This finding does not deny that there is a difference by class, since the number of reportedly working-class families in the sample was small, but it suggests that the difference may not be as great as originally supposed.

The role of the child increases almost directly with their age in the year of changing schools, from Year 1 to Year 11, while the role of the parent remains fairly steady in comparison (Table 7.3). It is the concept of a shared choice that decreases with age. Older children are more likely to claim that they made a choice alone, rather than with the help of a parent. Of course, these snapshot figures cannot reveal how the individual child's role varies over time, as discussed in Chapter 9, but there is a clear indication of at least one time-sensitive change. The majority of respondents in this survey relate to Years 6 and 7. In most of the schools in which Year 6 were surveyed, the majority of the families were intending to use one of the schools in which the Year 7 were also surveyed. If the survey had been carried out a year earlier, most of the Year 7 respondents would have been involved, and if a year later, most of the Year 6 would still have been involved. Thus, apart from the calendar difference of one year, there is no reason to suppose that the two year groups are any different, as they effectively represent different cohorts from the same schools. The differences between them can therefore be used to shed light on how the reasons of families change during the process. Since there is no reason *a priori* why the Years 6 and 7 should differ in this respect, it is interesting to note that the majority of respondents, 60%, feel that the choice is a joint one before it has been made, while the majority, 54%, see it as made by one party or the other, after the event.

Table 7.3
The main role in choosing by year group

	Parent's choice	Child's choice	Joint choice
Year 1	44	-	56
Year 6	33	7	60
Year 7	45	9	45
Year 8	24	30	46
Year 11	37	20	42
Chi-Square	DF	Significance	
65	8	0.0000	

An alternative pattern appears in a breakdown of the figures for the choice roles in terms of the types of schools (Table 7.4). Each of the state primary schools involved fed directly into one of the two secondary schools, so that a large proportion of the users of these schools would be common from year to year, but these are the schools in which the largest variation is apparent. In fact, the pattern for the state secondary schools is similar to those of the fee-paying schools, who are all relatively uniform in terms of who, in the family, plays the main role in choosing. It is the state primaries that display a clear difference to the rest. There is no reason for the roles to vary so much from Year 6 to Year 7 in state schools, since the process of choice that the two groups are describing is, of course, the same one, with the difference being merely one of perspective. The parents are seen to have a much greater role in choice before it occurs, while, in retrospect, the choice is more commonly seen as a joint one, in these schools alone. The role of the child apparently increases over time in some families.

Table 7.4
The main role in choosing by school type

	Parent	Child	Both
State primary	71	12	18
Stand-alone	45	10	45
Catholic	43	8	50
State secondary	42	5	53
Grass-roots	38	8	54
Feeder proprietary	38	9	53
Traditional	38	13	48
Chi-Square	DF	Significance	
24	12	0.0189	

It is well-known locally by the schools, and is apparent from the interviews with parents, that one of the state secondary schools is considered particularly desirable and heavily over-subscribed. One of the focus primary schools is a feeder for it, and is assured that there will be a place for all of its leavers. Parents plan ahead, and use the appropriate primary school accordingly (Chapter 8). This may involve moving to the area, or sending children to the primary from outside the catchment of the secondary school. Such moves and applications take place while the child is of primary age, and cannot be expected to play a large role in the process. In summary, many of the choices represented in rows one and four of Table 7.4 are long-prepared, and planned by parents alone. The exaggerated role of the child in Year 7 is therefore anomalous. This confirms two ideas which are central to the models of choice presented in this book. Firstly, the apparent role of the child increases as the choice process takes place, and secondly, if there is a dispute between the parents and children, there is some evidence here that the parents are more reliable on this question (Gorard 1997f). The issue of who is really making the choice of schools is a complex one which can be elucidated by the stories from interviews, and is therefore taken up again in Chapter 9.

The differences between religions have already been linked to class, parent's education, and the use of particular types of schools. It is clear that both Catholics, and families with no religion, are more parent-centred in their choosing, while Protestants, and families with a minority religion more often make a joint selection of school. The users of Catholic schools overall are, however, not noticeably different in this respect from those using any other fee-paying schools.

Sources of information about schools

For most respondents, the most significant source of information used in making a choice about schools is a personal acquaintance, whether another parent, or a child at the school (Figure 7.2). This kind of second-hand information is even more popular than visits to the school. Prospectuses and examination results are used, and acknowledged by many parents, but few feel that they are really useful, despite the publication of league tables and the pressure to use them as performance indicators. These findings are generally in line with those of other studies outlined in Chapter 2 (e.g. GPDSA 1995), while they have implications for the likely outcome of any attempt to improve the quality of schooling via increased choice based upon formal performance indicators. The sources of information listed as "other" in Figure 7.2 include a few not coded as one of the other four, such as visits to exhibitions, and the Holy Spirit appearing in a vision, but this category mainly represents families who had relied on more than one main source of information.

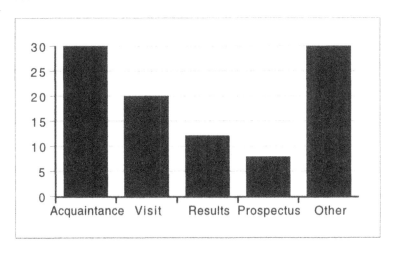

Figure 7.2 The main source of information

The overall figures mask certain differences between the information sources used by various families when considering diverse schools. In addition, each family may use different approaches at different times for different children. It is clear from Table 7.5 that visits and prospectuses are far more important to the process of choosing a boarding school, while acquaintances and examination results are more relevant for day schools.

Table 7.5
Sources of information by day or boarding

Source of information	Day pupils	Boarders
Acquaintances	31	11
Visit	23	44
Results	10	-
Prospectus	8	28
Other	27	17
Chi-Square	DF	Significance
14	4	0.0053

Day pupils represent 94.3% of the sample, meaning either that they were day pupils, if in Year 1 and 7 at the time of the survey, or they intended to be day pupils next year. The very few boarders arises partly from the lower response rate from boarding schools, but it is also a reflection of the current trends in private education, away from boarding. Boarding is more common for children in Year 8, and for boys, since respondents in Year 8 represent the users of one traditional preparatory school.

Visits may be more important for boarders, because their choice involves the evaluation of accommodation, as well as the selection of an educational establishment. It is likely that boarders rate prospectuses as more useful because there is a tendency for their schools to be further from their homes. In this case, literature can be used to limit the number of long journeys to schools unlikely to be selected. This idea is supported by the fact that families from rural mid-Wales, Dyfed and Powys, rate the relevance of prospectuses much more highly than those in cities such as Cardiff, perhaps because remoteness makes visits difficult, and perhaps because a restricted choice in rural areas leads to more boarding and so to consideration of schools from even further afield (Table 7.6). Families from the valleys north of Cardiff also differ from the norm of rating acquaintances as the most important source. For them, visits are more important, which is perhaps due to the nature of the grass-roots fee-paying schools available in Mid Glamorgan. Regardless of the area, users of grass-roots schools do not rate examination results as highly as others, but as the child gets older, examination results become a more important source of information for all schools and users. There are no significant differences in the use of the various types of information by class or by parent's education.

Table 7.6
Sources of information by area

	Acquaint.	Visit	Exam	Pros	Other
Cardiff	30	19	14	3	33
Valleys	22	36	18	14	9
Vale Glam.	30	23	5	13	29
Gwent	32	27	-	14	27
Swansea	18	24	-	12	47
Mid-Wales	9	18	-	55	18

Chi-Square	DF	Prob.
69	20	0.0000

The choice set

The "choice set" refers to the set of schools considered by each family at the start of the choice process. On the survey form, parents were asked to name the schools in this set and, in a clear majority of cases, all of the schools in each set were of the same type, as defined in Chapter 6. This finding further confirms the typology of schools, and suggests that in many families, the choice of a type of school is the first, perhaps unconscious, step in the process. Families report seriously considering around two schools on average (Table 7.7). They tend to read more prospectuses, but visit fewer schools than the number of schools they seriously consider. This suggests a coherent whittling-down process of reading about schools, rejecting some, and then visiting a smaller number.

Table 7.7
Size of the choice set

Schools	Mean	Standard Deviation
Number considered	1.70	0.95
Number visited	1.47	1.46
Prospectuses read	2.02	2.12

Parents also report that they considered a larger number of schools than their children do. This ties in with the finding above that the participation of the child increases as the process progresses. In this case, one would expect children to report only the number of schools in the choice set from the point at which their involvement becomes significant. They may therefore be unaware of some of the schools initially considered by the parents, before whittling down. This suggestion is confirmed by Table 7.8, which shows the magnitude of the difference between the views of the two generations in this respect, and which showed up despite the unfortunate restriction on the number of schools that parents could mention, as described in Chapter 5.

Table 7.8
Size of the choice set by generation

	Number considered	Standard Deviation
Parents	1.88	0.950
Children	1.57	0.923
t-value	DF	Probability
5.18	883.16	0.000

Despite the differences between the three measures of the choice set - schools, visits, and prospectuses - all three are also highly correlated with each other, and after allowing for the inevitable measurement error, there is a suggestion that the three variables may, in fact, be measuring nearly the same thing - perhaps a level of engagement with the choice process. The correlation between the number of schools considered, and the number visited, is 0.57, and between the number of prospectuses and the number visited is 0.77, for example. Thus, people who consider more schools, in general also visit more, and read more literature. Confirmation of the reliability of these results comes from the finding that those families rating prospectuses or visits as more important sources of information, also tend to read more literature and to visit more schools, for example (i.e. the respondents are being consistent).

It is also true that among all respondents, families with more children in private schools tend to consider, and visit, more schools, and read more prospectuses, perhaps because of the link between private schools and boarding, as outlined above.

Ratings of the reasons for choice

Tables 7.9 to 7.12 show, in descending order, the mean ratings given by all 1,267 respondents to each of the 73 variables representing choice criteria. On a scale from zero: "not important" to two: "very important", the mean ratings ranged from 0.19 to 1.84, and this range is notionally divided into four sections. "Very important" is from 1.5 to 2.0, rounding up to 2. "Important" is from 1.0 to 1.5, rounding down to 1. "Less than important" is from 0.5 to 1.0, rounding up to 1, and the "not important" section is from 0 to 0.5.

Also shown alongside the mean ratings in each figure are the standard deviations, and it is clear that these rise in the middle of the list, and fall way at both ends, in a kind of flattened normal distribution. This suggests two mutually supporting explanations. First, that there is firmer agreement between all respondents on what is very important and what is of no importance, while those ratings in the middle are there not because most respondents see them as moderately important, but because some see them as more important and some do not. As an example, "dissatisfaction with state schools" is rated as less than important overall, but has the highest standard deviation, indicating that respondents are split on this issue. Secondly, the lower standard deviations of responses near the top and bottom of the list may indicate the effects of truncation by the scale used for measurement.

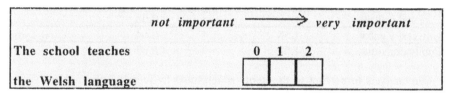

Figure 7.3 The appearance of the questions

Respondents may have felt constrained by the scale, and unable to express particularly strong or negative support for an item (this is a disadvantage of using the three point scale). This explanation is confirmed by the behaviour of some respondents when they wished to show hostility, or occasionally very strong support for an item. In addition to writing many blunt and thought-provoking comments, some people also "redesigned" the question before answering. The reasons used in the survey all appeared in the same form (Figure 7.3). It was felt unnecessary to provide a negative scale in the design, since all of the questions related to seemingly positive characteristics of a school, but some respondents added extra boxes to the left of the diagram for questions, such as that about the Welsh language, and then ticked these. Such responses appear in the results as a zero, equivalent to "not important", but to treat them as such may be to ignore an interesting, if unanticipated, finding. The implications of some of these editions are discussed in Chapter 10.

Table 7.9
Very important reasons for choosing a school

Criterion	Mean	SD
Happiness	1.84	0.40
Good teaching	1.77	0.51
No bullying	1.76	0.53
Pupil safety	1.75	0.49
Qualified teachers	1.73	0.51
Work atmosphere	1.72	0.51
Teaches respect	1.71	0.51
Caring staff	1.71	0.53
Well-managed	1.71	0.52
Range of subjects	1.69	0.56
Later advantage	1.64	0.58
Well-equipped	1.63	0.59
Good facilities	1.63	0.57
Career prospects	1.61	0.60
Exam results	1.61	0.60
Balanced education	1.60	0.58
Care and welfare	1.59	0.60
University entry	1.58	0.64
Pupil behaviour	1.52	0.63

The analysis turns first to the items which most frequently appeared as "very important" reasons for school choice (Table 7.9). These very important reasons for choosing a school, come from only two of the categories for choice criteria defined in Chapter 2 - security and academic outcomes - in almost equal measure. The variable "pupil happiness" heads the list, as predicted by previous work. One surprise is what this list does not include. None of the variables rated as very important can be classed as situational, organisational, or selective criteria. In not finding an important role for situational criteria, such as travel, this study is very much in a minority (e.g. West *et al.* 1994). However, many families represented by these findings are using, or intend to use, a fee-paying school. Their occupational class backgrounds show that they are not, in the main, working-class, and this study has also found parents to be more instrumental in making the choice than previously suggested. Since, other work has also suggested that middle-class families are less concerned with situational variables, while children are more concerned with them, it is perhaps not surprising that users of fee-paying schools are using the more adult, middle-class selection criteria described in Chapter 2 (e.g. Smedley 1995). It is also very likely, that by presenting respondents with only a limited range of reasons, previous researchers have ended up over-emphasising certain variables, as noted in Chapter 3.

More surprising is the absence of direct evidence of a strong desire for any kind of pupil selection. Single-sex, religion, ability, and social class are all missing as significant influences on school choice. It could be argued that variables such as "pupil behaviour" actually represent a type of unconscious code for class or social background, or that a desire for good "examination results" from a school is actually a desire for high ability pupils in an era of raw score performance indicators, but there are two arguments against this. First, such variables are linked by later analysis with others, that have no such underlying selective message. The school's departmental facilities, for example, are strongly linked to examination results, but do not appear to imply any kind of pupil selection at all. Secondly, several other variables, not rated as nearly as important overall, explicitly measure views on selection, including "clever pupils", "nice pupils", "single-sex", "middle-class pupils", "religion", "ethnic mix", and "the proportion of 'British' pupils". It could also be countered that families want selection, but are not willing to state it openly, as was suggested by the findings of Bagley (1995), but this view is both unparsimonious, and unsupported by the frank and unembarassed comments of many respondents on their forms, and later in the interviews. Less surprising, except perhaps to those researching school effectiveness and improvement, is the lack of the majority of the variables to do with school organisation and ethos. This finding has important implications for public choice theorists, since unless a market in schools operates in such a way that popular schools improve over time, the market can have no beneficial effect on standards of education. Families are only making a decision for the present cohort in school, and they want their child to go a school that is safe, and currently obtaining good examination results. Whether the school improves or fails at a later stage is not so relevant to them (see Chapter 11).

The next category of variables are those ranked as "important" in school choice, as shown in Table 7.10. To a large extent these confirm the conclusions drawn above. Many of these reasons still relate to academic outcomes and the child's happiness, but a number are also concerned with the ethos of the school. The first few selection variables appear, although most of these are in fact to do with anti-selection, such as a "good ethnic mix", and "tolerance of all religions". While it must be considered that this finding is partly a consequence of what Bagley (1995) called a "category misinterpretation", it does confirm that selection is not reported to be as popular among these families as other studies may have suggested (e.g. Fox 1989). The first situational variable to be mentioned, ease of travel, only just makes it into this category.

Table 7.10
Important reasons for choosing a school

Criterion	Mean	SD
Learning difficulty	1.47	0.73
Nice pupils	1.43	0.65
Visitors welcome	1.40	0.66
Responsiveness	1.40	0.64
Exam emphasis	1.38	0.69
Equal opportunities	1.38	0.71
Child's wishes	1.37	0.67
High expectations	1.36	0.68
Competition	1.35	0.69
Firm discipline	1.33	0.70
Traditional morality	1.32	0.73
Religious tolerance	1.29	0.77
Sports range	1.26	0.73
Small class	1.24	0.81
Promotes confidence	1.24	0.77
Sixth form	1.23	0.80
National Curriculum	1.21	0.76
Clubs	1.16	0.72
Character building	1.14	0.77
Progressive style	1.12	0.78
Traditional style	1.12	0.78
Proportion at 16+	1.11	0.77
Sport reputation	1.10	0.77
A particular sport	1.07	0.84
Ease of travel	1.03	0.74
Ethnic mix	1.02	0.77

Perhaps the most surprising results are shown in Table 7.11, where several situational reasons found to be popular or significant in other studies (e.g. Woods 1992), such as going to the same school as friends or relatives, are seen as less than important . These low ratings are even more interesting, since the results of this study include the views of children who are thought to be more concerned with such practical issues. Although, it is possible that this finding is a result of the relatively elevated occupational class of the sample, it also confirms the suspicion that previous studies may have exaggerated the importance of some reasons for choice, by ignoring others. The lists of "less than important" and "not important" reasons for choice are reproduced in full here, chiefly to make this point. The 73 reasons suggested in this study probably comprise the longest list used in any comparable study, and therefore currently give the best estimate of the effects of bias through omission in other studies. Another possible explanation of the difference is that the situational variables are only important very early on in the choice process, during the creation of the "choice set", and that at the time of the survey this moment had passed. Such an interpretation is discussed further in Chapter 9. The list of "less than important" criteria for school choice, in Table 7.11, is mostly made up of situational, and organisational variables. The relatively high standard deviations suggest that some of these reasons are more important to some groups of respondents than others, and this possibility is examined once the reasons have been reduced by principal components analysis.

Table 7.11
Less than important reasons for choosing a school

Criterion	Mean	SD
Friends at school	0.96	0.80
Lenient discipline	0.95	0.72
Head style	0.94	0.77
State dissatisfaction	0.94	0.84
A particular subject	0.94	0.74
Useful social contacts	0.93	0.76
Mixed	0.93	0.82
Strict uniform	0.93	0.77
Lower fees	0.88	0.79
Higher status	0.88	0.81
Clever pupils	0.84	0.75
Fees help	0.82	0.82
Music reputation	0.82	0.74
Small school	0.76	0.80
Sibling at school	0.63	0.75
Boarding facilities	0.61	0.82
Attractive buildings	0.59	0.66
School bus	0.54	0.74

Finally, the least important criteria for school choice are shown in Table 7.12. The clear majority of the reasons rated as "not important" relate to pupil selection in some form. As well as containing all three of the variables relating to Welsh issues, this list shows that very little support exists for single-sex education, or for selection by social class, religion, or ethnicity. This is an important finding, especially as it comes from a study focusing on fee-paying schools, and one which needs to be examined seriously in the light of previous findings. Of course, despite the indications above, respondents might genuinely want selection and not be prepared to report it, but the absence of any such reports cannot be used to argue that selection is wanted. Also of interest is the finding that despite the high proportion of private school users in the sample, a family tradition of using a particular school is of no importance. This result can act as a corrective to those whose research concentrated on the elite private schools, but whose findings have been quoted as indicative of the whole sector (e.g. Fox 1989). This issue is discussed more fully in Chapter 10.

Table 7.12
Unimportant reasons for choosing a school

Criterion	Mean	SD
Mostly middle-class	0.49	0.64
Religion	0.47	0.70
No Welsh ethos	0.46	0.68
Professionals	0.46	0.65
Welsh language	0.38	0.61
Single-sex	0.34	0.67
Mostly British	0.34	0.64
Family tradition	0.32	0.60
Welsh ethos	0.27	0.52
Head gender	0.19	0.51

In summary, although various criteria may be found to be more significant to some groups of respondents than others, families are chiefly concerned with security, school resources, and academic outcomes, preferring tolerance and a pleasant ethos to selection, and convenience. These respondents express no great concern over management or discipline. The next section looks at the links between the 73 reasons listed here. It does so not by merely collapsing them into smaller groupings based upon theory and common sense, but by measuring the size of the correlations between them, and so uncovering the links in the minds of the respondents, rather than unwittingly confirming the prejudices of the researcher (Chapter 3).

Relationships between the reasons for choice

This section looks at the relationships between the choice variables listed above. These relationships are defined in terms of their correlations - the extent to which respondents tend to answer any two of them in the same way. As assessed by Pearson's r, all of the 73 choice variables show a correlation with several others, each of which would be significant at the 5% level if only one coefficient had been calculated. This suggests that there is common variance between groups of these variables, but the large number of respondents means that coefficients as low as 0.06 are tagged as significant. In order to reduce the number of associations, this section only considers coefficients of absolute value 0.3162 and above, so that 10% of the variance is common to the two variables concerned. This common variance is of a large enough size to suggest the existence of an underlying and unifying explanation. Although explanations of the common variance to be found in smaller associations might also be valid, their explanatory power would be weak, since the common variance they would explain could be as little as one third of one percent. All responses are included in the calculations, fee-paying and state-funded, parents and pupils.

For 20 of the 73 variables, all 72 of their correlation coefficients are below |0.3162|, and since these variables show so little variance in common with any others, they are omitted from the principal components analysis. In addition, 13 of these 20 variables were rated overall as being "not important" or "less than important", and so they will generally be excluded from any further analysis, since they have been shown to be neither important to selection of a school by themselves, nor to be part of a larger underlying concept of any real explanatory value. The most important variable of all "pupil happiness" also does not share much common variance with any other reason for school choice, which is in itself a finding of great interest, since it has been assumed in previous work that this reason is really a conglomeration of other contributory reasons (Coldron and Boulton 1991). Pupil happiness is, in fact, unrelated to any other reason for school choice, and one possible explanation of this is that there is so little variance in the responses to this question. This variable has the lowest standard deviation, as nearly all respondents gave it the highest rating. It is probable that happiness is an imprecise and non-technical concept which, although seen as important by all respondents, they may have differing interpretations of how to achieve. It is therefore of little use in explaining school choice until it can be examined in more detail in the light of interviews. This variable, and six other "important" but uncorrelated variables are excluded from the principal components analysis, but are later fitted into the resulting model as far as possible, as reflects their importance to the process of school choice.

Ten further variables correlate strongly only with one of the other ten. The provision of a sixth form is linked to the proportion of pupils at 16+, a good ethnic mix is linked to tolerance of all religions, help with school fees is linked to low school fees, having mostly middle class pupils is linked to having clever pupils, and provision for Welsh language teaching is linked to wanting a Welsh ethos. These variables are excluded from the principal components analysis, but are then fitted into the resulting model as far as possible, in the form of five concepts: sixth form, tolerance, fees, selection, and Welsh. A further six variables correlate strongly with only one other variable, which in turn is related to several others. These six are also omitted, and are subsequently correlated with the principal components which emerge, with interesting results. The remaining 37 variables all show high correlations to at least two other variables. Each was linked to every other one of the 37, either directly, or through linkage to a common variable. These are the variables that are used in the initial PCA. However it should be noted that the PCA has also been run with all 73 variables, then deleting the complex variables and minor factors and the outcome is broadly similar.

Seven factors underlying the reasons for choice

The reduced set of 37 variables was used in a principal components analysis, with orthogonal rotation to a Varimax solution, which yielded seven factors, accounting for 59% of the total variance in the responses, which is a reasonable figure since there is obviously some measurement error, and a recent review of school choice studies in the UK suggests that choice is frequently idiosyncratic anyway (Smedley 1995). The first figures in each of the next seven sections, such as Table 7.13, show the loadings of the variables for each of the seven factors, including all those with a value of |0.3162| or greater. The seven factors appear in descending order of the total amount of variance that they explained. However, this amount is not necessarily linked to their importance in the process of choosing a school. Those factors extracted later are generally linked to fewer variables than those extracted earlier, and explain less of the variance, regardless of the importance of those variables to the respondents. For this reason, the mean importance of each variable is also shown again for convenience, coded as Very important, Important, Less than important, and Not important. Assuming that the measurement error in the variables is around 30% - a miserly estimate as the split-half reliability was over 0.9 - loadings of 0.84 and above can be seen as representing "pure" factor variables (Chapter 5). The abbreviated names, such as the "sports factor", given to each factor are provisional, and intended to be mnemonic rather than fully descriptive at this stage. A factor score is calculated for each respondent, based upon their ratings of the reasons associated with each factor, and this new score is used in the later analysis instead of the "simple" elementary reasons. In this way, 37 variables are replaced by seven factors. As explained above, a further 36 variables were omitted from the initial PCA as they showed too little common variance with other variables, however, it is interesting to note that nine of these show correlations of greater than |0.3162| with at least one of the seven factors, and these are also discussed below.

The sports factor

Table 7.13
Sports factor (20.1% of the variance)

Variable	Loading	Rating
Range of sports	0.76	I
A particular sport	0.76	I
Reputation for sport	0.75	I
Useful contacts	0.55	L
Boarding facilities	0.52	L
Progressive style	0.46	I
Social status	0.44	L
Range of clubs	0.43	I
Visitors welcomed	0.34	I
Nice pupils	0.33	I

The first of the seven factors extracted is clearly related to sporting activities at the choice school (Table 7.13). The high correlations between the three sport variables - range of sports, sporting reputation of the school, and a particular sport - and their large loadings suggest that they, and the factor itself, are in fact measuring the same thing, after allowing for the inevitable measurement error, which is why the factor is provisionally named "sports". This factor is important in choosing a school, but none of the variables related to it are in the "very important" category. One reason for this, suggested by the relatively high standard deviations for some of the variables, is that this factor is of more relevance to some respondents only. It concerns the provision of non-academic, or extra-curricular, activities, chiefly sports, which, along with a progressive style of education, are more relevant to children than adults in this study. The inclusion of "boarding facilities" does not imply that this factor is only of concern to those considering boarding, since this variable has a low loading, but because boarding is more commonly associated with fee-paying schools, and all state-funded schools in the survey are day schools, this factor is surely of more relevance to choice within the private sector.

As stated above, this sports factor is more relevant to children, and Table 7.14 shows the surprisingly large difference between the mean ratings from each generation in this respect. Sports are almost irrelevant to parents. The factor is also significantly more important in those families where the child has the major role in choosing, but less important in families from Year 1, in which only the parents took part in the survey, presumably for the same reasons. This finding is the first indication that the factors may not represent different compound reasons used to varying extents by all families, but that some factors may stand for a particular group, or sub-set, of choosers.

Table 7.14
Rating of sports by generation

	Rating of sports	Standard deviation
Parent	-0.72	0.95
Child	+0.57	0.93
t-value	DF	Prob.
-16.81	584.44	0.000

The sports factor is more relevant for boarders (Table 7.15). This finding provides the first indication that different factors may apply to different types of schools, as well as to different types of families. Since the sports factor is related to boarding, it is not surprising that it is also rated as more important by respondents with all of the characteristics so far associated with boarding, including families with boys in Year 8, where the father attended a private school, and who make more visits, or read more prospectuses before choosing a school. To some extent, these findings are consistent with those of David *et al.* (1995).

Table 7.15
Rating of sports, by day or boarding

	Rating of sports	Standard deviation
Day	-.091	1.14
Boarding	+0.67	0.96
t-value	DF	Prob.
-5.00	53.38	0.000

Table 7.16 lists some of the uncorrelated variables, left out of the original PCA, but which now show a correlation of at least |0.3162| with the sports factor which emerged. The majority are also rated as more important to children than adults, and the first three situational variables have also been found to be more important to children in previous studies (e.g. Echols *et al.* 1990). This finding confirms that

163

the sports factor is one used as a criterion for choice, or justification, more by children than adults.

Table 7.16
Correlation of sports and omitted variables

	Sports
Having friends at the same school	+0.38
School runs a bus to your area	+0.38
Ease of travel	+0.33
Good ethnic mix	+0.34
Lenient discipline	+0.36
Reputation for music	+0.38
Lower fees	+0.32
Help with the fees	+0.37

The inclusion of "music" in the list above confirms that the factor is to do with extra-curricular activities in general, of which sports may be merely the most significant. The link to fees also confirms the initial feeling that this factor is likely to be of more relevance to the larger, more expensive traditional foundation schools, which tend to be better equipped, to take boarders, and to be part of the Assisted Places Scheme (but see Chapter 10).

This last point is backed up by analysis of the importance of the sports factor for the users of different school types. It is much more relevant to the choice of traditional fee-paying and state-funded schools, which can offer the facilities, staff, and grounds for many activities, than to any other school types (Table 7.17). In fact, its importance is in almost direct proportion to the standard of facilities available at the various schools. The sports factor is particularly irrelevant for users of grass-roots schools, which is probably just as well since their facilities for sports, and their resources for the other traditional extra-curricular activities are almost non-existent (see Chapter 6).

Table 7.17
Rating of sports by type of school

School	Sports	Grass roots	
Grass roots	-0.96		
Feeder	-0.22		
Stand alone	-0.16		
Catholic	-0.05		
State	-0.03	*	
Traditional	+0.18	*	
Source	DF	F ratio	Prob.
Between	5	4.2663	0.0008

Table 7.18
Welfare factor (10.4% of the variance)

Variable	Loading	Rating
No bullying	0.68	V
Caring staff	0.61	V
Visitors welcome	0.55	I
Nice pupils	0.54	I
Well-behaved pupils	0.54	V
Pastoral care	0.50	V
Good teaching	0.50	V
Work atmosphere	0.47	V
Range of subjects	0.44	V
Well-equipped	0.34	V

The second factor, welfare, is clearly "very important" in school choice, possibly because it is seen as equally important by parents and children, and so it displays less variation by sub-groups of respondents than the sports factor (Table 7.18). Those variables with particularly high loadings are concerned with the welfare and safety of the pupil. This factor represents a choice of school in which the parents feel their child will be safe, and allowed to get on with an education, since they will be taken care of. It is also a school in which parents are welcomed, and in which the other pupils are not much of a threat. As such, it is more important for families with children in Year 1, who may feel that the child requires more protection at that age, although it must also be remembered that the Year 1 respondents represent only parents from fee-paying schools.

Table 7.19
Welfare by school type

School	Welfare	Stand alone	State	Traditional
Stand alone	0.10			
State	0.14			
Traditional	0.16			
Feeder	0.26			
Catholic	0.27			
Grass roots	0.88	*	*	*
Source	DF	F ratio	Prob.	
Between	5	3.1422	0.0083	

The welfare factor is of more relevance to families in which the father has no degree, and who use visits as the main source of information, but consider fewer schools. These characteristics are linked to families with working class occupational backgrounds in Chapter 6, and are also those particularly associated with the users of grass-roots schools, so it is not surprising that the welfare factor is more important to them than to users of the larger schools (Table 7.19). To some extent, this is a contrasting factor to that of sports, which is less significant for families from Year 1, and more favoured by users of large schools.

The outcomes factor

The third factor, outcomes, is also "very important" in school choice. The variables with high loadings in Table 7.20 make it clear that parents and pupils want high quality provision of services from their schools, and that the desired outcome of such provision is an advantage in terms of certification, later career trajectory, or social standing. This is the factor upon which performance indicators, in the form of league tables of examination results, are based in the UK. When policy makers and researchers speak of "school improvement", it is these kind of outcomes that they generally seek to improve.

Table 7.20
Outcomes factor (5.0% of the variance)

Variable	Loading	Rating
Exam emphasis	0.64	I
Exam results	0.62	V
University entrance	0.60	V
Career prospects	0.60	V
Later advantage	0.50	V
Social status	0.44	L
High expectations	0.44	I
Teachers' qualifications	0.41	V
Competitive environment	0.33	I

The outcomes factor is more relevant to families with a local minority religion, such as Islam, who also find league tables more useful than visits in selecting a school, and who, in fact, make fewer visits than others (Table 7.21).

Table 7.21
Outcomes by family religion

Religion	Outcomes	Protestant	None
Protestant	-.030		
None	-0.08		
Catholic	+0.20		
Minority	+0.55	*	*
Source	DF	F ratio	Prob.
Between	3	7.7642	0.0001

This factor is forward-looking, being less concerned with the school itself than with what happens after school, and so it is not surprising that interest in the

166

examination and career outcomes of school rises almost directly with the age of the child in question.

The variable measuring the assertion that private schools produce more self-confident pupils, was left out of the principal components analysis, but it shows a correlation of +0.32 with the outcomes factor which emerged. It is an outcome in itself, but since it can only apply to private schools, it suggests that it is private school users who may be slightly more concerned with outcomes. Most fee-payers probably believe that they are buying an academic advantage, and so making an investment for the future (Chapter 10). In fact, although it is true that users of proprietary schools, among whom there are a higher proportion of families with minority religions, rate outcomes more highly, those using grass-roots schools stand out in their neglect of this factor, with state-funded schools somewhere in the middle, which again shows the danger of making simple generalisations about all fee-paying schools (Table 7.22).

Table 7.22
Outcomes by school type

School	Outcomes	Grass roots	Feeder	State	Traditional
Grass roots	-1.3				
Feeder	-0.20	*			
State	-0.16	*			
Traditional	-0.14	*			
Catholic	-008	*			
Stand alone	+0.35	*	*	*	*
Source	DF	F ratio	Prob.		
Between	5	10.6447	0.0000		

The tradition factor

Table 7.23
Tradition factor (4.2% of the variance)

Variable	Loading	Rating
Traditional style	0.70	I
Strict uniform	0.67	L
Traditional morality	0.57	I
Firm discipline	0.54	I
Competitive environment	0.50	I
Well-behaved pupils	0.42	V
High expectations	0.41	I

The fourth factor, tradition, is only of moderate importance overall (Table 7.23), perhaps because it really only appeals to adults. Two of the variables with high loadings contained the word "traditional" on the survey form; a "traditional style of education", and the "school teaches traditional morality". These, along with firm discipline and strict uniform code, probably appeal to the restorationists, reminding them of their own school days, or at least an image of schools which they retain from that era (Chapter 8).

Children show significantly less interest in uniform, morality, and competition, and more interest in progressive education, tolerance, and lenient discipline (Table 7.24). As the tradition factor is more relevant to parents than children, it not surprising that it is rated as least important in families in which pupils have the major role in making the choice. Tradition is also rated more highly by families with a child in Year 1, whose responses only represent those of parents, and less highly by the "young adults" in Year 11, presumably for the same reason.

Table 7.24
Tradition by generation

	Mean	SD
Parent	+0.44	0.826
Child	-0.44	1.114
t-value	DF	Prob.
11.08	573.89	0.000

Tradition is rated more highly by users of the smaller fee-paying schools, including Catholic schools, where Catholic parents have already been seen to have a larger role in the choice process, as well as grass-roots and feeder proprietary schools (Table 7.25). Of the first four factors, each has been rated more highly by users of different types of schools, and every type of school has at least one factor with which it closely linked. This is both an interesting research finding in its own right (worthy of more investigation), and a further confirmation of the fruitfulness of the typology of schools derived in Chapter 6.

Table 7.25
Tradition by school type

School	Tradition	Stand alone	Traditional	State
Stand alone	-0.18			
Traditional	-0.15			
State	-0.10			
Feeder	+0.30	*	*	
Grass roots	+0.30			
Catholic	+0.52	*	*	*
Source	DF	F ratio	Prob.	
Between	5	5.8231	0.0000	

The safety factor

This is the third of the very important factors. The unifying concept underlying the linked variables is not immediately apparent, nor is it entirely clear how it differs from the welfare factor, to which it should bear no statistical relationship, by definition (Table 7.26). It could be statistical artefact. The loadings for both the "pupil safety", and the "school is well-managed" variables are high enough to suggest that they are almost pure factor variables. Perhaps the difference is that whereas the welfare factor is a characteristic of the people in the school, such as "nice" pupils and "caring" staff, safety is more to do with school organisation.

Table 7.26
Safety factor (3.6% of the variance)

Variable	Loading	Rating
Pupil safety	0.65	V
Well-managed	0.65	V
Teaches respect	0.60	V
Later advantage	0.40	V
Good facilities	0.38	V
Teachers' qualifications	0.37	V
Traditional morality	0.33	I

Safety is less important to pupils, especially those in Year 11, while it is more important to parents, particularly those using state schools. It is likely that this factor chiefly concerns those families with a child still in primary school, whether state-funded or feeder proprietary. Whether any great meaning can be attached to this factor in isolation will emerge as a result of the interviews in the following chapters.

The size factor

The sixth factor, size, or more strictly, avoidance of large schools, shows the link in people's minds between "small schools", "small classes", and "dissatisfaction with state-funded provision". State-funded schools, and their classes, are frequently seen as too large (Table 7.27). The strong association between these variables suggests that this factor is a reason for choosing a private education in general, rather than a specific fee-paying school. This would partly explain the relatively low rating, and high standard deviations, of these variables, since not all families in the survey were considering a private school. The variable measuring the notion that private schools produce self-confident pupils, was left out of the principal components analysis, but shows a correlation of +0.32 with the size factor which emerged. This reinforces the suggestion that this factor is used to distinguish between the state and the private sector, rather than to decide upon a particular school.

Table 7.27
Size factor (3.2% of the variance)

Variable	Loading	Rating
Small school	0.76	L
Small class	0.73	I
Dissatisfaction with state	0.55	L

A small school is more important for families with children in Year 1, probably because it is more important to parents than children. Families looking for a small school also tend to consider more schools, as do users of private schools, confirming the relationship between the two groups. This factor is of much less relevance to families using the larger state funded and traditional foundation schools, but it is significantly more important for users of all private schools than users of state schools (Table 7.28). This factor can therefore be seen as a sector determinant.

Table 7.28
Size by school type

School	Size	State	Traditional
State	-0.55		
Traditional	-0.07	*	
Feeder	+0.25	*	
Stand alone	+0.37	*	*
Catholic	+0.42	*	*
Grass roots	+0.53	*	
Source	DF	F ratio	Prob.
Between	5	12.4843	0.0000

The resources factor

This is the fourth, and final, "very important" factor - the material provision and resources of the school - and it is a surprising one, given the poor facilities of most of the schools in the survey (Table 7.29). It would therefore be a good factor to use to discriminate between school types, since such descriptions as "well-equipped" can really only be applied to state-funded and traditional foundation schools. The other four types of school are relatively poorly equipped, with restricted facilities and curricula. Unlike size, it would be a school, not a sector, determinant.

Table 7.29
Resources factor (3.0% of the variance)

Variable	Loading	Rating
Well-equipped	0.58	V
Good facilities	0.46	V
Range of subjects	0.44	V
Range of clubs	0.44	V
Good teaching	0.30	V

The resources factor is more relevant to adults than children, which is also surprising, since equipment and facilities are just the sort of practical "holiday camp" reasons one might expect children to rate highly. It is also more important to families in which the parents have a degree; who use more than one source of information about schools, and who consider more schools. As suggested above, it is rated more highly by those using state-funded and traditional fee-paying schools, and less by proprietary and Catholic school users, and much less by the grass-roots families (Table 7.30). In fact, as with the sports factor, the rank order of the factor scores by school type, from grass-roots to traditional foundation, almost perfectly matches the relative resources and perhaps also the prestige of the various schools.

Table 7.30
Resources by school type

School	Resources	Grass roots	Catholic
Grass roots	-1.62		
Catholic	-0.28	*	
Stand alone	0.00	*	
Feeder	+0.11	*	
State	+0.21	*	*
Traditional	+0.25	*	*
Source	DF	F ratio	Prob.
Between	5	12.1031	0.0000

Conclusion

Even with the heuristics used here, the data are too large and rich for all associations to be considered in the space of one chapter, and even this neglects the fascinating subject of those associations which were not found, but which might have been expected. For example, there is no difference in the rating of any factors by occupational class or area of residence, which is, in itself, a surprising result. When looking at the means or frequencies of different sub-groups, many possible relationships are present, and a decision has to be made which to follow up. Those avenues generally ignored are where the link has an obvious and uninteresting explanation, such as the association between school type and year group, or where the link concerns a very specialised group. Some of the findings of specific relevance to fee-paying schools are discussed in Chapter 10.

In summary, although, the process of choice is commonly seen as a joint one, both generations emphasise their own role in it. Older children have a greater lone input to the process, but there is also a tendency for families about to make a choice to see it as a joint process, while those who have made the choice see it more clearly as having been made by one party or the other. On the other hand, the role of the child generally increases during the process of choice. A personal acquaintance is usually the most important source of information about a prospective school, but families considering a boarding school use more prospectuses, and make more actual visits. The differences could be that boarding families live further away, and are not plugged in to a local grapevine, so they use literature to help decide which schools to visit. The visit is perhaps more important in respect to the school as a place of residence than as a place of learning. Those living in rural areas make more use of prospectuses, perhaps to cut down on unnecessary travel, while examination results are more important to older children, and to girls, who are more likely to be day pupils. Families, in general, appear to seriously consider two schools, although they may previously have read about more than this, but to visit only one of these, on average. This suggests a two-step whittling down process, of first creating a choice set, and then reducing it by research.

Over half of the reasons for choosing a school, originally suggested to respondents, can be reasonably well summarised by seven factors. These are:

Safety and organisation, a very important factor, used by parents, particularly those considering state schools.

Welfare and happiness, a very important factor, used by less highly educated families, with younger children, considering small schools, such as the grass-roots establishments, and relying on visits.

Outcomes, a very important factor, used by families with minority religions, and older children, particularly those considering stand-alone proprietary schools, and relying on League tables of results.

Resources, a very important factor, used by highly educated parents, considering large schools, whether state or private, and who consider more schools than most.

Tradition, an important factor, used by parent-dominated families, especially Catholic ones, with younger children, considering small primary and preparatory schools.

Sports, other ECA, convenience criteria, and cost, all combine to create a factor which is reasonably important for children, particularly boys, considering state schools, and for parents considering traditional boarding schools, and relying on visits and prospectuses.

Size, a less than important factor overall, used by parents, of younger children, considering smaller schools in the private sector, who have rejected the state sector, and who consider more schools than most.

There is little place for pupil selection, school organisation, or convenience in this seven factor model. Some of the factors, such as size, are more clearly sector determinants, more relevant to choice of a type of school, or to a decision as to whether to use fee-paying education. Others, such as outcomes, are more relevance to individual school choice within either sector. This suggests that there may be three steps in the process of choice, with the choice of a school type predating the creation of the choice set, and the two steps described above. Families might choose the fee-paying sector, for the traditional education that they had or would have liked, perhaps represented by grammar schools, and not for modern curricula, progressive teaching methods, or child-centred discipline. Such a traditional education is thought to produce adults with valuable personal and social advantages. Families, in general, also seek smaller schools and classes. Individual schools are chosen for their academic provision, the safety of the pupil, career prospects, and their extra-curricular activities, particularly in the case of boarding schools

The attitude of parents and their children to five of the seven choice factors are quite clearly different from each other. The fact that the differences are so clear in terms of the generation of the respondents, and that some factors are so highly rated by one group while being almost irrelevant to the other, suggests that the factors extracted may be more than mere items on a check-list for potential consumers. Some may actually represent different categories of consumers. Parents are more concerned with a desire for a traditional type of education, the safety and welfare of their child, the size of the school, and its material provision. Since the size factor also represents dissatisfaction with state-funded education, this provides evidence that it is the parents who are making the choice of sector, and that some factors are more relevant to choice of sector, while others are more relevant to choice of a specific school within that sector. Children seem more concerned with the quality of extra-curricular activities, and the social value of a fee-paying school. The social value factor is only really of relevance to fee-paying schools, and may be the child's way of justifying the choice of this type of school.

The process of choice then, involves parents looking back to the schooling that they had, as well as looking forward to the child's life after school. As they relinquish their child to a school, they are concerned for the child's well-being in an institution which has a large proportion of older children. In response they prefer, and where possible actively seek, a well-run small school with a family atmosphere, where their child will be noticed, and mixing with other pupils that are seen as desirable. Children are the ones who will actually be going to the school day to day, and they also want this experience to be socially pleasant, and fun, which for them is more practical and immediate. They do not want to be bullied, and they do want the school to be easy to get to, but above all, it must offer fun activities and sports, which for them usually means a much larger school than their parents envisage. Although children are also concerned with later life, this is expressed in terms of social networking, as much as academic results. The sports factor, with its association to progressive style and good boarding facilities has a practical everyday theme, and may be seen as a *portmanteau* of reasons for a child to choose a traditional fee-paying school.

This ends the analysis of the bulk of the survey data. The findings summarised here are laid alongside data from the interviews in the next three chapters, in order to help explain the patterns and stories present, and to move away from talking about tendencies and probabilities, to listening to actual families and their narratives.

Part Three
THE PROCESS OF CHOICE

8 Family influences on choice

Introduction

It might be imagined that just as everyone is supposedly an art critic, everyone is an "expert" on education. Everyone has been to school, and that experience is likely to have helped them form opinions about educational issues, even though they have only ever seen the "front of house", to use the stage analogy from Lortie (1975). It is therefore hardly surprising that some families, while officially encouraged to be "consumers" of education, as described in Chapter 1, approach their new choice as a matter of nostalgia as much as a matter of calculated outcomes. For example, faced with a question on the quality of facilities, one parent in the study stated that "they are pretty good compared to what I had". This finding is similar to those of West *et al.* (1994) who reported that parents relied on memories of their old school days in creating the values that they used in judging current information about schools.

In using their own knowledge of the time that they were at school, the data here suggests that parents are using historical rather than current criteria, in making a choice for a child today (Gorard 1996$_d$). This yearning for tradition or a past system (Macbeth *et al.* 1986) may therefore contribute to conservatism and restorationism in market-based schools. Tradition appeals to those who enjoyed or benefited from their time at school, but other parents who may feel that they were let down in their educational opportunities may also select schools that are unlike their own. In this way, school choice today can be influenced by the parents' education, for better or worse, and this influence is described in the first section of this chapter. Some parents intending to use a state-funded school make long term plans concerning residence and primary school choice so that the child will be eligible for a currently over-subscribed secondary school, while some parents intending to use a private school, decide on the school while the child is still an infant. Still others decide to send a subsequent child to a school which was beneficial for an elder sibling, sometimes after a gap of seven or more years, and these matters are discussed in the second section. All of these stories are found in the interviews, and they all have a common theme which is that choice of a secondary school is made a long time before the child is eleven years old and is based on knowledge which, in many instances, is years out of date at the time of transfer.

The reflection effect

One link between parent's and children's schools was shown in Chapter 6, such that parents who had been to private schools themselves are more likely to be using traditional and proprietary fee-paying schools for their children. This is clear statistical evidence of a generational connection. The seven major factors used in choosing a school are described in Chapter 7 and many of these have a generational aspect to them as well. Of these, provision for sports, with its link to lenient discipline and a progressive style, is rated more highly by the children, whereas tradition, with links to firm discipline, uniform, morality and also small class size are rated higher by parents. These findings indicate that parents are concerned with a more conservative mode of schooling than their children and the likely explanation for this lies in their own experience of schools, which acts as a benchmark against which existing schools are measured. In fact, over 70% of the parents interviewed made at least one spontaneous comment in another context that related the child's and their own schooling. There were also some strong unprompted comments about tradition and restoration on the survey forms ranging from:

> I am totally non-interested in the negative aims of current education, and wish my children to pursue, as closely as possible, the traditional liberal education of the well-adjusted and confident citizen

through

> I confess to being a supporter of grammar schools and 11+ testing

to simply

> Bring back Grammar schools.

In addition to selection by ability, which was likely to be more prevalent when today's parents were at school, they want "stricter discipline in schools". Standards of behaviour are seen as having declined, with young people today, apart from the child in question in most cases, not showing sufficient respect for others. What is needed are "higher morals and a respect for other pupils, and people and their property; both inside school premises and outside, especially when in school uniform. In short, a return to old-fashioned values - schools today are far too lax". The parents in the sample generally show less interest than children in either religious and racial tolerance as well as progressive styles of pedagogy, again using emotional appeals to a bygone era. One parent in the survey rates better career prospects as not important since the child is a girl, saying - "I hope my girls will be housewives".

It was a father who originally used the term "reflection" that is used as the heading for this section, by saying "I mean, I, the education you give your child is a direct reflection of the education you had yourself", and when asked to explain further continued:

> If you went to a prep school and it was lousy, then you went to a secondary school which was quite good and you were struggling to catch up, you would always say, right I'm never... this happened at my age. I'm going to give that child of mine the best possible start because it's so difficult to catch up. If he's given a good grounding in all the 3 Rs, he's going to get into secondary school, and be able to at least keep up. Because I had a lousy primary education, all my secondary school education was spent catching up. I was determined this wasn't going to happen to Nigel. And I think however, if you went to a very good one, you'd say right my son's going to go there or whatever. I think it's directly reflected in your type of education.

In a similar vein, he said "I'm a believer in coeducation, probably a reflection that I went to an all boys school [and didn't like it]". He had wanted to be a veterinary surgeon, but had to settle for agricultural college, and has recently become unemployed in middle-age. Although he realises that some parents may select schools because of a good experience in their formative years, he is clearly selecting one as a reaction to his own disappointment. This father appreciates the obviously traditional aspects of some of the fee-paying schools he has visited, even where these conflict with his memory of his own school.

> I like the, it's steeped in tradition really, I like the old traditions which offer... traditional teaching. I like Christian schools with a good Christian philosophy. And I really disliked Hereward because of its total lack of tradition. And the sort of philosophy really, I didn't like the... which just seemed to be geared to being like a sausage factory. For instance, I find out about the early morning assembly and whether there's a religious input into that, and whether they are in uniforms or gowns or what. I also ask about any problems they have, particularly with drugs and what their attitude is towards that and how they sort it out. I find out as much about the extra-curricular activities, things like CCF [Combined Cadet Force], which I'm rather a kind of fan of, and all the other things like rowing, sports activities. For instance, I, at Oakley the headmasters office was in a tremendous old building, creaky oak, wonderful...And cabinets and honours boards. But you didn't feel like you did in the old days, you didn't feel that the kids were in any trepidation, in any fear, that they were totally natural. You just get the feeling that they're happy children. There's no sort of... I remember at school you were always looking over your shoulder to see if a prefect was coming to clout you one. But there's none of that sort of feeling. I'm sorry I'm not being very...There was a very happy relationship between pupils and the staff, it's a very easy relationship. I mean, OK, there's a certain amount of formality, that the children call the teachers 'sir' which is fine and I think that's good. But also they feel that teachers are completely accessible to talk to. There's no sort of ... I know the word but I can't think of it. There's no barrier.

He realises that credentials and qualifications are important both from his own experience, and his lack of them, but at the same time he also believes that they are coming to mean less and less about the person who has them.

> I just feel it is more and more important. I mean, my folks used to tell me that it was important. I wish I'd taken more notice of them. If only I had a better education, which wasn't the folks' fault, they did what they could at the time. My ambition was to become a vet. Vets, it's always been difficult to become a vet, you've got to do well, very very well, which is an absolute nonsense. Which is why I don't think academic results are the be all and end all. You sit and you take your GCSE and simply everyone gets A grades. Apparently it's similar with A levels. I gather that some universities take all A's and some people still can't write English.

This father introduces two themes relevant to a "reflection" account of school choice - the love of tradition, with its denigration of standards today, and the direct comparison of the educational experiences of both generations in the family. The term reflection is appropriate and so used in this book since it is as ambiguous as the role of the past experience in choice. A reflection can be seen as almost an identity, in the case of the more typical reproduction model of family influence, or it can be almost an opposite, as in a mirror, in which case it describes the parents, as here, who want more for their children, starting with avoidance of the mistakes that their own parents made. Either way, a reflection is a very close relationship to the education of a previous generation.

Love of tradition

Tradition, as exemplified by uniform, or discipline, is important in choice for parents, but not all parents have exactly the same views of which traditions are desirable. As an example, one mother shows a less symbolic and more pragmatic desire for a traditional education than the father described above. Indeed, several mothers suggested that it was their husbands who were more concerned with tradition than themselves, providing an indication of traditional gender roles in choice. Having been to a state school herself, and left at the earliest opportunity, this particular mother is not looking for polished floors, or display cabinets of sporting trophies, but complains that there have been too many changes recently in state education leading to low morale and industrial strife, just like in nursing - her own profession. In relation to the National Curriculum she comments:

> I don't know a great deal about it, there's been so many changes in education in the last few years. I'm not as well up in it as I probably should be. I'm very old-fashioned. I don't believe in calculators, they've got to be able to say their tables and to be able to read. Those are the basics. They've got to get the basics. I still know my tables now and going from here to Orange school every morning reciting our tables, really. And the reading had to be done every night and signed.

A similar discontent with "trendy teaching" was voiced by another parent. She moved her son to a private school, after a state primary education which she ended up dissatisfied with. The father has a state school background, and both parents left school at the earliest opportunity. Her family are looking for something that reminds them of a "proper school".

> The more I got to know the school, the more I felt they weren't bringing the best out in him. I remember collecting him one day, he didn't know that I was going to take him and he was playing with sand when all the rest were in the main hall having assembly. I said 'what on earth is Richard doing out here'? Oh they didn't want to go to assembly so we let them play outside. Well I'm not like that. To me you know he had to conform and do what the rest did. They were giving him too much space. It wasn't until he left there that they then just let out that it was very rare that they actually managed to get him to sit down.

She concludes with her reason for using a private school, presented almost as an excuse - "we are paying for an education that has now disappeared, what his father had as a child, sitting in rows". Similarly, another mother attended a state school, but is also pining for an education that no longer exists. She was enchanted by one school that had "little wooden desks with lift up lids that remind me of school and traditional values". She also emphasises discipline, believing in corporal punishment for her daughter, and uses a belt since "they need to know they've been hit". Her argument for using one of the most expensive and exclusive schools in Britain is partly based upon the following series of questions, but it also directly links the size of classes to standards of behaviour:

> When you drive through the streets of Cardiff, and you look at them all at the bus stops and you see how the girls are dressed and their behaviour and their short skirts up to here, and their actions and their trainers. If a school can't get children to wear their uniform correctly then how much control do you have over children of an age when they definitely need to be on a short rope?.... How do you control them outside of school afterwards, if you can't make then turn up as they should? It's not very encouraging when you see the size of the classes, you see how these teenagers are behaving outside school, what you see in the papers in the news, the one-off things.

One father attended a grammar school and initially felt uneasy using a private school for his daughter, while his wife, who had attended a local fee-paying school, did not. He was encouraged to use private by being posted abroad, and by the emotive appeal of tradition in a fee-paying school. He describes being in a corridor, and feeling at home, and "converted immediately from an anti-private school stance, almost by a whiff of pheromone". He also feels that state schools today are not as good as when he was young, and so his story acts as an introduction to those families making explicit comparisons between their own schooling and their child's.

Because of her starting a private school in Norway, which was the only way she could get an English education, and monitoring what's happening to education in the UK, I'm a lecturer and my wife is a teacher, so we're not talking tittle-tattle, we realised that the system in the UK is going down the tube. Luckily enough we've got the funds to opt out.

He feels that the family is "purchasing a right, not an advantage - a right denied by the government. They are putting her level of achievement at risk, and so we are buying the risk out". Several accounts suggest that families are reluctant users of private education, but are willing to pay (and in some cases suffer the hardships described in Chapter 10), for a school that relates in some way to their own, or to their memory of their own. This is one of the main reasons for private school choice which emerges from the survey and from the interviews. It may well be that private schools appeal to those who are attracted by old-fashioned schools and schooling. In fact, one mother, one of the few intending to use her old school for her daughter, decided against it in the end, because it was no longer the same as it had been thirty years ago.

Up until a week ago I wanted her to go to Henry's, apart from I'd been there, I knew it, I knew the ropes. It doesn't seem the same place. Obviously it's not 40 years ago, nearly 30 years? It's a long time. The whole feel of the place is not what I remember. It doesn't seem as academic, put it that way.

Intergenerational comparisons

Since parents clearly consider their own schooling in making a choice for the next generation, it is not surprising that direct comparisons between the two eras appear in several interviews. Like the father mentioned first, one mother wanted her children, who had encountered difficulties in local primary schools, to have opportunities that she and her husband had never had. She pointed out that her husband "Roger could have gone a lot further but his parents couldn't afford an extended education for him". Her comparisons therefore were between the education that they never had available as children, and the new possibilities for her two children today.

I was entering a field that I knew nothing about. If we'd gone to private school, and it was in our plans from the word go for our kids to be privately educated, I'd probably have looked at it all with a different pair of eyes.

Coming from a family who had never used private schools, and had never before considered using them, she wanted to dissociate herself quickly from the unreasoned users of private education that she had encountered:

A lot of them they've mapped out their child's education from cradle. They went through that system and that's the way that Beatrice is going you know, and there's never any question of whether we can afford it, or what the local comprehensives are like, that was the route. Never batted an eyelid about it. Those people I avoid like the plague.

Another family show how confusing the reflection process can be, since they talk about making judgements based on clearly out of date experiences, such as:

Because with [my husband] being in the system anyway he knew lots of schools. I know it was twenty-five years ago but to him, certain schools interpreted certain sorts of behaviour, and meant certain things, you know Gordonston is cold showers.

They are relying on his knowledge, gained generations before as a pupil, presumably visiting other schools for activities such as sports matches. On the other hand, The mother describes how both of them reacted badly to the unhappiness of boarding as a child, and complains that they did not really experience family life. At weekends when they went home it was as a guest, a big event, so they were taken out to dinner, for example. It was an adventure for this couple to keep their children at home.

We didn't have a lot of time actually in a home environment. So we now found that was quite difficult. It was fun in one way because we had to work out what we meant by a family, but as I say we felt we'd missed out on family life, the everyday running of a family, rather than it always being a special occasion, and so we decided that our children wouldn't go.

However "old habits die hard" and, at the time of the interview, the parents are just in the process of persuading their youngest child to go to a boarding school in Wales. Another mother, on the other hand, uses her own experience of boarding more directly to persuade her son, and perhaps herself, that traditional full boarding is less disruptive to the child than any modern compromise.

I don't know if he'll be able to weekly board as he does now because it was made clear that he would have to play in the Chapel on Saturday mornings and on the occasional Sundays. In some respects it might do him good to settle there a bit more without coming home each weekend. We'll play that by ear, because after all when I went to boarding school, I used to get all worked up coming home for the weekend and then when you were home you were all upside down so I just never seemed quite.... In the holidays it used to take days to settle.

Another shows that even where a parent is satisfied with their own schooling, but does not wish their child to repeat it, the old school still has an influence on choice - "we didn't choose Hillside...because my husband went there. Almost we tried not to". [Since this statement is ambiguous, it should be made clear that the family rejected Hillside school partly because of this past association].
Despite being frustrated at not being able to help their three children, as they "do not know the system", a father expresses his unhappiness at their progress in a local state school, and their apparent idleness, by comparing their experience with

his own and his wife's. He is therefore making a comparison across educational systems and states, as they were both at school in the Punjab, as well as across generations when he says "I didn't go to school in this country. School here is very easy. I used to ride 10 miles to and from school in Lahore". A similar story of working hard and "making good" is told by a mother.

> My husband went to one of two grammar schools. He didn't get into the brightest school, he went to the one, well the ones who passed the 11+ just scraped in, but in fact he worked very hard and he was the only one out of his friends, all his friends went to the brighter one and he was the only one that went to university. That's him, he's a bit obsessional about many things and sitting down and doing his homework was one of them.

It is perhaps not surprising that although able to afford private schools, but only considering them at the insistence of the mother "who failed my 11+ and went to a Catholic private school", both children are sent to a nearby state school. Interestingly, this mother was in favour of using private schools, but not Catholic ones, saying "NO.. not THE convent", which again shows the difficulty of drawing simple conclusions about the relevance of prior experience. Another mother, one of the traditionalists quoted above, is divorced, and has raised her daughter alone. Her anger and disappointment have clearly coloured the decision made to send her daughter to a single-sex boarding school.

> I have this fear, by the time she's 17, the worst thing she could do to me is you know, get pregnant, get married to a car mechanic who shortly loses his job, can't pay the mortgage, doesn't like the baby, she's got three by the time she's 22 and I end up putting a roof over their head and the food in the pantry and helping her with the double buggy down the lift. Which is going to cost me more in the long run. Five or six years more of private education and hopefully she will take life more seriously, see where all of her friends are, aiming for one thing and that's to do well for herself, get somehow, I'll probably have to have it grafted, a sense of ambition from somewhere. Hopefully she'll learn it from her peers, and follow a career which will make her independent of any other man, any chap. I'm not a hard out and out feminist but I do believe what's good enough for you should be good enough for her. That if she were to go to a comprehensive, I'm sure she would only get four or five O levels, would come out and end up working in a job, not furthering a career, a job that will fill the gap until she finds a man and settles down, or doesn't settle down and finds a man who will provide the children that give an excuse not to work any more. I'd hate that, I've been there, believe me.

A reluctant user of private education reinforces his argument by an appeal to the past, and a lost education system:

> Being a tight bugger I'd rather she followed the route that I did, through the state system, no cost, but as far as I can tell it's not available.

He hints at disputes in the family over the choice of schools based chiefly on the differing educational experiences of the adults. When discussing the merits of coeducation and single-sex schools he says:

> There's a difference why we were considering private schools between my wife and myself. The wife came through it and has always supported it. I came through the state system, and always thought it offered an unfair advantage. My daughter shouldn't take part in that. That's before I had a daughter of course! Single-sex was because the schools of the calibre we were hoping for in the area were both single-sex. I would read it as pure coincidence, my wife would probably say I think it would be better for her initially. I came from a coed school, she came from Henry's [a local girls school]. I'd rather her in a coed school.

A mother from another family makes an almost identical comment in the same context:

> Against that its boys only which my husband particularly feels is important, mixed education. That may be a difference because I went through a single-sex education and he went through mixed.

In explaining why her son was moved from a state school to a private one, this mother complained of unstructured teaching holding him back, and eventually leading to behaviour difficulties at home as well. Since there are several linked themes in her narrative, it is quoted from at length:

> Peter had led a very structured life, I suppose we are very organised as a family, and as individuals, and so his day had followed a structured pattern. But for example, we would stop at a certain time of the morning, I mean not rigidly, and have a break in the morning, watch, you know a children's programme on television..... He got to the school and it was completely unstructured. There might be a certain number of tasks written up on the board for them to get through in the day in whichever order they wished....Peter went to school in September at the age of four and a half and so raced forward that by the end, by Christmas term, he was so far ahead of the others apparently that some of the others were upset that they weren't doing what Peter was doing and I had the comment that at four and a half a child should not be in school to learn. They ought to be in school to play. Now he could not read before he went to school. Deliberately I didn't teach him because I thought that... he recognised letters because he'd asked me about them and he could count. But then in a couple of weeks he could read and he just wanted to work and work and work, and they were unhappy about that. Felt this was not right or normal, and it was a school where all the infants were in one group. And so he actually learnt an awful lot, after the Christmas for the rest of the year he learnt a lot but not by working at the work he was being set to do. Because he could write his name that was all you had to do in that class. It was not until you were on the table that you could write your address or your phone

number. So at the end of the day, my son used to take all day to write his name because if he wrote it, he just got sent and told to do it again. He learnt a lot, but he learnt by listening. He learnt his tables but that hadn't been taught to him. That was being taught to the top class. They were all in the same room, which is a wonderful way to learn but he wasn't learning how to work. I felt. The school could not understand my concern that yes I knew that he knew a lot and could read well and his Math's was good but I wasn't concerned about that. I was more concerned that he wasn't learning how to be in school and how to apply himself.... It changed almost immediately when he changed school. Almost immediately.

While starting to make a comparison between the schools today and those of her generation, this mother's story leads back to tradition, and thus reinforces the link between the two components of this account of the reflection effect.

The domino effect

Although parental choice research does not generally consider or make clear whether a child for whom choice is made is the eldest in a family or not, serial choices for a succession of siblings are assumed to have some effect on the process (Dennison 1995). A link is established in Chapter 6 between the types of schools used by siblings, which is statistical evidence of what Johnson (1987) termed a "domino" effect in school choice. In the interviews, all parents with a child older than the one being discussed make spontaneous comments about the education of the other, and more or less directly suggest a relationship between the experience of the first, and the choices for the second. The fact that some also link their own experiences to make an unbroken inter-generational chain of "educational dominoes" is exemplified by this mother. She learnt that she must treat her two children in the same way, from the bitterness that resulted between herself and her brother.

I always went to a boarding school, but my brother went to a private school only until 11 then he moved to the local grammar. The reason he didn't go to a boarding school was that my parents had a farm, and they needed him on the farm after school and at weekends, and so he's always held a bit of a grudge that he didn't have the opportunity. But then Neil happened to be bright, and he went away to college, and he's got his own business now anyway. At the time he was quite bitter about it for years. So I'm very aware that I must do the same for both.

There is quite a large age difference between the two children in the next family (five years), and educational decisions were initially made for the eldest, a son, on the assumption that he was an only child. His name was put down for an expensive private school when he was born, intending him to start at age five, but the plan had to be delayed when the second, a girl, was born. This change was partly financial, but it also became difficult for the mother to drive the son to school as planned. However, he encountered problems of control in his local primary school as described in Chapter 10, and was moved to a private school later as a result. This caused new problems with the younger daughter:

> Because each day she has been going to his school. She sees the wonderful grounds, the smart uniform, all the facilities that he has, and right from the word go 'why can't I go there?' Why am I here? So all I can do to that is to tell her that she doesn't need it quite the same. I have her coming home saying she's bored, she isn't pushed.... It isn't the ideal, I'd prefer to take her out of there and put her in a private school where I know that she will be motivated, and sit down and do lessons, and that is what she would like but I cannot afford it. Because when Robert was born I thought he was going to be the only child, we had a scheme going for him when he was born. We had one that helped us along until he was 11 and another that will last until he's 18. The returns on it when he was younger were altogether better than what they are now. Things have changed so with Christine we've only put one down for when she's 11 and I ended up putting it in savings bonds in the Post Office. I had to do it even if I have to sell the house so we live in a flat, I promised her that at 11 she would go to a private school.

The mother justifies the different amount she is prepared to pay for the two children on their specific needs, but it is clear that the compromise is an uncomfortable one. Despite illustrating the pressure on parents to treat siblings in the same way, this family are not alone in treating them differently. That such different treatment is slightly easier with children of different genders, whatever their age and order, is apparent in several stories.

> When we went round Tower schools, Christine said - perhaps I could do an academic scholarship to go here - and I said no. It's very difficult for her but I can't do it for her. Not to go to a school like that. It'll have to be a private school in Cardiff. Because Robert needs it.... It suits that he's away from us so that when he comes home at the weekend he appreciates us. He needs the space, he's just that type of child, whereas Christine is happy to read, to do tapestry. He isn't.

One family also considered using a private school but decided that it would be too expensive for their three boys, and they "need to treat all three the same". Another demonstrates a variation of the domino principle, and its link to finance in the case of fee-paying schools. With four children, they sent them all to a private school which offered compound reductions for siblings, and although dissatisfied with the school in many ways, they retained them all there until the eldest left at the end of compulsory schooling. The mother expresses the same fear as several parents, that a child will reproach her later for not offering the same opportunities to all.

> Well to be quite honest with you, we er, we had the boys in there first, because I suppose there wasn't an awful lot of choice for the boys. We had the boys in there first, and then we put the girls in there and the incentive

was because we had 4 children in private education, we had one free. That was our incentive... They all left together, yes, yes. David left, my oldest left to go to A level college, yes we did lose our discount there but I mean that wasn't the criteria at the time...The decision wasn't financial, it was purely for his, you know, his academic future, ... yes it did help... Whereas I had the intention of leaving all the other children where they were, was he going to look and say well I didn't have my fair share you know, you didn't leave me in private education, you took me out but the others were there. There was a gap of five years you see between him and the other children, so a bit of soul searching there a bit of heart searching and we decided you know, to make a change.

In addition to the moral arguments for using the same type of school for all children , and the financial incentives to use the same fee-paying school, there are, of course, very practical reasons for any parent to use the same school for all. A mother with two daughters commented on the convenience of the present arrangement.

I wouldn't want to send Celia to Needles school, in the opposite direction. If I've got a decent school on my doorstep which will satisfy my need, I see no need to go in different directions just to keep her away from her sister. I can see that if you've got one very bright child and one less bright, or very unbright, I wouldn't send those to the same school.

Another, having decided to use a fee-paying school, has the same view, saying "if Andrea had been willing to board, I would have preferred them to attend the same school". She realises however, that the specific learning difficulties of both children make this unlikely, and that her chosen school will only suit one of them.

Originally we'd anticipated both girls going there, but the older one is unable to cope with the idea of boarding. You have to look at the character of the child don't you. We have one child who is easily distressed and one who is self-confident, who on the [inaudible] index comes out as more dyslexic than her sister, but copes with it much better. She's had problems in that it's obvious to her that her classmates can do things that she finds more difficult, but her attitude is not a self-critical one. She just does her work without fuss really. The other one would be very conscious of the fact that she can't do things like the others, and that would increase the anxiety. Whereas for one boarding is attractive, for the other it just isn't.

One family sent their youngest child to a private school, while the three elder sisters had been to, or were attending, state schools. It is interesting that the child in question is a boy again, but their story also hints at the distressing outcome if children are given different education.

So we said to the girls, you know you could always have done the same if you had wanted to go, and the second daughter said "I did".

The next mother offers an even more intriguing insight into the mechanics of the domino process. It is well documented that state schools automatically offer places to younger siblings of existing pupils in most cases (Chapter 6), and that many private schools offer financial inducements. The implication in this story is that an over-subscribed private school has taken this process one stage further, as it will only agree to take one child if her sister also agrees to attend the same school.

> Mother - We decided to move Cherie to Henry's.... I looked at the junior school at Henry's for Lucy ... so I took her to sit the exam, and I sat outside a classroom and there was no control at all.... So we said 'Oh we didn't want the place'. They wrote back and said, 'we notice that you don't want the place for Lucy, and they kept her waiting all summer and right at the end they said they weren't going to accept Cherie [despite her coming first in the mock examinations at the very successful feeder school].
> Researcher - And you think the two things were related?
> Mother - Yes I do. I couldn't see why they suggested in the letter that we don't want the place.

Another parent is not sure that her second child should attend the same school as the older son, as the two are very different, but has allowed the daughter to go ahead and choose it. The mother is, in part, influenced by the presence of an even younger child, not at school yet, who represents another domino even further down the line.

> We've got a completely different kettle of fish with Geraldine from my son. Academically she isn't at all bright, although she's very bright in other areas, so she needs to go to a school where there is an all-round education. Going away [boarding] is out of the question. We have a 9 month old baby upstairs asleep, and she would feel pushed out because she's very good with the baby. I don't want her to feel ostracised because the baby's here, so she has to go away. We would send her away if we thought it was the right thing, but not now. Where else is there in Cardiff? She knows how happy Alan is, and that he's doing well and he's got lots of friends, and they're always ringing up for Alan now. So we thought right, they've got a good all round education in Ford's. I'm a little bit concerned that she might end up in the you know one of the lower streams. [The tutor] who's in there now doesn't think so because Geraldine's doing work that normally children of her age in the state system haven't even heard of. We're going to give her a year in Ford's, we're going to try it and see how she gets on.

Conclusion

The theme of this chapter is that choices being made today are critically influenced by events in the past, sometimes long in the past, and that opportunity, nostalgia, tradition, and convenience often combine to make school choice a far from "rational" process. This is not to say that the choices described in this chapter are bad ones, but rather that, whatever the outcomes, they are certainly not made in the way that some advocates of public choice suggest (Chapter 1). Decisions, commonly based upon knowledge which is five, or even forty years, out of date, are not catered for by those arguing that school choice will lead to school improvement, via the application of market forces. It was shown in Chapter 7 how very few families find the introduction of annual league tables of performance particularly useful in helping to make up their mind. It is also clear from the findings in Chapter 6 that the restorationist feelings among parents are deliberately played upon by the private schools, as a form of marketing. The relative unpopularity of fee-paying schools in Wales means that most are very small. Their very limited accommodation necessitates whole class teaching in rows of desks, and their lack of facilities often leads to concentration on the "basics" of education. All of these accidental characteristics are combined with other the factors described in Chapter 6, such as uniforms, and an ageing teaching staff, to create the very effect that many of the parents are looking for. What is interesting in this context, and in the light of previous research, is the absence of any great desire for single-sex schooling among the respondents, which coupled with the decline of single-sex Welsh private schools, suggests that this is not a characteristic that most respondents associate with their vision of the past. The children are anyway, not so keen on tradition, and realise the practical drawbacks of small schools. Chapter 9 examines the relative contributions of the two generations to the choice process.

9 The three step model

Introduction

This chapter mixes data from the interviews with findings from the survey, and examines them from four different but related perspectives, each of which builds upon the importance of prior educational decisions in the family, as discussed in Chapter 8. The first section expands discussion of the respective roles of the key players in the school choice process, previously addressed in Chapter 7, by adding data from the interviews to give a fresh perspective. The process of choosing a school is found to have three major components in many cases, and these are described in the second section. It describes the process of choice as a sequence of three steps - creating a "choice set", narrowing it down, and finally making the selection. This is termed the "three step" model (Gorard 1996$_e$). Previous writers have suggested a simple dichotomy between those who are, and those who are not, willing and able to engage in an educational market, but this is not sufficient to explain the diversity found in this study. Each step can be approached by families in very different ways, and five different approaches are identified from the stories of the families cited in this chapter. The third part of the chapter accordingly places the families into one or more of five categories as defined by the preceding sections. Using the model of three steps, the brief stories of five families are used to illustrate different approaches to each step. The final section describes some of the limitations on choice, and some of the strategies used by parents, and schools, to make children accept the final selection of a school.

Different roles in the choice process

A large part of the theoretical basis for the analysis used in this chapter comes from the survey results concerning the process of choice described in Chapter 7. A brief summary of the relevant findings follows.

Results from the survey

Most families reported that they were seriously considering only one of the types of school defined in Chapter 6, which is an indication that selection of the type of school for further consideration is usually the first, perhaps implicit, step in selecting a school. The importance of the seven factors underlying the families' reported reasons for choosing a school, varies for different sub-groups of respondents. Four of the factors are of more relevance to parents, and one to children, which suggests that the two generations are using different reasons for school selection, even where these different routes lead to the same choice. This, in turn, suggests that the factors are not merely items on a check-list used by consumers, or alternatives used by all families, but may in fact represent different types of respondents or families. For example, larger families are less concerned with the school having a pleasant ethos, perhaps because the child is more used to the "rough and tumble" of family life. Some factors clearly relate to the choice of a type of school, such as state-funded or fee-paying, rather than to the choice of a specific school within one sector. The high correlation between parents expressing dissatisfaction with a state school, and the desire for a small school, suggests that "size" is an example of a factor determining choice between the sectors. The fact that this is really only of relevance to parents, and is more important to families where the parent has the larger role, suggests that choice of a type of school is more usually the responsibility of the parents.

Families about to make the choice in Year 6 commonly report that the decision will be a joint one, whereas those who have already made a choice in Year 7 more often report that the choice was made by either the child, or the parent alone. Since there is no other reason for the families of the two year groups to differ, as they effectively represent different cohorts from the same schools, this may be seen as evidence that as the process of choice takes place, the role and responsibility of the pupil increases in some families, and disappears in others. Parents also report considering more schools than their children do, which suggests that some parents are pre-selecting which schools to discuss with the child, who, in turn, may not be aware of the full range originally considered by the parents.

More pupils report that they have the sole responsibility in making the choice than their parents do, and vice versa. Although it may be seen as natural for both groups to emphasise their part in this important process, in light of the evidence of parental pre-selection by type and number, above, it is also likely that this is a "true" result. The parents are reporting on their involvement in the whole process, while the pupils are understandably only able to comment on those aspects visible to them, in which they appear to have a larger role. This result may also be seen as evidence that the children are deliberately made to feel more responsible than they actually are, which leads to the discussion in the final section of this chapter on the micro-politics of choosing.

Stories from the interviews

A similar question to the one in the survey concerning the role of parents and child in the choice, was also used as a probe in the interviews. Rather than being easily divisible into categories where parent, child or both chose, these accounts show

how confusing it can be even to decide what choice is, in this context. These stories, revealing the power to choose within each family, are organised loosely into three groups - those primarily concerned with adult choice, those relating to a more combined choice, and a few choices made by those outside the family.

Adults Most interviews were held with only one adult from the family, but most interviewees tended to give the impression that where they had a partner, both had views which were equally valid, and that anyway they tended to agree. The fathers were keener on tradition and sport, and the mothers on "smallness" and safety, but the sample of interviewees is small, and consists mostly of mothers, so it is difficult to draw conclusions with any certainty. When one partner is seen as having a dominant voice among the two, it is the father, but when only one partner is involved at all, it is generally the mother, perhaps because she is looking after the child alone. This conclusion is broadly in line with the findings of David *et al.* (1994).

One mother confirms the first of these observations in response to the question about who makes the final choice:

> David really, my husband really. He's very much head of the house. You know, we would all give our input, you know give our opinion, but when it came down to it, he would know.... So we could all like a different school.

A father apparently jokingly describes the same situation:

> Researcher - Does your wife feel the same? Do you agree with her generally when you discuss these issues?
> Father - Generally speaking. She puts more emphasis on other points, but I bully her!

One mother who is a school teacher, is taking responsibility in her family, and explains:

> If I'm perfectly honest, it will end up - me. We all have an input but if there's something that I'm very unhappy about, you know because it's so difficult, then he won't go there because I was so unhappy with the first school he was at. I felt that if I was so unhappy ... My husband can go out to work and have other things to occupy his mind and not think about all the time during the day.... I know that unless I get it right, life is going to be hell for the next seven years.... I have a terrible choice to make in the next week.

As suggested by the survey results, most of the parents interviewed described a major role for themselves in the school choice, regardless of the type of school considered. The biggest differences between families in this respect can be explained by the age and birth order of the child in question. As one respondent wrote on the survey form when asked who chose the school - "he's only four"! This theme of youthfulness, being a barrier to making a decision appears in several interviews, even concerning much older children, and is often backed up by an assurance that even where the choice made is not popular, the child will come to appreciate it - in time. For some parents, their treatment of children aged 10 or more may be coloured by a convenient "ideology of immaturity" (Grace 1995).

Asked whether her daughters had played a major part in choosing a school at 11, a mother says:

> So, um, well, no, I think considering the age they were, no. I mean had they been teenagers and perhaps a bit more decisive, a bit more, more knowledgeable, you know, of what they really wanted to do.

On the same question, another is even more forthcoming, linking the lack of a role for her daughter to her age:

> How much influence can you allow an 11 year old to take? If it was down to Heather, she'd like a school because they had Paddington Bear wallpaper. The reason she wanted to go to Mousefield not Deacon was the fact that she stayed there and the girls were very friendly. You've got to explain to a child, you didn't stay at Deacon, and they would be just as friendly there. Heather might decide not to like a school because she doesn't like their uniform. Children of 11 are too fickle to see what is best for them. They have to follow your guidance.

She believes that her daughter will come to agree with her mother's choice in time:

> Anyway at the end of the day she'll probably love it.... but given the choice, she wouldn't be going. She would be going to Mordred comprehensive, because her friends are going, and she can stay at home with mummy, and we don't have to do all this bleeding hard work then. She sees that as the greener pastures. How can you expect her to see the down side? Sadly she's a bit bimbonic when it comes to anything she wants, if it takes a little bit of effort, oh forget that, she never tries. That's why I chose the school I did.

A mother with two daughters in Year 7 has already seen this process of settling down and acceptance take place, and is convinced, if not entirely convincing, that the girls are now happy with the change:

> Well at first they resisted a little bit, about leaving their school, just a little bit.... but a week into Orange school, and they were very very glad that they'd made the move, well even less than a week I think. A few days.... So as I say after the initial two days they were very happy with having made the choice. They were very pleased. Never looked back, never...

Another feels that the opinions of her children are too unstable to be of use long term:

Well I mean children are children aren't they? They, one day they think - that's a good idea, and the next "oh no we don't want to leave".

This is similar to the view of the mother who does not believe that her daughter knows what is in her own best interests:

We would not give them a free choice of anything since our criteria for educating them.... We wanted some sort of structure. The older one, given the opportunity of not having school structure the day, wherein she had to produce a certain amount of work, yes I'm sure she would [pick a progressive school]. She doesn't like school, she finds it hard, so given the option to do very little, she'd love it.

A further reason why children may be excluded from the real decision making is that it involves non-educational implications affecting the whole family, such as travel and housing which clearly would not normally be left to a child:

Why else do you think we moved here? We moved for that very reason. We were out in Cowbridge, my husband was working very long hours and never seeing the children. We had to move James in to the Village school, and so I said right, let's move in. It took a fair while, as I said there's no point in moving in to the city unless you're living on the doorstep..... So that's why we moved here.

Perhaps the clearest examples of denying the child any say in the choice of school, whether because of immaturity, or lack of decisiveness, comes when the decision is made a long time beforehand, perhaps at birth or even before. One parent describes how she moved ten years ago to be in the "correct area" for a popular state school. In the same context, another said - "when we were moving into the area twelve years ago, we asked around before buying the house". A third parent has a similar story concerning choice of a fee-paying school - "we knew a few teachers there and they were really nice, so we thought he'd always go there, and never considered anywhere else". A fourth mother could not remember when the decision had been made - "mm, how long ago? I think we'd always hoped she would go there". In each of these cases, there is a reminder of the stories in Chapter 8 where the choice of secondary school was made many years before the child could possible be involved. It is interesting to note also that such an approach to school choice makes a nonsense of current annual performance indicators such as league tables, since the parents are in fact choosing the school as it was ten or more years ago.

In other families, it is clear from early on in their stories that the parents are making the choice, but that they are now seeking to involve the child and so make the choice consensual. Some of these families have already been quoted above, and some appear again in the final section concerning the tactics used by adults to persuade the children of their own views. For the reasons given above, children are sometimes offered a school choice from a "stacked" deck, either containing only schools of the same type, or the favoured school, and a patently unsuitable alternative. In this way a dominant parent can make a child accept the decision more easily, by offering the appearance of participation.

One mother is probably more concerned to empower her son in the decision than many of those above, but like others, finds that the boy cannot make up his mind, although in this respect he may not be very different to his mother, who also speaks of the agony of indecision:

> He didn't like Cromwell, maybe because he goes there swimming and from a small age he'd seen the boys and larking about in the pool and I think he found it quite off-putting - "tremendously badly behaved mum, you would not believe it, I can't understand how the school allows them to do these things". I say to Peter, I think you'll find they are not as bad as in lots of places. Now he's got older and nearer them in age, I don't think that he'll be quite so concerned.... and that day completely changed his attitude and he was all for going to Cromwell. He said "you're right, I've only seen the bad side of it and now I've seen a good side". Then he went to Market school, and was shown round and he really liked the people there - "oh they're so nice, I'd like to go there". He can't make his mind up. he was quite happy for us to send him to Hereward... If you ask him today he doesn't know.

The decision that their child should board taken by one family, who "wouldn't force them, they choose to board", or the decision not to board taken by another because "he'd had a taste of both, and decided home was better", both required the compliance of the child. Even the father mentioned above who "bullies" his wife, hopes that his son will be happy with the choice:

> He likes them both. If he doesn't get into the boys school, he says he's quite happy to go to Market school.

Other families also appear to allow their child a veto:

> If Celia wasn't suited to the school, or couldn't handle the school, I wouldn't have sent her there.

One story shows what happens when a long term plan goes wrong because a child is not happy with the choice. This mother is now faced with the two daughters going to different types of school, one in England and one in Wales.

> Originally we'd anticipated both girls going there. The older one is unable to cope with the idea of boarding.... Andrea has become very reliant on us as she can't even read the questions on her homework, and she's possibly a little over-dependent, but at the moment she's so emotionally unable to cope with the thought of failure that it would be senseless to send her. So, yes they had a measure of choice, and Andrea has made the choice in not wanting to go away from home anywhere, which has narrowed down the choice considerably.

The role of the child As well as those families in which one or more parents dominate the choice process there are a large number in which the child is treated almost as an equal. The existence of these families can be predicted from the survey results. One mother is typical of this group when she says: "We were all in agreement over Hillside, we all came away saying exactly the same". It is not clear who made the choice, but all are involved and all are reported as happy. This compromise solution is also noted by two other families:

> Because it wasn't just my choice, it was my husband's choice, the child's choice. You had to strike a happy medium and what we could afford. So it made life a lot more difficult on the road. It was a joint effort really.

> Mother - We would have moved had she been willing but she just didn't want to move. We had two cats, they were both run over and they're buried in the garden, and she doesn't want to leave the cats. So we said would you like to weekly board? She said yes. I didn't want her to board, I don't mind her weekly boarding, as we'll see her. I don't want to just cast her off, it would be awful, but weekly's the best of both worlds.
> Father - If she said I want to go to Henry's daddy, there'd be no argument.

One family claimed to have left the choice of school entirely to their child. However, as with the supposedly "disconnected" type of family described by Gewirtz *et al.* (1994) in Chapter 3 they have an older child, and as suggested by the findings in Chapter 8, the younger simply wishes to follow the older:

> She really wants to go. She's decided to go. Mind you we don't know that we've got in yet. We've applied but we don't know. Second choice is at Cattlestation. We're just waiting to hear.

Other choosers Of course, in many cases, it is neither the child nor the parent who makes the final choice, because of standard numbers and entry requirements for the schools. In this case, the child is actually chosen by the school. In other cases, the parents and child do not even get to state a preference, or make the selection. One woman who works as a "missionary" for disabled children has to make a choice for one child that she barely knows:

> It is an unusual situation. I have only been a guardian for this child and her sister for 20 months. This child has a disability and is greatly affected by the loss of both parents. The total consideration has been the child's needs and happiness.... and the choice was made with advice from the education officer statementing this child for support.

More common is an attempt by parents to "pass the buck" to their God. One man states that the "Holy spirit" is the most important source of information about a school. Another states that

> God indicated through His Word that Christian Education was the right way to go for Christian children. He also specifically told us that our

daughter should attend Westward school. We obeyed knowing that His will for her was the very best. All else follows.

Taken literally, this comment states that the decision as to which school a child attends was taken by a being from another dimension. Several of the parents using grass-roots schools made similar comments. It is unlikely that such views are catered for in rational choice theory.

Another influence is, of course, the staff at the previous school, and sometimes they can come close to making the decision themselves. The Strakers use a feeder proprietary school with a widely respected Head who has very strong views on the placement of her ex-pupils. What is unusual for them, in comparison to the stories in the fourth section of this chapter, is that the Head is actually pushing the least prestigious of the schools in the choice set, because of the merits of its pastoral care system.

Three steps to choosing a school

The results from the survey, and the compromises over who chooses, as outlined above, can be captured in a model of three steps in the process of choosing a school (Gorard 1996$_e$). It is not suggested here that families formally engage in all of these steps, but in the first instance the model is a useful structure to facilitate further analysis of the interview data.

The Model

Step 1: the parents alone decide on a type of school, perhaps as a reflection of their own schooling, and that of siblings, including whether they can afford, and wish to use, the fee-paying sector. At this stage, convenience (for the parent), tradition, school size, and pupil safety would be the main determinants of choice.

Step 2: the parents alone consider some alternatives within that type, and select an appropriate subset of these, perhaps using the advice of the current school, local reputation, or school-based literature. At this stage, provision and educational outcomes become more relevant.

Step 3: the parents and child together come to a satisfactory agreement about one of the subset, perhaps by visiting one or more schools. At this stage, sports, other extra-curricular activities, pupil happiness, and convenience (for the child) become the important determinants, along with child welfare and outcomes.

These three steps are confirmed, and indeed were originally suggested, by the unprompted comments of respondents themselves in interviews. The stories of each family are different but the quotations below all have a common element of the parent undertaking some earlier research, before allowing the child a higher level of input. In each case, only one type of school was being considered.

A father offered his son a choice of two fee-paying day schools:

> Researcher - "You went to see three schools and just wrote one off"?
> Father - "Yes, and he sat the exam for both of the others... If he gets accepted for the boy's school, he wants to go there. We haven't heard ourselves and we're awaiting the results of the boys school. I've said it's his choice now. He wants to go to the boys school because all his chums are going there".

A mother intended to send her child as a boarder to a fee-paying school in England:

> Whereas when we went looking for James, for a boarding school, we looked at more. We looked at about four, and then whittled it down to two, and then took him with us to two, and between the three of us we decided which was going to be right for him.

A third parent is seriously considering two schools, having eliminated some possibilities and is now involving his son. In reference to a question concerning convenience, he says:

> Well I think it is a major factor in his mind, and you have to consider what he wants. It seems to me pointless if he was accepted at both schools, and he desperately wanted to go to Cromwell, and I said "no you're going to Market school". I think that would be wrong. So we've narrowed the choice down. He has the choice of which one he goes to.

A fourth parent summarised all three steps in the process. The parents decided on the use of fee-paying schools, made some initial selections and only then involved the children:

> We presented them with several options, and when we started to look at schools at the ISIS exhibition, we looked at prospectuses and brought them home and let them read them and say which they thought looked like nice schools. From there we narrowed it down.

These comments all illustrate the move from the second to the third step in the process of choice, and they explain why parents and children might disagree on the main reasons for choice, even after the choice has been made. The two generations may simply be describing the reasoning in the step that is most important to them, with the parents emphasising the initial selection of appropriate schools, and the child concentrating on the final judgement. In each case all of the schools considered are of roughly the same type as defined in Chapter 6, whether fee-paying or state-funded. Few families still have more than one type to consider at step three. One mother visited five schools, of different types, and selected three of these for her daughter to consider:

She went for the day to Henry's, she went for the day to Hood, she went to the open day at the Bishop's school, and she was asked her opinion of the schools.... She was told which schools she had a choice of, which she would prefer to go to.... If she'd been happy going to Henry's, it would have been better for her.... with a happy relaxed atmosphere and attitude towards the school than pushing her into a school that I felt was going to be better for her, and had her dragging her heels and being stubborn and awkward and setting her mind in the wrong direction.

This comment also suggests one of the main reasons for empowering a child. It is not necessarily motivated by a sense of natural justice, or a belief that children make good decisions, but that if they feel involved they are more likely to accept the outcome.

The first step, of selecting a type of school, was more rarely mentioned in interviews, possibly because it had been taken much earlier. Very few Assisted Places are available in Wales (Gorard 1996c), and the scheme is not widely publicised (Edwards *et al.* 1989), so most families are faced with a very limited choice of types of schools (Chapter 6). Many may be unaware of even their limited choices, and so the first step can be a default one, made in ignorance of the alternatives. Even those for whom a wider range of alternatives is possible might ignore some, such as state-funded schools, because of "urban myths" they had heard about class sizes, or simply because they had only ever considered one school, whether state-funded....

We knew a few teachers there and they were really nice, so we thought he'd always go there, and never considered anywhere else.

or traditional fee-paying....

I put his name down for Village school when he was born.

One parent made the following comment on the survey form:

It is the only private girl's school in South Wales within easy travelling distance with Assisted Places - in reality no choice.

This comment shows quite clearly that step one can be invisible to the choosers, and can lead automatically to the final choice where the initial parameters of the choice set are precise. It also shows the problems in using the word "choice", which can refer to a process, a result, or, as in the above case, a summary of the number of options available. Another parent, on the other hand, who initially considered many schools, both state-funded and fee-paying, shows how much work can go into the first step. Having selected six schools from their own literature, she visited them and made notes on her impressions. Once she, and her husband, had decided on use of a fee-paying school, her son was involved, and he was allowed the final choice.

So I started, I should think, almost two years ago, and looked at the state schools as well because where we are the county cannot decide .. we are on the line on the map.... I actually looked around Merriweather, Arthur's, and King John's, and also got information on the Village school in Hereford which had impressed me earlier on, and Cromwell school because that does seem to be where people just assumed Paul would go, and Redfields also. I asked for them all to send information to begin with. and then I asked for appointments to go round.... Which I did first on my own.

A similar idea was suggested by Martin (1995), when he identified two phases in the choice process, that of "becoming informed", and secondly of "expressing a preference". The description of these two phases are similar to the steps two and three of the three step model. The first step may not have been apparent in the Martin study which was dealing with a small number of families in one local area, all intending to use state provision.

More evidence from the survey

If something like this progression of three steps takes place in the choice process it would be expected that the ratings given by respondents to their reasons for choice and their sources of information would be different if surveyed during different steps. For example, if deciding on a type of school comes first, then reasons such as the level of fees, or tradition would be more important to parents early on. Later, once the choice set has been created, other factors would come into play. As the role of the child increases during the process according to the model, their reasoning and the factors relevant to them should be more important later. As explained in Chapter 7, apart from the calendar difference of one year, there is no reason to suppose that the responses from Years 6 and 7 would be any different, as they represent successive cohorts from the same schools. Any differences between them can therefore be used to shed light on how the reasons of families change during the choice process.

The wishes of the child get more important with age, which is perhaps to be expected between Years 1 and 6, or between Years 8 and 11, but the respondents for Years 6 and 7 are, in reality, describing the same choice. The difference is simply whether the choice has already been made or not, and so, if they are faithfully recalling and describing the process of choice, there should be no difference between them. Perhaps the reason that the value given by respondents to the importance of the child's wishes is below the mean for the population in Year 6 (1.37, standard deviation 0.67), is that at the time of the survey between October and February, most families were in stage one or two. Similarly, perhaps the reason that the value given to the child's wishes in Year 7 is above the mean for the population, is that at the time of the survey most families had just completed stage three. Such an explanation clearly supports the three step model.

Interestingly, the mean rating by the children does not change that much, from 1.38 in Year 6 to 1.39 in Year 7. It may be that they are not aware of the length and complexity of the three step process, although it is true that children consistently rate their wishes higher than their parents do. It is the parents, who are more involved in the early steps, who change their rating of the views of the child more significantly, from 1.25 to 1.36 over the course of the year. Another interesting difference is that before making the choice, parents claim to be seriously considering more schools, reading more prospectuses, and making, or intending to make, more visits than parents surveyed at the start of Year 7. This seems to confirm that parents with children already in Year 7 are forgetting things from earlier in the choice process, or perhaps re-evaluating them. They also seem to have forgotten, or re-evaluated, the sources of information that they used in making the choice (Table 9.1).

Table 9.1
Main source of information by age of child

Percentage using:	Year 6	Year 7
League tables	30	70
Personal acquaintance	42	58
Visit to school	63	37
Prospectus	56	44

The major difference shown in Table 9.1 is that visits are reportedly more important before the choice has been made, while league tables of examination results seem more important afterwards. It is therefore consistent that the choice factor termed "outcomes", including examination results (see Chapter 7), is rated as more important by respondents in Year 7 than those in Year 6. This is more likely to be a simple change of perspective than anything to do with the three step process. Families who have made a choice are now free to look ahead and might be tempted to use results, sixth form, university entrance, and career prospects which all lie in the future, as justification for the choice they have made. Also rated higher in Year 7, by both generations, are the more idealistic reasons for choice, such as lenient discipline, a good ethnic mix, and religious tolerance, which are also more important to children. This finding fits well with the three step process, since if the wishes and roles of children are more significant over time, the kind of reasons they use should also become more relevant to parents after the choice has been made.

In Year 6, respondents rate many of the practical and convenience reasons, including having friends at the school, having siblings at the school, school bus services, ease of travel, and low fees much more highly. These are exactly the kind of practical reasons that would be used by parents to help make up the initial choice set, which of necessity is only composed of schools nearby or, in a few cases, affordable boarding schools. Although these situational variables are, like the idealised ones above, more important to children, they are reported as more important to children of all ages. The difference here is with the parents, who use convenience more at the start of the process, than at the end, which is another confirmation of the three step model.

The big surprise in this context is that the choice factor "size of school" is rated more highly by those in Year 7. Since this factor relates to dissatisfaction with state schools, it is described in Chapter 7 as a criterion used to decide on a type of school, but if this were so, and the choice of a type of school takes place early in the process, the opposite result would be expected. This finding can either be seen as a potential weakness for the three step model, or it can be seen as a further significant result in its own right. Whatever their initial motivation, a family finding that they have rejected a free place at a large local school, to pay for a child to attend a poorly provided one, will need to provide further justification to themselves, as well as to others, in order to reduce dissonance (Eiser and van der Plight 1988). They can start to look ahead to better outcomes, as shown above, and justify their choice on those grounds *post hoc*, but they generally cannot cite lower fees, convenience, or better provision as a reason. Perhaps the emphasis on small schools and small classes, which although clearly visible, are anyway sometimes of dubious benefit, is their best short-term justification for using a fee-paying school for a child of age 11.

The five types of families

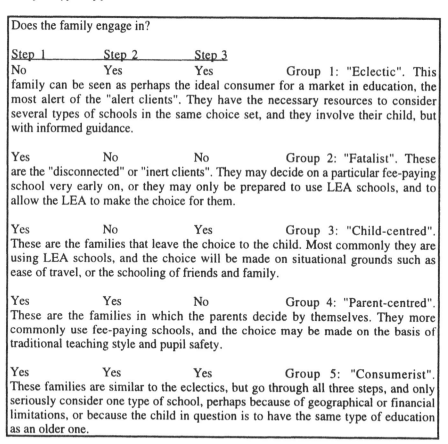

Figure 9.1 Five levels of engagement with the market

The model of three steps seems both elegant and plausible, agreeing with most accounts from the interviews and several of the unexpected findings from the survey. It has also provided fruitful ideas for further analysis of the survey data. However, it is quite clear from the interview data, as well as from results of previous work on choice in state-funded schools (Thomas and Dennison 1991, Hughes *et al.* 1994), that some families skip at least one of these notional steps. In the present study, some of the parents claim to be in charge of the process throughout, while a few seem to have given the child considerable responsibility. Some families only ever consider one type of school, while at least one family compared the merits of different types, such as fee-paying and grant-maintained up to the last moment.

If there are three such steps, and any of them may be skipped by any family, then the process of choice can theoretically develop in any one of eight different ways for each family, depending on which steps are skipped (since $2^3=8$). The eight ways would range from families that apparently did not engage in the choice process at all, through those in which parents decided on a type of school, and left the rest to the child, to those idealised "consumers" who formally consider each step. However, of these eight ways, four would be defined by skipping the first step of selecting a school type, and as was stated above, this was uncommon, particularly for subsequent children who are often offered the same type of school as the older one (Chapter 8). In fact, only five groups of families can be plausibly formed from those available in the interview data for this reason. All of the families that did not select a type of school first were otherwise clearly engaged with the market in both subsequent steps. However, the existence of even a few families that do consider state-funded, proprietary, and traditional fee-paying schools at the same time, for example, confirms that the others are making at least an implicit decision in this step. The five groups of families are therefore as outlined in Figure 9.1.

Stories from five families

This section contains brief accounts of five families who in their own words fit into one of the five groups suggested by the three step model. Each group could be represented by more than one family from the data, and although the frequency of each group differs, the families interviewed are only exemplars, and do not represent a stratified sample of any larger population. Accordingly, no statistical treatment of their characteristics is possible. Some of the families appear to have behaved very differently with different children, perhaps depending upon their birth order, their age, or their gender. Although the data on this is too sparse to draw any firm conclusions at present, it does indicate that the grouping of families probably only relates to their behaviour with the present child at the present age, and not to any immutable characteristics or tendencies.

The first family are "eclectics", since they are considering several types of schools at once, and have a history of using more than type of school for each child. The oldest son was sent to a traditional foundation school, but he became demotivated, and was moved to a stand-alone proprietary school for one year. This school was a long drive from home, and very small, with poor facilities. He asked his parents if he could move to the local comprehensive, which he did, and he has been happy there ever since. His sister also initially went to a traditional foundation school when very young, but left quickly because there were so few girls in her class. She is now in Year 6 at a feeder proprietary school, which is encouraging her to move to a local Catholic school. The parents have also considered a stand-alone proprietary school (not the same one as her brother), but they have now agreed that Geraldine should attend the local comprehensive as well. However, even this decision is seen as contingent, and for one year only in the first instance. The four quotations below, from the transcribed conversation, show firstly that the family is actually considering four types of schools, that the mother, who is speaking, has firm opinions, but that the final choice was made by the child.

> There's the convent, in Ealing Road. I was educated in THE convent. No, no, not THE convent!
> I would be delighted to send her to King John's if only they'd get better accommodation, with more sport, more .... because she is academically weak, it is no good sending her to a school that majors in academia.
> We went to Needles twice, and we weren't impressed at all. Potter's was her choice.
> She really wants to go. She's decided to go. Mind you, we don't know that we've got it yet. We've applied but we don't know.

The second family are "fatalist" which is very similar to saying that they are one of the "disconnected" described in Chapter 3, but since they are relatively privileged they would come from the upper quadrant of the Gewirtz et al. (1994) model. They had their own business, sent their son to a preparatory school in Scotland, and "put his name down" for a traditional fee-paying school very early. They quite clearly did not consider other school types, and they only appeared in this survey because the family business went bankrupt, and after a nearly a year of relying on relatives to pay the school fees, they had moved to Wales to start again.

> He was always going to Village school from the year dot. When he went to Harbour school, they felt that Village was his school because he's middle of the road. He's sporty, but he's not excessively good at anything.... and we loved it. We loved the layout, we loved the facilities, lots of grass.

The third family are "child-centred". They only seriously considered traditional fee-paying schools, since they had recently moved from Norway, and felt such schools would be more familiar in style for their only child. She went with them to several schools, and made her decision on the basis of travel, and where her class-mates were going. Her parents were reportedly prepared to move to a different area if she wanted to move to a distant school, but she wished to stay in the house where her cat was buried. Having made the decision, she changed her mind at the last minute, and decided on a school further away, that few of her class-mates were going to. Since she still did not want to move, she apparently suggested weekly boarding. After some hesitation the parents accepted the change. It is quite clear that both parents are concerned with the daughter's education, but that they feel it must be her choice in a relatively new country.

I know there are parental influences all along, but I could remember asking over the last 18 months, would you like to go to Cromwell? No was her answer.... Do you want to go to Henry's? Yes. And the decision about Henry's and the College in the end came down to her. She apparently wanted it. Then the attractions of the College were so intense that she went flip. My wife was the last to see that, but in the last week has been talking to parents....

The fourth family are "parent-centred", seemingly determined that Lucy should attend the school of their choice. The major difference between this family and the second one is that although they knew which type of school they wanted, they did not make an early decision on one school. The school they chose just happened, according to them, to be the first one they considered. Some families in this category considered more than school, but this family is used as an exemplar since the mother expresses such determination to be right.

I didn't look at other schools in the area. I went to look at Henry's and if that suited there seemed no need to go and look elsewhere. I think you have to be fairly positive in your own mind that it's right in the first place. If it really is wrong, first of all you've got to understand why it's wrong, who's made the fault, you or them? And hopefully you haven't made the fault, and .... if you do, I wouldn't rush the kids away fast. I'd have to get to have at least a year, preferably two years before I realised that it wasn't going to suit them. It's like anything, you've got to give it a fair crack of the whip.

The fifth family are "consumerist". They have two children, both of whom attended a state-funded Welsh language primary school, but who had run into problems there. Both are dyslexic, a condition which they felt was exacerbated by the bilingualism, while the school was also felt to be too secular. The family was in the process of moving around in the region, while the father was awaiting appointment to a diocese. The parents had no background in fee-paying education, but decided to use a religiously founded private school, at which the children could board, at least for the present. Since they also wanted the school to offer them a bursary for children of the clergy, which were only available at traditional foundation schools, these were the only type that they considered. This is why they differ from the eclectic families. The three quotations below, from conversation with the mother, clearly show that several schools were selected within the type, by the parents initially, and whittled down, but that the final choice was left to the child, as with the eclectic families.

She doesn't like school. She finds it hard, so given the option to do very little, she'd love it. We would not give them a free choice of anything since our criteria for educating them has to be one that's Christian. We wanted some sort of structure. We presented them with several options, and when we started to look at schools, at the ISIS exhibition, we looked at prospectuses and brought them home, and let them read them, and say which they thought looked like nice schools. From there we narrowed it down [pause]. The younger one first visited the school a year ago at their open day, and about 10 days ago she spent the day with them in class, and at the end of the day, she decided that was where she wanted to go. We were very happy with that choice, but we wouldn't have sent her if she wasn't.

The micro-politics of choice

David *et al.* (1994) have argued that researchers tend to ignore some participants in the choice process, and they stress its complexity in saying "we construe it as a multi-layered social process rather than an event at one point in time" (David *et al.* 1994 p.130). Others decry the fact that "surprisingly, though, there have been no studies centred upon the actual decision-making process" (Dennison 1995 p.5). By including both parents and children in this study, and mixing the methods of data collection, it has been possible to discover some of the conflicts embedded in that process, and to begin to describe some of the stratagems used by the participants. It is quite clear that parents exercise influence over their children's choices (Hunter 1991), and that "many parents exercise a good deal of subtle persuasion when choices are being considered" (Smedley 1995 p.99). What is also apparent from this study is that the schools have some influence over the families, and that the four "actors" in the play - parents, children, current school, and prospective schools - each put pressure on the others to achieve an outcome favourable to themselves.

Pressure on children from the parents

Sometimes, as in the parent-centred families, the pressure placed on children is simply the naked power of the parents due to their relative age, or legal and financial status. Sometimes this is accompanied by persuasion, spelling out the advantages, and slowly wearing down the resistance, if there is any. This was the case with one of their children in the following family. The parents appeared to offer the child a choice of two schools, but continued to push one of them at every opportunity:

> .... so by now I could see the way that the wind was blowing.... and you can talk them round at age.

They believe, as many families do, that the opinions of children are malleable. This is why children are not reliable according to them, and why they cannot be given complete control of their educational destiny. It also explains how some parents achieve their choice. Of course, other parents simply order their children to do what they are told, but even here such a display of strength is usually accompanied by a "refund period", described here by a mother who had already explained that the choice is hers alone:

> She's quite vain, and she can be a little too interested for my liking in boys.... I dread to think where 14 or 15 would lead her if they were accessible.... I will shield her from such things until I can't shield her any

more. By then she'll have got to 18 and not my problem.... But I have made a pact with her that if she went away and didn't settle, and was unhappy after the first term, I would start to look around for an alternative. If it continued that by the end of the third term she would move. It's not too short a period for her say "right I don't like it I'm coming home", and not an ongoing thing where she has to endure it forever if she really is not enjoying [it].... When.... I explain, she's resigned to the fact that mum's too strong a character to argue with.

These agreements for trial periods are quite common. One mother simply says "if it doesn't work she'll have to move", and another had just persuaded her son to board at secondary school:

And he did say last week, "the moment I tell you there's a problem you'll do something straight away, and you won't say its my fault will you?" So we said no, no.....

One family tell a story of the trial period not working:

Everyday we drove up there. My husband used to take him up there on Fridays and every Friday he said he felt inside although he never said to Alan, what are we doing up here? You know its such a, such an awful area, such an awful school, but we knew that academically it was very very good. Awful, the fabric, terrible, the area and of course the awful children coming down and threatening the ones with the red blazers.... and Alan was very frightened and say "please be there mum, they've got knives and things". We always said to him, please don't feel if you're not happy, you haven't got to stay here, but you've got to give the school two terms at least, if possible three. You've got to give it that, but we had to pass the Village school every day, and he cried and cried, the rugby and the cathedral and the green.... and he gave it a year and he restarted the next year, and in the middle of that term, where the half term was, he came out and said "you're going to be very cross with me", and I said what have you done? "I've given it a year mum, and I'm just not happy". Fine, daddy won't be cross, we'll discuss it.

Another have a similar story, except that for them the trial period was just a device to get the child to agree to try the school. Their eldest child remained in the school despite problems, and now resents his education. This is one reason why the younger children are now being treated more carefully.

We had to persuade him, er to go. He had his days trial, we had to persuade him really to go to er to private education, um he agreed in the end, but as I say he spent four unhappy years there. Didn't like, didn't fit in at all, didn't get on with the Headmaster.... It took him a couple of terms to settle in, um. It was quite a battle to get him there.

There are successes though. One family has a daughter who wanted to leave at the end of year 11, but was "pushed back". She is now glad of her parents pressure. She is deputy school captain, and has found a love of drama from producing the school play.

Most parents, perhaps particularly those dealing with a second child and feeling that they made mistakes with the schooling of the first, are clearly politically sensitive, and this runs across all family types. At one extreme, a "parent-centred" mother has ordered her child away to boarding school. She took her daughter to see two schools in England, one of which was patently not as desirable as the other. The outcome of this "two card trick" was that both mother and daughter then agreed on the better of the two, which was the one that the mother had wanted to use all along. The choice can now be recorded as consensual to some extent, despite the fact the daughter originally wanted to attend the local state school with her friends. One problem was that by loading the option in this manner, the daughter might be put off boarding altogether by the poor accommodation at the rejected school:

> I've explained to her sensibly why I think she should go to Trinity and to be honest, it was Heather, when we went to Moorlands who said "I don't want to go here". I wasn't there more than twenty minutes because I wasn't going to wreck my plans by leaving that as an impression of boarding school, so that she said "I'm not even going to look at the next one mummy". So I got in and out as fast as I could.

At the other extreme is one "child-centred" family, but even they eased their child's transition to boarding. Though the decision to board was clearly taken by the daughter, and she had a local day school as realistic alternative, as an only child, she was captured by the "glamour" of dormitories and midnight feasts after only one night as a trial. That the matter may not be as simple as that is suggested by a comment addressed by the father to his wife:

> She said 'I'd like to weekly board'. Didn't you give her some books to read and I remember you gave her one and said if you read this you'll find out what it's like to board. Enid Blyton?

Pressure on families from the schools

Schools can act for the best genuine interests of the child, as the agent of the parents, or in their own interests. Several parents mentioned pressure coming from fee-paying schools, forcing them to make a quick decision. One couple claim to have only considered one primary school for their daughter, because when they made an initial enquiry at one local school, they were "railroaded into entry". It is possible that at least some of the tactics used by schools are ruses, similar to the phantom contract races occasionally used by estate agents with hesitant buyers. The stories here centre on two small fee-paying schools, both in Cardiff. One is a stand-alone, and the other a feeder, proprietary school. They are therefore both run for profit.

One family describe how one of the schools, pushed them into moving their first child so quickly that they did not really think out the consequences. It was too small for him to have any friends, and poorly staffed and equipped. Their son was unhappy for four years. The mother says:

> So it was a decision that we had to make very quickly, as the Headmaster of St George's school sort of said that if you're going to move him, this is the time to move him. Otherwise he's going to lose out on his GCSE courses, that's right yeah! So we made the decision. We moved him.

It is possible that these parents are attempting to deflect any criticism of their decisions by blaming the school, not only for being a poor school for their child, but also for making them choose it. What is the difference between pressure from a school and normal marketing and promotional activities? Perhaps the story of the another family, concerning the same school, exemplifies the difference. They rang up to enquire about the possibility of their son changing school:

> And we rang up the headmaster, and he said "well he can start in two weeks". Two weeks! I was thinking perhaps next summer or next term. "Well we can't keep the place for you". My gosh!

Needless to say, they chose to take the place and were not happy with the school. What is interesting about this story is that after getting to know the school, they realised that it was both non-selective and under-subscribed, as are most fee-paying schools in South Wales. There really was no need to hurry the decision at all. Local boarding schools have a further enrolment problem, faced with a national decline in boarding. They need a certain proportion of boarders to cover the cost of providing accommodation. Those in towns and cities are converting to day schools, but rural schools, especially those bounded by the Brecon Beacons do not have a large enough catchment area. They may, however, find themselves over-subscribed for their few day places, and turn this to their advantage, as witnessed by one family:

> At that stage we thought we'd put him in at Cromwell as a day boy. The Headmaster said "lets get him interviewed and then we can negotiate", so that's exactly what we did. We put him in for the scholarship, and as I say he didn't get it, but he got a place. He didn't have to do Common Entrance. Then we approached Cromwell, and said - OK now you've got him, can we have him as a day boy, and they've come back at the moment and said "no".... Presumably because of finance they have to have a certain percentage of paying parents for the upkeep of buildings. So I would think it's a financial arrangement. Apparently if you want a day boy in Cromwell, you've got to have their name down years in advance. Thirteen year olds all go as boarders.

The family are considering playing the school at their own game, by accepting the boarding place and converting to day status after a few weeks. It will be interesting to see how it turns out.

Another strategy used by fee-paying schools to maintain their roll is to create a junior section, and this is a growing trend in Wales (see Chapter 4). Such a section can be used to compensate for a falling roll, and provide other uses for existing facilities. However, the major reason is to "capture" potential applicants for the senior section. Where the senior section is over-subscribed, as it is in one case, the reverse policy comes into play. Allocating a certain number of places in the senior school to those from the junior section, acts as a magnet, drawing in as juniors those who do not want to face open selection at age 11. This story was mentioned by two families, but was perhaps most eloquently expressed by a father who was concerned, not that his daughter would not get in, but that when she did, she would be with children of lower academic ability:

> Father - [The Head] said a fixed number of places will go to the juniors from Henrys, and then the rest to outside, and I was under the impression that it was open competition in the senior school, like all the applicants whether they be from Henrys or not. I didn't like to hear that, but to me that is a recent innovation, the inside track for the junior school. To see that inside track was a surprise and one I didn't appreciate. We are sacrificing things to send our daughter, and that inside track could or would dilute the standards in the upper school, if you haven't got that filter.
> Researcher - They claim to filter the previous year in the junior school.
> Father - Bullshit. Absolute bullshit. We had girls being pulled out of Orange school - this is all gossip between mums.... perhaps a quarter of them, to go to Henrys to get that inside track. Their mums are basically said that's why we're doing it. The local gossip on the doorstep is that they wouldn't stand a chance to get into Henrys via Orange. I'm a great believer in open competition. I wanted to know what the fees were. Whether the rolls were going up and down, because I start to get the feeling that.... [the Head] was manipulating the entrance arrangements, changing the curriculum to make it more appealing to everybody, so she could carry out her goal of making it a commercially successful school. The changes that were going on are degrading its character.

A "before and after" motif appears in several interviews, with schools promising one thing during the choice process, and not being able to fulfil the promise later. Of course, no one can predict the future, but there seems to be more than merely errors of judgement being made here. One family reported that they considered one school this year which had very poor accommodation, only because it has plans to move to larger premises in the near future. Another family told how they had moved all four of their children away from that same school, since there was no sign yet of the move to new premises that they were promised at interview seven years ago.

A further family were concerned about the difficulties of a move to a state school, which was much larger than the primary, and were reassured by the evident care of the school, but later had to move the child again:

> Before she went there they said can you tell us who your friends are, and we'll make sure you are in a class with your friends. [pause] In actual fact

they made sure there were no friends, that she was .... so she started off with no friends, and she struggled on for a bit.

This could be incompetence by the school, or even "sour grapes" from the parents, but taken together the stories presented here and the evidence concerning the schools literature in Chapter 6 suggest that the principle of *caveat emptor* rules, particularly in the fee-paying sector of education, from which all of these stories emerge. Perhaps these "survival techniques", to use the expression of Griffiths (1991), are the result of increasing competition for a dwindling customer base. If this approach is one outcome of the increased competition between schools due to marketisation, and the private sector is providing a clue to the future its state-funded equivalent, there is a need for much better safeguards for the consumer. These school businesses are often small, and under-subscribed. One cannot be surprised that they show parents the better of their two Chemistry laboratories on Open Day, for example. However, this also happens in the far wealthier and more prestigious traditional foundation, or "public", schools, and what might surprise Open Day visitors more is that the other laboratory has a gas leak, and unfilled trenches cut in the floor to runs pipes through, and that this is not a temporary state. Children have been taught in here for over two years, as happened in one case.

Ironically, in England, as opposed to Wales, the pressure from such traditional fee-paying schools is almost the reverse. They are well-equipped, but out of the price range of most families in South Wales:

> I think Jack would have loved it, but my husband didn't want him to go away, and I don't think I did either. Apart from that it would have been colossally expensive. He would have loved it. He could have gone to Springwater or Hillside, where they had a decent rugby team.

Influence on the family can also come from the existing school, sometimes clearly with the best interests of the child at heart, but sometimes also to increase its own prestige. If there is anything close to a performance indicator for primary and preparatory fee-paying schools, it is their record of placements, and scholarships, at prestigious senior schools. That is how they can sell themselves to the next generation of potential customers.

One mother obviously admires the Head of the feeder primary attended by her daughter, who is helping her decide between three schools. It is clear that the Head does have the best interests of the child at heart - the same Head has been praised by other families - but it is interesting that the school she vetoes is also the one that would look least impressive on an honours board:

> Before you start, so you don't think that I'm influenced, the greatest influence upon us is Jo, the Headmistress, otherwise he would have been moved [earlier], and we would not have considered Cromwells. Her personal qualities are the reasons why I sent him there in the first place, and my respect and admiration for her are such that what she says carries more weight than anything.... To begin with she felt that maybe the cathedral tradition, and the mix, that from a personal view, Wakeford

would suit Peter very well, but from an educational view Cromwell would suit him very well, and that we would have to be more active in making sure that he had a balanced social life outside school to compensate for it. I haven't asked her straight out. She probably favours Cromwell, but her comment to us in the summer was, "he has to go one of those two schools, he cannot go to Redfields". She's absolutely emphatic. I phoned her up, and said he'd been offered the major scholarship there - "You do not accept it". We'll wait and see. She is very very firm and that is why I find it difficult, as I like the people there.

A parent-centred family describe a situation which is unique among the interview transcripts, although probably not that unusual overall, where many of the micro-political strategies used in choice come together in the same story. The parents played the two card trick on their son, attempting in this way to reach an ostensibly consensual choice. They wanted him to board, and like the mother described above they achieved their goal by showing him two boarding schools, only one of which they actually wanted to use. The "phoney" school was even further away from home in this case, and not as appropriate. This risky strategy, aimed at getting the child to the more prestigious senior school, was suggested by his existing school. The deputy Head joined the parents in applying pressure on the child, and eventually the child "chose" the correct school, despite having hated boarding before. As the story is so complex, and the plot so devious, it is quoted from at length:

He's got somebody in the Village school, a teacher.... who's actually taking him on the side and helping him, because originally he said "no way. If I have to board, I'm not going". But I said to this teacher I'm sure something must have happened when he was at his other school because he will not tell us. But slowly since he's been here, he's said "you don't realise how much I was being bullied, and I couldn't tell you". So this teacher, the deputy head, he and Jack have a really really good relationship and he's been talking and sharing with him. Jack's nearly six foot now, and so he's explained to him how because he's physically so much bigger and stronger, he's more assertive, and not so timid and this sort of thing, and that Jack's not looking at it right. ... So he's talked it through to the point of accepting.... Also the teacher at Village, who was helping John with the problem over boarding, had recommended to us that we went to Hillside school. He thought that Jack's problem, when he saw something else, you know we said to Jack, yes at Cromwell you'd have to board, BUT the alternative could be this place here, over the bridge, what do you think of that? He felt it might have a psychological bearing on Jack. That if Jack went "no way, not on your life mate, I want to go to Cromwell". That's exactly what did happen. It was a risk, but he knew Jack.... It worked. You get teachers don't you, I expect there are other pupils who probably think he's the pits, but he's a real mans man, you know which suits Jack just down to the ground.

213

Although none of the interviewees admitted such practices themselves, many knew of cases or "friends of a friend", in which families had obtained a place at a school by deception. Unlike the stories of pressure from schools and parents on children, which all involve fee-paying schools, the stories of deception all involved state-funded schools. Their recent prevalence suggests they are a further result of the marketisation of education, but since they do not appear in the private sector, they have more to do with the artificial constraints of standard numbers of enrolment and catchment areas, than with increased choice *per se*.

One family applied to one of the most over-subscribed secondary schools in Cardiff, even though they lived on the other side of the city. Their child did have a cousin at the school, but the only justification accompanying their application was that they were intending to move closer to the school in a year or two, and did not want their son to have to move school again. They admit that they were lucky to get a place in a school in which every unsuccessful applicant goes to appeal. As English is not her first language, the mother found it difficult to explain her story at times, but her brief sentences are eloquent on this point:

> Some people just rent address to get in, or buy house and don't live there. We tell true, no lie. Want to move there.

Another family applied to the same school, with a similar story but were turned down:

> Again over-subscribed....that was part of it yes, because we weren't nearby and they were over-subscribed, but I think the, I don't really know, my husband went to that appeal.

The pressure on popular schools, unable to expand, faced with mounting appeals, and deceitful applications, and anxious to do the right thing, is now enormous, and some families, like the one below, do not take "no" for an answer. However, although like others they know of people who lie in applications, they, at least, were honest:

> Mother - Well, we went to appeals, you know we sort of um fought a bit of a battle. We tried to get into the Bishop of Merton, that was our first choice....We were very upset that we couldn't get into the Bishop of Merton.... but because we were not active Anglicans, chur, you know, that was ruled out. We did go to an appeal there as well. We went to a quite austere appeal, my husband and I. My husband is C of E but he's not practising and I am Catholic and practising, but that obviously went low, low down the priority, their list of priorities, um the school was over-subscribed and we were sort of well down the list, but that's what I would have liked....
> Researcher - Was your husband prepared to exaggerate his Anglican background for this purpose?

Mother - No, he didn't. He wasn't prepared to compromise, and we do understand that people do this. They sort of, they practise for a couple of months prior to their children going in, and then they lapse, but er no, he didn't, no he didn't. We were quite open with them and just sort of said we wanted Lionel to go there, A because obviously the school has a good reputation, B it is in the locality, C there is an emphasis on religion, and we are religious, and we would have liked him to be in that environment but obviously it wasn't taken onto consideration. We didn't battle again after that, having sort of applied and said no, then we went to an appeal, and then we were turned down, we didn't sort of battle after that. Maybe we should have done. We didn't really have much of a choice after that.

They visited the school they were offered, and hated it, but were eventually offered a place at their second choice school, after the start of the year:

They offered a place, I don't really know on what grounds, but he wasn't going into the Year 7, he was going into Year 8. They might have lost somebody. I don't really know.

Conclusion

British research on the process of school choice has focused on how families from different social class backgrounds go about selecting secondary schools for their children. This type of research also had the larger purpose of demonstrating the place of school choice in the wider processes of social and cultural reproduction. More recently, however, researchers have turned their attention to the micro-processes of school choice, at the level of the household, and the ways in which these are played out at the level of the family (Ball *et al.* 1995, David *et al.* 1994, Edwards *et al.* 1989, Fitz *et al.* 1993). Such research suggests that there is an intergenerational aspect to school choice, in addition to the dimensions of class and gender. The process of choosing involves both parents and children, even though in Britain it is only parents who have any statutory rights to "choice" in education.

It may be difficult for parents to distinguish between taking a child's preference into account (West and Varlaam 1991), and allowing the child as a person to choose, and this may account in some part for the differences reported by previous research. The evidence here suggests, however, that some parents have developed reasonably sophisticated strategies, which seem to empower children, and make "choice" decisions appear collective, but which also ensure that parental preferences are realised. The interview data reveal that parents may decide on a type of school first, sometimes without formal consideration of the alternatives, and generally without reference to the child, before selecting a few schools of this type, which are only then offered to their child as possibilities. The children may not be aware of the earlier steps, and so feel more empowered than they actually are. Some families have explicitly stated that this is their strategy - to direct the child while giving the appearance of choice - sometimes by "stacking" the choice, through the inclusion of patently undesirable schools.

Part of the significance of these findings is that they open a new avenue for exploring the issue of school "choice". Against this background, the sequence of the choice process is a significant factor in explaining the micro-politics of family decision-making, and suggesting why parental preferences can be made to prevail, even in an apparently consensual outcome. Future scholars investigating school choice may need to focus more rigorously on the intergenerational aspects of the process, perhaps looking for systematic variations in terms of gender, occupational class, and sector of choice. They certainly need to take account of the complexities of family-level negotiations in the construction of their research designs.

10 What are they paying for?

Introduction

This chapter concentrates on the 868 respondents from fee-paying schools in the sample for the survey, and relevant stories from the follow-up interviews (Gorard 1996f). The first section characterises the families involved, describing how they go about deciding to use the private sector, and then selecting a school within it. The second section looks at the reasons they report for making these choices, and the third one examines these reasons in light of the characteristics of the schools chosen. This chapter therefore seeks to answer several related questions, such as: who uses private schools, why do they use them, are private schools "good" schools, and are the users "good" choosers? The final chapter will use the tentative answers to these questions to discuss the light that they throw on the possible outcome of increased parental choice in the state-funded sector.

Choice of a fee-paying school

Who are the families using private schools, how do they fit with a concept of cultural or social reproduction, and how do they go about choosing their schools?

Families using fee-paying schools

A typical family using fee-paying education could be described as well-educated, living in the suburbs and with a parent in a non-manual occupation. However, the parents would have no background in private education themselves, and no particular loyalty to the fee-paying sector, or a particular school within it. Most will have sent, or intend to send, this or another child to a state-funded school. Thus, the majority of users of fee-paying schools have significant links with the state sector. It is important to realise that they are not an entirely different population from the users of state-funded schools. This finding makes it clear that the small private sector of schools is not simply acting as an agent of direct social

217

and cultural reproduction, packaging the advantages of the parents for their children. In addition to the minority of traditional users, there are those who experienced a selective grammar school education themselves (see Chapter 4), but who do not find such an opportunity in the current state-provision in Wales, particularly if they are not prepared to countenance education in the medium of Welsh at Ysgolion Cymraeg. It is perhaps therefore not surprising that some users of fee-paying schools appear to be avoiding the Welsh ethos, and sometimes the Welsh language, prevalent in the local state schools. They are prepared to pay for a little bit of England (Gorard 1997g). Some families have a strong religious motivation for using a private school. There are other families who are not prepared to use a state-funded school, because of a previous bad experience, or because their child has particular problems. Finally there are what may be a growing set of families, who are using a cheap fee-paying school because they were denied entry to the state school of their choice.

Perhaps the first myth to challenge about users of fee-paying schools is that there is often a family tradition of use. In this study, only 30% of the mothers, and 28% of the fathers of children in private schools went to a private school themselves, and even with these few, there is no indication that the child was commonly sent to the same school as either parent. With the present generation, there is also little evidence of fierce loyalty to the private sector. Only 52% of the parents using a private school had the intention that the child would remain in private education throughout their school life. If nearly half of the children in private schools are going to change sectors at least once in their life, this indicates a very volatile private sector. Secondly, in families where one child was in a private school, over 30% of their school-age brothers and sisters were currently in a state-funded school. The private sector in education then, is not the exclusive domain of a group of traditional family users, as perhaps implied by previous research at large English boarding schools (Fox 1990), and to that extent this finding is in line with that of Walford (1990).

However, the families described here are definitely privileged. As defined by the parent in each family with the most prestigious occupational class, parents of privately educated children are generally professional and highly educated. Only 3.4% of parents have manual occupations, and only 1.7% are unpaid, which includes those retired, as well as those out of work. The vast majority are in the service class, while 49.2% of the mothers, and 62.5% of the fathers have a first degree. The proportions of parents in the service class, and of those with degrees, are both considerably higher than the national averages. Surprisingly the figures are even higher in this respect than those reported by Whitty et al. (1989), and Fox (1985) in HMC schools in England, whereas it was assumed before the study that the users of the smaller private schools in Wales would be less advantaged than those using the genuine "public" schools in England. There are several explanations for this surprising result. The scale for measuring the notion of occupational class is far from perfect. Respondents may have "inflated" their position in their self-description, and the researcher may have inflated their position by misunderstanding those descriptions. Titles such as "scientist" or "sales manager" are very hard to classify. Perhaps there is also a trend towards what were traditionally middle-class occupations in society, discernible even since 1985, and the question has to be asked whether having a desk and working in an office puts a person in the intermediate or service class merely because they do not get their hands dirty. This is linked to what is probably the strongest explanation of the remarkable figures above. Occupational scales were traditionally devised for male wage-earners in nuclear families, and it is already reported that using the scale with females as well tends to "inflate" the middle-class. For example, West *et al.* (1994) reported a much higher proportion of mothers than fathers were in non-manual occupations in the same families. The present study used the same kind of scale, applying it to all families, and selecting the class on the basis of the most prestigious occupation, in families where there was more than one wage-earner. This procedure, although more realistic than using the least prestigious occupation, clearly exaggerates the class of the respondents, compared to 1985, for example. Even though such methodological reasoning accounts for part of the picture, it is clear that the class profile of fee-paying school users is high, and that the Assisted Places scheme, brought in to widen the class catchment of private schools, has had little apparent overall effect in the region since it applies to so few schools.

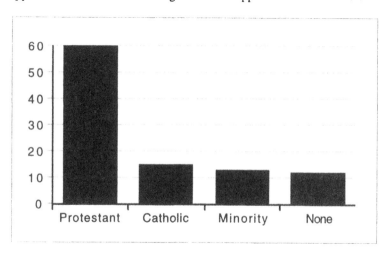

Figure 10.1 Frequency of family religion

So, the local users of private schools are privileged, but not traditionally committed to the private sector in education. They might be parents looking for entry to the service class for their children (Griffiths 1991), or those dissatisfied with an experience of the state sector. The Bursar of one of the focus schools claimed that the prospectus, and other advertising material, was deliberately made to appeal to those facing problems in state education, since "in most cases, applications are from families who are new to independent education". One such identifiable group are in-migrants to South Wales, perhaps from England, or beyond. No questions were asked concerning ethnic background, but the question about the main family religion revealed a surprisingly high proportion of families with a minority religion, such as Hinduism or Islam, in fee-paying education (Figure 10.1). Minority religion can be seen as a rough proxy for some of the families who would be described by the Census 1991 as "non-white". The Census reveals that "whites" are 98.5% of the population in Wales, and that the majority of the "non-whites" are from the Indian sub-continent (OPCS 1993), and who would have a family religion included in the minority category. Given that the other religious categories will also contain "non-white" minorities, such as those of African origin, it can be seen that fee-paying schools are attracting a disproportionately large number of families of minority ethnic origin. It is possible that these families are disproportionately wealthy but such an explanation seems far less likely than that there is either something about state-funded schools that such families are avoiding, or something special about what private schools are providing for them.

The gender breakdown of the children in fee-paying schools is interesting, in that there are a much larger number of girls. This result is also distinct from that of much previous work, which found a larger proportion of boys in fee-paying schools, and led one observer to conclude that there is a "discrepancy between what parents are prepared to pay for their sons and their daughters" (Griffiths 1991 p.86). She found, as this study did, that there were often many more boys than girls in the majority of ostensibly coeducational schools, and tried to explain this partly in terms of a difference in the willingness to pay for the different genders. There have been some indications in this study to support that notion. However, Griffiths does not include single-sex provision in her sample, and although it is true that girls-only schools are over-represented in the sample for the present study, it is also true that in South Wales, most single-sex schools are for girls only. There is no statistical evidence here to support the view that males are over-represented in private schools.

Choosing a fee-paying school

Most families using a fee-paying school, seriously consider between two and three schools before making a choice, which is significantly more than the average for the whole sample. There is a tendency for some to read a larger number of prospectuses before settling on their "choice set" (Table 10.1). The fact that some parents read prospectuses from schools that they are not "seriously" considering suggests that such information is used early in the selection process. Many families visit fewer schools than they are seriously considering which suggests that this step comes later in the selection process once the choice set has been whittled down. The possibility of distinct steps in the choice process is discussed fully in Chapter 9. In fact, the most influential source of information about a school is a network of friends and acquaintances, which is mentioned by 28.8% of respondents. Visits to the school are the next most influential, mentioned by 25.1%, which are only then followed by prospectuses, 10.4%, and lastly by tables of examination results, influencing only 9.4%.

Table 10.1
The number of schools in the choice set

	Number of schools	Standard Deviation
Number considered	2.10	1.05
Number of visits	1.84	1.50
Number of prospectuses	2.62	2.14

The parent nearly always play a major role in the selection of a new school, with only 3% leaving it mainly to the child. Most frequently, the decision is a joint one (51%), rather than made by the parents alone (46%). A further myth to be dispelled about private education is that boarding is common. Most schools do not cater for boarders, and 95.3% of users of fee-paying schools in South Wales are day pupils with no desire to board. However, it must be said that this figure is biased, since parents of boarders are, in general, harder to contact than those of day pupils. Although 24.1% of the respondents are receiving aid with the school fees in the form of Assisted Places, scholarships, and bursaries, 89% of them already pay, or are prepared to pay, the full fees. This finding suggests that there may be a hidden subsidy for some families, who do not really require the assistance with fees, and it confirms, and presages, some of the stories from interviews suggesting that the level of fees is not a major factor in the selection of a specific private school.

Reasons for choosing a fee-paying school

There is no particular reason to expect that any of the criteria, factors or models discussed in Chapter 7 should not apply to fee-payers, as well as to anyone else. Therefore, it is not necessary to repeat the foregoing analysis. What follows is a summary of the ways in which the fee-payers differ markedly either from the rest of the respondents, or from what might be expected, as well as a variety of accounts from the interviews relating specifically to those choosing to "go private".

Findings from the survey

Table 10.2
The advantage factor

Variable	Loading
Later advantage	0.62
Useful contacts	0.61
Social status	0.53
Career advantage	0.37

The principal components analysis was run again involving only those using, or intending to use, a private school. It is a tribute to the stability of the solution that, as with the split-half analysis, the same seven factors emerged. However, an eighth factor also appeared, which has been labelled "advantage" (Table 10.2). This factor became the basis of a prompt in the interview schedule for fee-payers, and interestingly was usually denied by them as a motivation. Although, of course, they could be being disingenuous on this point, the fact that this advantage factor is rated more highly by children suggests that the adult interviewees may be being perfectly candid, and that what the survey was showing up was the desires of fee-paying children, who have not appeared in previous studies, and who do not appreciate small poorly provided private schools, which is the reality of what most of them are faced with. They may be motivated therefore to look beyond their time at school in order to seek some justification for their supposed privilege.

Of the remaining seven factors, two of them - resources and safety - are rated lower by fee-payers as a whole, while three - outcomes, tradition and size - are rated higher. Whether these three are appropriate criteria to be used to select the schools concerned is discussed below. Of the variables not used in the PCA, several showed differences between the two sectors. The convenience variables, such as friends, siblings, and travel were reportedly less important for fee-payers, which is as predicted by the previous work quoted in Chapter 2 (e.g. GPDSA 1995). Perhaps the biggest surprise is that there is no evidence for a great desire for selection of any kind. Although the appearance of the advantage factor may have class overtones, the users of state schools actually rated the importance of having other middle-class children at school significantly more highly than the fee-payers. The fee-payers also clearly prefer other pupils to be from a mixture of ethnic backgrounds, and for there to be *no* Welsh ethos and *no* Welsh language teaching, while it is the state school users who prefer the majority of the other pupils to be "British". There is some evidence of families, particularly in-migrants, using private schools to avoid the "Welshness", and, in some cases, what is seen as the racism in local state-funded education (Gorard 1997$_g$).

Reports from the interviews

As suggested by the survey, many of the families using fee-paying schools in South Wales are doing so for the first time. Some parents, like the one below, spoke of their wonder at the new world of schools that was now available to them. They also felt that by being "prepared to pay", they were suddenly empowered with real choice, perhaps for the first time, but that the responsibility made them more critical. This is one of the few signs in this study that public choice theory may work out in practice, as well as some feel that it does on paper, at least for the parents described here. Choice, for them, leads to critical appraisal:

> I'm glad we have the choice. Mind you when you do decide to go for private education, the choices that present... all of a sudden you've got choices, whereas in the state system they go from junior school to comprehensive school to whatever and that's it. But all of a sudden when you have got choices, you obviously become more critical and you want results and just making the choices, are we doing the right thing? And that caused a lot of heartache... Every experience was a new one, I didn't know what common entrance was. How important is it? Why isn't it based on the National Curriculum?

The survey suggests that there are three major common reasons for choosing a private education. One of these, tradition, is clearly important to many parents, and as such is discussed separately in Chapter 8. The other two reasons are: the academic outcomes, and the size of the school and classes, which is linked by PCA to dissatisfaction with state schools. Both of these are discussed here, after a summary of the views of parents on that defining characteristic of private schools - the payment of fees.

Payment of fees Perhaps the first issue to be aired concerning fees should be the notion of a threshold of affordability. Are private schools an option for most families, or are they the preserve of a clearly privileged elite? Chapter 6 shows how low the fees are in some fee-paying schools, and how many of the other schools offer inducements in the form of assistance with fees. In general, the most expensive schools, the traditional foundations, offer the most scholarships and bursaries, and are more likely to be part of the Assisted Places scheme, providing free, or subsidised, places to families unable to afford private education themselves. The religious schools, and some of the proprietary schools, on the other hand, charge very little. It has already been shown in this chapter that most fee-payers went to state schools themselves, have used state schools for their children, or would be prepared to do so again. Chapter 7 reported that the sample as a whole, including the users of state schools, rated both of the variables concerning the level of the fees charged by schools as being "less than important". None of these findings suggest that private schools are only available to a financially privileged minority.

Many of the families made spontaneous comments at interview about the difficulties of paying fees, and the implications of their private school strategy on the rest of their life. Most of these were expressed in terms of clear alternatives, and chosen lifestyles. The family were consciously giving up something else, something that other families might see as normal and non-elitist, such as a package holiday. In this context, a mother using a proprietary school said:

> Don't mention the fees. I could have had a nice large house. It does make life very hard and its going to be hard for a long time to come as far as I can see. We are ordinary people who live in an ordinary house. We have one week a year at a cottage in Devon, and put it all into education.

During one interview, the daughter was sitting in the house with her coat on, as it was quite cold, but her mother would not allow her to put the heating on. To the same question, a mother using a traditional foundation school replied:

> No, yes, I can afford to buy it, but on the other hand they might not want to buy it. We don't go out very much, I drive around in just about the oldest car in Cardiff (X reg). I'm not pleading poverty, but there's no way... I'm not poor, but we don't eat out, we don't go out, we don't socialise. We choose to spend our money in a certain way on our children's education, and just because somebody else doesn't choose to do it that way, doesn't mean to say I'm right and they're wrong.

A third mother pointed out that the family only had an old car, and did not go on holidays, seeing education as an investment in the future, and concluded: "if that's the right school I've got to find the money somehow. We do without other things ". A fourth said, "I mean, we had to scrape to get him in and keep him in and all that...". Even a mother who was talking to the researcher in her "palatial" home with five sports cars in the drive, saw the fees as a replacement for something that others in her position might pay for - a wedding, for example.

When she leaves school and becomes a wage earner of her own, I don't think I will feel nearly as obliged towards providing for her than most people would, less so, because I feel then I've done it. So if she came to me and wanted a huge white wedding that cost £7000 I'd say you'd better start saving up girl. Or I want a little car because my friend's got one. When you earn enough you will. I'm concentrating it all into now and hopefully because of that she will become independent of a man, and able to go ahead and have her own career. I think its a much more secure foundation. All the expenditure's now.

She continues, although in the circumstances it was difficult to empathise with her talk of sacrifices:

I wasn't governed by fees, and all that will happen is that while Heather's away at school, one of my sales team is leaving. Instead of replacing them I'll take a bigger part in that. It's not without sacrifice, but I'll have more time to do it now instead of juggling both.

One family were so certain that their chosen school was right that they continued with their plans, despite a dramatic change in circumstances, and their story introduces a new theme. When in financial difficulties, families turn to their relatives, and to the schools themselves, for help, both of which happened in this case:

It's not really to do with money though. My husband's been bankrupt in the middle of it all, yes his business, as an individual, so we lost everything, house, cars the whole lot, and yet my mother paid one term, my sister paid one term, and through it all we gradually worked, and got the money together for him to keep going, because we believe in it so strongly.

So, a pattern begins to emerge of families seeing themselves as deprived of opportunities, that others in their financial position would take for granted, whether a large house, car, holiday, or heating, in order to pay for their schools. As a continuation of this theme, many of the same families pointed out that once they had made up their minds to use a private school, they did not necessarily go for the cheapest, which is confirmed by the low rating given to all of the fee-related variables in the survey. In fact, the most popular and larger private schools in Wales tend also to be the more expensive, which is the opposite of what is predicted as the result of a free-market. Larger schools with lower proportional unit costs should be able to offer their services cheaper. The irony for choice advocates is that small schools tend to be popular, according to the reports, while popular schools tend to grow larger. Thus, there are two ways in which schools are not a standard market commodity. Relative popularity does not reduce the cost, and consumers do not use cost as a major criterion of choice. One mother pointed out:

So you see I don't consider paying for it as a choice, it's not a financial decision... it doesn't matter what the fees were, if that was the school we felt was right, we'd find the fees from somewhere. Do you know what I mean?

A father, questioned about the chance of a scholarship to a traditional foundation school, stated:

We're always hopeful, that would be very pleasant , but I think no. It came down to the right school rather than that one's £100 cheaper than that one.

A mother looking at a cheaper school agreed:

I don't make a decision at all on which school because they've got cheaper fees, or he's a day boy because its cheaper. I wouldn't even consider those criteria.

It came as no surprise that the woman with the sports cars also denied wanting the cheapest:

Having been appalled at how expensive it was going to be anyhow, the actual difference in fees is only £2-3000 between the cheapest and the dearest. The way I looked at it, if you're going to be done for £11000 a year, you might as well be done for the 13 and have the name Roedean open doors for you.

One mother, whose daughter was offered a scholarship to a for-profit school, claims that this had very little to do with the choice of private education, or the specific school:

She didn't get the 50% but they wrote and said that because she was so desperate for work that they would make a second scholarship for her , so she's got 25%.... I think if it hadn't have been for the scholarship, she'd have gone anyway.

Although the absolute cost of each school does not appear to have much influence on the decision, the offer of an Assisted Place, or scholarship at this stage can help the family select a school. In some cases the decision is so finely balanced that the award can tip the balance, even when there is no financial need. The award suggests that the family is getting a bargain, and it also carries some prestige. In some cases the monetary value of the award is anyway passed directly to the child as a reward:

It was felt, let him sit all three and then maybe there would be an easy decision on what he was being offered. I think it's almost a case of there's got to be something that swings it one way or another. I think if it came down to it at the end of the day, it wouldn't be made on financial decisions but it is an indication of what the school wants to do. So, we're looking for something but at the moment the decision's still not being made easy.

On the other hand, there were some families currently using both state and fee-paying schools who reported a much more significant role for the cost of schooling in the choice process. The comment "please" next to the question on the survey about reduced fees has already been mentioned. Of those currently using state schools, the parents who made comments on this issue often regretted not being able to use fee-paying schools, and gave lack of finance as their reason. The following comments are very similar, but from two different families:

> We are not in a financial position to even consider private education.

> We live in a catchment area - so it was a foregone conclusion.....we did not feel that there were many options available to us. We briefly considered Henry's school but our daughter wasn't keen, and too expensive.

The children, who gave a higher rating to the importance of fees in the survey, were consistent with this when they made comments on the form, such as:

> I am here because I won a scholarship. If I hadn't we couldn't afford the fees, I would have gone to [state comprehensive] and I think I'd have been just as happy there.

Obviously, the parents of families already using the private sector could not really claim that they could not afford it, rather than that they had to make sacrifices, but a few went against the general trend, and claimed that the level of fees affected their choice of schools within the sector. One family with three daughters were relying on a bursary:

> And in our case, whether they offered a substantial clergy bursary has to be one of the ... deciding factors. Deacon offers 16.7% off which is a very nice sum. Tower with their own bursary, offered about £3,000 off the fees. So you have to look seriously at the school.

Two other families found their choice within the sector limited by cost:

> It was quite unsettling really when you realise what was out there, because we couldn't afford for him to go. I wanted him to go, and my brother has got three boys in Wellington school in Somerset.

> That definitely comes into it.... at the moment, yes. Both Cromwell and Wakehouse are very reasonably priced I'm told. If money were simply no problem, we wouldn't be excited about whether he got into Cromwell or Wakefield. We'd say fine and send him to Millfield or something. Yes, it is a problem. We are going to be struggling to keep him at private school, although we have a certain amount of help from my mama.

However, the fact that fee-payers cannot buy the most expensive model does not imply anything for the threshold of affordability. By way of analogy, most of them have a car, but would not consider buying the most expensive model, for example. Whatever the fees are, the people paying an "an arm and a leg" find them "one heck of a lot of money", as two parents put it. This feeling is transmitted to the children, several of whom mentioned the pressure to do well, and occasionally the guilt of failure, that comes from this. It was starkly put by one boy on his survey form: "when you pay there's more pressure".

Size   The survey suggests that one of the key reasons for using private schools is their small size, and the small size of their teaching groups. This finding is especially relevant for those families who have had some experience of the state sector, and their stories came up again and again in the interviews. In the first two examples, parents with children in Year 6 at the same state primary bemoaned their fate, and although their reasons for wanting to use a private school are various, they are both centred around a complaint about the size of the schools:

> From personal experience we know that our daughter would receive a better education if sent to private due to smaller classes, individual attention, wider curriculum, higher expectation.

> I think they are all in a state of decay. I only wish I could afford private education. It is a shame that our education system is this bad. The schools are too big, no one really seems to care.

Parents, who had previously used state schools, and decided to change, had similar views, in retrospect. One mother had been upset at the complacency of popular state schools, and chose a private alternative because it:

> ... offered small classes, and a caring attitude, as opposed to all local schools approached. The children were considered as a nuisance factor at interviews with heads because they brought up the numbers in the class.

Most private schools are under-subscribed on the other hand, and parents "have a pound in their pocket that they want". Others families, with children having special educational needs, felt that the size of the groups in state schools hindered the identification of the problem. The following is only one of several similar cases:

> Very dissatisfied with state schools. For this child to be statemented took one year!!! She has not needed special needs teacher here and has made good progress due to a very caring environment.

One family moved their son twice in two years because the shock of going from a small primary to a large state secondary school was too much. This was when they decided to "go private". However they mix their points about the size of the school with comments about the class backgrounds of the pupils, which were also reported to differ.

> We felt that after the first year there his standards just dropped academically and socially, ha, ha, having been in um you know in a small

community in the convent for, for all his primary school life, then we moved him for that one year to comprehensive, and we just found, as I say, the first term, the first half year's report wasn't too bad and then the second half the report went right down, and er we just felt we'd made a mistake. We tried it, but we thought it was a mistake. The size was a problem, the environment was a problem, and the social sort of scene wasn't there.

Another family found the problem of large schools so great for one child that they overrode the domino effect described in Chapter 8, and sent two children to different types of schools. However, as also noted in Chapter 8, the fact that the child being paid for is a boy, while the other child is a girl, would not unduly surprise some observers anyway.

That is why really he is at a private school, because the classes are small. Chris is in a class of twenty-six twenty-seven, but after the summer she'll be in a class of forty plus. Robert is in a class of only eight, but he's never been in class bigger than about sixteen, no he hasn't. He does get a lot of attention.

One of the subsidiary advantages of a small school is that the parents are easy to identify, as well as those children with problems. According to a mother:

I never walk in there and say I'm Mary Straker, I don't have to say that. At the parents' evening I say I'm Richard's mother and they immediately know who I am. Whereas possibly in this school [outside the window], would they know who I am? I doubt it. Such enormous amounts of people. I don't think the pupils can know half the teachers. That's sad isn't it. Because you take your school days to the end of your... that's where you get your first impressions, and I hope my children will look back on their school days as something happy.

Four other families tell similar stories of avoiding the anonymity, uncaring attitude, pupil mix, and above all the scale of state schools, even though these families have not used them for the current generation. However, they complete this tale of a consistent view, held by some at state schools, some who have used and rejected them, and some who have never used them. The schools are just too big. Two fathers say:

Elizabeth being an only child, she hasn't got the confidence and the panache that would mean she would survive to the best of her ability anywhere, so by going to a kinder environment, we're reducing the risks.

I think it is a major factor in state schools because you're given the 40 kids and essentially that class is going to go at the level of...of the middle group, or lower to middle group, whereas because there's been a selection process for private schools, there all going to be some sort of standard, they have to attain that standard.

228

Two mothers say:

> I wouldn't want Victoria to be in a class of state school size, thirty-five to one teacher.... I don't know how the state system works and whether you get the same access. I can't really comment as I haven't been myself and haven't investigated the state system.

> Orange is a very small school, and to go from the top of a little school like that and you are top dog and prefect at the age of eleven, to go to a huge school. I often think what would she be like if she went here to [large state school].

Finally in this section, to show that the size factor is not solely used to explain a choice of sectors, but can also determine the type of school within it, a father explains why his daughter was sent to a grass-roots school, the smallest school in the survey - with seven pupils at the time of writing:

> The essential reason for private education was the ability of a school to kick-start a young child into using its brain. A small class has this capacity. She needs a small caring school which encourages self-achievement and not the 'win at all costs' attitude of a lot of private schools.

Outcomes The third factor of especial interest for fee-payers, which emerged from the survey, was academic outcomes - referring to examination results, university entrance, and career prospects. However, the absolute size of the difference between fee-payers and others was small, (0.13), compared to the difference in the mean ratings for the size of the school (0.73). This finding is generally reflected in, and confirmed by, the stories from interviews. Parents, especially of older children, are concerned with good outcomes, which are seen as crucial, but which are also always assumed to be available in the schools of choice. This easy assumption that good academic outcomes are possible, which is confirmed by the relative lack of interest in league tables, means that the fee-payers almost take them for granted, and so report other reasons for choosing a private school, such as character development, social standing, manners, and frequently elocution. Parents of bright children explicitly claim that their child would do well in any school. It is the parents of what they describe as "average" children who see the private schools as acting as a spur to attainment. No one, in either sector, seems to consider the possibility that private schools may actually be less effective in this respect. One story introduces several of these ideas:

> No you can just go down and look at the Bishop of Llandaff and see their exam results, they've got fantastic results haven't they? And Cardiff High, I know they've got some which aren't, but at the end of the day, if you've got a child that's bright but they go to the state school, or a public school it's not going to stop them achieving their great heights. I don't consider it as buying an advantage. I'm buying a type of education. I don't see it as an advantage. If I couldn't afford it, I wouldn't be bitter and say my child

will be a second class citizen. It's more the values are different, this is what we both, we were both bought up in this way. If there was a grammar school on my doorstep, it would probably be different then.... But as they're not there any more...

The two schools mentioned are both state-funded, and the mother is denying the thesis that private schools help equivalent children gain better results, and suggesting alternative reasons for choice, although even here she appears to be pining for a type of education from the past (Chapter 8). One couple agree (eventually) that the outcome for a bright child does not depend on the sector of school. The mother seems to have few academic worries after moving both of her children to a local state school, however there are class-cultural concerns revealed in her concern about body-piercing and regional accents:

> There are plenty of entrants to Oxbridge from the Mash school, and we know that plenty of Alan's friends at the Village school [traditional foundation type] were doing very badly. My husband is adamant that if you've got it it doesn't matter where you go, state or private no matter what, it won't benefit you in the private system at all, and I perhaps agree now. I'm just a bit worried that if one is easily led, there might be a few more ruffians and people to disrupt in these large state classes and I worry that Geraldine might go down that road. If after two years we decide that she's now going to lots of discos and sticks rings in her nose and things then she'll be out straight away. Alan's certainly got more of a Carediff [sic] accent since going to Mash, I must say.

Another family have a similar view, but they see outcomes as a matter of probability. By using a traditional foundation school, they are attempting to buy out the risk:

> Although looking around some of the local schools here, the education she could get and possibly would get might be just as good certainly as Henry's. But very much more of a gamble.

On the other hand, many of the comments at interview assume, or directly state, that private schools lead to better results, for whatever reason. Three parents made almost indistinguishable comments in this regard:

> From my own experience in the state sector as a teacher and a parent, too much emphasis is placed on "special needs", meaning low ability. Children of average ability but willing to work also need special attention. The state sector is not providing this.

> The state sector tends to concentrate on the most and least able and the ones in the middle get lost.

The state system was totally inadequate for my daughter's needs. Being average she was being left behind in every aspect of education. This is not the case now.

One parent is in a minority in claiming that a private school is necessary because her son is clever, rather than of average abilities. The problem is that he is too clever:

Paul is academically bright, he's also musically very good. I got the distinct impression, and also from teaching children in the state system, he would be allowed to be one or he would be allowed to be the other, with the children. He could not be both. That's going over the top. He would find life difficult. That would be my worry.

Several parents, coincidentally all currently using feeder proprietary schools, and envisaging a move to a traditional foundation school, were clear that private education leads to better academic outcomes, but that they were paying for more, sometimes much more than this. The academic results are simply taken for granted. One mother probably puts this in a nutshell:

We choose private education because we believe it is the best, and yes I agree... but it is also character building.... to bring out whatever, no matter how thick he was, find where he was gifted and bring it out of him. You know, lift that potential in him, whatever it was, even if it was carpentry or metal work, it wouldn't matter, whatever it was it would bring out the potential in him, but I don't equate that with finance at all. Yes it definitely is an advantage. We want him to get A levels, he probably would have got A levels at another school, but I think it definitely is character building as well, it goes along with the A levels.

A father is even clearer that private schools lead to academic advantage:

I hope so. Otherwise you may as well not bother. I am buying an advantage, that is the long and the short of it. I'd be dishonest if I didn't say so. Hopefully we're going to have a few other things thrown in as well, a bit of elocution, a bit of deportment, opening the door, a little gentleman at the end, a little gentleman that might have a few qualifications. I think you get a bit more for your money than just that. There's precious few opportunities in the world today anyway. If they are not going to have that piece of paper, they're not going to get through the door to impress at the interview are they?

Another family also make the assumption about outcomes, and look for more, including, of course, tradition and size:

And it's not just the academic results, it's whether the child is happy. That's the most important thing as far as we are concerned, obviously we wanted the results too but I also wanted a well balanced child that

231

maximised his potential. It's costing us an arm and a leg. You do wonder sometimes if you did make the right decision. I do. How would they have turned out if they had gone to the local school? In a class of 35, Richard would probably have got away with murder and nobody would have been noticing or had time to notice much. I've got a polite presentable confident young man on my hands. He's 15, he likes the girls, but he's not one for hanging around the street corners, hopefully not doing drugs, and I know where he is at night. So far I'm very pleased with my son. Not terribly pleased with his exam results, but I don't blame the school for that. He's terribly disorganised. I think he will get A levels in excuses.

It sounds as though this family are going to be disappointed with the outcome, even if they do not blame the school. Do the schools only get the credit for successful outcomes, or do all parents really accept that the school does not make much difference in this respect? There is an indication in several interviews that runs counter to the finding in the survey that pupil selection is not important. Parents do care about who is also using the school. They do not really care about selection by ability, but want the school to be small and inhabited by "nice" people, people like themselves perhaps. This father is one of the few parents to make an explicit reference to "high culture". This is what he is paying for. In response to a question about outcomes he said:

> I think that's half, maybe a third of the equation. I think the other third of the equation is an education as opposed to just results. Do you see what I'm trying to say? I just don't want him to come out with three A levels and be a completely boring old thing without any appreciation of the arts, drama, of music, or anything else. I want a complete rounded appreciation of everything. I think that is perhaps the most important thing. Very equal thing is that he must come out with adequate results and go on to some sort of further education and obviously the more of a chance you give him, the easier he's going to find it. If the school consistently get 98% As, Bs or whatever, the chances are that he's going to do reasonably well, and go on to university. I've seen people completely mortgage their lives for their children's education and then their children turn out to be complete dickheads, druggies or hippies.

"If the school consistently get 98% As, Bs or whatever, the chances are that he's going to do reasonably well". This comment by this father should be put at the top of school league tables of examination results. It sums up their appeal with startling clarity, and states directly his belief in a form of "passive" intellectualisation. This is the superstitious notion that children can achieve good results simply by being with other children who are going to get good results, and it is at the school level what Edwards and Whitty (1996) described as "competitive advantage by association" for the fee-paying sector as a whole. Presumably such an environment can have an effect in the form of higher expectations, good models of study for the child to copy and stimulating competition. However, his comment implies more than this and suggests, in addition, that schools achieving good results are good schools. He is confusing outcomes with effectiveness. This issue is referred to again later on in the chapter.

Dissatisfaction with the state sector As explained above, many of the fee-payers who were interviewed had recent experiences of the state system, and the evident dissatisfaction which led them to change is not solely based upon the size of state schools, although they may argue that whatever problems emerged might have been spotted earlier in a smaller group. Several comments were also made about the "undesirable" type of children at the state schools, and this links, in their minds, to the important issues of safety and bullying, as well as the more trivial ones of snobbery and regional accents. One family moved one of their sons from a private school, to a state school, but then moved him to another private school because:

> The children he started mixing with.... were not entirely sociable, um fights in the school all the time, fights on the buses all the time, and um it just wasn't the scene that we'd been used to and Dominic had been used to.

A mother moved her son to a private school after several years of problems at her local state primary. She is quoted elsewhere as saying that one day she found him playing outside while the school was in assembly, and that it was only when she took him away that the school told her that he rarely sat down. She accepts that he was not an easy child to deal with, but was concerned with the limited attention he was given in the state school, as well as the punishments, the lack of reporting, and the influence of other children. Almost as soon as he was moved, there was an improvement. She is quoted at length.

> It didn't work, it didn't work for my son. If he'd have stayed there I dread to think what sort of child he would have grown up. Robert was always a handful, right from the word go. Very demanding, very insecure and as he was my first child, I hadn't any relations round. I had him quite late in life, I found things very hard indeed and possibly I didn't handle him right, I don't know. When he went to school they said that he always seemed a bit distant. He didn't cause trouble in class, he was on a par with the rest. He'd come home and say he'd been put on the prickly mat, a rather barbaric punishment that if you don't behave they were put on a prickly mat. He seemed to be spending a lot of time on this prickly mat.... He would do silly things. I would go into school to pick him up and he would have thrown a child's headband on top of the roof. Silly little pranks. I felt that they didn't handle it really correctly so I was very glad when he left anyway. At that age they didn't have yearly reports.... I dread to think what would have happened if he had remained where he was. And also some of the boys that Robert got in with, he always seemed to get involved with ones that were worse than himself. Typical, they never pick on a sweet quiet boy.... In fact because I had never been to a state school I found it quite an interesting revelation. Um, I was amazed how things were just sort of so slack. They didn't seem to be pushed or motivated much. It all seemed to be like play time to me. No I felt even at a young

age, yes learning can be fun, but somehow they seem to spend so much time on not really getting down to things.... At the Village school [traditional foundation] they sorted him out pretty quickly, I remember his teacher, his form teacher calling me in after school, after he'd been there two weeks and saying it was the worst two weeks of her career.... yes she did do wonders for him.

Another mother also has criticism of the lack of care and attention given to her daughter at her local primary. This is presumably the kind of care that she believes can be provided in a private school, because of the small class size:

She did two or three years there.... and they said she was becoming disruptive and I said why's that, and they said well we set her work , and they were sitting her and this other child on a desk together. And the two of them would finish their work. They were the two fastest, and as soon as it was over they would start gassing so instead of setting them extra work, the teacher just left them to it and called them disruptive. Then I looked at the work and all the writing was done on drawing paper without any lines and the teachers said she's terribly messy. I said well without lines how on earth can a child be expected to know whether or not a 'y' goes through the line or whether a 'd' goes above it or what? So that really just clinched it for us.

Other parents react badly to the social mix of pupils in the state schools that they have seen, which they feel contributes to the generally poor behaviour that they complain of. These parents are generally not those who have a recent experience of state school, and so they rely on a variety of sources for the information to make their judgements. One mother used the behaviour of children in shops to justify private schooling:

Our children will have to be educated privately in senior school as our local comprehensive is appalling. The children flock to [name deleted] village at lunchtime and are abusive and can only be let into shops a few at a time because of theft.

Another made similar comments based upon observation in the high street:

There are an awful lot more schools but they weren't offering the right sort of ... socio-economic group.. well Valhalla school for a start [almost 100 yds away]. I think I would have had to have been desperate to send my child to Valhalla. She spent 18 months next door to Valhalla and watching the general behaviour of the children, I would never have contemplated it. I mean I really would have had to have been desperate....I've seen the atti.. the behaviour of the children. Uh swearing, general lack of courtesy, to everybody and everything. I mean, its unbelievable. I cannot believe how children can actually behave like that. If my, even now, if my twenty-five year old behaved like that she'd get a clip. I wouldn't think about it twice. I mean, they wouldn't dare to behave like that. I don't understand the attitude these days of having no respect for anyone and anything, and that school is rife with it. Its got to be just the general slapdash attitude. I mean I don't blame the staff, because they don't have...

One mother used material from conversations with her baby-sitter to help her justify not using a state school:

One of the things I don't like about the state system even in the short time I've been in contact is the, and the baby-sitters I've had here, you chat to these young girls, in some cases the very left wing attitude which is fed to these children. There's one girl.... and she was doing politics and it was just staggering how she was... if you sat down and chatted to her she was actually being fed this information and you say hang on a minute 'have they told you that it could be seen in a another' and it was just black or white and that's what I don't like. I don't approve of that. I think Victoria's got a very left wing teacher but she doesn't actually take her politics into school which is what I would expect. What the heck she's doing at a private school I don't know, but that's up to her, that's her conscience to live with. As long as she's not feeding it to my children that's what I want and maybe that's what I'm paying, what I'm choosing to isolate my children away from.

Another fears her daughter would not survive in a state school. She might be bullied for her posh accent, and she would meet boys.

At this stage I would be mortified if I had a change of financial circumstance and Heather had to go to a state school. I would be horrified because, two major reasons. Perhaps I've got a paranoia, I feel that Heather has been protected and sheltered from society. You go and throw a child who's had that amount of protection into a state school of 1000 pupils, thirty-five to a class, I would be seriously worried about how she would adapt and how she would be treated by the other children and what she would do then to try and fit in, that would really backfire on us all. You've got a crowd of girls who can be very spiteful, especially at that age, then you've got Heather who speaks so well, who is different, has been used to mixing with children who speak the same, who's parents have a different attitude and then to be thrown into a class of 35. Academically when she got there she would probably be ahead of the class, but she would slip back so quickly. She would stand out and in the effort to be accepted, I think my daughter would be daft enough to do stupid things, she'd end up sort of just to be popular doing things she knows are wrong, and I don't know where it will all end up.

On the other hand, many of the same parents who abhor their local state schools because of the violent, badly dressed, badly spoken, and scruffy pupils, seem to have the concurrent illusion that because the private school of their choice offers Assisted Places, or takes wealthy overseas pupils, it therefore introduces their child to the full range of social backgrounds. For them, the children at private schools are not a uniform elite. Perhaps they are merely all the nice children, of whatever background, gathered together by their well-motivated parents. In speaking of one of the oldest, most academic traditional foundation school in South Wales, one of these parents said:

> There's a complete cross-section at Henry's of parents, politically and socially. And socially. One of Veronica's best friends lives in Splott, Splo sorry, huh, huh. That's what I really like, a real cross-section. That's the way they want to spend their money. They don't want to spend it on holidays abroad, if they'd rather spend it on their children's education that's up to them. It's to do with your standards of life, not living but life and your attitude to life.

Parents are not the only ones who make the choice however, and some children were also reported to be concerned about the effect of the other pupils in state schools:

> And then we started thinking what are we going to do about Karen. And what do you want to do? Do you want to stay in Valhalla. She was worried about her peer group, smoking and fighting, and saying she would have to join in. So she wanted to move to private as well.

Several parents suggested that they would have preferred to use a state school, but had ended up considering the private sector because their first choice of school might not be available:

> Most good state schools are not available if you do not attend the feeder schools.

> One Head actually said that as I was out of the catchment area, he would advise the authority to turn down my request.

> It is very sad that after all the recent legislation the state system still fails to provide an adequate schooling system for all.

> We only put [popular state secondary] on the form. If he had not got in, we would use private, Hood school.

One family had used fee-paying schools for both children for much of their early education, but were beginning to think that they had made a mistake, in terms of the academic results and resources available:

> We've spent an awful lot of money on their education when we've got a very good comprehensive school up the road that seems to offer, there's dram.... my daughter's really keen on drama, very good sports, eight tennis courts, she's very good at tennis, there's athletics, it seems to have

everything. Whether she's going to cope with very large classes, remains to be seen.

Other reasons for choice Of course, school choice is, to a large extent, idiosyncratic, which is partly why the seven factors in Chapter 7 only account for around 60% of the variance in responses, and why the survey showed differences in terms of sub-groups, such as religion, age or gender which are so ccmplex. Surprisingly, if it possible to make such a comparison, less diversity was displayed by the respondents at interview. Each family had different circumstances, and their level of engagement with the market also varied (Chapter 9). However, most of them seemed concerned that the child was happy and safe first of all. Fee-payers saw this primarily as a function of school size, teacher and pupil motivation, and traditional styles of control and discipline. These characteristics create the ethos in which successful outcomes are seen as sure to follow.

Some parents mention other reasons for choice as being particularly important. This is very different from those who simply acknowledge the value of several school choice criteria. The reasons given here were uncommon, but they were the single most important reason to the individuals concerned. One parent said that they chose the Hood school, a stand-alone proprietary, because of its ethnic mix. This family, of Indian origin, wanted their child to feel comfortable with his peers, and not to "stand out" in the class. There is a tradition in Wales for parents in some privileged families to send their children to English boarding schools. The evidence, presented here for the first time however, suggests that a number of not so privileged families are fleeing into the smaller fee-paying schools in Wales in order to avoid National Curriculum Welsh. The spokeswoman for one group of parents in West Glamorgan, fighting this issue, sees the "Welsh language lobby" as so powerful that English speakers are ignored in policy-making (Prestage 1995 p.5). She claimed:

> This is not an area where a lot of Welsh is spoken, and while we do not oppose anyone who wants to have their child educated in Welsh, we do not see why we should have it imposed on our local schools.

There are several related strands in this opposition to Welsh language teaching in schools, including those who begrudge the use of scarce curriculum time for what they see as a "futile" language, those who are new to the region like the family above, or for whom English is already a second language, and those who are simply hostile to Welsh and its related culture. What is described is not a new phenomenon, and is also evident in the USA where there is suspicion of "bilingual education programs that appear intended to maintain a non-English linguistic subculture" (Coleman 1990 p. x). In the survey, the mean responses for the teaching of Welsh language (0.38) and a Welsh ethos in the school (0.27) are two of the lowest of the 73 possible reasons suggested to parents (Chapter 7) and they are even lower among users of fee-paying schools, especially small for-profit and grass-roots schools which have a significantly higher proportion of families with minority religions. The problems caused to this minority, among others, by the implementation of a bilingual educational programme based on the principle of territoriality in a region where the majority of Welsh-speakers now live in

237

predominantly English-speaking areas such as Cardiff, are described further in Gorard (1997f).

Several parents made comments on their survey form about the fundamental role of religion in education, but none of these volunteered to be interviewed, or at least none of those interviewed made such comments. Examples include:

> It is important that the school teaches my child in a Christian and Biblical environment.

> The single most important aspect of the school my child will attend is an adherence to Christian principles (John 14v6).

Fortunately however, one of the survey respondents from a PACE school, included a lengthy and well-composed letter which gives a more detailed glimpse of these views. In fact there is some indication in the letter that this parent had discussed the matter with others, and was mandated to put their point of view across. It is important since it purportedly represents the views of working class families from an ex-mining community with high unemployment, in a valley north of Cardiff. These are not the archetypal fee-payers. They care nothing for elocution, and little for academic outcomes, but they have this in common with those above. They want a school which is small, and traditional, in their sense, and they want to avoid the National Curriculum.

> It seems to us that most of the questions are biased to assume that parents are middle-class who send their children to private schools. We are not middle-class, but a working class family and happy to be so. The reasons mainly we choose to send our children to the school is because states schools have fallen in morality and are generally ill-disciplined, far too big, far too competitive and uncaring of pupils. They are also generally atheistic in their beliefs and teach from an "Evolutionist" view rather than seriously considering the claims in the Bible that God created the heavens and the earth. We also do not like the pressure that is put upon pupils in states schools to "perform" to certain standards. The National Curriculum is too pressurised for school children. There is not enough value put on children for who they are. Education should not just concern itself with the intellect. The heart/soul or personality of a person is probably even more important. It is no help to a child if he ends up highly educated but emotionally bankrupt. We see this happening in many young people today. Education has become striven, driven and distorted - like much in our competitive/materialistic Western Society - too much in terms of academic prowess is expected of children, when what they really need to know is that they are special, cared for and infinitely precious. These values we find in the school to which we send our children, and those values are worth far more than the best academic education for our children - even if we offered that education free. We hope this also helps you understand why we will not answer some of your questions.

Are private schools a good choice?

Parents are attracted to private schools because they are small and traditional, evocative of a past age, as well as appearing to offer the chance of better outcomes in terms of certification. Children, and to some extent their parents, are chiefly attracted to the apparent social status of attending a fee-paying school. These are the chief ingredients of the mix, although freedom from the National Curriculum, freedom from SATs and the disputes over testing - what one parent described as "the mess the state system is in" - and in some cases, religious self-determination all contribute their part. It is clear that the schools in question are generally small, and old-fashioned. They are exempt from the provisions of the Education Reform Act 1988. Do they also offer the opportunity of better outcomes, or is their reputation based upon the performance of a few famous schools, on the present policy of using raw score indicators, and on the attribution of quality caused by the payment of such high level fees?

Table 10.3
Outcome performance indicators

	GCSE	1+ G	93-95	5+ C	93-95	A lev.	Entry	PPC	93-95
State-funded									
Wales	-	89	78	41	39	-	-	15	15
Cardiff High	189	100	97	80	73	127	110	19	18
Fee-paying									
Monkton	33	88	85	70	65	14	14	15	15
Llandovery	27	89	81	74	62	43	33	14	15
New College	-	-	89	88	78	6	4	-	18
Christ	46	96	86	85	80	66	64	20	19
Howells	82	100	99	100	98	67	67	20	20
St Clare's	36	86	87	75	79	16	13	16	20
Rougemont	40	98	92	93	83	33	33	22	21
St Michaels	44	94	86	68	75	17	16	19	21
Monmouth	81	99	96	98	95	88	81	22	22
Haberdashers	92	100	97	100	97	75	69	24	23
Our Lady's	29	100	95	83	74				
St John's	29	90	94	76	75				
Ffynone	36	97	92	83	79	3	3		
Westbourne	9	100	94	100	89				
St David's	7	100	-	100					

Table 10.3 shows a compilation of extracts from the Welsh league tables of school performance for 1995 (Western Mail 1995). It provides comparable figures on examination entry and results for state schools in Wales as a whole, for one of the more successful local state schools, Cardiff High, and the sixteen private schools in South Wales for whom figures were available. Three columns have been selected

for attention. The first shows the percentage of relevant children gaining at least one GCSE at grade G or above, and the inverse of this figure gives an indication of the proportion of school leavers with no qualification. It can be seen that on this measure, the private schools as a whole are doing little better than the average for Wales as a whole. Three private schools have a school "failure" rate higher than the average for the principality, and the majority are anyway doing slightly worse than the exemplar state school.

The second column shows an official benchmark figure, the percentage of children gaining at least five GCSEs at grade C or above. At this level, the picture for the private sector improves. All schools have a benchmark figure considerably higher than the average for Wales, even though five still have worse figures than the non-selective state secondary. The third highlighted column gives the average number of A level points gained per candidate. Here the picture reverts to that of the failure rates above. Private school candidates are not performing much better overall than the average for Wales, with several schools doing worse than the exemplar state school, some of them even worse than the average for Wales. As an extreme example, Llandovery College, one of the most expensive schools in Wales, entered only 33 of its 43 A level students for A levels. What happened to the other ten is unclear. Even so, they achieved overall results which are worse than the national average, and which have been so for the past three years.

These figures must be considered in the light of the reservations expressed about raw score tables, and the difficulties of isolating a school effect in outcomes, that were explained in Chapter 2. However, even if the results in Table 10.3 are taken at face value, they give very mixed support to the idea that private schools, as such, lead to better examination results. Some private schools in Wales, and, as shown in Table 10.3, some state schools gain excellent results. Others do not.

Conclusion

Parents using fee-paying schools, in general, come from educated, apparently service-class families. They have no particular background in private education, and most have used, or considered using, state-funded schools for the child in question or its siblings. Around a quarter receive help from the schools or government in the form of fees concessions, and probably many more are helped by relatives, especially grand-parents. There is no clear threshold of affordability, and to some families paying for education rather than a holiday, for example, is just a matter of priorities. The level of fees rarely dictates choice of school within the sector. The parents concerned seem more often to be upwardly mobile, with a high proportion of religious minorities, and in-migrants. Therefore if fee-paying schools are playing a part in social reproduction, it is not a direct in-family kind of reproduction. Perhaps private schooling is a badge, or emblem, of being in the service class, more than a direct cause of the current situation. It may also be seen by parents, and especially children, as an opening into social networks of privilege and influence. Whether it is actually so in most of the focus private schools is a debatable point.

The schools they are using are in the main, small coeducational non-selective day schools, with limited facilities and very limited space. The choice set is slightly larger for fee-payers, perhaps because they have a wider choice. The schools are chosen not for convenience, or their facilities, but because they are small, nostalgic, and obtain reasonable outcomes. Selection by gender and ability is not a big issue in the sector, but parents want their child to sit in class with other "nice" children. Many of the parents with unfortunate experiences of the state sector are making a negative choice - choice away from a type of school - and there is some evidence that this is partly motivated by dislike of the National Curriculum.

Part Four
WHITHER MARKET FORCES IN EDUCATION?

11 Conclusions and implications

Introduction

This final chapter returns to the questions which prompted the research, and which were listed in Chapter 1. It uses these as a structure to summarise the main findings and their implications. The first section reviews the contribution of the methodology, and the second describes the models of the choice process suggested by that methodology. The third section summarises the findings with respect to fee-paying schools, while the final section examines the implications that these findings have for the outcome of the UK marketisation experiment.

Researching school choice

Although there is sufficient common ground between this study and the literature described in Chapter 2 to reinforce its validity, the participants in this study have also suggested several aspects of school choice that were little emphasised in earlier choice research, as reviewed later in this chapter. It is suggested that these differences may arise partly due to the regional nature of the survey, while some are surely to do with the relatively high proportion of middle-class respondents. In addition, it must be noted that the sampling frame and the geographical area for this research were appreciably wider than in many other studies, which may therefore have been describing more localised and limited phenomena in school choice.

The third major explanation of the emergence of these new findings is, as suggested in Chapter 3, that this study differs methodologically from most UK school choice research. This study differs from many others in the following respects. The large sample size has already been mentioned, but this is linked to a much higher response rate than is perhaps accepted as normal. In addition, the survey component included children who although found to be important in other studies were rarely the direct subjects of research in this context, with some notable exceptions. The range of types of schools was also unusual, particularly the inclusion of the volatile "reluctant private sector". The creation of a more complete list of possible choice criteria than is standard was shown to be crucial in school choice research, raising the possibility that previous studies may have been unacceptably biased by their instrumentation. Finally, the use of an interval measuring scale for some variables led to factor analysis, which allowed the criteria to be collapsed more usefully, and more safely, than in prior studies. In these circumstances it is not surprising then that the results outlined below differ in several significant ways from the field of established work.

Since prior work has been shown, in at least some cases, to contain lack of attention to detail, and errors of analysis, it is hoped that the results of this study will provide a challenge, and perhaps a stimulus to further investigation, since it provides such a strong indication of the primary importance of listening to the data in research. For example, the case for researchers trying to collapse choice criteria into fewer categories based on their judgement alone, has now been weakened. This study calls for the data from participants to speak for them, as has been demonstrated here. Thus, even those most basic of choice variables, "ease of travel" and the "schooling of siblings", assumed to be related by Coldron and Boulton (1991) for example, and by this researcher before the study, are clearly shown to be unrelated to each other, and to any larger group of criteria. Also, while criteria such as pupil selection, and school management are not important to the families described here, there are indications that it is the biasing effect of the sampling strategy, and omitted variables, that have produced a larger role for them in other work. These are the kinds of shock to the unwary or complacent that a change in methods can provide.

The process of choice

The first set of questions, voiced at the outset of this study, related directly to school choice as a process in all families and types of schools (i.e. the complete school market in South Wales).

How are schools chosen?

Previous work has suggested the existence of distinctions between groups of families with differing approaches to school choice, such as "alert" or "inert", and "privileged" or "frustrated" (e.g. Gewirtz et al. 1994). Some studies have examined the roles of the different family members in the choice process, and explored variations in the pattern in terms of age, class or sector of schooling (e.g. West et al. 1994). The present study has suggested the existence of a larger range of family groups, based partly on their levels of engagement with the market, and partly on variations in the roles assigned to the various family members. The resultant three step model of choice helps to explain disagreements in previous studies as to the relative role of parents and child in the choice process, and differences between the findings for studies using Year 6 families and those using Year 7. It also creates a background for analysis of the motives of players in the choice process, as they seek to gain advantage in family-level negotiations. The three steps are the selection of a type of school, the creation of a choice set, and the final choice. The typology of families described here ranges from "consumerist/eclectic" who go through all three steps, through "child (or parent) centred" who miss out either the second or third steps, to "fatalist" who miss out both the second and third steps.

This study also suggests a link between two phenomena affecting the choice process, which have consequently turned those schools which are responsive to the demands of a market, into more conservative and traditional institutions. One of the ironies of market forces, in the private sector at least, is that change leads to restoration of a more traditional style. The reflection effect, which is the two-way influence of the schooling of the parents, has not been noted before in the form described here. The domino effect, which is the influence of the schooling of elder siblings on school choice, has been noted before, but not always given as much emphasis as it deserves. This study has shown the similarities of these two processes of "dominoes" and "reflection", which are discernible across both sectors, in leading to judgements based on out-of-date information. This finding draws a sharp contrast to the supposed outcomes of market theories of choice, based upon current performance indicators. "Reflection", a term suggested by one of the participants, is carefully chosen, since in-family reproduction, of the type suggested by Bourdieu and Passeron (1992), and apparently observed by Bernstein (1977), does not feature strongly in this study. If the fee-paying schools of South Wales are leading to some kind of social reproduction, it would probably be the regeneration of the class structures at a different level of abstraction than was observed here. In this way, the conclusion of this study is similar to that of Halsey *et al.* (1980) - private schools are more involved in social mobility for an aspirant intermediate class, than in reproducing elite family advantages over generations - but for different reasons, and in a climate in which the class structure profile is anyway changing towards a society with a lower proportion of families that are clearly working-class, in terms of the 1980 scale. Many children at fee-paying schools in Wales today do not come from privileged families anyway, and there is no evidence here that simply paying for a school in Wales has, in the past, led to any advantage in terms of certification or later careers.

What are the common reasons for school choice?

In showing that the categories of choice criteria set up by previous studies without empirical support, are not those in the minds of the participants in this study, it is also clear that the number of such categories have been underestimated. The majority of the reasons for choice can be explained by a model of seven factors, but there also remain a number of other important idiosyncratic reasons, unrelated to the overall model. Of the seven factors described here, one, the size of schools and classes, is less than important overall in choice, and applies chiefly to parents switching from state to fee-paying schools. The remaining six in approximate ascending order of importance are sports and ECA, a traditional style, good academic outcomes, the welfare and development of the child, the safety of the child, and the resources of the school.

Of the variables that did not fit the seven factor model, only two - pupil happiness, and a broad and balanced education - were very important. Analysis of the responses to these two variables, in terms of the other variables and the interviews did not uncover any further general meaning. The interview data help to explain that such concepts are not clearly defined. The vast majority of participants

247

rated them very highly, and yet all may have different reasons for doing so. In interviews, for example, some saw happiness in terms of safety, some in terms of fulfilment, some in terms of the child's wishes, and so on. This lack of clear pattern reinforced the lack of statistical variation, and leads to the paradoxical conclusion that although happiness is reported as important in school choice, the finding itself is of little value since the term itself has no universal meaning. In the same way, most respondents might have responded that they wanted a "good school" for example, if the question had been asked, without having any clear agreement on what makes a school "good".

In general, the variables relating to pupil or social selection in any form, those relating to convenience, and those relevant to school management were not important. The very existence of some categories of choice criteria, such as convenience, are called into question by the lack of correlations between items which have been simply assumed to be related in previous studies.

Fee-paying schools

Several of the research questions specifically concerned the fee-paying schools in the study region, their characteristics, the shape of the sector, and its users.

What types of schools are there in the private sector?

Five distinct types of fee-paying schools have emerged from this study. The traditional foundation schools, of the type which have been the object of most educational research in the sector in England, are rare in Wales. Many of those that do exist are clearly at the elite end of local fee-paying provision, but they are in no way comparable to the English public schools, and the notion of a Welsh Eton is still an "absurdity". To these, predominantly rural schools, must be added a sizeable number of urban ones, which clearly emulate the traditional schools, but which are smaller, or newer, and excluded from the Assisted Places Scheme [at the time of the study], and from the more prestigious associations, such as HMC. The Catholic fee-paying schools also come into this category [although by the time this book appears only one of the three Catholic schools remains]. The privately owned schools, run for profit, are, on the other hand, smaller and more numerous, set in the towns and cities of the South coast. The fee-paying schools which are the most different from the popular image have been termed here the grass-roots schools. These are the smallest schools, charging fees reluctantly, and forming a even more volatile but significant and under-researched part of the sector.

Despite the differences between schools in terms of size, prestige, history, and financing, there is a trend towards overall similarity of provision in the fee-paying sector. Single-sex, selective, rural, primary, secondary, preparatory and boarding schools are in decline, as evidenced by both falling pupil numbers and the changing nature of schools. Non-selective, urban, coeducational day schools, taking pupils of all ages, are on the increase. These schools are mostly poorly equipped, under-subscribed, and using adapted premises, to deliver a narrow curriculum. They are also quite traditional. Their classes are small, their pupils are well-behaved, and while their outcomes in terms of certification are generally good, there is considerable variation within public examination performance.

Why is the private sector in Wales so small?

Several possible explanations have been outlined for the distinctively small size of the Welsh fee-paying sector in comparison to England. Comparison between areas with similar measures of mean socio-economic status has not suggested that the reason is solely to do with deprivation, and this conclusion is backed up by the low threshold of affordability for private education in Wales today. Evidence concerning the relative effectiveness of schools does not suggest that state schools in Wales are outperforming local fee-paying schools, at least not in a way that is not also happening in England. Confirmation that relative effectiveness is not a useful explanation comes from the finding that the fee-paying sector is in fact smallest in those areas of South Wales in which the results from the state-funded sector are seen at their worst.

Part of the explanation for the small scale of the private schools sector in Wales today undoubtedly lies in its history. For a variety of demographic, legislative, and social reasons, and despite the existence of one school in Wales dating back to the sixteenth century, the fee-paying sector did not emerge as early, or as strongly, in Wales as it did in England. The size of the sector today, and the newness of many of the schools, means that the whole is economically unstable. The sector is marked by frequent school closures, mergers, and sales, making overall growth difficult, but tempting new schools to open and compete for what has turned out to be a dwindling supply of "customers". Even so, this is only part of the explanation. It may also be that education of the kind provided by fee-paying schools, leading to certification appropriate to non-manual jobs, and probable exodus from the rural and mining communities of South Wales, has not been appropriate for, or valued by, local families. What has been missing in Wales until recently is a large and influential middle-class, and even today the users of fee-paying schools may be weighted towards in-migrants from England and further afield.

What kinds of families pay for schooling?

Families using fee-paying schools are often well-educated, with parents in prestigious occupations. However, they are no different in this regard to the users of popular state-funded schools in South Wales. In fact, there is enormous variation between the different kinds of fee-paying schools in terms of the backgrounds of their users. Many families are not wealthy, using very cheap schools, relying on assistance to pay the fees, or being prepared to forego some consumer commodities that others take for granted. Most parents have no background in using private schools themselves, and most have used state-funded schools for at least one of their children. Many of the users of the proprietary schools come from ethnic minority backgrounds. In this respect, the work described here has findings in line with some studies in the USA, reporting that private schools are offering a positive educational environment for some low-income and minority families escaping large urban schools (Schneider 1989). The findings make it easy to agree with the observer who stated that "private schools are not just schools for the wealthy. Many poor and minority parents who choose them, most at great financial sacrifice, value education highly and want what is best for their children" (Bauch 1989 p.301). This conclusion is certainly a better description of the situation in Wales than the findings of some studies of elite private schools in England.

Do different types of families use the different schools?

The answer to this question has to be a guarded "yes". Fee-paying schools are still more often used by parents who attended private school themselves. Children attending fee-paying schools have a higher proportion of siblings also attending such a school. However before the conclusion can be drawn that this finding represents a simple case of traditional users of private schools trying to reproduce their class advantages for the next generation, the exceptions must be noted. It is only the users of traditional foundation schools, and to a lesser extent the proprietary schools, who have these characteristics. The variations within the fee-paying sector in this regard are greater than the differences between the sectors. The users of grass-roots schools, and to a lesser extent the Catholic schools, actually have a lower educational and social class profile than users of the focus state-funded schools, and this pattern has also been previously observed in other countries, such as the USA.

Why do families elect to pay for education?

As this study shows, parents using fee-paying schools do so for many of the same reasons cited by users of good state schools. They are not a class apart. The differences between the users of private schools, in this respect, are larger than those between the two sectors in general. Fee-paying parents seem to be motivated, in addition, by a combination of dissatisfaction with the local state schools in the light of a recent experience, a desire for smaller teaching units, and, in some cases, a wish to avoid the National Curriculum provision for Welsh. Children rate schools in terms of their extra-curricular "holiday camp" facilities, or seek to justify their use of fee-paying schools in terms of social networking,

Is private schooling better than state-funded education?

It has been shown that questions concerning the relative value of different schools are difficult to answer, for two main reasons. It is difficult to determine the prior question of what schools are actually for, while many commonly used measures of school performance are difficult to assess objectively. Nevertheless, it is possible to say that there is no indication here that private schools, in general, are better staffed, resourced, or equipped than their state-funded equivalents. There is no evidence that they produce better long-term effects, in terms of job prospects, lifestyle or individual happiness. The overall public examination results, retention rates at 16, and rates of entry to Higher Education, are better in private schools, but this is not evidence that private schools produce better results for equivalent pupils.

There is, in addition, very little prestige attached to an education in the majority of fee-paying schools in South Wales.

Within the local fee-paying sector, it is clear that more curriculum time, smaller classes, and higher fees do not necessarily lead to better examination outcomes. On the other hand, the schools and their classes are smaller than their state-funded equivalents, and this probably makes teaching easier, leading to greater individual attention for the children. Such attention may not produce clearly better academic outcomes, but it may make life at school better for all concerned. It is this focus on school as a major component of the life of the children, rather than as a process to be assessed at age 16 for example, that is lacking in much writing about school choice. The parents appear to be attracted by the traditional feel of many of the schools, but perhaps the principal gain purchased through the payment of fees is the profile of the other families involved. It is clear from this study that pupil selection, with its commonly understood meaning applied to ability, or gender, is not important to the families, and anyway, is not a characteristic of most fee-paying schools. In fact, some state-funded schools in this study routinely turn away more prospective users than the private schools can even dream of. Private schools are generally under threat financially, under-subscribed, and changing themselves through the introduction of wider age intakes, coeducation or special needs provision, in order to be able to sustain their "market share". The main value of most private schools may well be their defining characteristic - the payment of fees - which represents the true selection process for the school. In the case of free places through scholarship or the Assisted Places Scheme, selection is overt. As this study indicates, for the other families using what are, in the main, relatively cheap schools, the payment of the fee is a symptom of their commitment. Covert selection arises from the fact that the payment also buys into a school in which the other families are similarly committed.

Whatever the reasons given for using a private school, and whatever the nature of their supposed advantage, one fact emerges very clearly from this study. The fee-paying school sector in Wales as a whole cannot be seen as particularly elitist, nor to cater for particularly privileged families. In the religious grass-roots schools, the proportion of working-class families is high, while in the proprietary schools, the proportion of ethnic minorities is high. The Catholic schools, and their users, have many similarities to local state-funded schools. It is, perhaps, only the few traditional foundation schools that are anywhere near the common image of English private schools in terms of their users, if not their results.

Whither market forces?

Many of the research questions in Chapter 1 are related to the possible effects on schools of the recent programme of increased parental choice in the UK (Gorard 1997h).

How much choice and diversity is there?

It has been shown that there is little diversity among Welsh state-funded schools, and that because of the relatively low population density of parts of South Wales, and the covert catchment areas operated by the LEAs, there is also little choice for most families. In the fee-paying sector, the situation is slightly different. In most cases, the "consumer" able to cross the "threshold of affordability" has a genuine choice, in that the school selected is usually very happy to accept all comers. On the other hand, while there are organisational differences between the schools, the economic threats described here are making them more similar over time. Choice and diversity are not linked in this market.

How much do families really know about the schools?

In a market system of schooling any beneficial effect on education as a whole relies on parents and children making "good" choices. In some formulations of choice theory this might be tautologous, in that popular choices are by definition good and unpopular schools are bad. However a theory cannot survive as a tautology, and so it must be possible to consider the quality of the decisions made in this study in order to assess the likely outcome of the experiment. This in turn, depends on the quality of the information available to choosers. It should also be mentioned, in light of the role of children in choice, that children, and the information available to them, are too often ignored. "There is little evidence for equating 'popular' with 'good' in terms of parental choices, and none at all in terms of the choices of ten year-olds" (Walford 1991a p.73). The knowledge of choosers is imperfect for several reasons, because of the complexity and volatility of the system they are required to judge (Echols and Willms 1995).

In a section entitled "Choosing the right school", a recent Welsh Office publication explained how to understand annual school performance booklets and prospectuses, with the clear implication that these are the sources of information to use (Welsh Office 1994c). In a later section, an aside mentions other parents, and visits to the school, as possible extra sources of information. In fact, as this study has confirmed, the relative emphasis of these sources should be reversed. Parents do not readily use current information about a school and are rightly suspicious of what they see and hear on official school visits. The local reputation of a school is very important to the impression gained by prospective parents, but such a nebulous source of information can be misleading. The local stories about schools are often wildly inaccurate, or based on out-of-date information, and as such may be no more reliable than the image presented by the schools themselves.

One mother said of her local state schools "you don't need to go to know they have classes of thirty-five". Another mother claimed that one school she was considering was "quite an academic school and quite a fair size". The secondary school in question has around 300 pupils in total, and sixth form results equivalent to the average for all schools in Wales. A third mother said of the private school with the worst examinations record in Wales "[school name] has a benchmark of 63%, which is good". She also stated "they have an excellent department for art, they do pottery and so on". The art department in this school is in an unheated converted army storage hut, around 300 yards from the main building across an unlit field. Its facilities are clearly worse than an average state-funded school. Many of the comments of parents at interview betray just such a lack of awareness of what local fee-paying schools are offering, and how they compare to state schools. Some of these parents may be "bad" judges, but to write them all off as such would be to miss the point. It does not matter whether it is the schools misleading parents, or parents comparing the schools today to those they attended, the relevant finding is that even the predominantly service and intermediate class families taking part in this research were making decisions concerning schools based on inadequate research.

This conclusion is in general agreement with that of West *et al.* (1994), who found that although families take the choice of a new school seriously, they may not act competently in some cases. Their choices may not be rational, but more impressionistic, and evolving over a period of time, using local "grapevines" as sources of information. Parents may not know their rights under the law, or may not use them through lack of skill or fear of the consequences. Some were not even sure whether they had made a choice or not. Similarly, Martin (1995) found that even parents who were active choosers sought schools that were nothing like the criteria that they set initially. In one case a family decided what they wanted from a school, and without changing their minds applied for a school that could not provide it, but which they knew was over-subscribed and which would refuse them a place according the schools' published decision criteria. The final nail in the coffin of rationality was provided when the child was in fact offered a place. The author concluded that "the existing literature related to parental choice indicates that parents have neither the skills or the information about schools to act in such a rational way" (Martin 1995 p. 13).

On the other hand, the West study found that, in general, parents considering all types of schools had concerns that the government and policy-makers would approve of, such as discipline, exam results, and teaching. It also concluded "that private education may represent an absence of active choosing" (West *et al* 1994 p.14). These conclusions are not borne out by the present study. Some participants reported periods of extremely active investigation of schools. The safety and welfare of their child were their main concerns, while officially designated performance indicators, in examinations and truancy, were not. Unfortunately, the results also suggest that these investigations have frequently not been very successful. As in the Hughes *et al.* (1994) study, parents did not see themselves as consumers, and several found the idea puzzling or distasteful.

Are market forces leading to improvement?

As far as it can be deduced from the foregoing, the prognosis for the improvement effect of markets on schools is not good. Bearing in mind the length of time needed to measure the effects of previous educational reforms (e.g. McPherson and Willms 1987), early research in the state-funded sector is so far merely indicative. There are indications that the purportedly damaging effects of the market in schools may be more of a problem in the short term transition and changeover. In the USA choice experiments it was observed that "poor parents take longer to acquire information; over time they catch up and become aware at the same level as non-poor parents" (Bauch 1989 p.302). A similar trend is observable in Britain, with a rise of 120% in the number of appeals from 1990 to 1994, and the rate of increase rising every year. As reported in the present study, every parent refused entry to a selected secondary school appealed, almost as a matter of course, and the hearings were held *en masse*. However, in reality, nothing much has actually changed. Schools still operate a system of catchment, or selection by mortgage, creating educational ghettos in some areas. Parents can still only express a preference. Some of the purportedly damaging effects of marketisation are in fact based on the lack of a market structure in state schools. The rise in appeals puts pressure on the popular schools to expand, which they are unable to do, except in a very few cases, such as those hoping to benefit from the "Redwood" plan in Wales to give an extra £23 million to 12 schools (Pyke 1995).

Since the fee-paying sector has been in existence as a market for so much longer, it is possible to draw some conclusions on the costs and benefits of "consumer choice". On the positive side, applicants to private schools are not generally turned away, and so despite the very small number of fee-paying schools in Wales, several parents spoke of the enormity of the choice, especially, but not exclusively, in urban areas. Given the relatively large number of state schools in the region, it can be imagined what the impact of a genuine market incorporating free choice would be. Because there are no "standard numbers" in most private schools, applicants do not generally have to resort to the deceits and subterfuges becoming more obvious in the state sector. Because private schools users are charged for examination entry, their public examination entry policy is one of the areas where parents can make a difference. Private schools are therefore generally more adventurous in making entries, especially in entering candidates through two examining boards, and selecting ambitious tiers and modes for marginal candidates. This is a high-risk, high potential gain policy, and the better results for local private schools at GCSE level, but their high overall failure rate may be partly due to this.

On the other hand, the market is pulling towards similarity of provision, with some evidence that larger schools are establishing a quasi-monopoly. The fragmentation of the sector, and the lack of a co-operative infrastructure may presage what will happen in the state sector, in the context of an enforced break up of the LEAs. Private schools still seem more concerned with promoting themselves than with what parents actually want. Thus, there is little evidence that the schools in this study actually provide the characteristics demanded by the six important choice factors, such as pupil safety (e.g. Hugill 1993). If state schools follow suit, and in a competitive environment, spend increasing amounts on promotion, education as a whole may be the loser, whatever the benefits of choice for the individual. An education market, as displayed by the volatile fee-paying sector in South Wales, is a zero-sum game (Smedley 1995). As one school wins, another loses, and so as schools put more and more into marketing, they may, like Alice in Wonderland, find themselves running faster and faster just to keep up.

Bibliography

Aberystwyth Policy Group (1990), *Secondary Education in Rural Wales*, Faculty of Education: University of Wales

Adair, J. (1973), *The Human Subject,* Boston: Little, Brown and Co.

Adler, M., Petch, A. and Tweedie, J. (1989), *Parental Choice and Educational Policy*, Edinburgh: Edinburgh University Press

Allsobrook, D. (1990), Technical Education in Wales: influences and attitudes, Webster, J. and Jones, O. (Eds.), *The Welsh Intermediate Education Act of 1889: A centenary appraisal*, Cardiff: Welsh Office, p. 27

Alston, D. (1985), *Secondary Transfer Project, Bulletin 3*, London: ILEA

Ambrose, J. and Williams, C. (1991), Language Made Visible: Representation in geolinguistics, Williams C. (Ed.), *Linguistic Minorities: society and territory*, Bristol: Longdunn Press, p. 298

Anderson, T. and Zelditch, M. (1968), *Basic Course in Statistics*, New York: Holt, Rinehart and Winston

Arnot, M. and Barton, L. (1992), *Voicing Concerns: Sociological perspectives on contemporary educational reforms*, Wallingford: Triangle Books

Arons, S. (1982), Educational Choice, Manley-Casimir M. (Ed.), *Family Choice in Schooling*, Toronto: Lexington, p.23

Ashford, S. (1990), *Cycles of Disadvantage: Parental employment status and labour market entry*, London: City University

Averch, H., Carroll, S., Donaldson, T., Kiesling, H. and Picus, J. (1974), *How Effective is Schooling?*, New York: Rand Corporation

Bagley, C. (1995), *Black and White Unite or Flight? The racial dimension of schooling and parental choice*, paper presented to the British Educational Research Association Annual Conference, Bath 1995

Bagley, C., Woods, P. and Glatter, R. (1995), *Barriers to School Responsiveness in the Education Quasi-market*, paper presented to the American Educational Research Association Annual Conference, San Fransisco 1995

Baker, C. (1990), The Growth of Bilingual Education in the Secondary Schools of Wales, Evans, W. (Ed.), *Perspectives on a Century of Secondary Education in Wales*, Aberystwyth: Centre for Educational Studies, p. 77

Ball, S., Bowe, R. and Gewirtz, S. (1992), *Circuits of Schooling: A sociological exploration of parental choice in social class contexts*, paper presented to the British Educational Research Association Annual Conference, 1992

Ball, S. (1993), Education Markets, Choice and Social Class: The market as a class strategy in the UK and the USA, *British Journal of Sociology of Education* 14, 1, pp. 3-19

Ball, S. (1994), *Education Reform: A critical and post-structural approach*, Buckingham: Open University Press

Ball, S. (1995), Intellectuals or Technicians? The urgent role of theory in educational studies, *British Journal of Educational Studies*, 43, 3, pp. 255-271

Ball, S., Bowe, R. and Gewirtz, S. (1996), School choice, social class and distinction: the realization of social advantage in education, *Journal of Education Policy*, 11, 1, pp. 89-112

Bates, I. (1990), *'Designer' Careers. An initial analysis focusing on the influence of family background, gender and the vocational track on female careers*, London: City University

Bauch, P. (1989), Can Poor Parents Make Wise Educational Choices?, Boyd, W. and Cibulka, J. (Eds.), *Private Schools and Public Policy: International perspective*, London: Falmer Press, p. 285

Bellin, W., Farrell, S., Higgs, G. and White S. (1996), A strategy for using census information in comparison of school performance, *Welsh Journal of Education*, 5, 2, pp. 3-25

Bennett, N. (1996), Class Size in Primary Schools: Perceptions of headteachers, chairs of governors, teachers and parents, *British Educational Research Journal*, 22, 1, pp. 33-55

Bentley-Ball, W. (1982), Parents in Court, Manley-Casimir, M. (Ed.), *Family Choice in Schooling*, Toronto: Lexington, p. 43

Bernstein, B. (1977), *Class, Codes and Control, Volume 3: Towards a theory of educational transmission*, London: Routledge

Blair, M. (1994), Black Teachers, Black Students and Education Markets, *Cambridge Journal of Education*, 24, 2, pp. 277-291

Blackburne, L. (1994), Heads Spurn 'too tough' Exam Boards, *Times Educational Supplement*, 18/2/94, p. 6

Blackledge, D. and Hunt, B. (1985), *Sociological Interpretations of Education*, Kent: Croom Helm

Bolam, R., McMahon, A., Pocklington, K. and Weindling, D. (1993), *Effective Management in Schools*, London: HMSO

Bolton, V. (1992), *Pastoral Care in Two Cardiff Private Schools*, M.Ed. Thesis, Cardiff: University of Wales

Bone, A. (1983), *Girls and Girls-only Schools*, Manchester: Equal Opportunities Commission

Borg, W. and Gall, M. (1983), *Educational Research: An introduction*, New York: Longman

Bourdieu, P. and Passeron, C. (1992), *Reproduction in Education, Society and Culture*, London: Sage

Bottery, M. (1992), *The Ethics of Educational Management*, London: Cassell

Bowe, R., Gerwirtz, S. and Ball, S. (1994a), Captured by the Discourse? Issues and concerns in researching 'parental choice', *British Journal of Sociology of Education*, 15, 1, pp. 63-78

Bowe, R., Ball, S. and Gerwirtz, S. (1994b), 'Parental Choice', Consumption and Social Theory: The operation of micro-markets in education, *British Journal of Educational Studies*, 42, 1, pp. 38-52

Boyd, W. and Cibulka, J. (1989), *Private Schools and Public Policy: International perspective*, London: Falmer Press

Boyd, W., Crowson, R. and van Geel, T. (1994), Rational Choice Theory and the Politics of Education: Promise and limitations, *Politics of Education Association Yearbook 1994*, pp. 127-145

Brown, S. (1994), School Effectiveness Research and the Evaluation of Schools, *Evaluation and Research in Education*, 8, 1 and 2, pp. 55-68

Bryk, A. and Lee, V. (1992), Is Politics the Problem and Are Markets the Answer? An essay review of Politics, Markets, and America's Schools, *Economics of Education Review*, 11, 4, pp. 439-451

Budge, D. (1994), Skills to Beat the Sexists, *Times Educational Supplement*, 17/6/94, p. 16

Burgess, R. (1985), *Field Methods in the Study of Education*, East Sussex: Falmer Press

Bynner, J. (1989), *Transition to Work: Results from a longitudinal study of young people in four British labour markets*, London: City University

Cahn, S. (1970), *The Philosophical Foundations of Education*, New York: Harper and Row

Charles, C. (1988), *Introduction to Educational Research*, New York: Longman

Child, D. (1970), *The Essentials of Factor Analysis*, London: Holt, Rinehart and Winston

Child, H. (1962), *The Independent Progressive School*, London: Hutchinson

Chubb, J. and Moe, T. (1990), *Politics, Markets and America's Schools*, Washington: Brookings Institute

Clark, P. and Round, E. (1991), *Good State Schools Guide*, London: Ebury

Clune, W. and Witte, J. (1990), *Choice and Control in American Education, Volume 1: The theory of choice and control in education*, London: Falmer Press

Clune, W. and Witte, J. (1990b), *Choice and Control in American Education, Volume 2: The practice of choice, decentralization and school restructuring*, London: Falmer Press

Cohen, L. and Manion, L. (1989), *Research Methods in Education*, London: Routledge

Coldron, J. and Boulton, P. (1991), 'Happiness' as a Criterion of Parents' Choice of School, *Journal of Education Policy*, 6, 2, pp. 169-178

Coldron, J. and Boulton, P. (1996), What do parents mean when they talk about 'discipline' in relation to their childrens' school?, *British Journal of Sociology of Education*, 17, 1, pp. 53-64

Coleman, J., Campbell, E., Holson, C., McPortland, J., Mood, A., Weinfield, F. and York, R. (1966), *Equality of Educational Opportunity*, Washington: US Office of Education

Coleman, J., Hoffer, T. and Kilgore, S. (1981), *Public and Private Schools*, Chicago: National Opinion Research Center

Coleman, J. and Hoffer, T. (1987), *Public and Private High schools*, New York: Basic Books

Coleman, J. (1990), Choice, Community and Future Schools, Clune, W. and Witte, J. (Eds.), *Choice and Control in American Education, Volume 1*, London: Falmer Press, p. ix

Comrey, A. (1973), *A First Course on Factor Analysis*, London: Academic Press

Cookson, P. and Persell, C. (1985), *Preparing for Power*, New York: Basic Books

Cookson, P. (1994), *School Choice*, London: Yale University

Corrigan, P. (1979), *Schooling the Smash Street Kids*, London: Macmillan

Cox, C., Balchin, R. and Marks, J. (1989), *Choosing a State School*, London: Hutchinson

Cresser, R. (1993), Take Three Girls: A comparison of girls' A-level achievement in three types of sixth forms within the independent sector, Walford, G (Ed.), *The Private Schooling of Girls*, London: Woburn, p. 174

Cureton, E. and D'Agostino, R. (1983), *Factor Analysis: An applied approach*, London: Lawrence Erlbaum

Dale, R. (1974), *Mixed or Single Sex School? Volume III: Attainment, attitudes and overview*, London: Routledge

Daly, P. and Shuttleworth, I. (1995), *Public Examination Entry and Attainment in Mathematics in Single-sex and Coeducational schools*, paper presented at British Educational Research Association Annual Conference, Bath 1995

David, M., West, A. and Ribbens, J. (1994), *Mother's Intuition? Choosing Secondary Schools*, East Sussex: Falmer Press

Davies, J. (1993), *The Welsh Language*, Cardiff: University of Wales Press

Dean, C. (1994$_a$), Class Divide Deepens in Poll, *Times Educational Supplement*, 11/2/94, p. 5

Dean, C. (1994$_b$), Boarder Numbers Fall Again, *Times Educational Supplement*, 29/4/94, p. 6

Delamont, S. (1980), *Sex Roles and the School*, London: Methuen

Dennison, W. (1995), *Researching the Competitive Edge: Detractors and attractors in school marketing*, paper presented at ESRC/CEPAM Invitation Seminar, Milton Keynes 1995

DES, (1988), *Secondary Schools: An appraisal by HMI*, London: Department of Education and Science

Devlin, T. and Knight, B. (1990), *Public Relations and Marketing for Schools*, Essex: Longman

DfE, (1994), *Department for Education: Statistics of schools, January 1993*, London: Department for Education

Donelly, J. (1993), *Managing Primary/Secondary Links*, Leicester: Secondary Heads Association

Dooley, P. (1991), Muslim Private Schools, Walford G. (Ed.), *Private Schools. Tradition, Change and Diversity*, London: Chapman, p. 98

Douglas, B. (1993), *Managing Within the Education Act 1993*, Leicester: Secondary Heads Association

Douse, M. (1985), The Background of Assisted Places Scheme Students, *Educational Studies*, 11, 3, pp. 211-217

Echols, F., McPherson, A. and Willms, J. (1990), Parental Choice in Scotland, *Journal of Educational Policy*, 5, 3, p. 207-222

Echols, F. and Willms, J. (1995), Reasons for School Choice in Scotland, *Journal of Educational Policy*, 10, 2, p. 143-156

Edwards, T., Fitz, J. and Whitty, G. (1989), *The State and Private Education: An evaluation of the Assisted Places Scheme*, London: Falmer Press

Edwards, T., Gewirtz, S. and Whitty, G. (1992), Whose Choice of Schools? Making sense of City Technology Colleges, Arnot, M. and Barton, L. (Eds.), *Voicing Concerns: Sociological perspectives on contemporary educational reforms*, Wallingford: Triangle Books, p.143

Edwards, T. and Whitty, G. (1997), Marketing Quality: Traditional and modern versions of educational excellence, in Glatter, R., Woods, P. and Bagley, C. (Eds.) *Choice and Diversity in Schooling. Perspectives and Prospects*, London: Routledge, pp. 29-43

Eiser, J. and van der Plight, J. (1988), *Attitudes and Decisions*, London: Routledge

Emler, N. and Abrams, D. (1989), *The Sexual Distribution of Benefits and Burdens in the Household: Adolescent experiences and expectations*, London: City University

Emler, N. and St James, A. (1989), *Staying on at School after Sixteen: Social and psychological correlates*, London: City University

Erickson, D. (1989), A Libertarian Perspective on Schooling, Boyd, W. and Cibulka, J. (Eds.), *Private Schools and Public Policy: International perspective*, London: Falmer Press, p. 21

Eurostat (1995), *Education across the European Union - Statistics and indicators*, Brussels: Statistical Office of the European Communities

Evans, L. (1970), *The Evolution of Welsh Educational Structure and Administration 1881-1921*, London: Methuen

Evans, L. (1971), *Education in Industrial Wales 1700-1900*, Cardiff: Avalon

Evans, W. (1981), *A History of Llandovery College*, Cardiff: CSP

Evans, W. (1990$_a$), *Perspectives on a Century of Secondary Education in Wales*, Aberystwyth: Centre for Educational Studies

Evans, W. (1990$_b$), The Welsh Intermediate and Technical Education Act, 1889: a centenary appreciation, *History of Education*, 19, 3, p.195-210

Everitt, B. (1980), *Cluster Analysis*, London: Heinemann

Farber, J. (1969), *The Student as Nigger*, New York: Pocket Books

Filstead, W. (1970), *Qualitative Methodology: Firsthand involvement with the social world*, Chicago: Markham

Firestone, W. (1987), Meaning in Method: The rhetoric of quantitative and qualitative research, *Educational Researcher*, 16, 7, pp. 16-20

Firestone, W. (1990), Alternative Arguments for Generalizing from Data as Applied to Qualitative Research, *Educational Researcher*, 22, 4, pp. 16-23

Fitz, J., Edwards, T. and Whitty, G. (1986), Beneficiaries, Benefits and Costs: An investigation of the assisted places scheme, *Research Papers in Education*, 1, 3, pp. 169-193

Fitz, J., Halpin, D. and Power, S. (1993), *Education in the Market Place: Grant Maintained Schools*, London: Kogan Page

Fletcher, J. (1981), Education, Merthyr Teachers' Centre Group (Eds.), *Merthyr Tydfil - A Valley Community*, London: Joint Publishers, p. 143

Forster, P. (1992), Whose Choice is it Anyway?, *Managing Schools Today*, 1, 6, pp. 36-37

Fowler-Finn, T. (1994), Why Have They Chosen Another School System?, *Educational Leadership*, December 1993/January 1994, pp. 60-62

Fox, I. (1985), *Private Schools and Public Issues: The parents' view*, London: Macmillan

Fox, I. (1989), Elitism and the British "Public" schools, Boyd, W. and Cibulka, J. (Eds.), *Private Schools and Public Policy: International perspectives*, London: Falmer Press, p.331

Fox, I. (1990), The Demand for Public School Education: A crisis of confidence in comprehensive schooling?, Walford, G. (Ed.), *Privatisation and Privilege in Education* , London: Routledge, p.45

Frazer, E. (1995), What's New in the Philosophy of Science?, *Oxford Review of Education*, 21, 3, pp. 267-281

Frude, N. (1993), *A Guide to SPSS*, London: Macmillan

Gabbitas, Truman and Thring (1992), *Which School?*, Edinburgh: Bell and Bain

Gaffney, E. (1981), *Private Schools and the Public Good*, Indiana: University of Notre Dame

Garner, W. and Hannaway, J. (1982), Private Schools: The client connection, Manley-Casimir M. (Ed.), *Family Choice in Schooling*, Toronto: Lexington, p. 119

Gaunt, H. (1991), *Could Do Better*, West Yorkshire: Horton

Gephart, R. (1988), *Ethnostatistics: Qualitative foundations for quantitative research*, London: Sage

Gewirtz, S., Ball, S. and Bowe, R. (1994), Parents, Privilege and the Market Place, *Research Papers in Education*, 9, 1, pp. 3-29

Gewirtz, S., Ball, S. and Bowe, R. (1995), *Markets, Choice and Equity in Education*, Buckingham: Open University Press

Gilbert, N. (1993), *Analysing Tabular Data: Loglinear and logistic models for social researchers*, London: UCL Press

Ginzberg, E., Ginzberg, S., Axelrad, S. and Herma, J. (1951), *Occupational Choice*, New York: Columbia University Press

Glaser, B. and Strauss, A. (1970), Discovery of Substantive Theory, Filstead W. (Ed.), *Qualitative Methodology: Firsthand involvement with the social world*, Chicago: Markham, p. 288

Glatter, R., Woods, P. and Bagley, C. (1995), *Diversity, Differentiation and Hierarchy: School choice and parental preferences*, presentation at ESRC/CEPAM Invitation Seminar, Milton Keynes 1995

Glatter, R., Woods, P. and Bagley, C. (1997a), Diversity, Differentiation and Hierarchy: School choice and parental preferences, in Glatter, R., Woods, P. and Bagley, C. (Eds.) *Choice and Diversity in Schooling. Perspectives and Prospects*, London: Routledge, pp. 7-28

Glatter, R., Woods, P. and Bagley, C. (1997b) *Choice and Diversity in Schooling. Perspectives and Prospects*, London: Routledge

Goldring, E. (1997), Parental Involvement and School Choice: Israel and the United States, in Glatter, R., Woods, P. and Bagley, C. (Eds.) *Choice and Diversity in Schooling. Perspectives and Prospects*, London: Routledge, pp. 86-101

Gorard, S. (1996a), *School Choice in an Established Market: Families and fee-paying schools*, Cardiff: University of Wales (Ph.D. thesis)

Gorard, S. (1996b), *An Uneasy Alliance: Parents, children, and school choice*, presentation at British Educational Management and Administration Society Research Conference, Cambridge

Gorard, S. (1996c), Fee-paying Schools in Britain: A peculiarly English phenomenon, *Educational Review*, 48, 1, pp. 89-93

Gorard, S. (1996d), *Reflections of the Past: The generation of school choice*, presentation at British Educational Research Association Annual Conference, Lancaster, also submitted to *Educational Studies*

Gorard, S. (1996e), Three Steps to "Heaven": The family and school choice, *Educational Review*, 48, 3

Gorard, S. (1996f), *What Are They Paying For? Families using fee-paying schools*, presentation at British Educational Research Association Annual Conference, Lancaster, also available on Education-*line* - http://www.leeds.ac.uk/educol/

Gorard, S. (1997a), *A brief history of education and training in Wales 1900-1996*, Cardiff: School of Education, ISBN 1 872330 05 3

Gorard, S. (1997b), The family micro-politics of choice, in Stott K. and Trafford V. (Eds.) *Partners in Change: Shaping the future*, London: Middlesex University Press

Gorard, S. (1997c), A choice of methods: the methodology of choice, *Research in Education*, 57, pp. 73-88

Gorard, S. (1997d), Uncharted Territory: the missing schools, *Welsh Journal of Education*, 6,2

Gorard, S. (1997e), *The region of study: Patterns of participation in adult education and training*, Cardiff: School of Education, ISBN 1 872330 02 9

Gorard, S. (1997f), Who pays the piper? Intergenerational aspects of school choice, *School Leadership and Management*, 17, 2

Gorard, S. (1997g), Paying for a Little England: School choice and the Welsh Language, *Welsh Journal of Education*, 6, 1

Gorard, S. (1997h), Whither market forces in education?, *Oxford Review of Education* (submitted)

Gorard, S., Rees, G., Furlong, J. and Fevre, R. (1997), *Outline Methodology of the study: Patterns of participation in adult education and training*, Cardiff: School of Education, ISBN 1 872330 03 7

Gorsuch, R. (1972), *Factor Analysis*, London: Saunders

GPDSA (1995), *School Marketing/PR: Key points*, handout to member schools

Grace, G. (1995), *School Leadership*, London: Falmer Press

Gray, J. and Jones, B. (1986), Towards a Framework for Interpreting Examination Results, Rogers, R. (Ed.), *Education and Social class*, East Sussex: Falmer Press, p. 51

Gray, J. and Sime, N. (1989), *Extended Routes and Delayed Transitions Among 16-19 year olds: National trends and local contexts*, London: City University

Griffiths, J. (1991), Small Private Schools in South Wales, Walford G. (Ed.), *Private Schools. Tradition, Change and Diversity*, London: Chapman, p.85

Grubb, W. (1994), The Long-Run Effects of Proprietary Schools: Corrections, *Educational Evaluation and Policy Analysis*, 16, 3, pp. 351-356

Guilford, K. and Fruchter, B. (1973), *Fundamental Statistics in Psychology and Education*, London: McGraw-Hill

Hackett, G. (1995), A Flawed Spur to Improve, *Times Educational Supplement 15/12/95*, p. 12

Haertel, E., James, T. and Levin, H. (1987), *Comparing Public and Private Schools, Volume 2*, Lewes: Falmer Press

Hahn, F. (1988), On Market Economies, Skidelsky R. (Ed.), *Thatcherism*, Oxford: Blackwell, p.107

Hallinger, P. and Leithwood, K. (1994), Introduction: Exploring the impact of Principal Leadership, *School Effectiveness and School Improvement*, 5, 3, pp. 206-217

Halpin, D., Power, S. and Fitz, J. (1997), Opting into the past? Grant Maintained Schools and the reinvention of tradition, in Glatter, R., Woods, P. and Bagley, C. (Eds.) *Choice and Diversity in Schooling. Perspectives and Prospects*, London: Routledge, pp. 59-70

Halsey, A., Heath, A. and Ridge, J. (1980), *Origins and Destinations: Family, class and education in modern Britain*, Oxford: Clarendon

Halsey, A., Heath, A. and Ridge, J. (1984), The Political Arithmetic of Public Schools, Walford, G. (Ed.), *British Public Schools: policy and practice*, Lewes: Falmer Press, p. 9

Hammersley, M. (1990), *Reading Ethnographic Research*, Essex: Longman

Hammond, T. and Dennison, W. (1995), School Choice in Less Populated Areas, *Educational Management and Administration*, 23, 2, pp. 104-113

Hargreaves, L., Comber, C. and Galton, M. (1996), The National Curriculum: Can small schools deliver? Confidence and competence levels of teachers in small rural primary schools, *British Educational Research Journal*, 22, 1, pp. 89-99

Harris Research Centre (1988), *Secondary Education in Kent: Research among customers*, Kent County Council

Hartley, D. (1994), Mixed Messages in Education Policy: Sign of the times?, *British Journal of Educational Studies*, 42, 3, pp. 230-245

Headington, R. and Howson, J. (1995), The School Brochure: A marketing tool?, *Education Management and Administration*, 23, 2, pp. 89-95

Hedderson, J. (1991), *SPSS/PC+ Made Simple*, California: Wadsworth

Hirschman, A. (1970), *Exit, Voice, and Loyalty: Responses to decline in firms, organizations, and states*, Cambridge: Harvard University Press

Hughes, M., Wikeley, F. and Nash, T. (1994), *Parents and their Children's Schools*, Oxford: Blackwell

Hughes, M. (1995), *The Effect of Parent's Views on Schools at Key Stage One*, paper presented at ESRC/CEPAM Invitation Seminar, Milton Keynes 1995

Hugill, B. (1993), Teacher "in charge" 25 Miles Away as Boy Burnt in Blast, *The Observer* 26/9/93, p. 9

Hunter, J. (1991), Which School? A study of parents' choice of secondary school, *Educational Research*, 33, 1, pp. 31-41

ISIS (1992), *Choosing Your Independent School*, London: Independent Schools Information Service

ISIS (1993 Reprint), *Independent Schools in Wales 1993-94*, London: Independent Schools Information Service

ISIS North (1993), *A Guide to Independent Schools in Northern England and North Wales*, Lancashire: Independent Schools Information Service

ISIS (1994), *Planning an Independent Education*, London: Independent Schools Information Service

ISIS (1995$_a$), *Wales 1995-96*, London: Independent Schools Information Service

ISIS (1995$_b$), *Annual Census 1995*, London: Independent Schools Information Service

Istance, D. and Rees, G. (1994), Education and Training in Wales: Problems and paradoxes revisited, *Contemporary Wales*, 7, pp. 7-27

Jackson, D. and Borgatta, E. (1981), *Factor Analysis and Measurement*, London: Sage

James, C. and Phillips, P. (1995), The Practice of Educational Marketing in Schools, *Education Management and Administration*, 23, 2, pp. 75-88

Jenks, C., Smith, M., Ackland, H., Bane, M., Cohen, D., Gintis, H., Heynes, B. and Michelson, S. (1972), *equality: A reassessment of the effect of family and schooling in America*, New York: Basic Books

Johnson, D. (1987), *Private Schools and State Schools. Two systems or one?*, Milton Keynes: Open University Press

Jolliffe, I. (1986), *Principal Component Analysis*, New York: Springer-Verlag

Jones, B. and Lewis, I. (1995), A Curriculum Cymreig, *The Welsh Journal of Education*, 4, 2, pp. 22-35

Jones, G. (1982), *Controls and Conflicts in Welsh Secondary Education*, Cardiff: University of Wales Press

Jones, G. (1990$_a$), *Which Nation's Schools?*, Cardiff: University of Wales Press

Jones, G. (1990$_b$), From Intermediate to Comprehensive Education, p. 60, Evans, W (Ed.), *Perspectives on a Century of Secondary Education in Wales*, Aberystwyth: Centre for Educational Studies

Keeves, J. (1988), *Educational Research, Methodology and Measurement*, Oxford: Pergamon

Kim, J. and Mueller, C. (1978$_a$), *Introduction to Factor Analysis. What it is and how to do it*, London: Sage

Kim, J. and Mueller, C. (1978$_b$), *Factor Analysis: Statistical methods and practical issues*, London: Sage

King, R. (1987), No Best Method: Qualitative and quantitative research in the sociology of Education, Walford, G. (Ed.), *Doing Sociology of Education*, Lewes: Falmer Press, p. 231

Knoke, D. and Kuklinski, J. (1982), *Network Analysis*, California: Sage

Kruskal, J. and Wish, M. (1978), *Multidimensional Scaling*, London: Sage

Labovitz, S. (1970), The Assignment of Numbers to Rank Order Categories, *American Sociological Review*, 35, pp. 515-524

Lake, M. (1992), Under the Influence, *Managing Schools Today*, 1, 9, pp. 12-14

Larkin, J. (1994), Walking Through Walls: The sexual harassment of high school girls, *Gender and Education*, 6, 3, pp. 263-280

LeCompte, M. and Preissle, J. (1993), *Ethnography and Qualitative Design in Educational Research*, California: Academic Press

Lee, E., Forthofer, R. and Lorimor, R. (1989), *Analyzing Complex Survey Data*, London: Sage

Lee, V., Croninger, R. and Smith, J. (1994), Parental Choice of Schools and Social Stratification in Education: The paradox of Detroit, *Educational Evaluation and Policy Analysis*, 16, 4, pp. 434-457

Lee, V., Marks, H. and Byrd, T. (1994), Sexism in Single-Sex and Coeducational Independent Secondary School Classrooms, *Sociology of Education*, 67, 2, pp. 92-115

Levin, B. and Riffel, J. (1995), School System Responses to External Change: implications for school choice, paper presented at ESRC/CEPAM Invitation Seminar, Milton Keynes

Levin, B. and Riffel, J. (1997), School System Responses to External Change: implications for school choice, in Glatter, R., Woods, P. and Bagley, C. (Eds.) *Choice and Diversity in Schooling. Perspectives and Prospects*, London: Routledge, pp. 44-58

Levin, H. (1992), Market Approaches to Education: Vouchers and school choice, *Economics of Education Review*, 11, 4, pp. 279-285

Levine, G. (1991), *A Guide to SPSS for Analysis of Variance*, New Jersey: Lawrence Erlbaum

Levine, J. (1993), *Exceptions are the Rule: An inquiry into methods in the Social Sciences*, Oxford: Westview

Lortie, D. (1975), *School-Teacher: A sociological study*, Chicago: University of Chicago Press

Lowe, C. (1988), *Education Reform Act 1988: Implications for school management*, Leicester: SHA

Mac an Ghaill, M. (1991), Black Voluntary Schools: the "invisible" private sector, p. 133, Walford G. (Ed.), *Private Schools. Tradition, Change and Diversity*, London: Chapman

Macbeth, A., Strachan, D. and Macaulay, C. (1986), *Parental Choice of School in Scotland*, Glasgow: University of Glasgow

MacDonald, M. and Woods, P. (1977), *The Education of Elites*, Milton Keynes: Open University Press

Macleod, F. (1989), *Parents and Schools: The contemporary challenge*, Lewes: Falmer Press

Maddala, G. (1992), *Introduction to Econometrics*, New York: Macmillan

Madsen, J. (1994), *Parent Efficacy in Independent Private Schools: Lessons for Public Schools*, paper presented to American Educational Research Association Annual Conference, New Orleans 1994

Manley-Casimir, M. (1982), *Family Choice in Schooling*, Toronto: Lexington Books

Marradi, A. (1981), Factor Analysis as an Aid in the Formation and Refinement of Empirically Useful Concepts, Jackson D. and Borgatta E. (Eds.), *Factor Analysis and Measurement*, , London: Sage, p. 11

Martin, S. (1995), *Choosing a Secondary School: Can parents' behaviour be described as rational?*, paper presented at British Educational Research Association Annual Conference, Bath 1995

Massey, R. (1993), *Parent Power*, Cambridge: Harmsworth

Maxwell, A. (1977), *Multivariate Analysis in Behavioural Research*, New York: Chapman and Hall

Maxwell, J. and Maxwell, M. (1995), The Reproduction of Class in Canada's Elite Independent Schools, *British Journal of Sociology of Education*, 16, 3, pp. 309-326

Maynard, A. (1975), *Experiments with Choice in Education*, London: Institute of Economic Affairs

McCracken, G. (1988), *The Long Interview*, London: Sage

McEwen, A. and Robinson, E. (1994), Evangelical Beliefs, Attitudes Towards Schooling and Educational Outcomes, *Research in Education*, 52, pp. 65-75

McPherson, A. and Willms, J. (1987), Equalisation and Improvement: Some effects of comprehensive reorganisation in Scotland, *Sociology*, 21, 4, pp. 509-539

McRae, K. (1983), *Conflict and Compromise in Multilingual Societies: Switzerland*, Ontario: Wilfrid Laurier University Press

Measor, L. and Woods, P. (1991), Breakthroughs and Blockages in Ethnographic Research: Contrasting experiences during the 'Changing Schools' Project, Walford, G. (Ed.), *Doing Educational Research*, London: Routledge, p. 59

Meighan, R. (1986), *A Sociology of Educating*, London: Cassell

Meighan, R. (1992), *Learning from Home-based Education*, Derbyshire: Education Now

Meighan, R. (1995), Home Based Education Effectiveness Research and Some of its Implications, *Educational Review* 47, 3, pp. 275-287

Menter, I, Muschamp, Y and Ozga, J (1995), *The Primary Market-place: A study in small service providers*, paper presented at American Educational Research Association Annual Conference, San Francisco 1995

Merthyr Teachers' Centre Group (1981), *Merthyr Tydfil - A Valley Community*, London: Joint Publishers

Microsoft (1991), *User Guide: Microsoft Word for Windows*, New York: Microsoft

Miles, M. and Huberman, M. (1994), *Qualitative Data Analysis*, London: Sage

Morgan, W. (1990), Curricular Problems of Small Rural Secondary Schools in Dyfed, p. 208, Evans, W. (Ed.), *Perspectives on a Century of Secondary Education in Wales*, Aberystwyth: Centre for Educational Studies

Morris, A. (1994), The Academic Performance of Catholic Schools, *School Organisation*, 14, 1, pp. 81-88

Mortimore, P. and Mortimore, J. (1986), Education and Social Class, p. 1, Rogers, R. (Ed.), *Education and Social class*, Lewes: Falmer Press

National Commission on Education (1993), *Learning to Succeed*, London: Heinemann

Norusis, M. (1985), *SPSS^x Advanced Statistics Guide*, Chicago: SPSS inc.

Norusis, M. (1988$_a$), *SPSS PC+ V2.0 Base Manual*, Chicago: SPSS inc.

Norusis, M. (1988$_b$), *SPSS PC+ V3.0 Update Manual*, Chicago: SPSS inc.

Norusis, M. (1991), *The SPSS Guide to Data Analysis*, Chicago: SPSS inc.

265

Nuttall, D. (1986), *Assessing Educational Achievement*, London: Falmer Press

O'Connor, M. (1995), After Eleven Shopper's Guide, *The Observer schools' report* 15/10/95, p. 3

OECD (1994), *School: A matter of choice*, Paris: Organisation for Economic Cooperation and Development

OPCS (1970), *Office of Population Censuses and Surveys*, London: HMSO

OPCS (1993), *1991 Census. Report for Wales. Part one*, London: HMSO

OPCS (1994), *1991 Census. Welsh language. Wales*, London: HMSO

Oppenheim, A. (1992), *Questionnaire Design, Interviewing and Attitude Measurement*, London: Pinter

OHCMI (1993), *Achievement and Under-achievement in Secondary Schools in Wales 1991-92*, Cardiff: OHCMI occasional paper 1

Packer, A. and Campbell, C. (1993), *The Reasons for Parental Choice of Welsh-Medium Education*, paper presented at Minority Languages Conference, Cardiff 1993

Partington, J. and Wragg, T. (1989), *Schools and Parents*, London: Cassell

Payne, S. (1951), *The Art of Asking Questions*, New Jersey: Princeton University

Peterson, P. (1990), Monopoly and Competition in American Education, p. 47, Clune, W. and Witte, J. (Eds.), *Choice and Control in American Education, Volume 1: The theory of choice and control in education*, London: Falmer Press

Petrie, A. (1994), *Home Education in Europe*, New Jersey: paper presented at the Comparative Education Society of Europe Conference, 1994

Phillips, D. (1992), *The Social Scientist's Bestiary: A guide to fabled threats to, and defences of, Naturalistic Social Science*, Oxford: Pergamon Press

Pifer, L. and Miller, J. (1995), *The Accuracy of Student and Parent Reports About Each Other*, paper presented at American Educational Research Association Annual Conference, San Francisco 1995

Popkewitz, T. (1984), *Paradigm and Ideology in Educational Research*, Lewes: Falmer Press

Power, S., Fitz, J. and Halpin, D. (1994), Parents, Pupils and Grant-Maintained schools, *British Educational Research Journal*, 20, 2, pp. 209-225

Prestage, M. (1995), Parents Fight Welsh Closure, *Times Educational Supplement*, 15/12/95, p. 4

Pyke, N. (1995), Parents Appeal for Real Choice, *Times Educational Supplement*, 29/12/95, p. 1

Pyke, N. (1996a), Jewish Faith Settled Out of Class, *Times Educational Supplement*, 16/2/96, p. 16

Pyke, N. (1996b), New Focus for Islamic Grievance, *Times Educational Supplement Extra*, 16/2/96, p. II

Rae, J. (1981), *The Public School Revolution*, London: Faber and Faber

Raven, J (1989), Equity in Diversity, p. 59 in Macleod, F. (Ed.), *Parents and Schools: The contemporary challenge*, Lewes: Falmer Press

Redpath, R. and Harvey, B. (1987), *Young people's Intention to Enter Higher Education*, London: HMSO

Reynolds, D. (1990), The Great Welsh Education Debate, *History of Education*, 19, 3, p. 251-260

Reynolds, D. (1991), Doing Educational Research in Treliw, p.193, Walford, G. (Ed.), *Doing Educational Research*, London: Routledge

Reynolds, D. (1995), Creating an Educational System for Wales, *The Welsh Journal of Education*, 4, 2, pp. 4-21

Reynolds, D. and Cuttance, P. (1992), *School Effectiveness*, England: Cassell

Reynolds, H. (1977), *Analysis of Nominal Data*, London: Sage

Robson, M. and Walford, G. (1989), dependent Schools and Tax Policy Under Mrs. Thatcher, *Education Policy*, 4, 2, pp. 149-162

Roderick, G. (1990), Industry, Technical Manpower, and Education, South Wales in the nineteenth century, *History of Education*, 19, 3, p. 211-218

Rogers, M. (1992), *Opting Out*, Wiltshire: Cromwell

Rogers, R. (1986), *Education and Social class*, Lewes: Falmer Press

Roker, D. (1991), *Gaining the Edge: The education, training and employment of young people in private school*, London: City University

Roker, D. and Bankes, M. (1991), *The Political Socialisation of Youth: the effects of educational experience on political attitudes*, London: City University

Riley, K. (1994), The Active Parent Myth, *Education*, 1, April 1994, p. 251

Rutter, M., Maughan, B., Mortimore, P., and Ouston, J. (1979), *Fifteen Thousand Hours*, Somerset: Open Books

Salter, B. and Tapper, T. (1981), *Education, Politics and the State*, Suffolk: St Edmundsbury Press

Schachter, S. and Singer, J. (1962), Cognitive, Social and Physiological Determinants of Emotional States, *Psychological Review*, 69, pp. 379-399

Schneider, B. (1989), Schooling for Poor and Minority Children, in Boyd, W. and Cibulka, J. (Eds.), *Private Schools and Public Policy: International perspective*, London: Falmer Press p. 73

Sen, A. (1982), *Choice, Welfare and Measurement*, Oxford: Blackwell

SHA (1990), *Sport for All?*, Secondary Heads Association Update Series, 10, Bristol: Central Press

Sharp, D., Thomas, B., Price, E., Francis, G., and Davies, I. (1973), *Attitudes to Welsh and English in the Schools of Wales*, London: Macmillan

Shipman, M. (1981), *The Limitations of Social Research*, London: Longman

Siegel, S. (1956), *Nonparametric Statistics*, Tokyo: McGraw-Hill

Singh Ghuman, P. (1995), A Study of Multicultural Education in Welsh schools and PGCE Students' Attitudes to Multicultural Education, *Welsh Journal of Education*, 5, 1, pp. 82-95

Skidelsky, R. (1988), *Thatcherism* , Oxford: Blackwell

Smedley, D. (1995), Marketing Secondary Schools to Parents - Some lessons from the research on parental choice, *Education Management and Administration*, 23, 2, pp. 96-103

Smith, D. and Tomlinson, S. (1989), *The School Effect*, London: PSL

Smyth, J. (1993), *A Socially Critical View of the Self-Managing School*, London: Falmer Press

Spencer, D. (1994), Staff Say No to More Sport Hours, *Times Educational Supplement* 25/2/94, p. 11

Spender, D. (1989), *visible Women*, London: Women's Press

Spender, D. and Sarah, E. (1980), *Learning to Lose*, London: Women's Press

Spring, J. (1982), Dare Educators Build a New School System?, p. 33, Manley-Casimir, M. (Ed.), *Family Choice in Schooling*, Toronto: Lexington

SPSSx (1988), *SPSSx User's Guide*, Chicago: SPSS inc.

Statham, J. and Mackinnon, D. (1991), *The Education Fact File*, London: Hodder and Stoughton

Steedman, J. (1983[a]), *Examination Results in Mixed and Single-sex Schools*, Manchester: Equal Opportunities Commission

Steedman, J. (1983[b]), *Examination Results in Selective and Non-selective Schools*, National Children's Bureau

Stevens, J. (1992), *Applied Multivariate Statistics for the Social Sciences*, London: Lawrence Erlbaum

Strauss, A. (1987), *Qualitative Analysis for Social Scientists*, Cambridge: Cambridge University Press

Sudman, S. and Bradburn, N. (1982), *Asking Questions*, San Francisco: Jossey-Bass

Terrell, I. and Clinton, C. (1992), Voicing their Views, *Managing Schools Today*, 2, 1, pp. 26-28

TES (1993), *Times Educational Supplement Secondary School Performance Tables '93*

TES (1994[a]), *Times Educational Supplement Secondary School Performance Tables '94*

TES (1994[b]), Rough Justice for the Independent-minded, letter to *Times Educational Supplement* 15/7/94, p. 16

TES (1995), *Times Educational Supplement School and College Performance Tables 1995*

Thiessen, E. (1982), Religious Freedom and Educational Pluralism, Manley-Casimir, M. (Ed.), *Family Choice in Schooling*, Toronto: Lexington, p. 57

Thomas, A. and Dennison, B. (1991), Parental or Pupil Choice: Who really decides in urban schools?, *Education Management and Administration*, 19, 4, pp. 243-251

Thomas, S., Sammons, P., Mortimore, P. and Smees, R. (1995), *Differential Secondary School Effectiveness*, paper presented at British Educational Research Association Annual Conference, Bath 1995

Tomlinson, S. (1994), What is Really Going on in School?, *Parliamentary Brief on Education* December 1994, pp. 103-110

Turner, G. (1983), *The Social World of the Comprehensive School*, Beckenham: Croom Helm

Tyack, D. and Hansot, E. (1990), *Learning Together*, London: Yale

Tymms, P. (1992), The Relative Effectiveness of Post-16 Institutions in England, *British Educational Research Journal* 18, 2, pp. 175-102

Tyrell, C. (1992), *The Parents' Guide to Independent Schools*, Berkshire: SFIA

Van Zenten, A. (1995), *Market Forces in Education*, paper presented at British Educational Research Association Annual Conference, Bath 1995

Venkatraman, N. and Grant, J. (1986), Construct Measurement in Organizational Strategy Research: A critique and proposal, *Academy of Management Review* 11, 1, pp. 71-87

268

Wales on Sunday (1996), The school that time forgot, *Wales on Sunday*, 12/5/96, p. 1

Walford, G. (1984), *British Public Schools: Policy and practice*, Lewes: Falmer Press

Walford, G. (1986), *Life in Public Schools* London: Methuen

Walford, G. (1987a), How Important is the Independent Sector is Scotland?, *Scottish Educational Review* 19, 2, pp. 108-121

Walford, G. (1987b), *Doing Sociology of Education*, Lewes: Falmer Press

Walford, G. (1987c), Research Role Conflicts and Compromises in Public Schools, Walford, G. (Ed.), *Doing Sociology of Education*, Lewes: Falmer Press, p. 45

Walford, G. (1989), *Private Schools in Ten Countries: Policy and practice*, London: Routledge

Walford, G. (1990), *Privatisation and Privilege in Education*, London: Routledge

Walford, G. (1991a), Choice of School at the First City Technology College, *Educational Studies*, 17, 1, pp. 65-75

Walford, G. (1991b), *Doing Educational Research*, London: Routledge

Walford, G. (1991c), *Private Schools. Tradition, Change and Diversity*, London: Paul Chapman

Walford, G. (1991d), Researching the City Technology College, Kingshurst, Walford, G. (Ed.), *Doing Educational Research*, London: Routledge, p. 82

Walford, G. (1991e), The Reluctant Private Sector: Of small schools, politics, and people, Walford, G. (Ed.), *Private Schools. Tradition, Change and Diversity*, London: Chapman, p. 115

Walford, G. (1993), *The Private Schooling of Girls*, London: Woburn

Walford, G. (1995), The Christian Schools Campaign: A successful educational pressure group?, *British Educational Research Journal*, 21, 4, pp. 451464

Waters, H., Jones, F., Fisher, V., and Evans, K. (1973), *A Hundred Years of Schooling*, Cardiff: St German's School Managers

Webster, R. (1990), Education in Wales and the Rebirth of a Nation, *History of Education*, 19, 3, pp. 183-194

Webster, J. and Jones, O. (1990), *The Welsh Intermediate Education Act of 1889: A centenary appraisal*, Cardiff: Welsh Office

Weiss, J. (1990), Control in School Organizations, Clune, W. and Witte, J. (Eds.), *Choice and Control in American Education, Volume 1: The theory of choice and control in education*, London: Falmer Press, p. 91

Weller, S. and Romney, A. (1988), *Systematic Data Collection*, California: Sage

Welsh Language Society (1991), *The Eleventh Hour: Welsh in education in South Glamorgan*, Cardiff: CNAP

Welsh Office (1990), *Welsh in the National Curriculum*, Cardiff: HMSO

Welsh Office (1993), *School Performance Information 1993 South Glamorgan, Mid Glamorgan, West Glamorgan, Gwent, Powys, Clwyd, Dyfed, Gwynedd*, Cardiff: HMSO

Welsh Office (1994a), *Statistics of Education and Training in Wales: Schools, No. 2*, Cardiff: HMSO

Welsh Office (1994b), *Using Your Welsh*, Cardiff: HMSO

Welsh Office (1994c), *Education: A charter for parents in Wales*, Cardiff: HMSO

Welsh Office (1995$_a$), *Statistics of Education and Training in Wales: Schools, No. 2*, Cardiff: HMSO

Welsh Office (1995$_b$), *Welsh in the National Curriculum*, Cardiff: HMSO

West, A. and Varlaam, A. (1991), Choosing a Secondary School: Parents of junior school children, *Educational Research*, 33, 1, pp. 22-30

West, A. (1992), Factors Affecting Choice of School for Middle Class Parents: Implications for marketing, *Educational Management and Administration*, 20, 4, pp. 212-221

West, A., David, M., Hailes, J. and Ribbens, J. (1995), Parents and the Process of Choosing Secondary Schools: Implications for schools, *Educational Management and Administration*, 23, 1, pp. 28-38

Western Mail (1995), Western Mail Schools Performance Tables, *Western Mail* 22/11/95, p. 11

Whitaker's Almanac (1994), *Whitaker's Almanac*, 127th Edition, Whitaker: London

Whitehead, C. (1994), Boarders in the Best of Both Worlds, *Times Educational Supplement Section 2* 17/6/94, p. 2

Whitty, G., Edwards, T. and Fitz, J. (1989), England and Wales: The role of the private sector, Walford, G. (Ed.), *Private schools in Ten Countries*, London: Routledge, p. 8

Whitty, G., Edwards, T., and Gewirtz, S. (1993), *Specialisation and Choice in Urban Education: The City Technology College experiment*, London: Routledge

Willms, J. and Echols, F. (1992), Alert and Inert Clients: The Scottish experience of parental choice of schools, *Economics of Education Review*, 11, 4, pp. 339-350

Williams, C. (1991), *Linguistic Minorities: Society and territory*, Bristol: Longdunn Press

Witte, J. (1990$_a$), Introduction, p. 1 in Clune, W. and Witte, J. (Eds.), *Choice and Control in American Education, Volume 1: The theory of choice and control in education*, London: Falmer Press

Witte, J. (1990$_b$), Choice and Control: An analytical overview, Clune, W. and Witte, J. (Eds.), *Choice and Control in American Education, Volume 1: The theory of choice and control in education*, London: Falmer Press, p. 40

Witte, J. (1992), Private School Versus Public School Achievement: Are there findings that should affect the educational choice debate?, *Economics of Education Review*, 11, 4, pp. 371-394

Woods, P. (1992), Empowerment Through Choice? Towards an understanding of parental choice and school responsiveness, *Education Management and Administration*, 20, 4, pp. 204-211

Woods, P. (1996), Choice, Class and Effectiveness, *School Effectiveness and School Improvement*, 7, 4, pp. 324-341

Young, S. (1994$_a$), Inquiry Call on Services Pupils' Fees, *Times Educational Supplement* 18/3/94, p. 3

Young, S. (1994$_b$), League Table Revamp on Cards, *Times Educational Supplement* 25/3/94, p. 2

Young, S. (1994$_c$), Beware the Perils of Parental Power, *Times Educational Supplement* 6/5/94, p. 7

Young, S. (1994$_d$), Fears Over 'fairer' League Tables, *Times Educational Supplement* 15/7/94, p. 3

For Product Safety Concerns and Information please contact our EU
representative GPSR@taylorandfrancis.com Taylor & Francis Verlag GmbH,
Kaufingerstraße 24, 80331 München, Germany

Printed and bound by CPI Group (UK) Ltd, Croydon, CR0 4YY

08/05/2025

01864370-0010